CIPS Study Matters

Level 6

Graduate Diploma in Purchasing and Supply

# Advanced Project Management

**Dave Smith**
Positive Purchasing

THE
CHARTERED INSTITUTE OF
PURCHASING & SUPPLY

**Published by**

The Chartered Institute of Purchasing and Supply
Easton House, Easton on the Hill, Stamford, Lincolnshire PE9 3NZ
Tel: +44 (0) 1780 756 777
Fax: +44 (0) 1780 751 610
Email: info@cips.org
Website: http://www.cips.org



First published September 2006



Study sessions 8 – 10 originally drafted by Alan Pilkington, Royal Holloway, University of London.

Technical reviewer: Paul M Gaffney, Oxford Brookes University Business School

Instructional design and publishing project management by Wordhouse Ltd, Reading, UK

Content management system, instructional editing and pre-press by Echelon Learning Ltd, London, UK

Index prepared by Indexing Specialists (UK) Ltd, Hove, UK

ISBN 1-86124-163-1
ISBN 978-186124-163-4

## Contents

# Introduction

This course book has been designed to assist you in studying for the CIPS Advanced Project Management unit in the Level 6 Graduate Diploma in Purchasing and Supply. The book covers all topics in the official CIPS unit content document, as illustrated in the table beginning on page xi.

Purchasing and logistics aim to deliver strategic value into the organisation. That value has to be more than just negotiating a price freeze this year or gaining 10% off delivery charges. To fulfil a strategic role, purchasing and logistics need to achieve substantial results and this calls for radical change.

This book is about managing the projects which deliver those radical changes. It covers understanding projects from delivering a small contract to revolutionising the purchasing organisation. From the birth of the first idea to the continuous process of learning and improving, this book provides a structured way of understanding the challenges of succeeding where other projects fail.

The established tools are here, but project management involves far more than a time plan, a budget and a risk register. This book incorporates up to the minute initiatives such as category management, lean, supply chain and six sigma and uses purchasing and logistics examples to explain current ideas. Can critical chain help deliver supplier relationship management? What will project maturity actually do for my company? This is the only text to draw together all these ideas and apply them within purchasing environment.

## How to use this book

The course book will take you step by step through the unit content in a series of carefully planned 'study sessions' and provides you with learning activities, self-assessment questions and revision questions to help you master the subject matter. The guide should help you organise and carry out your studies in a methodical, logical and effective way, but if you have your own study preferences you will find it a flexible resource too.

Before you begin using course this book, make sure you are familiar with any advice provided by CIPS on such things as study skills, revision techniques or support and how to handle formal assessments.

If you are on a taught course, it will be up to your tutor to explain how to use the book – when to read the study sessions, when to tackle the activities and questions, and so on.

If you are on a self-study course, or studying independently, you can use the course book in the following way:

Scan the whole book to get a feel for the nature and content of the subject matter.

Plan your overall study schedule so that you allow enough time to complete all 20 study sessions well before your examinations – in other words, leaving plenty of time for revision.

For each session, set aside enough time for reading the text, tackling all the learning activities and self-assessment questions, and the revision question at the end of the session, and for the suggested further reading. Guidance on roughly how long you should set aside for studying each session is given at the beginning of the session.

Now let's take a look at the structure and content of the individual study sessions.

## Overview of the study sessions

The course book breaks the content down into 20 sessions, which vary from three to six or seven hours' duration each. However, we are not advising you to study for this sort of time without a break! The sessions are simply a convenient way of breaking the syllabus into manageable chunks. Most people would try to study one or two sessions a week, taking one or two breaks within each session. You will quickly find out what suits you best.

Each session begins with a brief **introduction** which sets out the areas of the syllabus being covered and explains, if necessary, how the session fits in with the topics that come before and after.

After the introduction there is a statement of the **session learning objectives**. The objectives are designed to help you understand exactly what you should be able to do after you've studied the session. You might find it helpful to tick them off as you progress through the session. You will also find them useful during revision. There is one session learning objective for each numbered subsection of the session.

After this, there is a brief section reproducing the learning objectives and indicative content from the official **unit content document**. This will help you to understand exactly which part of the syllabus you are studying in the current session.

Following this, there are **prior knowledge** and **resources** sections if necessary. These will let you know if there are any topics you need to be familiar with before tackling each particular session, or any special resources you might need, such as a calculator or graph paper.

Then the main part of the study session begins, with the first of the numbered main subsections. At regular intervals in each study session, we have provided you with **learning activities**, which are designed to get you actively involved in the learning process. You should always try to complete the activities – usually on a separate sheet of your own paper – before reading on. You will learn much more effectively if you are actively involved in doing something as you study, rather than just passively reading the text in front of you. The feedback or answers to the activities are provided at the end of the session. Do not be tempted to skip the activity.

We also provide a number of **self-assessment questions** in each study session. These are to help you to decide for yourself whether or not you have achieved the learning objectives set out at the beginning of the session. As with the activities, you should always tackle them – usually on a separate sheet of paper. Don't be tempted to skip them. The feedback or answers are again at the end of the session. If you still do not understand a topic having attempted the self-assessment question, always try to re-read the relevant passages in the textbook readings or session, or follow the advice on further reading at the end of the session. If this still doesn't work, you should contact the CIPS Membership and Qualification Advice team.

For most of the learning activities and self assessment questions you will need to use separate sheets of paper for your answers or responses. Some of the activities or questions require you to complete a table or form, in which case you could write your response in the study guide itself, or photocopy the page.

At the end of the session are three final sections.

The first is the **summary**. Use it to remind yourself or check off what you have just studied, or later on during revision.

Then follows the **suggested further reading** section. This section, if it appears, contains recommendations for further reading which you can follow up if you would like to read alternative treatments of the topics. If for any reason you are having difficulty understanding the course book on a particular topic, try one of the alternative treatments recommended. If you are keen to read around and beyond the syllabus, to help you pick up extra points in the examination for example, you may like to try some of the additional readings recommended. If this section does not appear at the end of a session, it usually means that further reading for the session topics is not necessary.

At the end of the session we direct you to a **revision question**, which you will find in a separate section at the end of the course book. Feedback on the questions is also given.

## Reading lists

CIPS produces an official reading list, which recommends essential and desirable texts for augmenting your studies. This reading list is available on the CIPS website or from the CIPS Bookshop. This course book is one of the essential texts for this unit. In this section we describe the main characteristics of the other essential text for this unit, which you are strongly urged to buy and use throughout your course.

The other essential text is

*Project Management a Managerial Approach*, 6th edition, by Jack Meredith and Samuel Mantel published by John Wiley & Sons in 2006.

The great strength of Meredith and Mantel is the breadth of coverage. If there is a subject you need to find out about or a project management tool you need to understand, the odds are that Meredith and Mantel can help. From a very comprehensive look at the time planning or value measurement tools to some ideas on management and team building, there is a wealth of information. It is a reference book rather than an exciting read, but as a reference book it works well.

The greatest weakness of Meredith and Mantel is probably a result of this detailed view: they cover the day-to-day management of projects and incorporate the wealth of established techniques. This means they tend to follow the established and limited view of project management to achieve fixed objectives rather than project leadership to gain competitive advantage. Don't go to Meredith and Mantel for a structured critical view or a high level view of project management: their book reflects practice in teaching and doing project management with all the strengths and weaknesses that implies.

# Unit content coverage

In this section we reproduce the whole of the official CIPS unit content document for this unit. The overall unit characteristics and learning outcomes for the unit are given first. Then, in the table that follows, the learning objectives and indicative content are given in the left hand column. In the right hand column are the study sessions, or subsections, in which you will find coverage of the various topics.

## Unit Characteristics

Projects can range from construction to refurbishment of premises, introduction of new information technology systems, outsourcing/offshoring of work previously done in-house, and re-design or re-engineering of products, services and processes. At the same time projects should align and contribute to the overall strategic objectives of the organisation.

This unit will enable students to develop a knowledge of principles, practices and techniques for the leadership and commercial management of projects, with a particular emphasis on the role of the purchasing and supply chain professional;.

The supply chain specialist in both the private and public sectors should have a vital role in the initiation, planning and control of projects, and the development and on-going management of resulting contracts with suppliers and customers.

The role of Projects is concerned with the achievement of objectives relating to Quality, Cost and Time. The supply chain specialist will have a high degree of involvement in developing the procurement strategy for contracts with suppliers, and the operational activities of monitoring and administering supplier performance.

The student needs to understand the architecture of project-orientated organisations. The focus is subsequently directed to roles such as project leader, project-team members, project-coordinator/coaches and project-mentor, from the project management point of view.

### Learning Outcomes:

On completion of this unit, students will be able to:

- Identify and critically evaluate organisational and management issues concerned with project management, including the power and influence of different stakeholders.
- Critically assess and justify the approach to managing Projects of a variety of different methodologies.
- Develop and systematically apply project management concepts, models and tools and techniques to derive solutions to a range of practical project management problems.
- Critically evaluate the key success factors in successful project management in the context of the contemporary business environment.
- Initiate, plan and implement projects in purchasing, logistics and supply chain management.
- Critically evaluate project management processes and their relationship to current strategic practice.

## Learning objectives and indicative content

| | | |
|---|---|---|
| 1.0 | **Identify and critically evaluate organisational and management issues concerned with project management, including the power and influence of different stakeholders. (10%)** | Study session 1<br>Study session 2 |
| 1.1 | Explore various definitions of a 'Project' and seek to understand similarities and differences<br>• Project Management 'Body of Knowledge' definition<br>• Burke (1999) definition<br>• Meredith and Mantel (2003) definition<br>• Maylor (2003) definition<br>• Seek a common view of 'what is a Project' | Study session 1 |
| 1.2 | Summarise the key distinctions between leadership and management relating to projects.<br>• Bennis and Nanus (1985) – efficiency and effectiveness<br>• Kotter (1990) leadership versus management<br>• Mintzberg's (1977) – ten roles of leadership | Study session 1 |
| 1.3 | Explore why organisations do projects.<br>• Rapid change in the external environment, products, processes, technology, markets<br>• Globalisation<br>• Impatient customers<br>• More need for 'unique and customised' solutions via a Project approach | Study session 1 |
| 1.4 | Assess the different sorts of activities which can be implemented as projects, and distinguish between 'hard and soft' projects.<br>• New product development<br>• New process development<br>• Re-design of products and processes<br>• Technology development<br>• 'People' based approaches to 'culture, structure, training and development' | Study session 1 |

| | | |
|---|---|---|
| 1.5 | Analyse the 'external environment' within which a project is undertaken.<br>• PEST factors<br>• Stakeholders<br>• Resource constraints<br>• Time Constraints<br>• Overall strategy of the Organisation | Study session 2 |
| 1.6 | Demonstrate an understanding of 'power and influence' relating to a project.<br>• Stakeholder Assessment<br>• Stakeholder Mapping – Mendelow (1981)<br>• Changing Stakeholder position over the life of the project | Study session 2 |
| 1.7 | Identify, map and assess project stakeholders, and how their power and influence may change over the duration of a purchasing and logistics project.<br>• Characteristics of a Purchasing and Logistics Project<br>• Various types of Purchasing and Logistics Project<br>• Stakeholder Assessment of Purchasing and Logistics Project<br>• Stakeholder Mapping – Mendelow (1981) - of Purchasing and Logistics Project<br>• Changing Stakeholder position over the life of the of Purchasing and Logistics Project | Study session 2 |
| **2.0** | **Critically assess and justify the approach to managing Projects of a variety of different methodologies. (25%)** | Study session 3<br>Study session 4<br>Study session 5<br>Study session 6<br>Study session 7 |
| 2.1 | Beware of the variety of different methodologies of approaches to Projects.<br>• Projects as a 'conversion' process – Maylor (2003)<br>• Project as 'low volume/high variety' process – Slack et al (2004)<br>• Meredith and Mantel (2003) | Study session 3 |
| 2.2 | Describe the approach of the Project Life Cycle, and its various phases.<br>• 3-stage PLC Meredith and Mantel (2003)<br>• 4-stage PLC – Maylor (2003)<br>• 5-stage PLC – Weiss and Wysocki (1992)<br>• 7S Project Approach – McKinsey, adapted Maylor (2003) | Study session 4 |
| 2.3 | Link the PLC to a variety of Problem Solving processes.<br>• 5-stage Problem Solving Approach (PSA)<br>• 6-stage PSA<br>• 8-satge PSA<br>• Linking PLC and PSA – The BT Way (1988) | Study session 5 |
| 2.4 | Critically evaluate Six-Sigma, DMAIC, PRINCE2, Critical Chains and other contemporary Project approaches.<br>• Six-sigma methodology – General Electric and Motorola<br>• DMAIC – product/service improvement<br>• PRINCE2 – Projects in Controlled Environments<br>• Critical Chain – Goldratt (1997) | Study session 6 |

| | | |
|---|---|---|
| 2.5 | Synthesise the various approaches and be prepared to justify an approach which is suitable for purchasing and logistics projects in various industry sectors.<br>• Exploring the pros and cons of each approach<br>• Examining each approach in the context of different industry/market conditions<br>• Assessing each approach in the context of a purchasing and logistics project. | Study session 7 |
| **3.0** | **Develop and systematically apply project management concepts, models and tools and techniques to derive solutions to a range of practical project management problems. (40%)** | Study session 8<br>Study session 9<br>Study session 10<br>Study session 11<br>Study session 12<br>Study session 13<br>Study session 14<br>Study session 15 |
| 3.1 | Understand the various phases of a Project, and the activities to be considered at each phases:<br>3.1.1 Initiation and Definition<br>• State the problem<br>• Identify project goals<br>• List the objectives<br>• Determine preliminary resources<br>• Identify assumptions and risks<br>3.1.2 Planning<br>• Identify activities<br>• Estimate time & cost<br>• Sequence activities<br>• Identify critical activities<br>• Write project proposal<br>3.1.3 Organisation and Implementation<br>• Determine personnel needs<br>• Recruit Project Manager<br>• Recruit Project Team<br>• Organise team<br>• Assign work packages<br>3.1.4 Measurement, Monitoring, Control and Improvement<br>• Define management style<br>• Establish control tools<br>• Prepare status report<br>• Review project schedule<br>• Issue change orders<br>3.1.5 Closure<br>• Obtain client acceptance<br>• Install deliverables<br>• Document the project<br>• Issue final report<br>3.1.6 Review, Evaluation and Learning<br>• Conduct project audit<br>• Lessons Learnt<br>• Communicate the Review, Evaluation and Learning | Study session 8 |

| | Learning objective | Study sessions |
|---|---|---|
| 3.2 | Appraise the range of tools and techniques which are available to the project team, in terms of appropriateness, selection and implementation.<br>• Appropriateness – pick the right tool for the task<br>• Selection – be aware of the limitation of tools and techniques<br>• Implementation - be able to use the tool correctly | Study session 10<br>Study session 11<br>Study session 12<br>Study session 13<br>Study session 14 |
| 3.3 | Use a range of tools and techniques to assist in robust and systematic data collection, analysis of options and decision-making.<br>• SIPOC<br>• 7 tools of 'quality control'<br>• Financial appraisal<br>• Voice of the Customer<br>• Quality Function Deployment<br>• Project Initiation Document (PID)<br>• Moments of Truth<br>• Work Breakdown Structure<br>• Critical Path Analysis – Network Diagrams<br>• Risk analysis and assessment – mitigating risks<br>• Risk/Impact Matrix<br>• Suitability/Feasibility/Vulnerability | Study session 9<br>Study session 10<br>Study session 12<br>Study session 13 |
| 3.4 | Demonstrate the approach of 'systems thinking and process focus', utilising process mapping techniques and procedures.<br>• Understanding end-to-end processes<br>• Flow-charting the process<br>• Understanding the interfaces – swim lanes<br>• Simplifying 'flow' – redesign and re-engineering | Study session 14 |
| 3.5 | Appreciate the range of Project Management Software and its utility in project environments.<br>• MS Project software<br>• Primavera software<br>• ACE software<br>• PRINCE2 software<br>• Critical Chains software | Study session 15 |
| 3.6 | Select and use a range of project management concepts, models, tools and techniques, which are particularly relevant to purchasing and logistics projects.<br>• Assess the characteristics of purchasing and logistics projects.<br>• Practical application of concepts to purchasing and logistics projects.<br>• Practical applications of models to purchasing and logistics projects.<br>• Practical application of tools and techniques to purchasing and logistics projects.<br>• Practical application of Project software to purchasing and logistics projects. | |

| Learning outcome | Study session |
| --- | --- |
| **4.0 Critically evaluate the key success factors in successful project management in the context of the contemporary business environment. (10%)** | Study session 16<br>Study session 17 |
| 4.1 Critically evaluate the concept of the Iron Triangle (Quality, Cost, Time)<br>• Quality, Cost, Time – Project Objectives, Slack et al (2004)<br>• The balance between QCT – contingent approaches | Study session 16 |
| 4.2 Contrast the Iron Triangle and other contemporary approaches.<br>• Critical chains – Goldratt (1997) – crashing project 'float' | Study session 16 |
| 4.3 Recognise the importance of the human aspects of project management, including leadership, management, teamwork and communication.<br>• The role and skills of the 'project manager' – Maylor, Meredith and Mantel, Lock<br>• Leading and managing projects – Managing in Four Directions – Buchanan and Boddy (1992)<br>• Teamwork – Belbin (1981), Body of Knowledge (2000) | Study session 17 |
| 4.4 Describe and apply to purchasing and logistics projects:<br>• Greer (1999) 'elements of project success'<br>• Greer (1999) 'ten ways that projects fail'<br>• Other contemporary approaches to 'successful projects' – Van Aken (1997), Grundy (2001), Gardiner (2005) | Study session 16<br>Study session 17 |
| **5.0 Critically evaluate project management processes and their relationship to current strategic practice. (15%)** | Study session 18<br>Study session 19<br>Study session 20 |
| 5.1 Describe and assess the architecture of project-orientated organisations; structures, cultures and project organisation and management.<br>• Function structures<br>• Matrix structures<br>• Process structures<br>• Culture and project approaches – organisational readiness – Hammer and Stanton (1995) | Study session 18 |
| 5.2 Describe and explain Buttrick(2002) – Project Management Maturity Matrix, and relate to contemporary project environments and issues.<br>• Maturity of organisations towards Project Management<br>• Unaware - sophisticated | Study session 19 |
| 5.3 Evaluate the utility of the concept of Project Excellence (Westerveld 2002) and how it links to the principles of the Business Excellence Model.<br>• The Business Excellence Model<br>• The Project Excellence Model – Westerveld (2002) and different approaches to Project Organisation and Management | Study session 19 |

| | |
|---|---|
| 5.4 Describe the principles of Knowledge Management, Knowledge Communities, and Organisational Learning, and demonstrate how this links to the successful implementation of strategy through projects, particularly in the purchasing and logistics areas.<br>• Knowledge Management and links to Project Management – the role of ICT and special interest groups in capturing and disseminating good practice.<br>• Knowledge Communities and Knowledge Creation – Nonanka and Tageuchi (1995) | Study session 20 |

Study session 1

# Managing and leading projects

1

## Introduction

What? Why? Who? How? The fundamentals of managing projects.

Projects and project management are becoming more and more widespread. Many businesses launch initiative after initiative as 'improvement projects', people talk of their 'pet' projects and, in the public sector, there is a reliance on projects to transform efficiency and effectiveness. Problems, delays, costs and failures are blamed on 'bad project management'.

Projects and project management have a substantial impact on the way we work, yet there is no one clear definition of what a project is. The project manager is frequently seen as key to success, yet the role is not always clear and the nature of project management has shifted from large, tangible projects such as ships or aeroplanes to a broader description including far more change management.

This first session aims to lay the foundations for the book by exploring what projects and project management are, what they can do and what project managers can expect to face and need to do.

## Session learning objectives

After completing this session you should be able to:

1.1 Identify the nature of a project and what characteristics differentiate projects from other types of operation.
1.2 Analyse the difference between leadership and management and identify the key responsibilities of an effective project leader.
1.3 Explain why organisations in different sectors, public, private, services and goods need to engage in projects and consider some of the different types of project in each sector.
1.4 Consider some different types of IT projects from your own company or newspaper reports and evaluate the importance and relationship of project management processes (hard) and people management (soft) in achieving project goals.

## Unit content coverage

This study session covers the following topic from the official CIPS unit content document.

### Learning objective

1.0 Identify and evaluate organisational and management issues concerned with project management, including the power and influence of stakeholders.

1.1 Explore various definitions of a 'Project' and seek to understand similarities and differences.
- Project Management 'Body of Knowledge' definition
- Burke (1999) definition
- Meredith and Mantel (2003) definition
- Maylor (2003) definition
- Seek a common view of 'what is a Project?'

1.2 Summarise the key distinctions between leadership and management relating to projects.
- Bennis and Nanus (1985) efficiency and effectiveness
- Kotter (1990) leadership versus management
- Mintzberg (1977) ten roles of leadership

1.3 Explore why organisations undertake projects.
- Rapid change in the external environment, products, processes, technology, markets
- Globalisation
- Impatient customers
- More need for 'unique and customised' solutions using a project approach

1.4 Assess the different sorts of activities which can be implemented as projects, and distinguish between 'hard and soft' projects.
- New product development
- New process development
- Redesign of products and processes
- Technology development
- People-based approaches to culture, structure, training and development

## Prior knowledge

Leading and Influencing in Purchasing and Strategic Supply Chain Management could provide a useful foundation.

## Timing

You should set aside about 6 hours to read and complete this session, including learning activities, self-assessment questions, the suggested reading (if any) from the essential textbook for this unit and the revision question.

## 1.1 The basics: what is a project?

### Learning activity 1.1

Below is a list of different businesses activities.

Identify which you believe are 'projects'.

Use these or other examples to build up a definition of what a project is.

*(continued on next page)*

### Learning activity 1.1 *(continued)*

You should aim to identify what feature or features separate projects from other activities:

1. Running an assembly line producing televisions.
2. Setting up that assembly line.
3. Introducing a new supplier with a product never sourced before.
4. Introducing a new supplier to replace a well-established single source for an important product.
5. Introducing one of 100 new suppliers for products which are re-sourced each year.
6. Developing a new manual for purchasing processes, documenting and standardising activity which has never been written down before and which is done differently by different people.
7. Developing a simple manual of your own purchase processes which define what you do but are not used by other people.
8. Leading a team to investigate potential for restructuring.

*Feedback on page 14*

Projects and project management form part of everyday life. A large piece of schoolwork is 'a project', organising a musical event might be 'a big project', if someone buys a run-down house for renovation, it is 'a tough project', bringing a large family together for Christmas might be 'an impossible project'. Part of the reason some projects are managed badly may be that what people describe as projects covers a very wide spread of activities. Managing the renovation of a house will take very different skills and knowledge from bringing a large family together.

To set a solid foundation, this section aims to use a range of definitions to build a common view of what a project is in management terms.

The Association for Project Management defines projects in terms of achieving agreed outcomes:

> 'Projects are unique, transient endeavours undertaken to achieve a desired outcome.'

Project management becomes the process of achieving these:

> 'Project Management is the process by which projects are defined, planned, monitored, controlled and delivered such that the agreed benefits are realised.'
>
> 'Projects bring about change and project management is recognised as the most efficient way of bringing about that change.'

Burke (1999) focuses more on what is needed to achieve the objectives:

> 'A group of activities that have to be performed in a logical sequence to meet preset objectives outlined by the client'.

Meredith and Mantel (2006) keep the definition broad:

> 'A specific, finite task to be accomplished' combined with seven factors common to projects: importance, performance, finite due date,

interdependencies (between departments and competing projects), uniqueness, resources and conflict.

They also suggest that all projects have the same 'direct' objectives or goals: performance (or scope), time and cost, and that project management focuses on managing the trade-off between these three.

Maylor (2003) uses a discussion of what is not a project to identify three agreed characteristics:

- constraints (time, resources and others)
- projects are a process
- the goal shows a project is 'a focused activity and often this is change'.

Turner and Muller (2003) discuss a series of definitions before defining using Cleland and Kerzner's: 'a combination of human and non-human resources pulled together into a temporary organisation to achieve a specified purpose'.

Each definition offers different features and has different weaknesses as follows.

### Objectives or outcomes

The idea of 'agreed benefits' and 'preset objectives' is attractive, but some projects start with a very vague idea of the outcome, while some objectives drift: 'scope creep' is a term for the changing requirements put on a project by stakeholders or clients. If a project takes two years or more, it is quite likely that some stakeholders or clients will be replaced let alone change their minds and requirements. It seems likely that for many projects, there will be some general objectives but the specifics will change. The goalposts should be expected to move.

### Uniqueness or novelty

Project management tools and techniques have been developed on the basis of managing new activities. Parts of the project will be unique, even if there are some well-established activities. A project to introduce a new major supplier in an innovative company will probably follow a similar path to the last major supplier change, but there will be new aspects. The general approach might be: learn from experience and use established processes, but project management must deal with unique and unknown activities and factors.

### Constraints and timing

Most definitions touch on the idea of constraints: time, resources and quality, for example. Meredith and Mantel (2006) focus on them as central to project management. All human activity is constrained, however, and these 'constraints' seem to be flexible. Major projects frequently overrun on cost, for example building the Channel Tunnel or Wembley Stadium. Many are delivered late – Wembley Stadium again, or almost any major IT project for government. A project which may have scarce resources at the outset often gathers momentum and wins resources as it succeeds, or as it begins to go wrong and fear of failure leads clients to 'throw' money or people at it.

Project management involves juggling factors such as cost, time and quality, but once again, these are often flexible and changing.

### Complexity and interdependence

This fits with project management: if an activity is very simple, even if it is unique and all the other things, the complex project management tools and ideas are unnecessary. If there is just one, simple activity with no impact on other departments or work, planning becomes straightforward.

### Change

All activity involves some change, but projects tend to involve *unique, novel, complex* change. Different people react differently to change and reactions can be severe and damaging. As a result project management needs to incorporate management of change.

These features may not give the perfect definition of what a project is, but they point at something equally valuable: what the demands on project management are.

### Summary

Definitions of projects differ but project management needs to offer ways of achieving objectives which will change and develop while:

- managing changing resources such as people and money
- coping with time constraints
- managing complex situations and activities, frequently with interdependence on people, departments and stakeholders spread across and beyond the organisation
- planning and managing activities which are new, hence experience is limited
- managing human reactions to change.

### Self-assessment question 1.1

What does a project mean to you? Set a definition of a project from your perspective.

*Feedback on page 14*

## 1.2 'Ours is a project organisation': the increasing importance of projects

### Learning activity 1.2

Select two or three projects from your experience or research of newspaper articles. What were the driving factors behind them? Identify the main reasons these projects were undertaken.

*Feedback on page 15*

More and more organisations appear to be using project management to drive change. Some organisations say 'ours is a project organisation'; in other words, all of their activity is changing all the time, they must constantly renew what they do. Even in the public sector – hospitals, schools, social services, local authorities – projects are becoming commonplace and new funding is often allocated only to projects.

This raises two questions: Why is project management becoming more widespread? What is it that project management can deliver for these different organisations?

### Hotter competition

Japanese manufacturing challenged and overcame US and European manufacturers of cars, motorcycles and electronics in the 1960s, 1970s and 1980s. Through the 1990s, other Asian 'tiger' economies such as Korea and Thailand brought more competition. Currently China is expanding manufacturing at a rate never seen before and offering competition which is very hard to beat. These are just examples of changes in the competitive environment, often grouped as globalisation and economic progress. To respond to these, companies need to change and change faster and better.

Predictions for the future of companies point at more and more rapid change, leaving behind the relative stability of 20 years ago. Kanter (1990) describes giant organisations as learning to dance: to be nimble and change rapidly. Handy (1989) predicts more change in organisations and also in individual careers: people will need to have 'transferable skills' which they take from one job to another.

### Demanding customers

Mass production is a fairly stable way of working, but Davis (1996) predicts a future of mass customisation, where each customer requires the value of mass production with a product tailored to their needs. As the cost of delivering goods and services is driven downwards, customers can demand more variety, while holding the price stable. In computing and mobile phones, sales can only be sustained by delivering new products rapidly which persuade customers to buy new and replace their old purchases. To respond to rapidly changing customer requirements and to feed the cycle of new products requires rapid and effective projects.

### Changing technology, changing demand

In medicine, technological advances are a constant. The demand, however, is changing. With an older population and greater success at overcoming illness, more and more different and more complex medical issues become important. People with profound and multiple illnesses are saved from death and require more complex treatments. This leads to a rapidly growing demand overall, with new challenges to management through size, complexity and technology.

### Better project management

Looking back 30 years, project management was considered part of engineering, and not necessarily successful at managing that. The understanding of project management has developed and linked with change management to produce a discipline which can offer far more effective management of a wide range of projects. The demands of each project may be different, but the portfolio of project management tools and techniques can be adapted and tailored to respond. The difficulties and failure of large public projects such as IT systems for the CSA, Passport Agency, the National Fingerprint Database and the London Ambulance Service demonstrate the impact of poor project management, but these failures can be reversed through comprehensive and effective project management and coordination.

So to return to those questions:

- Why is project management becoming more widespread? Project management is about achieving objectives which change and develop within constraints and a complex environment. The change driving industries and public organisations provides a need for strong project management.
- What is it that project management can deliver for these different organisations? A way of coping with change, and successfully managed change which can give competitive advantage or cost-effective improvement.

### Self-assessment question 1.2

Identify two possible projects for each of these two organisations: a large public hospital and a manufacturer of automotive parts, both based in the UK.

Suggest some of the factors which might be driving these four projects.

*Feedback on page 15*

## 1.3 The soft ones are often harder: two sides of project management

Much of the background to project management developed from large engineering or scientific projects. Time planning tools such as Gantt charts and PERT (Program Evaluation and Review Technique) were developed to build ships more effectively in the First World War and for the management of the Polaris nuclear missile system respectively. Project selection tools are frequently focused on financial analysis.

For large engineering projects, a very strong time plan is critical. For example, when building a large office block, each piece must be ready and in place like a giant jigsaw before the next stage can proceed. The steel frame must be complete before any cladding can go on, stairs must be in place before the next floor can be laid and so on. Where a critical piece is missing and work is stopped, costs escalate rapidly and the delay is hard to recover. Where activities happen out of sequence, for example cladding the frame before it is complete, there can be structural failures and safety problems.

For these projects it is also relatively simple to break down the project into smaller, measurable activities which can be identified as complete, for example assemble steel frame, put stairs in position.

The balance is different for projects which involve people in change, for example the restructuring of an organisation, changing the function of a purchasing team or even moving a department to new offices. In these cases, the physical, measurable change may be small: a movement of offices, changes to the organisation chart. Far more important will be the human factors: allowing people to understand the change, involvement in planning, acceptance of new roles.

### Hard and soft

The tangible, measurable activities and processes such as laying a floor in a building are termed **hard** elements. The human factors and processes like gaining acceptance and communicating are termed **soft** elements.

### Learning activity 1.3

Select a completed or near complete project with which you are familiar.

1. Try to categorise it as a 'hard' or a 'soft' project.
2. Identify hard and soft factors and suggest to what extent each contributed to success or failure.

*Feedback on page 16*

Projects are frequently divided into 'hard' and 'soft' because the management of these involves very different skills. As a very simplistic example, compare the two situations:

1. On a building project, part of the steel frame is late. Calling the supplier and demanding they hurry, with threats of penalties may be effective.
2. On a product development project, one supplier will be providing a key and complex new technology and they are a close partner in the project. Delivery is also late in this case and they do not seem very involved or committed. An angry phone call may not be so appropriate.

The division between hard and soft should more accurately be applied to aspects or elements of the project. Almost all projects involve some hard and some soft elements. A project constructing a new building could be mainly 'hard', but soft aspects would include communication and consultation with people living nearby, involvement of and consultation with the people who will use the building, managing the relationships between architect, structural engineers, builders and other subcontractors. A project restructuring a department may involve the physical relocation and changes to contracts as hard elements.

To understand the link between hard and soft factors civil engineering offers an excellent example. In the UK, large civil engineering projects overran budget and deadlines for 40 years until 1990, almost without exception.

Many civil engineers believed it was impossible to deliver on time and to budget because of uncertainty in the projects, in spite of the best and most advanced tools for time and work planning and management, using statistics and a wealth of experience. The management of hard factors became stronger and stronger yet the outcome stayed the same. This problem was solved by tackling soft factors: the relationship between different companies involved in the project. Funding for public projects was changed to 'Design Build Fund Operate'. Essentially, the project team gained income only for a finished project; it was in everyone's interest to overcome any problems quickly and effectively. Since then, almost all projects have been completed on time and on budget: the soft factors of commitment, incentive, shared goals, collaboration and teamwork have changed the way the industry operates.

### Summary

Projects consist of hard factors: the measurable aspects such as work, time and cost, and soft factors such as commitment, morale and teamwork. Most projects have a mixture of the two, some projects are biased to the hard, some to the soft, but both will need to be managed with very different management skills.

### Self-assessment question 1.3

Meredith and Mantel (2006: 631) use Pinto and Slevin's list to explain the critical success factors of projects:

1. Project mission: initial clearly defined goals and general directions.
2. Top management support: willingness of top management to provide the necessary resources and power/authority for success.
3. Project schedule/plan: a detailed specification of the individual action steps for project implementation.
4. Client consultation: communication, consultation and active listening to all impacted parties.
5. Personnel: recruitment, selection and retention of the necessary personnel for the project team.
6. Technical tasks: availability of the required technology and expertise to accomplish the specific technical action steps.
7. Client acceptance: the act of 'selling' the final project to its ultimate end users.
8. Monitoring and feedback: timely provision of comprehensive control information at each stage in the implementation process.
9. Communication: the provision of an appropriate network and necessary data to all key actors in the project implementation.
10. Troubleshooting: ability to handle unexpected crises and deviations from plan.

Suggest which of these factors are influenced by soft factors, with a very brief explanation.

*Feedback on page 16*

## 1.4 Managing projects: lead from the front or plan from the back room?

### Learning activity 1.4

Your company is launching a project to reduce the supply base dramatically. Currently there are 130 suppliers of indirect goods and services and this will be reduced to 50.

Draft an advert or specification for the project leader. What attributes, experience, knowledge, skills and attitude would you expect him or her to have?

*Feedback on page 17*

In section 1.1 above, project management was identified to involve:

- managing changing resources such as people and money
- coping with time constraints
- managing complex situations and activities, frequently with interdependence on people, departments and stakeholders spread across and beyond the organisation
- planning and managing activities which are new, hence experience is limited.

If these demands are applied to the project manager, the role begins to look very demanding. The project manager's role can involve challenge, collaboration confusion and conflict. The role is temporary, the project adds to existing workloads, not everyone will be supportive or enthusiastic and the inherent uncertainty means that setbacks and problems are almost certain to crop up.

To look at what is needed from a project manager, this section will divide the attributes into three parts: competence in managing the project, leadership, specific technical skills.

### Competence in managing the project

There are tools, techniques and skills involved in planning and executing the project. These include scope management, time planning and management (Gantt and Critical Path Methods), risk management (risk analysis and assessment), activity planning (Work Breakdown Structures, task allocation and milestone planning) and resource management or managing the team. These tools and skills often form the focus for basic project management books or courses and are very important in managing success. Software is available to support the use of many of the tools, for example Microsoft Project combines the ability to set up Gantt and Critical Path charts with resource identification costing and planning. Competence is not just about 'book smarts' or a theoretical understanding, professional bodies such as the Association of Project Management attach great importance to experience gained. Experience in applying tools and coordinating and linking them is needed to build competence.

## Leadership

Given a challenging project, some managers can apply the tools well, allocate tasks to the team, communicate to other departments and still fail. There is something beyond the project management activity which is needed to guide, inspire, coax, coach, cajole and provide vision. This falls under the heading of leadership and cannot be described as easily as management, in terms of activities and tools, but involves providing direction for the project and the work entailed in ensuring everyone involved achieves what is needed.

## Specific technical skills

Surely for a purchasing project, experience in purchasing is necessary? For an engineering project, isn't an engineer needed to lead the project? There is an unresolved argument about the need for experience and competence in the field in order to manage a project effectively. The two sides can be characterised simply:

1. Knowledge and experience of the field is vital for project managers. It reduces time wasted learning about purchasing, engineering or whatever, avoids basic mistakes, allows the manager to know when people are exaggerating or understating difficulty or problems, helps gain respect and acceptance from the team involved and speeds up the process.
2. Project management ability is more important, a technical expert can get bogged down in technical detail. A good project manager relies on the people around them for subject expertise. Time spent questioning the accepted ways of doing things can lead to breakthrough. Bringing new ideas and competence from other fields can challenge stale and rigid ways of working.

There is probably no best answer and the solution depends very much on the situation. Many project managers fall into the role and the luxury of selecting an ideal is not available. The warning from this argument could be summarised as shown in table 1.1.

**Table 1.1**

| | Strong technical knowledge | Strong project management knowledge |
|---|---|---|
| Dangers | • Tends to do things as they have always been done<br>• Accepts received wisdom<br>• Gets buried in detail<br>• Tends to focus on their area<br>• May lack project management or leadership skills | • Can be 'bamboozled' or misled by experts<br>• Can take time to understand the situation<br>• May not be accepted by technical experts |

## Leadership and management

Historically, the leaders of companies have rarely risen from the purchasing field. Purchasing may be well managed but the role of purchasing itself rarely leads a company or radical change. In the future, if purchasing is to be involved in projects which drive change, which deliver value beyond simple cost reductions, that leadership ability will become more and more necessary.

There are plenty of ideas on leadership and how it relates to management. Bennis and Nannus (1985) have a catchy explanation:

> 'Managers are people who do things right and leaders are people who do the right thing'

and

> 'Management means to bring about, to accomplish, to have charge of or responsibility for, to conduct. Leading is influencing, guiding in direction, course, action, opinion.'

This gives leadership the responsibility for overall direction, and a softer guiding of people. John Kotter extends this. He suggests that management includes planning and budgeting, organizing and staffing, controlling and problem-solving. All these are necessary but focused on the shorter term and the visible. Leadership includes establishing direction (vision and strategies), aligning people (communication and team-building), and motivating and inspiring (overcoming barriers and satisfying human needs).

This begins to form two very different but linked roles for leadership and management:

- Management focuses on the here and now, problem solving, applying rational ideas, plans and activities to bring order.
- Leadership focuses on the longer term and is far more creative, using vision and communication to find direction and inspire the people involved to work together to get there.

'Leadership' can conjure up images of heroes, dictators and demagogues, people you may not want to work with. These are not necessarily the best models for effective leaders of projects. Although leadership is an idea which arouses argument, for a simple concept, look at the people being led. A leader is a leader because people follow their direction, example, wish or ideas. A successful leader can be forceful and very visible, or subtle and nearly invisible. The success of a leader is in the outcome.

Finally, Henry Mintzberg (1973) looked in detail at what managers do and identified ten separate roles: figurehead, leader, liaison, monitor, disseminator, spokesman, entrepreneur, disturbance handler, resource allocator and negotiator. These may not be a perfect description of project management, but they highlight the variety of roles needed to manage effectively and drive change. Figurehead and leader are at the top of the list.

### Summary

The demands on the project manager are many and fall into three areas: competence in managing the project, leadership and specific technical skills. There is some debate on the need for specific technical skills, but to manage a project which will drive change, the project manager will need to combine a range of managerial skills with leadership which will direct the project and inspire the participants to achieve.

### Self-assessment question 1.4

You are looking for a leader for a project. This project is to purchase and commission a large ventilation unit for a building in your company.

Identify key requirements of the project leader.

*Feedback on page 17*

### Revision question

Now try the revision question for this session on page 319.

### Summary

This session has looked at the what, why and how of projects.

What are projects? There seems to be no clear definition, but the common factors are timing and goals. Some see projects as activities to deliver specified objectives, some take a more complex view of projects as temporary organisations, brought together to achieve goals which change and develop. The first definition may be of something easier to manage, but the second encompasses projects which can drive radical change.

Radical change is sometimes the 'why' of projects. There are many factors, including globalisation and technological developments driving projects and sometimes radical change is needed to keep up or compete. At the same time, a better understanding of how projects can be managed to success has helped spread the use of project management techniques.

'How' is really the subject of most of this book, so this session has looked at some of the basic elements. There are soft and hard parts of projects, sometimes the soft parts are harder to achieve. A project manager will need to manage both aspects to reach success, and expanding the role to go beyond management to leadership is a part of anything but basic projects.

### Suggested further reading

- Ayers (2004); Chapter 1.
- Bennis and Nannus (1985).
- Davis (1996).
- Handy (1989).
- Kanter (1990).
- Kotter (1990).
- Lock (2003); Chapter 1.
- Maylor (1996); Chapter 1.
- Meredith and Mantel (2006); Chapter 1.
- Mintzberg (1973).
- Turner and Muller (2003).

## Feedback on learning activities and self-assessment questions

### Feedback on learning activity 1.1

Using the discussion in this section, it becomes clear that there is no one definition for projects, so you could answer in many different ways. This feedback uses the list of features which define projects to examine which of these could be described as projects

1. *Running an assembly line producing televisions*: This could involve a clear objective with time and cost constraints, for example '1,000 televisions per day with 24 staff'. This is repetitive, though, and each day will be similar to previous days, so this is more of a process than a project.
2. *Setting up that assembly line*: This fits the definitions of projects better: it is a one-off with a clear objective and should involve cost, resource and time constraints.
3. *Introducing a new supplier with a product never sourced before:* Again, this is a one-off with clear objectives, etc and fits the definitions of projects.
4. *Introducing a new supplier to replace a well-established single source for an important product*: Although the product is well known, this is an important and complex activity of novel change: it still fits most definitions.
5. *Introducing one of 100 new suppliers for products which are re-sourced each year*: This is repeated frequently and is not novel or unique. It should be treated as a process rather than a project.
6. *Developing a new manual for purchasing processes, documenting and standardising activity which has never been written down before and which is done differently by different people*: This hits most of the features, including change and interdependence on other people.
7. *Developing a simple manual of your own purchase processes which define what you do but are not used by other people*: This is not especially complex and there is little change, so while some project management tools may be useful, for example time planning, this does not fit many definitions of a project.
8. *Leading a team to investigate potential for restructuring*: This may have vague and developing objectives, but it involves change, constraints, complexity and novelty. It is a project and probably quite a difficult/risky one.

### Feedback on self-assessment question 1.1

You could select any of the different definitions or combine some aspects.

Using some of the examples from learning activity 1.1 and comparing them with your definition may help.

The five aspects discussed at the end of the section feature in many of the definitions:

- objectives or outcomes
- uniqueness or novelty

- constraints and timing
- complexity and interdependence
- change.

Your definition will probably depend on your experience and attitudes, so there is plenty of room for variety. The two aspects which are in almost every definition are:

- Temporary: Not lasting indefinitely
- Objectives or goals: There is an intention to achieve something, even if that changes.

### Feedback on learning activity 1.2

Here is a list of reasons why more projects are used:

- Some projects may be driven by these reasons: demanding customers, increased competitive pressures, changes in technology and so on.
- Some, however, are triggered by causes which are stable: a new building to replace an old one, a new management structure to replace one which no longer works, a pilot for a new product.
- Some may be triggered by fashion: many companies are adopting a new initiative, so others follow, without necessarily needing to.
- Some projects are triggered by the human need to change: few people are content to do the same thing, day in day out, and need to try new ways of working to improve.

Most projects have a number of factors, so if you found it difficult to isolate one, instead finding a combination, this is similar to many other projects.

### Feedback on self-assessment question 1.2

There are many different potential projects, of course, some of which are mentioned in this section.

Either might be restructuring, training for some specific need, building, moving site, introducing some large technology or equipment, improving the customer/patient service, simulating to improve their process flows.

- The hospital may be involved in medical research into developing techniques or a large project to reduce infections or reduce cost, for example.
- The manufacturing company may be involved in quality, supply chain development, projects moving towards lean production or sourcing.

The detail of the projects may differ but the drivers are likely to be very different. Again, a review of the section may give some ideas:

- The hospital is public and government-funded, so many if not most of the factors will be related to government requirements or initiatives. Changes in staff, for example the limited supply of UK-based staff, may prompt projects, the changing requirements of patients may encourage some change projects, but the funder has the most impact.

- Customers fund the manufacturing company so they will impose some requirements and projects, but the competitive environment will also have a strong influence. If other companies are changing, then this company may need to follow; if new competitors emerge, then a response may be needed.

Some of the factors and detail are different, but it is worth noting that many of the projects could be similar in both organisations.

## Feedback on learning activity 1.3

The factors will vary from project to project. Here are some general comments:

1. You should have been able to assess the majority or balance of factors and categorise the project as 'mostly hard' or 'mostly soft', but categorising as entirely one or the other is unusual. Most projects are a mix of hard and soft and both need managing. If the majority of factors are 'hard', for example building, or a change with little impact on stakeholders, management should focus on those hard factors. If the majority of factors are soft, management effort should be weighted accordingly.
2. Hard factors may have included elements such as resources allocated, clear time plan, benefits hugely outweighing cost, large profits to be made. Soft factors may have included commitment of one key person or a group, people clearly understanding the need for change, the impact of senior management commitment. The interesting part is the link between hard and soft factors: a really profitable new product can fail because no one quite knows what to do. A really committed team needs a clear plan of action to succeed in achieving the goal.

If your analysis led you to categorise your project as totally 'hard' or 'soft', it may be worthwhile examining again to try and identify linked factors from the other side.

## Feedback on self-assessment question 1.3

There is an argument to be made for each of them to be influenced by soft factors:

1. Project mission: This is influenced by the stakeholders and is defined by the team: whatever the stated mission, unless the team accept it, it is unlikely to be achieved.
2. Top management support: Intrinsically soft.
3. Project schedule/plan: This depends on the speed at which people work and their willingness to take on or reschedule the work.
4. Client consultation: Intrinsically soft.
5. Personnel: Intrinsically soft.
6. Technical tasks: The technical tasks can be defined as hard, but sourcing the expertise and using it is influenced by soft factors.
7. Client acceptance: Intrinsically soft.
8. Monitoring and feedback: Measurements and reports could be described as hard, but monitoring and feedback is far more than

circulating a standard written report. Understanding progress and feeding that back to stakeholders brings in soft factors.

9 Communication: Intrinsically soft.

10 Troubleshooting: Intrinsically soft.

The success factors combine soft factors with hard and it seems difficult to separate the two.

## Feedback on learning activity 1.4

How does your description break down between the three areas below: competence in managing the project, leadership and specific technical skills?

The key is the balance between the three. Extensive experience in supplier management, experience with a similar consolidation project could be useful. This is unlikely to lead to success without the competence in planning and managing the project, however, and those skills are important. Finally, the best analyst, the best planner, the most intelligent and experienced purchaser may hit trouble without the ability in leadership to direct and inspire the project.

## Feedback on self-assessment question 1.4

Look at the three aspects from this section:

- Competence in managing the project: There is a strong need in this area. The project could have an impact on a lot of people and the cost is substantial, so skills in this area will be necessary, such as scheduling, coordination, budget management. You may believe experience is necessary, you may believe training will be enough.
- Specific technical skills: There are several areas of knowledge: ventilation engineering, a broader understanding of facilities management and, of course, purchasing. It is unusual for anyone to have the right mix of all three, so a choice has to be made. Can the ventilation and facilities management skills be brought in as required, perhaps by having someone with those skills on the team? Perhaps purchasing expertise can be brought in and a ventilation engineer should lead. Balancing skills is a complex issue and it seems certain that whoever leads will need to draw in expertise from other people.
- Leadership and management: This project has a lot of 'hard' factors: the nature and goal is well defined and it would be fairly easy to identify some measures of success: good and reliable ventilation with minimum disruption and minimum cost.

You may, quite rightly, have focused on management and coordination skills. In this case, an inspirational leader would probably be ill suited. There are skills required in leading and managing different people and drawing out different expertise, but the project is never likely to involve radical change and the management of complex and conflicting objectives.

Study session 2

# Power and influence in projects

2

## Introduction

Projects take place in a complex environment. A change in the market can tip a project from marginal benefit to huge value, or from shining star to dog. Social changes can make a project redundant overnight. Above all, stakeholders define, determine and drive success and are frustratingly varied.

Markets, governments and stakeholders: uncontrollable forces and unpredictable people.

This session aims to unravel some of the complexity in the project environment and provide some ways of managing projects successfully in spite of the uncontrollable forces and unpredictable people.

## Session learning objectives

After completing this session you should be able to:

2.1 Demonstrate an understanding of external business environmental factors and how they may affect a project.
2.2 Identify the key forces likely to affect successful project completion and evaluate their impact.
2.3 Demonstrate an understanding of who the key stakeholders in a project might be and identify their main requirements.
2.4 Analyse typical purchasing and logistics projects in order to identify the key stakeholders and how their power and influence changes throughout the life of the project.

## Unit content coverage

This study session covers the following topic from the official CIPS unit content document.

### Learning objective

1.0 Identify and evaluate organisational and management issues concerned with project management, including the power and influence of stakeholders.
1.5 Analyse the external environment within which a project is undertaken.
- PESTLE factors
- Stakeholders
- Resource constraints
- Time constraints
- Overall strategy of the organisation

1.6 Critically evaluate the concept of power and influence relating to a project.

- Stakeholder assessment
- Stakeholder mapping, Mendelow (1981)
- Changing stakeholder positioning over the life of a project

1.7 Identify, map and assess project stakeholders, and how their power and influence may change over the duration of a purchasing and logistics project.
- Characteristics of a purchasing and logistics project
- Various types of purchasing and logistics projects
- Stakeholder assessment of purchasing and logistics projects
- Stakeholder mapping of purchasing and logistics projects, Mendelow (1981)
- Changing stakeholder positions over the life of a purchasing and logistics project

## Prior knowledge

Level 6, Strategic Supply Chain Management, study session 1 would also be useful since there are clear linkages.

## Timing

You should set aside about 7 hours to read and complete this session, including learning activities, self-assessment questions, the suggested reading (if any) from the essential textbook for this unit and the revision question.

## 2.1 Tossed by tide and waves: the impact of the project environment

Study session 1 looked at a range of factors which were driving the growth in project management, such as technology and competition. These factors, external to the project and many external to the company, can have a strong impact on the management and the success and failure of a project.

### Learning activity 2.1

Consider the three projects below and the suggested changes to the environment. What impact would you expect on the projects?

1 A project to develop a new luxury car to compete with Rolls-Royce, Maybach and Bentley:
   (a) An economic slump or recession.
   (b) A coup in an oil-producing country forcing oil prices up.
   (c) A competitor launches a product with breakthrough technology in the car.

2 A project to re-source mobile communications for a company of 20,000 people:

*(continued on next page)*

Learning activity 2.1 *(continued)*

(a) An economic slump or recession.
(b) A coup in an oil-producing country forcing oil prices up.
(c) A merger between the two largest service providers (your suppliers) who control 45% of the market.

3 A project to move production of simple steel pressed parts to India:
(a) An economic slump or recession.
(b) A coup in an oil-producing country forcing oil prices up.
(c) Takeover of your company by a larger group.

*Feedback on page 35*

From the learning activity, the range of factors which can impact on the project becomes clear. These form part of the environment the project must take place in: the 'project environment'.

### External factors

Factors which affect the project externally can come from individual sources or groups and can be intentional or unintentional.

Governments can legislate or act to drive business behaviour. For example, tax incentives on IT investment have changed almost annually in the UK in an attempt to promote and direct investment. This can heavily influence IT projects. Some legislation has unintended consequences, for example it is often argued that increased employee protection encourages projects which outsource work to less-regulated countries.

Changes in economies can have a radical impact. Growth and slump, as in the learning activity, can have direct and indirect effects, but other factors, such as exchange rate trends and seasonal changes can be just as strong.

On a smaller scale, changes in markets can be important. The example of a takeover mid-project may seem unlikely, but in some industries takeovers or radical management restructuring happen on average every three years. If a project is planned to take two years, it is likely to suffer or enjoy one of those changes. Changes in the external market are even more frequent and can, of course, dramatically effect suppliers and the supply market. The entrance of new companies to insurance markets, for example, has changed competition, opening up low-cost, low-service options. Mergers and competition between retail companies are frequently reviewed by governmental agencies, but many business-to-business markets are dominated by a few key players. Finally, radical innovative products can transform demand or supply.

### Internal factors

Looking inside the organisation, the list of potential factors lengthens again. Management restructuring has been mentioned, but even more frequently managers and senior staff change posts and responsibilities. If the person driving the project – the sponsor – moves, their sponsorship, drive and support can disappear. Other competing projects may be launched, starving the project of resources, interest or time.

The strategy and policies of the organisation must be taken into account. A strategy of outsourcing may be reversed following failure or changed priorities. A project to re-source packaging can be blocked by the introduction of a Corporate Social Responsibility policy.

As individuals or groups, the people involved in the project or affected by it in some way can make the difference between success and failure. People who support the project at the outset can become disillusioned, enemies can become strong supporters and suddenly remove critical objections.

### Summary

The project environment is complex and fluid. An excellently planned and resourced project can be stopped by a small change to the market or management team, a relatively weak project can be revitalised by new policy.

At times the environment seems so complex it is tempting to ignore it and accept any changes as fate. It is almost like being at sea in a small boat, being tossed by waves, tides and currents too huge to understand or predict. There are, however, some tools to help understand the different factors and how they are likely to impact. The next sections look at the use of those tools and how they can support effective project management.

### Self-assessment question 2.1

What environmental factors might impact upon a project for a large energy company to re-source new supplies of gas for the long term?

*Feedback on page 36*

## 2.2 Understanding the environment: simple tools for a complex challenge

Section 2.1 above discussed some of the factors which formed the project environment. This section brings a series of tools and approaches to bear to help understand and respond to the environment.

A project may have been developed and specified before the project manager is appointed. That specification may have been based on a very strong understanding of the external environment. There is a temptation to accept the project and deliver it as specified, relying on a sponsor or other departments to identify changes, but there are two important reasons for developing a strong understanding of the environment:

- Understanding the forces on the project gives a far deeper understanding of what is needed from the project, where emphasis must be placed and why.
- The environment will change over the course of a project.

### Learning activity 2.2

From a report of your choice on a particular purchasing and logistics project identify the forces likely to contribute to its success or failure.

*Feedback on page 36*

### Scanning the future: PESTLE analysis

This has been discussed elsewhere, for example in Strategic Supply Chain Management, so this session provides only an overview.

**Figure 2.1:** PESTLE analysis

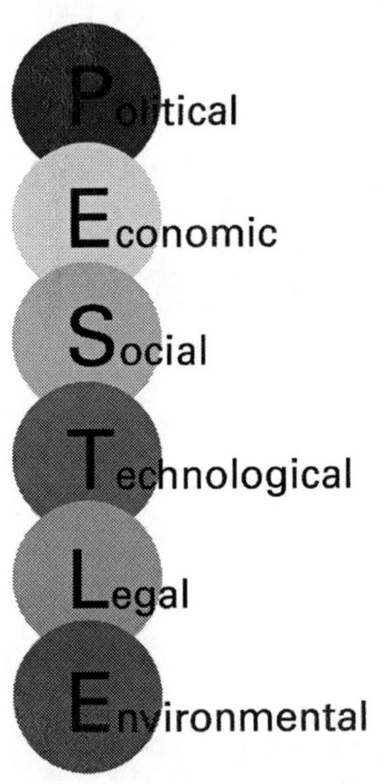


The essence of the tool (see figure 2.1) is to scan the environment for factors in each area which could have an impact on the project. As examples:

- *Political*: As in self-assessment question 2.1 above, political changes can affect supply, also tax and other incentive policies or new regulatory bodies can have a big impact.
- *Economic*: How sensitive is the project to growth and slump, foreign exchange, fluctuating demand, etc?
- *Social*: Will the project be affected by changing demographics, fashion, attitudes or consumption? A growth in activism on animal rights could have a strong influence in a livestock logistics project.
- *Technological*: Technology can replace or change products, but it can also change supply: online airline ticketing, for example, could become a key part of souring a travel category.
- *Legal*: Legal changes tend to be high impact but slow, hence it should be relatively easy to prepare. For example, changes in employment law should be taken into account in a project to source temporary labour.
- *Environmental*: With increasing interest in 'green' issues, environmental factors are of growing importance. A logistics project which is marginal

in terms of cost savings may offer great benefits in promotion and company profile in environmental awareness, for example.

A PESTLE analysis can be used to drive data gathering on the environment. What sources or intelligence does the project have on these factors? Is there enough information on impending legal changes or technological development? Of course a PESTLE analysis is imprecise and can only give an indication of the important factors, but repays time spent over and over when change is predicted and prepared for.

## Understanding the market: Porter's Five Forces Analysis

**Figure 2.2:** Porter's five forces

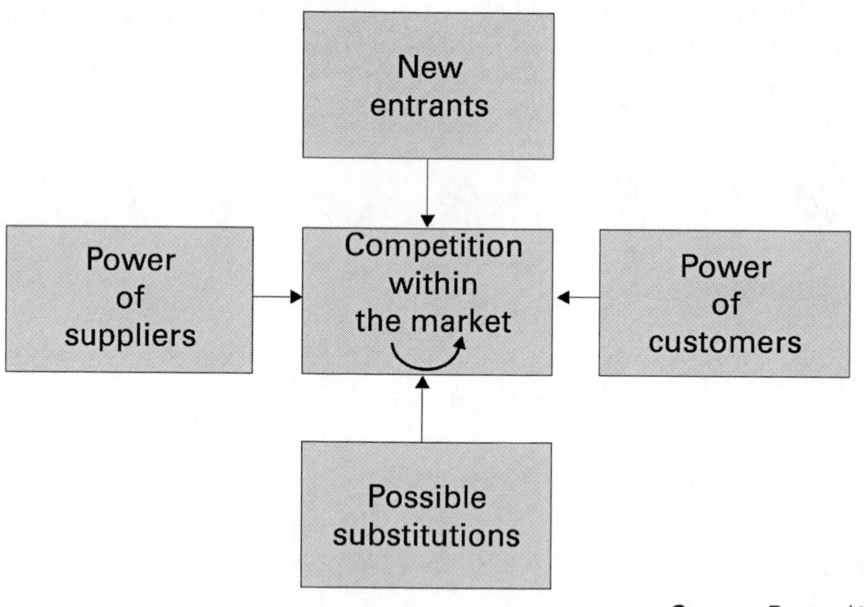


*Source: Porter (1985)*

Once again, this tool has been introduced elsewhere in the CIPS course, so this is just an overview (see figure 2.2).

The basis of Five Forces Analysis is to understand the forces and how they currently work, as well as how changes will impact. For most sourcing projects, the most important markets are generally upstream, supply side. Each of the five forces has a different value, as follows.

### *Competition within the market and new entrants*

Understanding the market is central to sourcing projects and that understanding should be strong enough to provide insight into how the market is developing. A project to develop and implement a sourcing strategy in mobile communications will have to take into account frequent mergers and changing competition over the time it will need to run.

### *Supplier and buyer power*

In many cases the buyers will include your organisation, so that is a good position to gauge power: can you influence specifications for example. Gaining information about suppliers to the market may be more complex, but as in the mobile communications example, understanding the power of the suppliers to telecommunications companies is vital to understanding the way the market works.

*Possible substitutions*

Once again, going beyond the immediate state of the market is essential for strategy and can be important for other projects. Developments in established modes of logistics can transform the market, for example the growth in internal air travel in India has been a major factor in the way business has developed.

### Inside the company: stakeholders

The people or groups inside (and outside) the organisation who can influence the project can be grouped together as stakeholders. Stakeholders is a term that has become used more and more. Handy (1998) suggested moving from a 'shareholder' to a 'stakeholder' economy; in the UK, employees are offered 'stakeholder' pensions. Definitions vary: Meredith and Mantel (2006) talk about 'parties at interest'. Maylor uses a common description: individuals or groups who have an interest in the project process or outcome. Turner (1993) separates stakeholders from the project team: supporters who supply resources, etc, the project manager and sponsor, limiting the term to people who have an interest but do not otherwise take part.

Most sources agree that managing stakeholders is one of the activities central to success. They also agree that stakeholders are likely to be complex, in identity, behaviour, attitudes and influence. To start on a simple basis then, the definition of stakeholders used here will be:

> An individual or group likely to have an *influence* on the success of the project, positive or negative.

Stakeholder mapping and management is covered in more detail in section 2.3 below. The central point is that stakeholder management is one of the most important activities in the project environment, indeed in project management itself.

### Cost quality and delivery: the 'iron triangle'

**Figure 2.3:** The 'iron triangle'

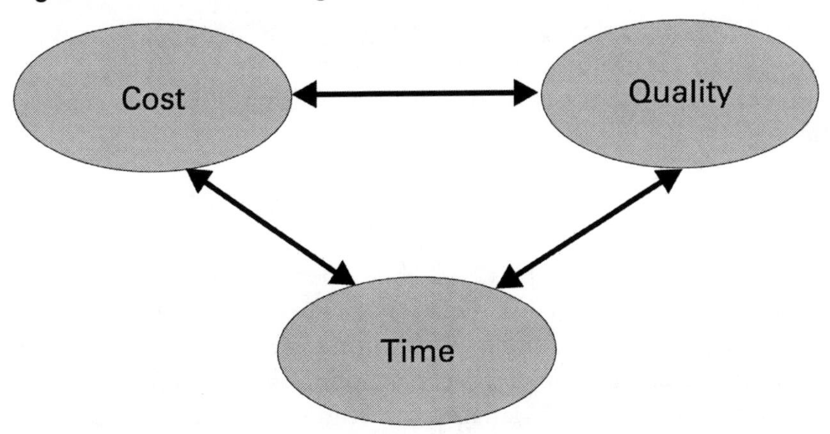

Cost quality and delivery are three aspects of project management sometimes called 'the iron triangle' (see figure 2.3). Managing these three is certainly central to much of project management and they are frequently predefined or fixed outside the project.

The objectives of a project can be characterised by positioning it inside the triangle. Which is most important: cost, quality or time? For a development of a product competing on price, cost might be uppermost. For developing a new drug, cost is still important, but quality comes to the front. If the project is to train a team of athletes for the Olympics, money may be tight, but the deadline is fixed and has to be most important. One factor need not dominate: for some projects, the importance of cost and quality may be balanced, while some may be placed in the centre of the triangle with totally balanced objectives. Position of the project makes clear what is most important and informs the planning process.

Through the life of a project, these aspects can change. Quality demands will tend to increase, resources may be taken away to serve other projects. The deadline may be moved to respond to external factors. It is important not to rely on having 'enough' money or time: few projects do.

There is a relationship between the three: some projects can be rushed by spending more money. If quality is compromised, sometimes costs can be reduced or the project can be finished more quickly. The relationship is not simple, however:

1. Delivering poor quality does not always reduce costs, frequently it has the opposite effect. There is not sufficient space here for a detailed look at quality, but improving quality can frequently reduce costs. For a more complete explanation, see 'Quality is Free' (Crosby, 1979).
2. Time has a complex relationship with cost. The standing costs of running a project, such as the project team and the manager, increase with time. If the project takes a long time, some aspects will have to be repeated, especially if they are sensitive to environmental changes.
3. Time and quality are only loosely related. A slow project does not guarantee quality, for example in software, where technology moves rapidly, a slow project can ensure old technology is embedded in the end result, leading to a lower-quality product which may become more difficult and expensive to support in the future.

As Atkinson (1999) suggested: cost time and quality are 'two best guesses and a phenomenon'. It can be important to manage all three, but the relationship between them is not rigid and their availability/demand can change through the life of the project.

### Bringing factors together: Lewin's Force Field

The different factors can be complex and while a detailed understanding is important, it can be useful to link them together on a common ground. Lewin's Force Field offers one simple way of bringing together and assessing the factor (see figure 2.4; a more detailed description is in section 5.1 and Level 6, Strategic Supply Chain Management, study session 9).

**Figure 2.4:** Lewin's Force Field

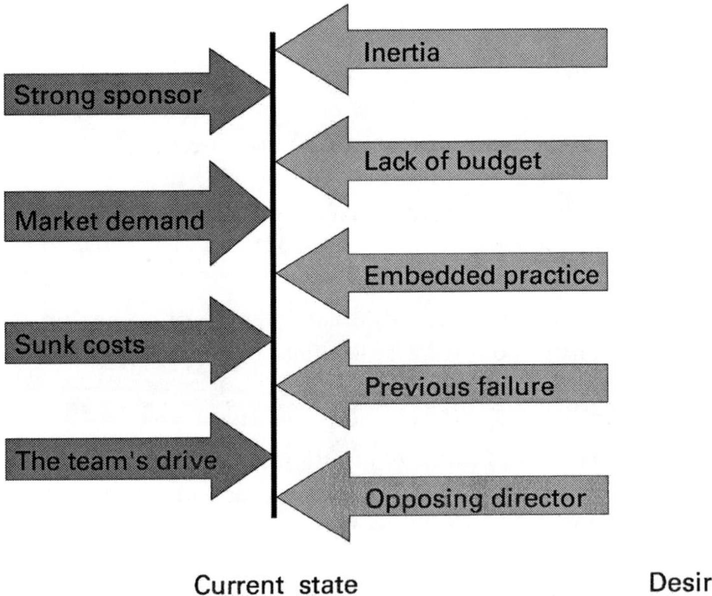


Current state

Desired state: we want to be here

*Source: Lewin (1943)*

## Self-assessment question 2.2

Explain the different functions of the tools and ideas identified in this section: what are they for and what is different about them. Use no more than two sentences each.

*Feedback on page 37*

## 2.3 Stakeholders: the people who define, determine and influence success or failure

## Learning activity 2.3

From a case study or newspaper article of your choice identify the key stakeholders in a project and what their main requirements are likely to be.

*Feedback on page 37*

In section 2.2 above, stakeholders were mentioned as critical to project success; in this section, the management and mapping of stakeholders will be explored in more detail.

The first stage is to explore what makes stakeholders important, and consider success and failure of different projects.

Consider a large IT project to introduce a customer information management system. Success will be defined by four groups of stakeholders:

- For the client: does it do what is needed? Not necessarily what was specified at the start, but what is needed after implementation.
- For the users: does it meet their needs of ease of use, speed, etc?
- For customers: does it support good service and provide privacy, etc?
- For the developers and installers: does it make a profit, was it a rewarding or a painful project?

Or take a project for a food producer to consolidate secondary packaging supply for all sites across Europe to one best supplier. There are again four stakeholder groups who will define success or failure:

- The 'client': Does it make the savings required, does it achieve a single source, without excessive cost of implementation and future management? Does it fulfil the other business requirements such as service, delivery, innovation?
- The users: People in sites who order and use the packaging: does it meet their needs of reliability, ease of use, etc?
- The project manager/team: Was it worth it? Would they do it again?
- The supplier: Is this a valuable new contract or a loss-making nightmare to operate?

In each case, success is defined and influenced by the stakeholders, and their decision on whether the project is successful outweighs all other consideration. As Obeng (1996) says, 'success is and can only be defined by the stakeholders'.

Unfortunately it is not simply a matter of defining each stakeholder's requirements at the start and meeting them, even if that were possible, stakeholder satisfaction is also a complex idea. Maylor (2003) uses the ideas of service quality to define satisfaction for the stakeholders:

Satisfaction = perception – expectation

This holds two important and frustrating ideas:

1. Satisfaction is based on *perception*, not necessarily on any hard facts.
2. Higher *expectations* can reduce the satisfaction of stakeholders.

Without diving too deeply into service quality concepts, it seems clear from this that stakeholder management will need to deal with managing expectations, and with managing perceptions.

### Judging stakeholder influence

The definition of a stakeholder was an individual or group likely to have an *influence* on the success of the project, positive or negative. Stakeholders can have influence through seniority of position or authority, some through their control over particular resources or their weight with other people, or power.

To gain a clear view of stakeholder influence it is useful to separate *influence* from *power* and *authority*. These three are complex constructions, so discussion here is restricted to simple definitions.

- **Influence** is causing some change in behaviour, affecting the thought, attitudes or actions of others. So influence is the application of power or authority.
- **Authority** is the legitimate power to influence, for example due to position in the organisation. The CEO or managing director has the authority to direct employees within limits. It is tempting to think of stakeholder management in terms of getting a sponsor or stakeholder high in the organisation to mandate any change or order it to be done. There are several problems with this. First, the higher the position, typically the less time is available for individual projects; second, support of just one stakeholder may vanish rapidly; thirdly, managers are often sensibly cautious about wielding their authority because ordering employees' actions is of limited value: it can breed resentment and reluctant compliance.
- **Power** is the ability to influence another person. This can come from authority or a wealth of other sources, such as controlling a scarce resource. Finance can be an example. Power can come from technical sources. A Quality Assurance or Compliance department has enormous power to block or support change for example. Personal power can come from friendships, favours or charisma. A front-line customer-service agent with a wide network of colleagues may have more power and potential to influence than the head of the organisation in some circumstances. In some cases, using this power could be wrong, harmful or damaging but it is important to recognise its existence and potential to influence. Weber (translated 1947) explained:
  'By power is meant that opportunity existing within a social [relationship] which permits one to carry out one's own will even against resistance and regardless of the basis on which this opportunity rests.'

## Stakeholder mapping

There are many stakeholders for any project and their power, motivation and interest will vary widely. In order to manage them effectively, some means of differentiating between them is necessary

There are many ways of looking at stakeholders, one of the most widely used is from Mendelow (1981) (see figure 2.5).

**Figure 2.5:** Mendelow's stakeholder matrix

| | | Level of interest | |
|---|---|---|---|
| | | Low | High |
| Power | Low | A<br>Minimal effort | B<br>Keep informed |
| | High | C<br>Keep satisfied | D<br>Key players |

*Source: Mendelow (1981)*

This gives a rapid and clear differentiation on a rational basis. By using power rather than authority or current influence, stakeholders who may have a strong influence in the future are identified as well as currently vital stakeholders. The use of 'interest' positive or negative accepts the importance of both.

One of the important aspects to bear in mind is that stakeholders can move. A key player can lose interest, while increased interest will shift a stakeholder from C to D. In extreme cases, a particularly negative but low power stakeholder may work hard to gain power and shift into the key player segment.

Other people use different factors: Archer (1995) divides between connections with the project: are they necessary or contingent (not necessary) and interests: compatible and incompatible with the project aims (see figure 2.6).

**Figure 2.6:** Archer's stakeholder matrix

| | | **Connections** | |
|---|---|---|---|
| | | Necessary | Contingent |
| **Interests** | Compatible | A | B |
| | Incompatible | C | D |

*Source: Archer (1995)*

Ignoring the slightly obscure labelling, this has the advantage of focusing on positive and negative attitudes as well as questioning the need to manage the stakeholder. As a result, it becomes clear that any stakeholder in segment D must be very carefully managed, since their interests conflict, yet they are necessary for success. Compromise, loss or change will be necessary.

The different ways of mapping suit different environments and personal choice. The methods can be adapted and developed for best effect. The results of any form of stakeholder analysis should include three things, however:

1. Identification of the individuals or group
2. Some indication of their attitude and potential influence
3. Implications: what should happen as a result?

Figure 2.7 shows an example stakeholder map using a simple scale:

- AIH: Against it Happening
- LIH: Lets it Happen
- HIH: Helps it Happen
- MIH: Makes it Happen.

**Figure 2.7:** Example stakeholder map using the 'IH' scale

| Stakeholder Map: Production Packaging category 12th July | | | | | | |
|---|---|---|---|---|---|---|
| Name & Role | AIH | LIH | HIH | MIH | Comments | Action |
| John Parsons Production Manager | | | X | | Currently positive and very important for success | Invite to be part of the project team |
| Sam Merton Technical Manager | | X | | | Can facilitate the work or slow it | Regular interviews and meetings |
| Billy Williams Finance Director | | | X | | Supports and controls the budget | Weekly detailed updates, including projected finances |
| Sheila Smith Logistics Manager | X | | | | Resisting the change, disruption will make her task harder in the short term | Convert if possible, use sponsor to 'reach out'. Repeatedly highlight long term benefits and existing support |
| Peter Ayres Sponsor | | | | X | Behind the change, tends to get bored quickly | Weekly positive updates, use to remove obstacles |
| Trisha Norton Stores | | X | | | Limited supporter, sees no need and a lot of work | Interviews and regular communications |

### Confidentiality

As a final note, stakeholder maps contain descriptions and perspectives which are potentially very inflammatory. It is best in many circumstances to keep them confidential.

### Self-assessment question 2.3

Write a brief memo suggesting the use of an analytical tool for identifying and assessing the impact of the main stakeholders upon a project of your choice.

*Feedback on page 37*

## 2.4 Stakeholders do not stand still

Unfortunately stakeholders change throughout the life of a project: they change in attitude and power, while different stakeholders are important at different stages. The case study below follows just four stakeholders at three points in a project. As stakeholder behaviour is sensitive, to protect confidentiality two real projects have been merged, and identities obscured.

### Case study: Magenta Foods

Magenta Foods is a PLC with £800 million turnover consisting of seven companies involved in food production. These companies have a total of 22 sites across Europe, mainly in France, Germany, the UK and Spain.

The project is to re-source secondary packaging (essentially packaging which does not touch the food). The objectives set early on were to single source everything, with a few specialist exceptions, and make direct savings of 12.5%.

The case will look at four example stakeholders at three different points in the project: three 'snapshots'.

The four sample stakeholders to be considered are:

1. The project team, considered as one group. They are working part time on the project from different departments.
2. A site logistics manager: Tessa Burns. She is currently responsible for most secondary packaging at a large site in the UK.
3. A supplier: Alcopak. They are one of perhaps eight companies capable of bidding for the contract.
4. The sourcing director: Sam Dinuraz. This project is part of Sam's work to achieve substantial performance targets.

*Snapshot 1: One month in*

The team are gathering the data necessary for analysis before contract decisions can be made.

1. The project team:
   (a) *Attitude and motivation*: The team are excited and optimistic about the potential they could achieve.
   (b) *Power and interest*: They have a strong potential to influence the project at this stage and are very interested, positively.
2. Tessa Burns:
   (a) *Attitude and motivation*: With a lot of experience, Tessa is worried about disruption, does not believe the project will succeed and believes her site will lose out. It is quite likely she will be blamed by the people around her if supply fails. She has all the historic demand data the project needs and holds the up-to-date specifications and part numbers.
   (b) *Power and interest*: Tessa can disrupt progress by withholding, selectively releasing and distorting the information she has. She also has power with her peers – people in similar positions at other sites. She has a strong negative interest.
3. Alcopak:
   (a) *Attitude and motivation*: They see reduced competition for a larger contract so are actively trying to put together a consortium to bid covering all sites.
   (b) *Power and interest*: They cannot influence the project much, but have a strong interest.
4. Sam Dinuraz:
   (a) *Attitude and motivation*: Keen to see the project succeed as soon as possible but not actively involved.
   (b) *Power and interest*: Some power, but would need to work with colleagues to make radical changes in other departments. Very positively interested.

*Snapshot 2: Pre-contract*

The demand is well understood, Sam Dinuraz has decided this will be the company's first e-auction and the team is preparing hard for that now. Just four suppliers have qualified and agreed to participate.

1. The project team:
   (a) *Attitude and motivation*: The team are worn out by the effort involved and disheartened by the way an e-auction was chosen without consultation.
   (b) *Power and interest*: Their power is currently far more limited, their interest still aligned with project success and quite strong.
2. Tessa Burns:
   (a) *Attitude and motivation:* The negative attitude remains but she is resigned to project progress and interested in the e-auction.
   (b) *Power and interest*: Power is reduced, interest reduced.
3. Alcopak:
   (a) *Attitude and motivation*: The potential sales remain high, but the auction means a strong focus on price and they have lost business at auction before.
   (b) *Power and interest*: The interest remains, but power has increased. If Alcopak pull out, the auction is at risk, with just three suppliers it may not work. If they know this, power is increased still further.
4. Sam Dinuraz:
   (a) *Attitude and motivation*: Now actively involved and with this project as a pilot, Sam's motivation is very strong.
   (b) *Power and interest*: Power still high, interest increased to an almost unsurpassable level.

*Snapshot 3: Post-contract*

The auction was successful with a predicted 18% price reduction, averaged across all part numbers. The next stage is to roll out across all sites.

1. The project team:
   (a) *Attitude and motivation*: The success of the e-auction has increased morale.
   (b) *Power and interest*: Interest is still aligned with project success and strong, power has increased again: they can have a strong influence on the success of the rollout.
2. Tessa Burns:
   (a) *Attitude and motivation*: Resigned to the project happening, she has become more active in helping implementation, though guarded about success.
   (b) *Power and interest*: Power returns: she can have an influence on implementation at her site and some influence with her colleagues. Interest lies strongly with project success.
3. Alcopak:
   (a) *Attitude and motivation*: The contract is signed and the focus is on managing the contract most profitably for the future.
   (b) *Power and interest*: Power to make this work or fail is now very high. Interest is also high. They will be a key player in this phase.
4. Sam Dinuraz:

(a) *Attitude and motivation*: The project is moving out of Sam's area and into logistics and operations. Sam sees the savings as 'in the bag'.
(b) *Power and interest*: Both have dropped away. Failure would be a problem, but direct interest and power to influence are limited.

## Learning activity 2.4

If you were the project manager in the Magenta Foods case, how would you manage each of the different stakeholders at each stage highlighted?

Note: you should have 12 separate answers: four stakeholders at three points.

*Feedback on page 38*

Now look at the broader, self-assessment question on stakeholders.

## Self-assessment question 2.4

Outline three different projects associated with supply chains from your experience or research. Use stakeholder mapping to identify key stakeholders from the above projects and the nature of their influence on the project. *Focus on one point in each project.*

*Feedback on page 38*

### Revision question

Now try the revision question for this session on page 319.

### Summary

Successful project management relies on using simple tools to help understand the complex environment and to support decisions, actions and choices which lead to overall success.

The project environment is complex. The use of a series of simple tools can help analysis and understanding:

- PESTLE Analysis can help structure understanding of the external environment as a whole, focused on the future. Five Forces gives an understanding of any markets key to the project and can inform analysis of any future changes.
- The Iron Triangle can help assess project objectives and manage these three important factors.

- Force Field Analysis can be used to draw together a range of factors.
- Stakeholder mapping and management are frequently central to success, looking inside the organisation at people and groups with an impact.

Unfortunately, the forces on the project change and develop as the project progresses. The environment changes, the stakeholders appear, disappear, change their attitude and become more or less important. There are many ways of dealing with this, but ignoring the external environment and stakeholders is rarely an option.

## Suggested further reading

- Archer (1995).
- Atkinson (1999).
- Crosby (1979).
- Handy (1998).
- Kotter (1985).
- Lewin (1943).
- Lock (2003); Chapter 6.
- Maylor (1996); Chapter 2.
- Mendelow (1981)
- Meredith and Mantel (2006); Chapter 3.
- Porter (1985).
- Weber (1947).

## Feedback on learning activities and self-assessment questions

### Feedback on learning activity 2.1

1 A project to develop a new luxury car to compete with Rolls Royce, Maybach and Bentley:
  (a) *An economic slump or recession:* This may hit the demand for luxury cars, reducing the market to the point that the project is shelved.
  (b) *A coup in an oil-producing country forcing oil prices up:* For the consumer, the cost of fuel is tiny compared to other costs in this market, so demand may not be directly affected, but costs of production will increase and indirect effects may be important: the fuel price rise may trigger an economic slump.
  (c) *A competitor launches a product with breakthrough technology in the car:* This is likely to cause radically different demands on the project. Time and cost pressures may increase or the project might have to be reversed and the design changed. There will almost certainly need to be a change in the project management.
2 A project to re-source mobile communications for a company of 20,000 people:
  (a) *An economic slump or recession:* The direct impact may be good: a slump will reduce demand making competition stronger. There may be an impact reducing your demand for communications however, so it may be worth revisiting the predicted demand.
  (b) *A coup in an oil-producing country forcing oil prices up:* Fuel costs are probably a relatively low proportion of the service providers'

costs, so the direct impact may be low. There is still potential for knock-on effects such as recession or increased demand.

(c) *A merger between the two largest service providers (your suppliers) who together control 45% of the market:* This could dramatically change the competitive environment and with it the project. A fast deal may get ahead of the effects of the merger but reduces the time to optimise. The change in the market could reduce the objectives dramatically.

3 A project to move production of simple steel pressed parts to India:

(a) *An economic slump or recession:* Demand may be reduced, the impact on the project will depend on the investment involved, the capital available and the potential savings.

(b) *A coup in an oil-producing country forcing oil prices up:* The added cost of transport may make the project marginal and balance some of the cost savings.

(c) *Takeover of your company by a larger group:* The policy of the group may be completely different and low-cost outsourcing may conflict with strategy. Another factor is indecision: people will be reluctant to make big decisions in the short term and energy will be focused on the takeover.

## Feedback on self-assessment question 2.1

An effective sourcing policy in this market would naturally involve a detailed understanding of the factors involved; for this exercise, you need only a basic overview.

The focus here should be on political and market factors. You should have identified a series of geopolitical factors: location of resources, transport pipelines, potential for disruption of supplies. For example, in 2005 Russia stopped supply of gas to Ukraine, and European gas prices soared as a result. In addition, war and dispute are common problems in some countries with large gas resources.

Market factors would cover the whole supply chain including a detailed understanding of the supply market; big players and their reach; and potential changes. Upstream of them is the activity of exploration: what resources lie where in the world. The competition with other large users is also important: what is their likely demand and an understanding of their behaviour will be critical both to assuring supply and controlling cost. Downstream, likely future consumption patterns will be important.

## Feedback on learning activity 2.2

Each project has a different profile of forces, some of them only become understood when it is too late to adapt.

Were there external forces? The way the market worked, mergers which eliminated competition, new regulation which increased cost, disruption to supply in other countries?

Were there internal forces? Resistance from users, a weak sponsor behind the project, power battles or poorly understood objectives?

Did the opposition never have a chance? Were the forces behind the project so strong that it was bound to happen?

You may have identified forces in a range of different areas, the tools and ideas in this section are aimed at structuring and understanding the wealth of possible forces which could contribute to success or failure.

### Feedback on self-assessment question 2.2

The uses can vary slightly, so here are some sample answers:

- *PESTLE analysis*: This is a structure for examining a range of factors which can impact on the project or market. It is focused on predicting future changes.
- *Porter's Five Forces Analysis*: This is to give an understanding of current market dynamics to allow choices for the future to be made.
- *Stakeholders:* Looking at stakeholders gives an understanding of the internal environment and likely support and obstruction which could make or break the project.
- *The iron triangle:* This is a reminder of three factors important to the project and considered by some to be the limited measures of success.
- *Lewin's Force Field:* This is a way of looking at all the forces acting on the project and assessing whether they are likely to ensure the move from the current to the desired position.

### Feedback on learning activity 2.3

The stakeholders will depend on the project. Using ideas from the discussion in this section may help:

- The client or sponsor is usually key: who is paying for the project is one way of defining the client, or who is behind it happening. Their requirements usually include success with minimum cost or problems, but defining these more closely can be difficult.
- Users or consumers, the people who will work with the outcome of the project, can be important. Their requirements can range from minimum disruption to something radically different from the status quo.
- The people doing the project: the leader and the team are central to success and their requirements are too often neglected. Their motivation may vary but support, recognition, encouragement, a sense that it is worthwhile and enjoyment are likely to crop up.
- External stakeholders like suppliers are frequently undermanaged. The relationship with a supplier can be formed by a project and if they see the customer as badly managed, reactive, poor at communicating and badly aligned with what they want, the ongoing relationship can be difficult.

### Feedback on self-assessment question 2.3

As suggested in the discussion, there are many ways of analysing and mapping stakeholders, including the examples here.

The mapping you prefer will depend on the stakeholders you are dealing with as well as visual impact, etc. The map using the IH scale is well organised but very simplistic. Mendelow's concept is visual and can show gradations, as well as recommending generic actions. It does not reflect positive or negative attitudes however, something that is corrected in Archer's version.

The choice is yours, but as a reminder, the three key elements are:

1. Identification of the individuals or group
2. Some indication of their attitude and potential influence
3. Implications: what should happen as a result?

## Feedback on learning activity 2.4

Managing stakeholders is complex and subtle without right answers. Consider your answers and see if they match with Mendelow's approach: Key Players, Keep Informed, etc. If not, is it a failing of the four-segment approach or could your answers improve?

In some cases, doing nothing may be appropriate, as with Sam Dinuraz at snapshot 2. For some, active management may pay off in the future, for example with Alcopak through implementation, where their power is high and their motivation – profit – may conflict with yours.

## Feedback on self-assessment question 2.4

The vital part of this exercise is to identify a range of stakeholder groups with a variety of motivations or attitudes and a variety of different ways of influencing the project.

Review your answers and examine the spread of stakeholders:

- Are there people from across the hierarchy, groups and individuals?
- Are there different motivations?
- Are there positive and negative stakeholders?
- Are there different forms of power: authority, knowledge, etc?

Study session 3

# Approaches to project management

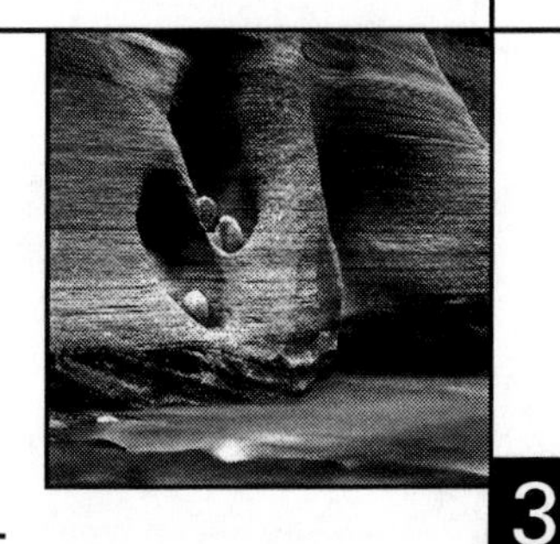



Back to basics: what are projects and what do project managers do all day?

## Introduction

Understanding what you are managing and what you should be doing is a key part of becoming an effective project manager. Unfortunately the discussion in study session 1 seemed to uncover a wide variety of opinions on what a project is and expanded the role of project manager to include leadership.

This session looks at projects from fundamentally different perspectives: as a conversion process and as low-volume high-variety processes. Using either has an impact on what projects are and how they should be managed. Finally, some of the guidance for project managers is drawn together to outline what the role involves and offer some insight into how to fulfil it.

## Session learning objectives

After completing this session you should be able to:

3.1 Evaluate and explain the idea of the project as a conversion or transformation process.
3.2 Evaluate the concept of variety and volume as applied to project management.
3.3 Describe the role of a project manager.

## Unit content coverage

This study session covers the following topic from the official CIPS unit content document.

### Learning objective

2.0 Assess and justify the approach to managing projects using a variety of methodologies.
2.1 Critically evaluate a variety of methodologies used in approaches to projects.
- Projects as a conversion process, Maylor (2003)
- Projects as low volume/high variety processes, Slack et al (2004)
- Meredith and Mantel (2003)

## Prior knowledge

Level 6, Strategic Supply Chain Management, study sessions 1 and 2 would provide a good foundation.

## Timing

You should set aside about 4 hours to read and complete this session, including learning activities, self-assessment questions, the suggested reading (if any) from the essential textbook for this unit and the revision question.

## 3.1 In and out: the transformation model

How projects are approached and managed, and to some extent their success, depends on the way they are defined, the underlying idea of a project. The way we see projects determines how we treat them.

As an example, Meredith and Mantel (2006) use an implicit understanding that project management is a set of tools, techniques and activities, many developed in large engineering-based projects, which can be applied to different projects in different ways. Meanwhile, Obeng (1996) uses an understanding that a project is about change and overcoming problems, largely from a human perspective. The result can be seen from their very different books: Meredith and Mantel (2006) explain that set of tools, techniques and activities in detail over more than 600 packed pages; Obeng (1996) uses perhaps 10% of the words to explain radically different approaches centred on overcoming problems largely generated by people.

The different perspectives can be useful and applicable in different ways to different projects and for a strong understanding of project management it is valuable to look at some different underlying ideas and definitions.

### Learning activity 3.1

Using a project well known to you, identify two lists: what are the 'inputs' and 'outputs'. What were the things needed to complete the project and what were the results?

*Feedback on page 49*

### The transformation model

Slack (2004) uses a widespread idea to define operations management, that of the transformation process model (figure 3.1).

> 'Put simply, operations processes take in a set of input resources which are then used to transform something, or are transformed themselves, into an output of goods and services which satisfy customer needs.'

**Figure 3.1:** The transformation model, adapted from Slack (2004)

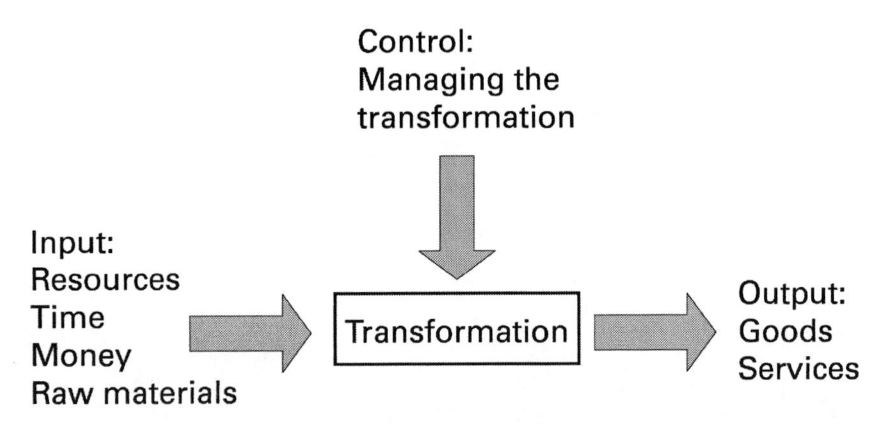


This is a useful definition for operations such as manufacturing: inputs such as raw materials, factory space, people's time, money, etc is transformed into goods. It also helps focus on inputs and outputs, the balance between which will define efficiency, profit and so on. Operations management involves the management or control of that transformation, with regard to the business environment.

Maylor (1996) uses this input output, transformation idea to define projects, but uses the definitions slightly differently, adding to inputs and outputs, constraints and mechanisms (see figure 3.2).

*Inputs*

The input will be wants or needs from a stakeholder who is effectively a client. Maylor does not define people's time, money or other resources as inputs.

*Outputs*

These logically follow as 'satisfied needs' such as a building, people changed through training, new information, or a specification for a product, for example.

*Mechanisms*

People, money, technology, knowledge, tools and so on are *mechanisms* by which the transformation is achieved.

*Constraints*

This includes cost, time, quality, but also environmental constraints (see study session 2). These could be legal, ethical, competitive or political.

**Figure 3.2:** Maylor's model of a project

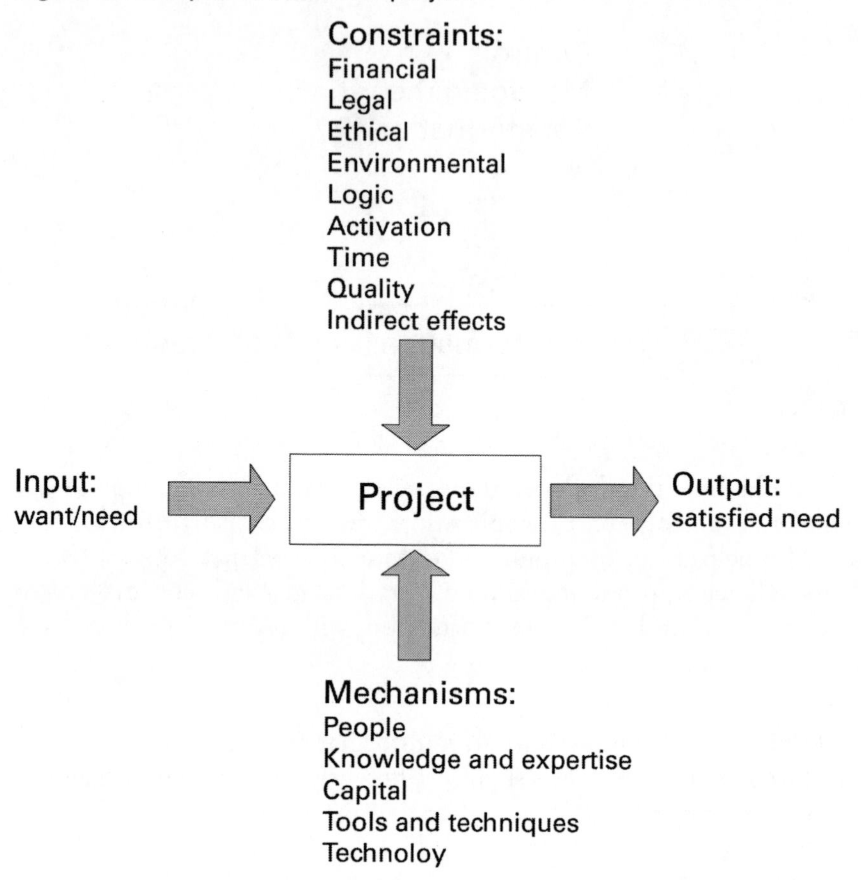


*Source: Maylor (1996)*

This development of the transformation fits with some process mapping approaches but raises some questions. Does this mean that a project always requires a defined need as an input and that satisfying the need is the activity of a project? This fits to some extent with projects such as road building but is problematic for projects where the objectives develop. The move of capital, people's time, etc from inputs to mechanisms makes defining a mechanism difficult: is it something which is used but does not change, like tools, or which is consumed to produce a later output, like capital? Finally, constraints include cost, quality and time, and as touched on in study session 2, these are moving factors in many projects, as well as overlapping with mechanisms, for example capital and people.

### Using the transformation model

The use of the transformation model for projects focuses attention not on the *how* (the tools and techniques) but on the *what* (the output of the project). This shifts attention away from an established 'body of knowledge' to what is done. By understanding what will be used and what will be achieved, cost benefit and effectiveness become clearer, while rigid adherence to past behaviour is avoided. It is not, of course, a tool for planning, scheduling or analysing projects.

To look at drawbacks, the model tends to focus on a stable and well-defined 'need', which conflicts with many projects and effectively defines project management as a subset of operations management. This is not a problem in itself, but can bring a range of 'baggage': it will tend to mean that operations management approaches will be used.

### Self-assessment question 3.1

Take the example project used in the learning activity and use the two examples of the transformation model above to define inputs, outputs and the other factors, described variously as control, constraints and mechanisms within the models.

Write 100 words on each model and the value and drawbacks of looking at projects in this way.

*Feedback on page 49*

## 3.2 How many and how different? Defining projects by volume and variety

In section 3.1 above it was mentioned that defining projects as a transformation process effectively makes them a subset of operations management. What then separates them from other operations management processes, like production? Slack (2004) suggests it hinges on volume and variety. The *volume* of products produced this way and the *variety* of those products. At one end of the scale, canned drinks, bank transactions or cars are produced/processed in high volume and low variety. At the project end of the scale, each project is unique (high variety) and large, so not many are produced (low volume).

### Learning activity 3.2

For the following projects, identify where they would sit on the two scales of volume and variety, and indicate why:

- the NASA Apollo 11 programme
- a multi-million-pound advertising campaign for a soft drink
- building an office block in Shanghai
- developing a new 300-passenger jet aircraft
- a process improvement project within a programme of such projects
- developing a new car for mass production.

*Feedback on page 49*

### The implications of defining projects by volume and variety

The first implication is that projects are no different in essence from any production process: they are there to deliver a product to a customer.

This definition also indicates what project management is *not* and what management ideas cannot be used. Tools used on other operations, process mapping and flow layouts are hard to apply as variety is high; continuous improvement is challenging due to the low volume. The definition indicates that the tools of project management must be different.

It would follow that tools used for processes close on the spectrum (jobbing processes) should be useful. Unfortunately there are few generic tools and concepts widely available for jobbing processes, in fact jobbing process management often relies on production management tools.

Slack (2004) identifies professional services in a similar position to project processes. Examples might include the work of architects, solicitors on large legal cases, or consultants on a large change project. This is certainly a good comparison, with the drawback that, once again, many of these use tools from project management. This comparison does, however, highlight some aspects often neglected: the fluid nature of some projects. A legal case can be very difficult to scope at the outset and objectives may well be revised as it progresses. In addition, the client brief is not handed over complete to the professional, it is developed in consultation between stakeholders. The objectives, expectations, scope, cost, time and quality may well develop throughout the project. Architects and solicitors are frequently excellent at managing key stakeholders and see this as a central part of their role. Some projects could learn from this.

*Projects and other processes*

If projects are the extreme of low volume high variety, what is the implication for repeated projects: a company with many research projects, or new product development projects, or process improvement projects (see section 6.1 on Six-Sigma)? Here the definition helps develop project management. Repeated projects become more like jobbing, batch or even mass processes. The tools can be transferred or adapted. These could include process mapping, standardised processes and continuous improvement. Projects can begin to follow a standardised best practice to avoid errors, the steps involved can be planned, checked and measured, and learning can be formalised. This is indeed what happens: companies can develop 'new product development process' and 'project checklists'. Building a new length of motorway is essentially similar to the other motorways around the world and managing road resurfacing projects could be close to the efficiency of mass production. As soon as a project has been done once, it should be possible to learn for the next.

### Self-assessment question 3.2

Some projects do not seem to fit into the Slack definition of low volume high variety, for example advertising campaigns and repeated process improvement projects (see learning activity 3.2 above).

In 100–200 words, identify whether managing these 'projects' is in fact different from project management or could they too benefit from project management techniques?

*Feedback on page 50*

## 3.3 Stairway to heaven or the job from hell: being a project manager

The role of project manager is at the centre of a lot of work on project management and often central to the project itself. In study session 1, the need for leadership was discussed, but what else does the role entail? What is a project manager?



### Learning activity 3.3

The manager of an IT department of three people supporting a site of 500 people is taking on her first project, changing the way IT is sourced and supported, drawing on help from people working in other departments. Identify the key new management challenges facing her.

*Feedback on page 50*

Looking back at the definition of project management in study session 1, it involves achieving objectives which will change and develop while:

- managing changing resources such as people and money
- coping with time constraints
- managing complex situations and activities, frequently with interdependence on people, departments and stakeholders spread across and beyond the organisation
- planning and managing activities which are new, hence experience is limited
- managing human reactions to change.

In addition, section 1.4 identified the very different skills needed for hard and soft projects and section 1.2 suggested that a project manager needed competence in managing the project, leadership and potentially specific technical skills.

If we take the example of the IT manager in learning activity 3.3 above, she apparently needs to continue doing her existing 'day job' well, while becoming a leader, developing competence in this range of project management tools and techniques, then applying this to a project where the objectives keep changing and cannot be pinned down, money, time and resources will never be enough and a whole range of stakeholders will be interfering, fighting, supporting then changing. In addition, in many organisations, advancement will not come from success in projects but through success in the normal hierarchy. A successful project is frequently claimed by everyone involved, a failure is often blamed on the project manager.

This seems an unenviable and more likely impossible role.

### Start at home

There must be a limit to the additional skills, knowledge and activities heaped upon the project manager. As a result, the first part of the role of project manager must be to manage themselves and their workload. This involves delegation, coordination rather than control, avoiding or refusing excessive demands and dealing with only the most important activities. It may seem trivial to identify this aspect, but many project managers accept an excessive workload and a sizeable minority suffer from stress for part or all of the project. To avoid this, managing the manager is a necessary activity at every stage of the project.

### Avoid micromanagement

Meredith and Mantel (2006) highlight the problem of micromanagement (managing the detail of other people's work). This has the twin problems of taking a lot of time to do and discouraging any effort from the person being managed. According to Meredith and Mantel (2006):

> 'It stamps out creativity or initiative…frustrates almost anyone…And generally ensures mediocre performance if not failure.'

The remedy is difficult, but as Semler (1989), a strong exponent of empowerment, suggested:

> 'Look at the list of things you have to do and identify which can only be done by you. If there are more than four of these and you are not president of your country, start again.'

### Systems not analytic

According to Meredith and Mantel (2006), the functional manager takes an analytical approach. This involves breaking down a system into smaller and smaller chunks in order to understand it and how different elements work and build up to the whole. Following this idea, in functional management it may be necessary to ensure each part of the department and activity is working well and linked well and to understand how they work and link. The project manager's role is far more about a *systems* approach. This involves understanding only that the system is working well and investigating parts of the project only when they are problematic. The example they cite is a software and database project where the project manager knows nothing of the software, the decision rules to be used or the hardware. This systems approach fits neatly with some of the needs of project management, although it is possible to question why it does not fit functional management, as Meredith and Mantel (2006) seem to suggest.

### Avoid the ostrich

The danger of being blamed for failure causes some managers to avoid warning about problems early on, sometimes waiting until the problems become massive and insurmountable. This 'ostrich' behaviour of burying the head in the sand is almost always counter-productive and highlighting and dealing with risks, problems and failures is an important part of the project manager's role. The responsibility for this lies partly with the project manager, but more with those overseeing the manager. The fear of blame comes from the way the project is set up and directed. As a passing note, it is probably well known that ostriches do not bury their heads in sand at the sign of danger, but they do have remarkably small brains and a tendency to lash out when challenged, so legendary or real, the ostrich model is probably best avoided.

### Attitude

If the project manager is not enthusiastic about the project, few others will be. The attitude of the project manager is reflected in the others involved and in the outcome. Few projects proceed smoothly from rational selection, through careful planning and well resourced execution to expected success. The project is likely to go through peaks and troughs of enthusiasm and despair magnified compared with functional management, both dangerous. In bad times when the project seems to be stuck and will never move, there will be a tendency to abandon it. When a great success has been achieved, the team may tend to drift away because the project is unlikely to match that success in the future. Weathering these times is part of the territory of the project manager. More difficult still will be carrying the rest of the team through them.

### The project-specific knowledge

One of the best ways to work out what is needed is to use other people's experience, success and failure. As a shortcut to this the Association of Project Managers (APM) in the UK and the Project Management Institute (PMI) in the US have consulted their members to develop 'Bodies of Knowledge'. These offer guidance on what technical project management expertise managers should have. These also categorise project manager roles into different levels to separate what might be expected in different categories. Maylor (2003) also offers a reflection of these throughout different project stages.

### Anything else?

Just in case the description of what is needed for project management is not extensive enough, the APM suggests the project manager needs:

- an open, positive, 'can do' attitude
- common sense
- open-mindedness to new ideas and practices
- adaptability
- inventiveness
- to be a prudent risk taker
- fairness
- commitment.

### Self-assessment question 3.3

Review the aspects of a project manager's skills and ability above and identify which are exclusive to project management and which can be

*(continued on next page)*

Self-assessment question 3.3 *(continued)*

or should be found in functional management. Take 200–300 words to explain your answers.

*Feedback on page 51*



## Revision question

Now try the revision question for this session on page 319.

## Summary

This session looked at two things: different ideas or concepts of a project and the role of the project manager.

The way a project is approached has a subtle but substantial impact on the way it is managed. The transformation model can usefully focus attention on inputs and outputs, to the results and the 'cost' in resources. It can also lead to a limited or hamstrung definition of projects: an input of a need passed to the project which results in a satisfied need. This ignores any more complex understanding of how projects develop.

The low-volume high-variety definition moves away from the focus on inputs and outputs but opens up a wealth of understanding in how projects can be managed. By linking project management to operations management, a comparison and diffusion of ideas is possible.

Definitions of the project manager's role are problematic. First, projects are hard to define: a project developing a new aircraft will require a different manager from one implementing structural changes in a small organisation in a short time frame. The more important problems are in adding to the project manager role. A set of project-specific tools can be identified, but many of the skills beyond that are extensions of 'normal' accepted management traits used in any other fields and any description of a project manager tends towards describing any ideal leader/manager. The key identifiable difference is in the balance of those traits. The temporary and novel nature of projects, the limited time, the need to work without line management authority and the wider spread of stakeholders mean that the skills related to change become far more important. Perhaps a project manager is like any other leader, but with added work, more change to cope with and accelerated time pressure.

## Suggested further reading

- Association of Project Management (2006).
- Ayers (2004); Chapter 1.
- Grant et al (1997).
- Lock (2003); Chapter 2.
- Maylor (1996); Chapter 1.
- Meredith and Mantel (2006); Chapters 1 and 3.
- Project Management Institute (2000).
- Semler (1994).

- Smith (2000).
- Weiss and Wysocki (1992).


## Feedback on learning activities and self-assessment questions



### Feedback on learning activity 3.1

This activity is placed before the definitions below to give you a chance to identify what you believe are inputs and outputs, to compare with the transformation model. The range of definitions is wide (see below), so these are some ideas.

Possible inputs:

- Things which are consumed: people's time, money, space, materials.
- Things which trigger the project: a need, a change in the environment, an idea.
- Things which are activities or support the project: a specification, a time plan, risk management.

Possible outputs:

- The product: a building, a plan, a changed organisation.
- The effects of the product: a need fulfilled, happy stakeholders, greater efficiency, greater competitiveness.
- By-products: experience, skills in project management, learning.

### Feedback on self-assessment question 3.1

There are of course some general points on the value and drawbacks identified in the text which you may have used or disagreed with as a basis for your answer. Your discussion should go further and build on your example. As a check on your work, does it answer the following questions for each model?

- Does this model fit my project?
- How easy was it to define my project according to this model?
- Was my definition and understanding of the project any different after using this model than before?
- What distinguishes between these models in terms of use and value?

### Feedback on learning activity 3.2

- *The NASA Apollo 11 programme:* This is pretty extreme on both scales: almost a one-off, packed with new challenges. Space Shuttle missions, however, shift along both scales: far more volume, less variety, suggesting management should become more standardised.
- *A multi-million-pound advertising campaign for a soft drink:* Although the creative element may be unique, there are many similar projects across the world and the variety is limited. A more process-based management should be possible.

- *Building an office block in Shanghai:* Many, many office blocks have been constructed around the world each year for 100 years, and Shanghai is a huge and fast-developing city with many office blocks. Some features of the design might vary, but the process should be stable and efficient. This moves away from Slack's definition of a project.
- *Developing a new 300-passenger jet aircraft:* Very few such projects take place; although airliners look very similar, each new one will incorporate much new technology. Very low volume, fairly high variety.
- *A process improvement project within a programme of such projects:* This is medium volume, medium variety. It moves away from Slack's definition and could be thought of as a process.
- *Developing a new car for mass production:* The mass car assemblers develop many new cars each year, typically launching several each week across the world. Each company will have several projects running concurrently. While these projects are large and complex, volume is not extremely low and variety is limited within certain technological and specification boundaries. The challenge here, therefore, comes not from the volume or variety but the size: learning from one project to another is difficult and the risks are high.

### Feedback on self-assessment question 3.2

There are several parts to this question.

First, some project management techniques may be useful in a range of environments and can be used for managing processes or other activities. Stakeholder management can be valuable in a range of areas, for example, not least in an advertising campaign or building an office block.

Some techniques could be adapted. Gantt charts can be used for production scheduling, for example, and certainly could be useful in building an office block.

Finally, Slack's definition could be wrong and these could be projects, hence they should be managed as projects and are likely to benefit from the use of project management techniques. The discussion in study session 1 centred on the lack of a clear definition for projects.

In summary, the definition of projects as very low-volume high-variety activities is interesting but does not define how projects should be managed or provide a definition which is superior to those derived in study session 1. It seems to isolate a small group of projects which are 'extreme': at one end of a spectrum.

### Feedback on learning activity 3.3

As a manager with three people reporting to her, she is likely to have a range of skills and experience, so the new challenges are likely to centre on the novelty, uncertainty and change involved in the project. They could include:

- a change from stable to very varied work patterns and requirements

- a new team, not reporting directly to her with other demands on their time
- needing to absorb project management tools and techniques such as time and resource planning
- having to negotiate with a wide variety of stakeholders with changing views, attitudes and requirements
- facing conflict and negotiation
- all the factors surrounding the implementation of change
- a change to her role for the future.

## Feedback on self-assessment question 3.3

Competence in managing the project and project-specific tools can be separated out: these are designed for projects and may be useful elsewhere but there is no necessity. Stakeholder management may be more intense and demanding in a project, but many functional roles will need it.

The remainder of the aspects could arguably be valuable in functional or day-to-day management.

The APM's list is a good example: an open, positive 'can do' attitude, common sense, open-mindedness to new ideas and practices, adaptability, inventiveness, being a prudent risk taker, fairness, commitment – all are valuable outside project management. Leadership, and managing money, time and resources are central to much management, as is the 'start at home' workload management issue.

Some aspects may be intensified by projects. The need to avoid micromanagement, use a systems approach, avoiding the ostrich way of ignoring problems and maintaining a positive attitude are relevant to functional management but the effects are far stronger in projects.

Study session 4

# The project life cycle

'It started well, but then…': managing the project life cycle.

4

## Introduction

The difference between getting a project started and making a successful completion is huge. Through a project the demands change, the focus changes and the required skills change.

What are the skills needed to get a project started? What needs to be done at each stage? What is often forgotten or done badly? By looking at the project through its life, it becomes easier to structure the activity of project management.

## Session learning objectives

After completing this session you should be able to:

4.1 Evaluate the concept of the project life cycle (PLC) as a management tool.
4.2 Explain the relevance of different approaches to the project life cycle and the stages they represent.
4.3 Identify the different stages of the project life cycle and their key characteristics and demands.

## Unit specification coverage

This study session covers the following topic from the official CIPS unit content document.

### Learning objective

2.0 Assess and justify the approach to managing projects using a variety of methodologies.
2.2 Describe the approach of the project life cycle, and its various phases.
- 3-stage PLC, Meredith and Mantel (2003)
- 4-stage PLC, Maylor (2003)
- 5-stage PLC, Weiss and Wysocki (1992)
- 7S Project Approach, McKinsey, adapted Maylor (2003)

## Prior knowledge

Study sessions 1 – 3.

## Timing

You should set aside about 5 hours to read and complete this session, including learning activities, self-assessment questions, the suggested reading (if any) from the essential textbook for this unit and the revision question.

## 4.1 What happens when: introducing the project life cycle (PLC)

Projects develop as time passes. If you consider the Magenta Foods case study from section 2.4, the project was to re-source secondary packaging (essentially packaging which does not touch the food). The objectives set early on were to single source everything, with a few specialist exceptions, and make direct savings of 12.5%.

If you look back to the start of the project, before it was formed, there will be some environmental drivers which push for a new project. Cost pressures or a perceived need to change might be encouraging a CEO or CPO to develop project ideas. The first idea might be vague: cost reductions from direct or production purchases, for example. The idea may change as it is discussed or examined, but at this stage it has no clear form or objectives, no resources attached to it and uncertainty is high. It may work, it may be useful, there may be potential savings there, but little is known with any confidence.

Next the idea begins to take shape and more information is gathered. Spend analysis in a coarse form will help identify the juiciest areas. A look at the market will suggest what potential is there, can suppliers offer savings? A rough benchmark against other companies will help guide the formation of clearer objectives. The cost of the project will also take shape: how much time is needed, how many people will be involved. Finally, who will drive it and be the project 'champion' or 'sponsor'? Where will it live in the organisation? At this stage many projects die away. People lose interest, the potential is not there or other projects take up all the available resources. For Magenta Foods, the project came out of this stage with clear objectives: 12.5% savings, single sourcing.

At some point, a project manager is appointed or found and detailed planning and definition can start. The team drawn from logistics, finance, purchasing, production and marketing is drawn together. Work on the project speeds up or intensifies and the team carry out detailed spend analysis, identify and standardise specifications and examine the market in real detail. The project does not stop developing. It may be found that single sourcing is not a good option or that savings will be greater than target. Some small benefits or 'quick wins' are found by eliminating the most expensive packaging which is still used for historical reasons.

The work on delivering the project grows, more time and money is spent and the potential results become even clearer. The sourcing director fixes on using an e-auction and the nature of the project is well defined.

Following the auction, work shifts to implementation. The team changes and the stakeholders change dramatically. The timing is replanned and a new project plan is set out.

Towards the end of implementation, the needs change. People start drifting away to focus on new projects, it becomes clear some of the specification changes will not be finished, the project overruns slightly. A new project manager takes over to finish off and make sure the project achieves maximum savings and all sites are using the new contract. This new project manager is told to pass on the lessons from it to other projects.

What worked well? What were the biggest barriers? What took longer than expected? What could really help next time?

## Learning activity 4.1

Using the example of Magenta Foods and projects you have been involved in or understand well, define a series of 3–6 stages you believe projects tend to go through from beginning to end

*Feedback on page 63*

4

The case should demonstrate that projects travel through a series of different stages. These can be divided up in a number of different ways (see section 4.2 below), as identified by Meredith and Mantel (2006). They suggest that most projects go through three similar stages:

1. The project is born, a manager is selected, initial resources and team are assembled: the start-up phase.
2. Work gets under way and momentum quickly builds, progress is made.
3. Completing the final tasks, which seems to take an inordinate amount of time.

According to Meredith and Mantel, these three stages (see figure 4.1) typically involve very different work and different work rates. The effort involved can be identified (figure 4.2) if effort and progress are proportional. Minimal effort is required at the beginning, a lot of effort in implementation, which drops away again in stage 3, when, presumably, the loose ends are tied up.

They accept that different types of project will follow different patterns, for example an 'inverse S' curve with high effort at the start and finish and a plateau in the middle (figure 4.3), or projects such as software development or cake baking, which remain largely incomplete until near the end of the project when the different parts of the project are united or the cake ingredients finally bind together (figure 4.4).

**Figure 4.1:** Meredith and Mantel project life cycle

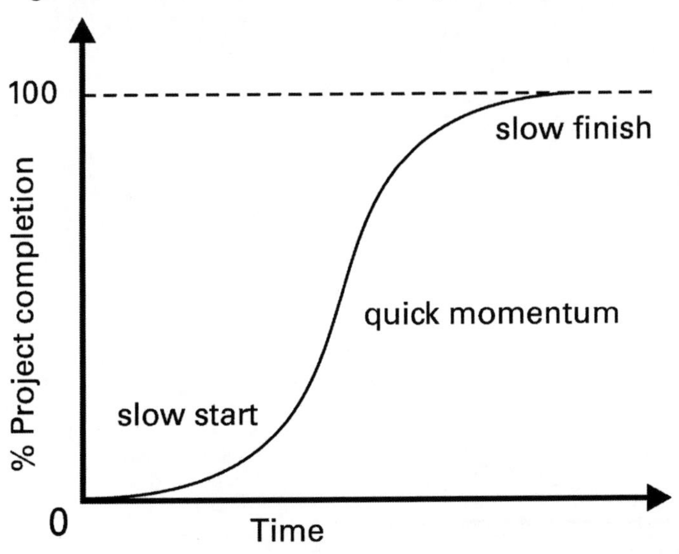


*Source: Meredith and Mantel (2006)*

**Figure 4.2:** Effort across the project life cycle

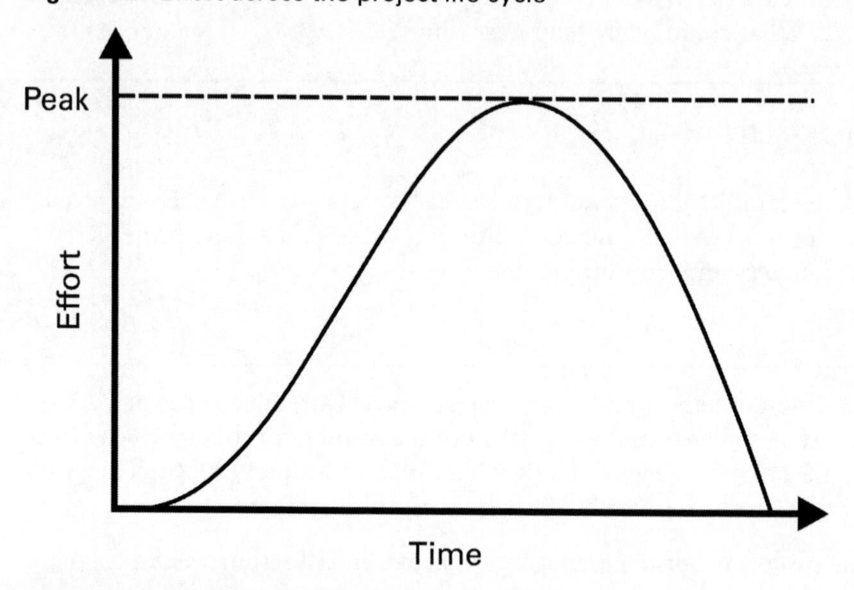


**Figure 4.3:** The 'inverted S' curve

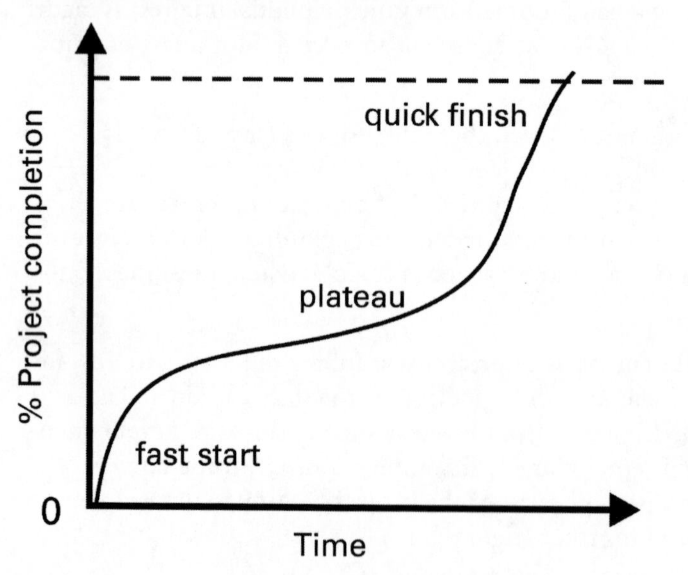


**Figure 4.4:** The software or cake curve

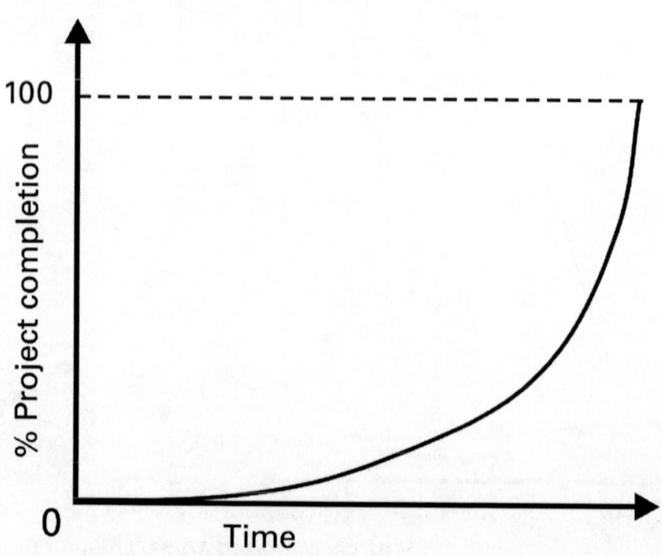

Given that effort across the PLC does not conform to a single shape, there must be some other value for it. Although understanding the potential spread of effort across time can be useful, the PLC gives more valuable insight. Different activities are relevant at different times, emphasis moves as the project develops, conflict changes and intensifies and understanding the life cycle can help avoid missing activities or hanging on to the wrong activities.



### Self-assessment question 4.1

From your analysis of the project life cycle, for example the analysis carried out for the learning activity, suggest problems which may affect the project team at each different stages of the life cycle.

*Feedback on page 63*

## 4.2 The value of the PLC: different views

Section 2.1 introduced the project life cycle and suggested the value but didn't define that value. This section attempts to put this right, looking at different ways the project life cycle is used.

Frigenti and Comninos (2002) build on the three stages identified already and extend it to five, dividing up the effort across the project (figure 4.5) and forms 'objective-directed project management'.

**Figure 4.5:** Frigenti and Comninos' stages of the life cycle

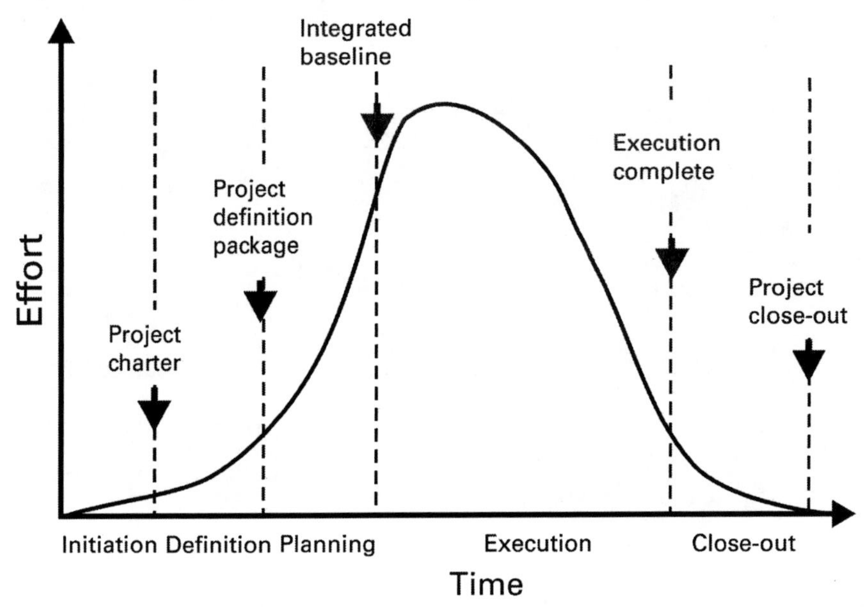


*Source: Frigenti and Comninos (2002)*

Each of these five stages is defined in terms of the inputs, activities involved and the outputs.

- *Initiation*: The brief and the business case with supporting documentation. A project manager is selected, briefed, accepts accountability and is given authority for the project. All parties are made aware of that authority and of the project itself. Stakeholder management is started and the output is a project charter: a document specifying the project and the roles and authority of the people involved.

- *Definition*: This brings together the team and sometimes stakeholders in defining the project and producing a project definition report. This shifts from an outline understanding of the project to something more concrete, with a mission, objectives, breakdown of deliverables, scope and definition, outline timings, costs and responsibilities, a risk analysis and communications plan.
- *Planning*: This takes the definition and involves detailed planning on time, resources, cash flow and procurement as well as details of the information system used for control and key performance indicators. It may involve several iterations to derive a practical, viable plan. The output is a detailed baseline plan for the execution phase.
- *Execution*: Monitoring, analysing, controlling and problem solving are key activities, along with reporting to stakeholders, sponsors or the project board. Regular meetings, accurate reports and change control are all included. There is no clear output or trigger for the next phase, but it occurs when 'progress begins to slow and it seems that the project will never end'.
- *Close-out*: Given changes to the project, the last stage must be replanned, performance criteria reviewed, resources released and the product delivered. Finally, a review looks back at the project as a whole and a final report is the last output.

## Learning activity 4.2

Suggest some of the strengths and drawbacks of the Frigenti and Comninos PLC described above. Focus on high-level rather than detailed specifics such as names or the location of minor activities.

More detail can be found in Frigenti and Comninos (2002).

*Feedback on page 64*

Weiss and Wysocki (1992) used a similar five-stage model, the only substantial differences being the separation of 'Planning' into two stages: 'Plan' and 'Organise' and the omission of the first stage, some of which is incorporated into 'Definition'.

Maylor (2003) takes a less prescriptive approach with what he terms the 4D process. First he notes that many projects will follow different patterns and that it is common for the cycle to be repeated for sub-projects or small parts of the project. The 4D process takes an organisational perspective, focusing on the important areas at each stage rather than the activity or tool to be used. It is defined in terms of fundamental questions and key issues in table 4.1.

**Table 4.1**

| Phase | Key issues | Fundamental questions |
|---|---|---|
| Define the project | Project and organisational strategy, goal definition | What is to be done and why? |
| Design the project process | Modelling and planning, estimating, resource analysis, conflict resolution and justification | How will it be done?<br>Who will be involved in each part?<br>When will it start and finish? |
| Deliver the project (do it!) | Organisation, control, leadership, decision making and problem solving | How should the project be managed on a day-to-day basis? |
| Develop the process | Assessment of process and outcomes of the project, evaluation, changes for the future | How can the process be improved continually? |

The first two stages map closely onto Frigenti and Comninos' Conception and Initiation, 'do it' combines planning and implementation, while 'develop it' takes the learning element from project close-out.

This higher-level perspective allows more flexibility for different contexts and projects, although the trade off is in less detailed direction. With Frigenti and Comninos, the project planning becomes more of a join-the-dots exercise, Maylor's process requires you to draw the dots, although he provides an example of a plan developed from the 4Ds.

Two interesting parts of Maylor's cycle are the emphasis on learning and the more general first stage. It is not necessary to enter the cycle with a defined specification, as with Frigenti and Comninos. It can develop in the first stage. The focus on learning is important as this is frequently very badly done in projects. In some projects the learning would be more valuable than the other outputs all together, yet it is hard to do and frequently done badly, as the list of failed projects suggests.

Maylor goes on from the life cycle to suggest the '7-S' of project management, claiming it is 'a comprehensive set of issues to be considered'. These are: Strategy, Structure, Systems, Staff, Skills, Style/Culture, Stakeholders. This bears strong resemblance to the long-established McKinsey's 7-S and is a framework for organisation rather than a reflection of the project life cycle.

Whether you use a prescriptive PLC like Frigenti and Comninos' or a more generic process like Maylor's it allows a strong overview of the project and the different activities, attitudes and focus needed at different points. A clear view of the project life cycle is also useful as part of the common language needed to communicate (Ayers, 2003: 72) and common processes in an organisation which seeks to manage projects effectively. The graph of effort against time, the completion curve and the detail may vary from project to project, the life cycle may be repeated by sub-projects within a larger project, but the project life cycle is a useful way of positioning the wealth of detail that makes up project management.



### Self-assessment question 4.2

Compare the stages you have defined in learning activity 4.1 above with the life cycles defined here. Take 200 words to explain how your stages map onto these cycles and identify where your stages need to be extended and any aspects you feel are missing in the cycles given.

*Feedback on page 64*

## 4.3 Bringing the views together: a summary of the PLC

The different descriptions of the project life cycle in section 4.3 offer different ideas of the stages a project goes through and different levels of detail. This section brings those together and looks at three things at each stage: the focus, the risks and the questions. The four general stages used are birth, planning and development, execution, and exit.

### Birth

This is the creation of the project and involves the development and selection of an idea along with some momentum, progress or enthusiasm which gives that idea life as a potential project.

*Focus*

- A creative leap to develop an idea responding to the environment or a problem.
- Getting people involved and committed – the project manager and team, for example.
- An outline set of aims or objectives agreed between the people involved, defining roughly what the project is.

*Risks*

- A rigid process of selection or definition applied too early can stifle creativity.
- The converse is that a project with a poor payoff could get through this stage unless there is some selection mechanism.
- People do not buy into the aims of project.
- An unbalanced team pulling the project in one direction or likely to conflict.

*Questions*

- The justification, through cost benefit analysis or other reasoning.
- What will the style of the project be: Open? Participative? Authoritarian?

### Planning and development

This stage defines the project more clearly and builds a firm foundation for success.

*Focus*

- A sound plan for cost, money and deliverables. Clear enough, but not too detailed, especially further into the future. Early deliverables are particularly valuable in building momentum and commitment.
- Building the team involved and a good working relationship.
- Building accountability and ownership for each part of the project: activities, management and control.
- A good control system for the future, with strong communications and measures.
- A structure for meeting and other communication between the team and stakeholders.

*Dangers*

- Stakeholders do not buy in.
- This stage is often skimped. Projects are launched late and a lot of planning can be boring and time-consuming, leading people to rush straight into the excitement of execution.
- As the converse, too much analysis can kill the momentum of the project, leaving a perfect plan with no project.

*Questions*

- Who is responsible for what, when and how?
- Is there still momentum?

### Learning activity 4.3

Before moving on to the next two stages, complete this section for yourself. Use your previous work on different stages in the PLC to identify what you believe should be the focus, risks and questions for execution and exit.

*Feedback on page 65*

### Execution

Execution is usually the most exciting and frustrating part of the project, with visible progress, conflicts, problems, barriers and challenges.

*Focus*

- Achieving the work needed for the objectives.
- The 'doing': plenty of activity.
- Managing problems.

*Risks*

- Drift of any aspect of the project: cost, time, objectives, stakeholder involvement.

- As the most exciting part, this can attract attention away from other stages in the project.
- Problems and fire-fighting are exciting and can bias the activity of the project.
- Stakeholders are often left behind by the progress of the project.
- The team become absorbed by the work itself and neglect the objectives and planning.

*Questions*

- How can we be sure it is going well?
- When does exit start?

### Exit

This is in some ways the hardest part of the project. Work seems to be very slow, and the objectives have to be revised and delivery matched to stakeholder expectations. The delivered result often does not seem as exciting or radical as at the start, while the team will have to be disbanded and the project wound up. At the same time, there is an expectation that learning should be identified from reviewing the whole project while everyone is working flat out and the team is leaving.

*Focus*

- Delivery of expected outputs.
- Embedding the outputs: the users are trained, maintenance is in place, people are moving to the new structure.
- Handing over the results.
- Ensuring all the stakeholders recognise the success of the project.
- Disbanding the team and returning resources.
- Learning.
- Celebration, whatever the outcome.

*Risks*

- The project drifts on or dies away.
- Objectives are reached but success is not recognised.
- The same mistakes are made in other projects.

*Questions*

- What are the outcomes?
- Project: the objectives?
- For the team?
- For the next project?

### Self-assessment question 4.3

At which points in the project life cycle is the effort needed on stakeholder management likely to be higher and why? Take about 30 minutes to identify different points.

*Feedback on page 65*

## Revision question

Now try the revision question for this session on page 319.

## Summary

Projects change in nature as they progress. The work of generating a project and getting momentum at the start is very different from the work of finishing, handing over and winding up. Activities carry on throughout, for example stakeholder management, but the things needed change, as seen in self-assessment question 4.3 above. These changes form the project life cycle.

There are many different views of the PLC. It can be used to define a process very clearly (Frigenti and Comninos, 2002), it can be a framework for risk and quality management (Meredith and Mantel 2006), or it can be an overview of the activity in different phases (Maylor, 1996). These views overlap and can be linked but offer different value.

One thing stands out. Understanding the different phases of the PLC makes it easier to tailor the management focus and effort and ensures key aspects of the management are not neglected.

## Suggested further reading

- Ayers (2004); Chapter 5.
- Frigenti and Comninos (2002); Chapters 7–11.
- Lock (2003); Chapter 1.
- Maylor (1996); Chapter 2.
- Meredith and Mantel (2006); Chapter 1.
- Weiss and Wysocki (1992); Chapter 1.

## Feedback on learning activities and self-assessment questions

### Feedback on learning activity 4.1

What you have defined is a 'project life cycle' (PLC). Different views of the life cycle are discussed in this session, yours could compare with any of those or be a combination. The work of project management changes throughout the lifetime of the project and the key aspects of a life cycle are that it starts at the very outset, when the project is formed, and ends only after completion and handover.

### Feedback on self-assessment question 4.1

If we use the three-stage cycle identified by Meredith and Mantel:

*Stage 1*: The project is fluid, the team is very new. There may well be early conflict as the team begins to try and find roles and ways of working with each other. There may be difficulties in focusing the team on the objectives because they are not set. The wrong people may be involved in the team and it could need to be changed.

*Stage 2*: There is a lot of work involved, the early enthusiasm could die away and morale could drop. At the same time, team members can be replaced as staff change roles, causing disruption. Team members can drift apart, each working on their own area, uncoordinated.

*Stage 3*: The project is drawing to a close and the team will be disbanded. Members may drift away early and the remaining team must take up extra work. Time pressures may become harsher, leading to problems, team members may not be ruthless enough with their pet areas, trying to finish at the expense of other areas of the project.

## Feedback on learning activity 4.2

The strengths and drawbacks will depend on your experience, attitude and perhaps the type of project. If your environment requires detailed, signed-off plans, this will be a strength; if it requires swift action and progress above all else, it will be a drawback. These are some general points.

*Strengths*

- The clear inputs, activities and outputs make for an easy-to-follow procedure.
- As a link to that, in the detailed description given in the source text, the activities at each stage are detailed and easy to understand.
- It focuses on planning rather than diving into the doing or execution phase unprepared. This can ensure a well-thought-through project rather than a rapidly changing problem in the making.
- The two-stage planning – outline and detailed – is useful. Different people and different skills may be needed for each.
- The first stage which ensures the manager is signed up, authorised and publicised is useful and often happens in a slightly haphazard way.
- The shift from execution to a close-out phase is important, if ill-defined, here.

*Drawbacks*

- The start assumes a clear and well-defined brief which is handed over to the project manager who then develops it with stakeholders in *Definition*. This is not always a viable pattern.
- There is a lot of planning before any progress starts. This could raise the risk of paralysis by analysis.
- The fairly rigid structure could be valuable but will fit some cultures well and others less so.
- There is little emphasis on the project team, instead it focuses on the project manager as leader, perhaps a solitary and heroic role, but not always the most effective.

## Feedback on self-assessment question 4.2

The key to this activity is in bringing together different cycles. The three discussed above do not align exactly so there is no reason yours should.

Questions which might help if you struggle to map the stages include:

- What are the activities in this stage?
- What are the outputs?
- When would this happen?
- Is there a reason why the location of the same activities varies or is one version more likely?
- Is the behaviour, team membership or key focus different in two neighbouring stages? If not, consider combining them.

## Feedback on learning activity 4.3

There are obviously answers within the section, the important part of this exercise is to reflect on any differences between those and your own. Ignore any small differences of when one changes and the other starts. What are the differences? Is your experience different? Are there things you missed? Are there parts where your answers better reflect reality for you?

## Feedback on self-assessment question 4.3

Consider the four stages.

*Birth*: The project is not yet formed so although some work with key stakeholders may be vital to give the project momentum, unless there are few stakeholders throughout, detailed stakeholder management can wait.

*Planning and development*: Here, the detailed identification of stakeholders and the first stages are needed. There is an old saying that you can only make one first impression and that applies to projects. There is a strong argument that this could be a time of high activity.

*Execution*: At this stage there can be a lot of impact on stakeholders and interaction with them. Stakeholder management is typically very important and sometimes neglected, as mentioned above. For many projects, execution will hold periods of intense activity managing stakeholders, especially when things have gone wrong.

*Exit*: If stakeholders define success (see study session 1) then managing those stakeholders is an important part of exit. The work will not just involve handing over the results, but managing expectations and communicating success. It would be a bit late to start stakeholder management, but it is definitely too early to stop.

## Study session 5
# Problem-solving techniques

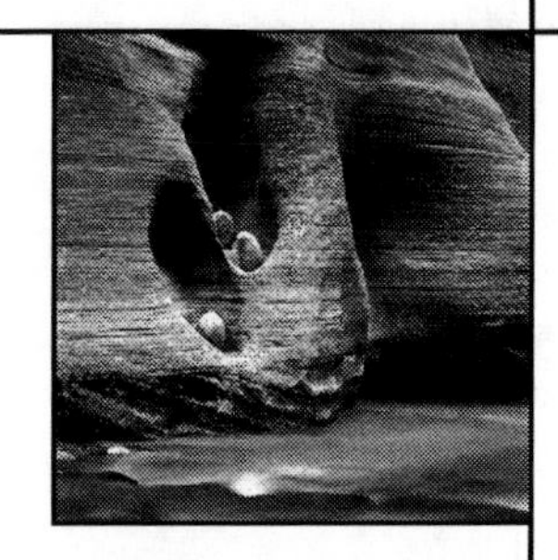

Emptying the garbage can: solving the project's problems.

### Introduction

Most managers are busy. Not every one is efficient, but most are busy. Project managers are no exception, in fact the unique challenges of projects result in many project managers complaining of being overloaded at some points through the project life.

The problem of overloading is all too often caused by poor problem solving. Many problems are part solved or hidden, then return later. This leads into an upwards spiral, or positive feedback loop, where old problems keep coming back, appearing more and more difficult to solve, while new problems keep arriving until the time to deal with all of them disappears.

Over 30 years ago Mintzberg (1971) described how managers often operate a 'garbage can' approach to storing and solving problems. The overloaded manager cannot deal with all the problems, but stores them all, like putting them in a garbage can. When an idea or solution comes up, the manager rummages through the problems until one of the problem fits it.

There has to be a better way of managing problems than the 'garbage can' approach. A structured, cause-based approach to solving problems is not only more effective at finding better solutions but is far more time efficient. This session looks at a wide variety of approaches to problem solving, aimed at delivering effective and efficient solutions.

### Session learning objectives

After completing this session you should be able to:

5.1 Investigate a number of problem-solving tools and techniques and understand how to apply them appropriately.
5.2 Identify the types of problem most likely to be encountered at each stage of the project life cycle. (Meredith and Mantel, 2006; Chapter 4).
5.3 Identify the benefits of 'cause-effect-cause' and 'decision tree' approaches to problem solving and decision making.

### Unit content coverage

This study session covers the following topic from the official CIPS unit content document.

#### Learning objective

2.0 Assess and justify the approach to managing projects using a variety of methodologies.
2.3 Link the PLC to a variety of problem-solving processes.
- 5-stage problem-solving approach (PSA)
- 6-stage PSA

- 8-stage PSA
- Linking PLC and PSA, The BT Way (1988)

## Prior knowledge

Study sessions 1 – 4.

## Timing



You should set aside about 7 hours to read and complete this session, including learning activities, self-assessment questions, the suggested reading (if any) from the essential textbook for this unit and the revision question.

## 5.1 Different tool for different jobs: five problem-solving approaches

### Clearing your view: Pareto analysis

According to Pareto's suggestions 80% of your delays are caused by just 20% of your problems; 80% of your overspend comes from just 20% of your activities. The number may not be exactly the same but the pattern is repeated over and over again: a few problems cause most of the delays, cost, work and irritation. Solve those problems and the situation becomes far better, not just because the delays and cost are eliminated, but because so much time is freed up to work on the next problems.

Analysis is a rather excessive term for what is involved. Measure the problems or activities. Rank them in order of frequency or impact. Work on the largest until they are solved at the root cause. Measure and rank again, and the cycle continues.

Figure 5.1 shows a ranking of the problems or requests that were passed to a project manager over two weeks. This was carried out to try and clear a backlog of work which had grown beyond manageable proportions.

**Figure 5.1:** Sample Pareto ranking

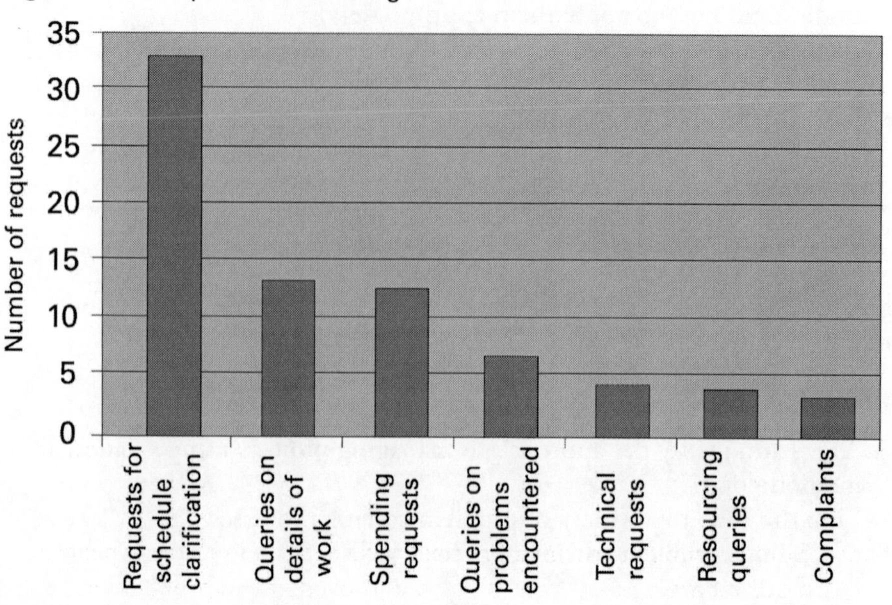

This ranking showed that the most requests were because people did not understand the schedule or the work involved, causing a constant flow of problems and requests. Two days were spent rewriting the schedule and work plan into a form people readily understood, then communicating it. The workload dropped radically, allowing important problems to be tackled, in this case the few complaints.

The huge advantage of Pareto analysis is that it clears away the noise of too many things happening at once and highlights the most important.

### Attacking the right problems: 5 Whys

One difficulty with problem solving is that symptoms are often different from root causes and treating the symptoms can be ineffective or even make things worse. To take a simple characterisation of the old problem of civil engineering projects: contracts used to overspend and overrun. One action taken was to increase estimates. Still the projects overran and the problem was worse. One action was to focus hard on specifying and planning, still the projects overran. One action was to accept it, and predictably the problem got no better.

By asking the 'why?' five times, it is sometimes possible to work back to the root cause.

- Our projects continuously overspend...Why?
- Because changes to the specification cost more...Why?
- Because we fight with the contractor over changes...Why?
- Because contractors make their profits from these arguments...Why?
- Because we set up the contracts like that...Why?
- Because it is standard industry practice.

If this is true, the problem of overspend is standard because standard practice encourages or even ensures it. The root cause is the contracting relationship, although being industry standard made it hard to change.

Using '5 Whys' is not simply a case of asking 'why?' five times like an irritating teenager and the answer magically appearing. The questions have to be carefully put to the right people and there may be false leads. In the example above, one false lead is to try and tie down the specification and eliminate changes. A '5 Whys' investigation may take a little time, depending on the complexity of the problem.

Why 5 Whys? Why not 4 or 6? The truth is that five is not a magic number, but it commonly takes five steps to get to a root cause. It could be three or seven, but if you get there in one leap, there is a danger you have missed the true cause.

### Breaking from the standard answers: brainstorming

Management Madness has been defined as doing the same things you have always done and expecting better results. When you try the same solutions to the same problems, you are likely to get the same failed results.

When you are constrained by established behaviour, a creative leap is what is needed to break the constraints. Most people are not particularly creative at work, but they can be.

Brainstorming is about creating a temporary revolution in the way people work and think to generate a creative leap and overcome a problem or exploit an opportunity. It involves a group working in a freewheeling, creative way focused on one outcome, not afraid of failure, success or looking stupid. It involves three stages:

1 Prepare well. A neutral, isolated but attractive environment and the right team at the right time of day help. Set the focus and work out how you will organise the team.
2 For the session, set the ground rules, then guide and prompt without directing. Getting the ideas flow going, working through the lulls and helping people maintain a creative frame of mind is not straightforward. Rules that welcome wild ideas, make sure all are treated as equal, encourage building and stop judgement help. There will be blanks and silences, very often some of the group will want to wander off-focus. Using new games or ideas, holding the focus and knowing when to stop are all important skills
3 After the event, make sure the best ideas that have come out are used in some form. Sometimes a shift from brainstorming to action planning is needed. By the nature of brainstorming most of the ideas will not be used, so make sure people do not feel their ideas are worthless, ignored or discarded.

Brainstorming is not just listing all current ideas or getting people in a room to think hard about a problem or finding the best solution, it is about changing the way people work temporarily to generate valuable creativity. The effort in doing that can be very well repaid.

## Learning activity 5.1

You are leading a project with a small part-time team which has just been brought together. Make brief notes on the potential advantages and dangers of using Pareto analysis, 5 Whys and brainstorming at this stage.

*Feedback on page 83*

### Uncertainty and fuzzy numbers

Much of the data for purchasing and logistics projects is patchy and uncertain. Predicting into the future is very difficult. One approach is to use probability, which gives an estimate of likelihood and can be valuable in risk assessment. However, as Pender (2001) points out, it relies on a number of assumptions which fit project management poorly, for example randomness, a basis on experience and 'black and white' states: something happens or it does not. Using different approaches can give different results.

Futures and options can be used. Complex markets deal with uncertainty by buying and selling 'options'. Options trading is common in commodities such as oil and foodstuffs. This approach is underused in projects as many hold the simple view that options which are bought and unused are waste. Options can be used in booking transport or deliveries, booking flights, products or even staff. The growth of low-cost airlines with extremely low fares well in advance allows tickets to be bought six months ahead for 10% of a scheduled or flexible fare, effectively an option to fly. A deposit given to a busy subcontractor to be available in a certain time slot removes the risk of unavailability at modest cost.

Fuzzy approaches can be used. The maths may be complex but the principle is straightforward. As an example, someone may ask: 'What is the likelihood of success in this project?' For anything but the simplest project, success is not a clear state. A project can be a success and a failure at the same time. As discussed elsewhere, it could be on time, within budget and to specification but still fail if the output remains unused. Fuzzy logic allows a project to be a success and a failure at the same time.

## Lewin's force field

This simple method of looking at the forces for and against change helps to get a clear view of what needs to be done to get over a problem, or indeed to get the project moving.

The starting point is to describe the current position and the 'desired position': where we want to be (figure 5.2).

**Figure 5.2:** Current and desired position

The next stage is to identify the forces which are pushing for change, which are likely to drive towards the desired position (figure 5.3).

**Figure 5.3:** Forces for change

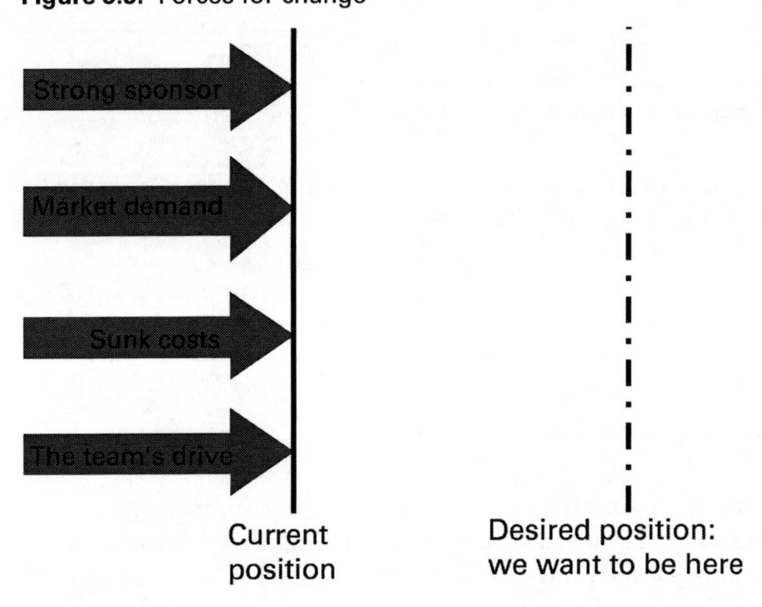

5

Finally, what forces are resisting the change: what will stop or resist the move? (See figure 5.4.)

**Figure 5.4:** Lewin's Force Field completed

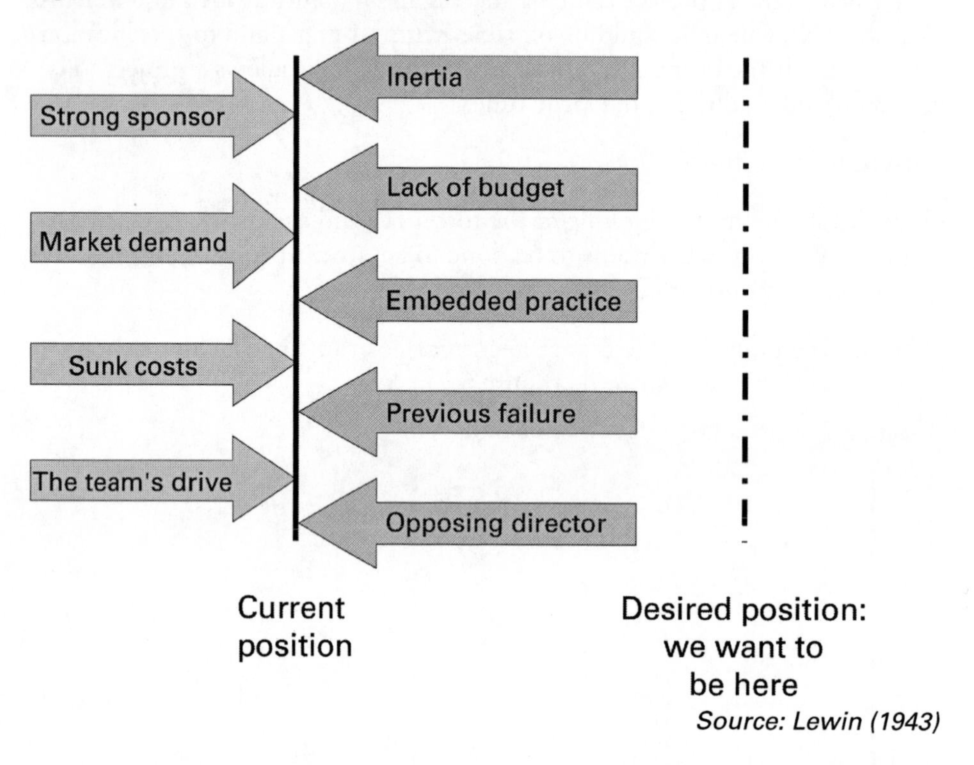


*Source: Lewin (1943)*

By comparing the forces, it is possible to get an impression of the balance of forces for change. In the example given, the forces opposing seem larger and the resulting drive for change will be small: movement is difficult. Implications could be: communicate market demand to help reduce inertia, use the sponsor to increase the budget, work hard on the opposing director, or try to gather supportive stakeholders to counterbalance.

## Self-assessment question 5.1

Examine each of the five approaches listed in this section: Pareto analysis, 5 Whys, brainstorming, fuzzy numbers and options, Lewin's force field.

Make brief notes for each on where they may be useful. Where they are less useful, what is needed to make them work?

*Feedback on page 84*

## 5.2 Different day different problem

Through the progress of a project, some conflict is likely. Some conflict is valuable or even essential as it is a part of team building and developing a shared understanding of the project. The nature of the conflict is likely to change as the project develops through its various stages; problems which will be of burning importance at the start of the project will fade to nothing, while issues ignored at the start can flare up as progress is made and the reality of the project sinks in.

Several studies have looked at the conflicts at different stages, notably Thamhain and Wilemon (1975). Their study suggested that conflict rose to a peak after formation, during early activity, then dropped away towards the end of the project. More notable was how types of conflict developed at different stages. Thamhain and Wilemon divided conflict into schedules, priorities, labour, technical, procedures, cost and personality.



### Schedule conflict

Schedules were consistently a high-conflict area, becoming a dominating theme towards the end of the project. This would fit with the decreasing time available: at the start there may be urgency but once the deadline looms, problems of time become real.

### Priorities and procedures

Priorities and procedures are the reverse of schedules. Participants argue more early on about what is more important and how it should be done, reducing the focus on this as time moves on. This fits with the reducing flexibility to change these aspects: trying to change priorities late on in the project will have limited impact and procedures will also have become more fixed.

### Labour and technical conflict

Disputes in this area generally followed the averaged level of conflict. Conflicts rose in the early stages of implementation but declined as the project continued.

### Cost and personality

The results for these two were relatively stable. Effectively there was always about the same level of conflict about cost and personality disputes.

### Learning activity 5.2

The conflict over schedules and priorities changes as the project develops. Identify how these two change and suggest three ways of resolving such conflicts.

*Feedback on page 84*

### Resolving conflict

Successful conflict resolution depends on several things. The type of people involved, the nature of the conflict, the personal relationship between the parties and the skill and knowledge of whoever is trying to resolve it. Many frameworks have been developed; one of the simpler and widely used ones was developed by Thomas and Kilmann based on a grid used by Blake and Mouton (see figure 5.5).

**Figure 5.5:** The Thomas Kilmann model of conflict management

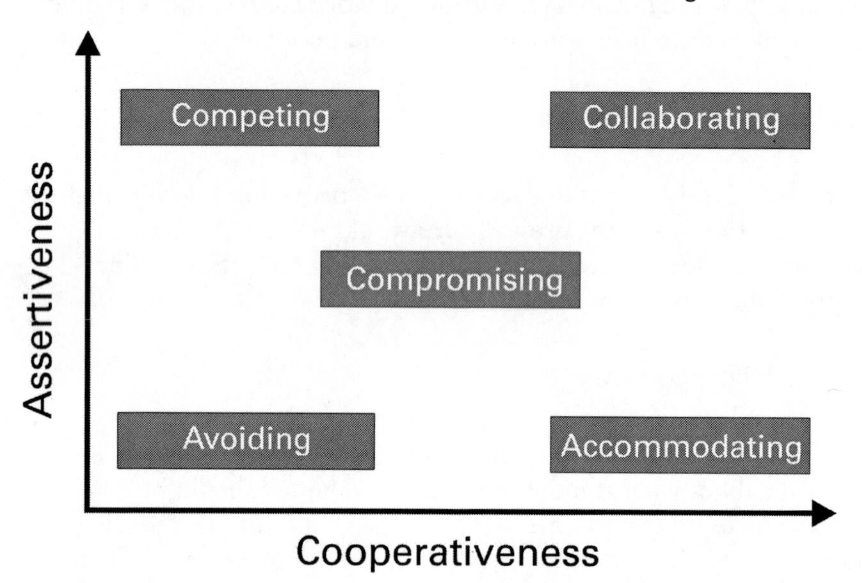


*Source: Thomas and Kilmann (1974)*

This model plots five different modes of conflict resolution on two axes: concern for others, or cooperativeness, and concern for self, or assertiveness. Each of these five modes has strengths and weaknesses in different situations, and different people will find them easier or harder to apply. The key is to be able to use more than one mode and to understand where each might work well.

### Competing: 'it is my way or the highway'

This can be useful where quick action is needed, for unpopular decisions or where an open debate would be dangerous and inappropriate. Stating your position then holding to it based on power, rank or other strengths can break a conflict quickly and it is effectively the method teachers use to break up fighting children in the playground. It is useful in certain circumstances and can be used as a show of strength, but there are drawbacks. It does not encourage initiative or empowerment, just assent, reluctant or otherwise. It does not involve the team and there is no learning from the decision-making process.

### Accommodating: 'it would be my pleasure'

This is the opposite of competing, where you adapt to the other person's needs or wishes. It is useful where the conflict is about something unimportant, where entrenched views are held or to develop the other party's behaviour. This shows flexibility and accommodation and encourages people to air their views or requirements. Using it too much or in the wrong place can undermine your authority or encourage people to ignore your requirements.

### Collaborating: 'two heads are better than one'

This involves working through your needs and the other party's needs to arrive at an agreed solution based on a balance of the two. It takes a lot of time compared with competing or accommodating but that is time well spent if it brings out different perspectives and ideas which can then be merged together to form a successful resolution. Doing this successfully is quite skilled, it requires involving the other parties, drawing out and identifying the different requirements, managing conflict where requirements cannot be merged, and synthesising the result. It can lead to a lot of time spent on trivial concerns and too much importance being laid on each person's requirements, but it is very effective at achieving commitment to the decision.

### Compromising: 'let's make a deal'

This is as balanced as collaborating but is more about negotiation and trade-off. Even if you are entirely in the right (or the wrong), you yield something to make a compromise deal. It is valuable where time is tight or where views are entrenched and power is evenly balanced. All the negotiating skills good purchasers have in abundance are valuable here: understanding both positions, managing the discussion, knowing when to yield and when to hold fast, knowing how to close. Compromising helps to get over problems but encourages negative behaviour. As an example, if you know there will be a compromise, your opening offer might be far less than you really expect to get, generating conflict where there need be none. There is little focus on what is better or more important, such as the goals of the project or organisation; this mode is about splitting the difference.

### Avoiding: 'I will think about that tomorrow'

Avoiding a decision is a valid way of dealing with some conflict. It may not please the parties involved, but where you have little control, where emotions are running high, where a decision would be dangerous or damaging, avoiding may be the best mode. Used too much it can cause problems: issues build up, people become afraid of decisions, the chance to decide may pass and one resolution may be forced on you, but skilfully 'kicking a problem into the long grass' is an option for conflict resolution which should be considered.

### If you cannot fix it, someone else usually can

When a conflict grows up between two parties, some attempt is usually made to resolve it by the people involved. If this does not work, a few other attempts may be made, but if these fail, there is the potential that it will rumble on without resolution. Even if one party is reasonable and attempts rational resolution, the emotions may be too high to allow this to work.

There is often a resistance to bring in third parties, people outside the conflict, to help find a resolution. Where help from these third parties is sought, it can be on a partisan basis: reaching up the hierarchy to get a director to 'back you up', for example. This limited use of third parties misses a very powerful and effective way of resolving conflict. Neutral third parties can bring swift and lasting success.

The first level of third-party help is negotiators: one or both of the sides engages someone to negotiate on their behalf to remove personalities from the conflict. One extreme example would be to engage a solicitor to help resolve a dispute. That solicitor is working on your behalf and will follow your instructions, but their aim is to achieve resolution and they should recommend actions and results you may not find palatable.

Beyond this, a mediator can be very valuable to bring the sides together. A mediator is neutral and manages the discussion between the two sides, sometimes as a go-between, sometimes more like a referee. Just bringing the two sides together and ensuring the problems are aired and discussed fairly can help resolution and this is often used to avoid disputes reaching legal action. A common example would be employers and unions who have reached a stalemate in negotiations using a third party to manage discussions.

The final level is an arbiter. This is someone who will listen to both sides and make a binding decision which both must accept. A current example would be judges presiding over disputes.

These third parties do not need to be formal, legal or paid – anyone neutral or uninvolved can act and mutual agreement on mediation or arbitration by someone else from the organisation can be the first step to a quick and lasting outcome.

### Self-assessment question 5.2

From your experience identify three instances of conflict where different Thomas Kilmann resolution modes have been used. For each of the three different cases suggest:

1. Was the mode appropriate for that conflict and why?
2. Was the conflict resolution successful?

*Feedback on page 84*

## 5.3 Different causes for different outcomes: understanding connections between cause and effect

There are several different ways of mapping out complex choices and systems, each one has different uses, different strengths. This section focuses on three tools: Fishbone or Ishikawa diagrams, cause-effect-cause diagrams and decision trees.

### Fishbone diagrams

Imagine you have just run a brainstorming session on the problem of late deliveries from one supplier. You are frequently running out of one medium-use packaging product based on PVC. The brainstorming session results in the list of possible causes on post-its (figure 5.6).

**Figure 5.6:** Brainstorming output

The challenge now is to put these problems into some order. The next step is to separate out one group of causes which can all be grouped and investigated as one (figure 5.7). In this case, causes which come through our ordering system have been picked out.

**Figure 5.7:** The start of an Ishikawa/Fishbone diagram

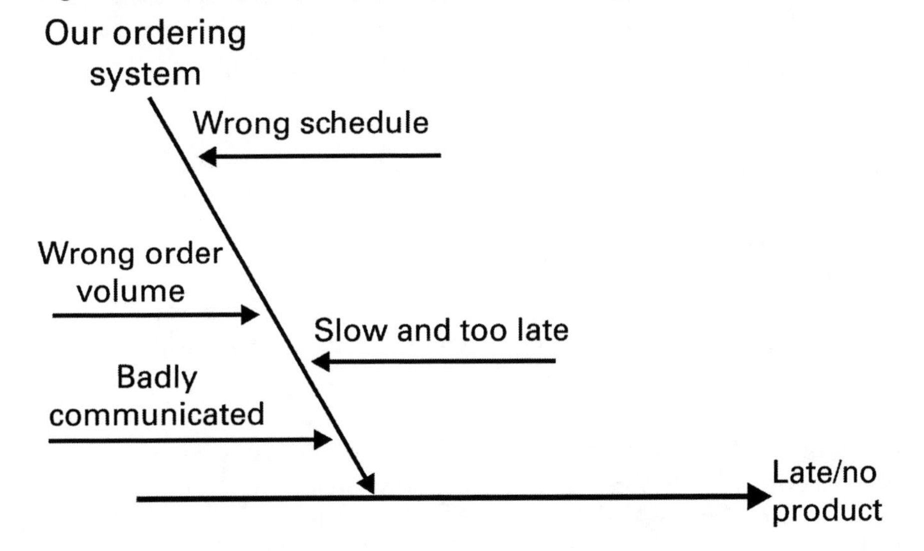

The rest of the causes are grouped similarly: the supplier's system, acts of God, our materials handling, until all of the causes are incorporated in some way.

**Figure 5.8:** The completed Fishbone/Ishikawa diagram

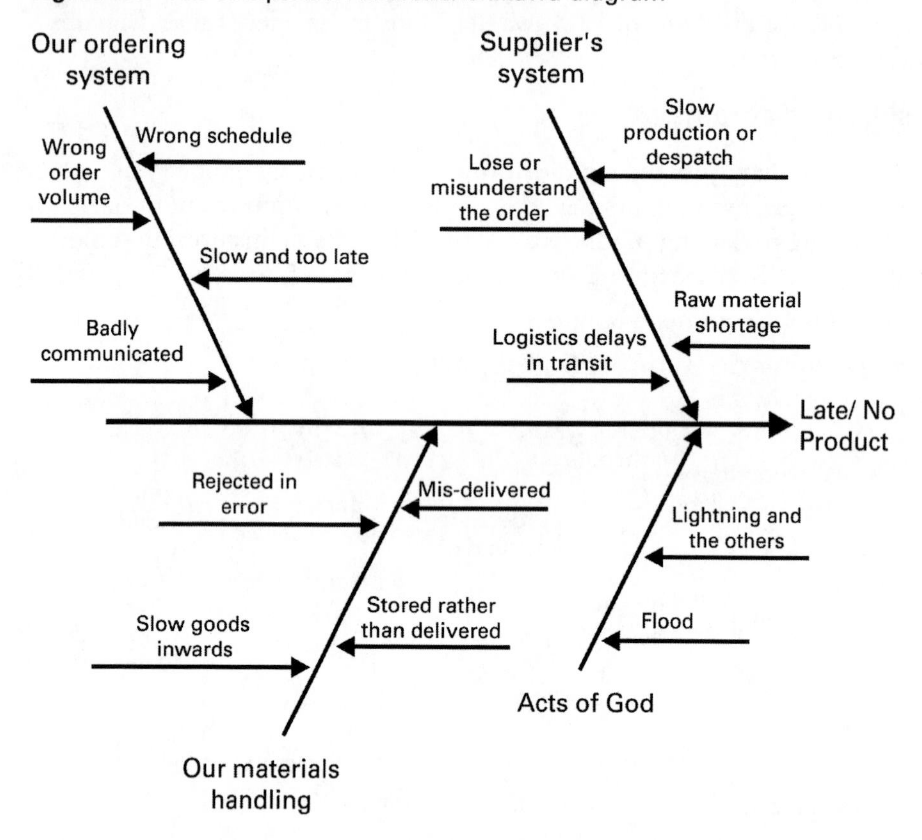


## Using the diagram

The first thing the diagram does is bring some order to the storm if possible causes. More importantly it simplifies testing: all of the causes related to materials handling could be tested by comparing delivery times to the time the product is available to use, for example all the ordering system causes can be tested by checking the output of that system. In this case, there may be several root causes, including raw-material shortages, because PVC has been in short supply recently, and internal scheduling problems. The Ishikawa diagram supports a methodical approach to tackling the potential causes.

### Cause-effect-cause diagrams or blowing bubbles

Sometimes the causes of problems are more complex and interlinked than the Fishbone/Ishikawa diagram allows for. Then the cause-effect-cause diagram (Maylor, 2003) or blowing bubbles (Obeng, 1996) approach can be useful. Maylor and Obeng both have good, detailed explanations of using this technique.

Start with the problem, a statement of what it is that is wrong. Using the Ishikawa example, the problem is not necessarily late deliveries, it is late or no product where it is needed.

An example might be: my ideas and recommendations are not used. There are several possible causes, as shown in figure 5.9.

**Figure 5.9:** Possible causes linked to the problem

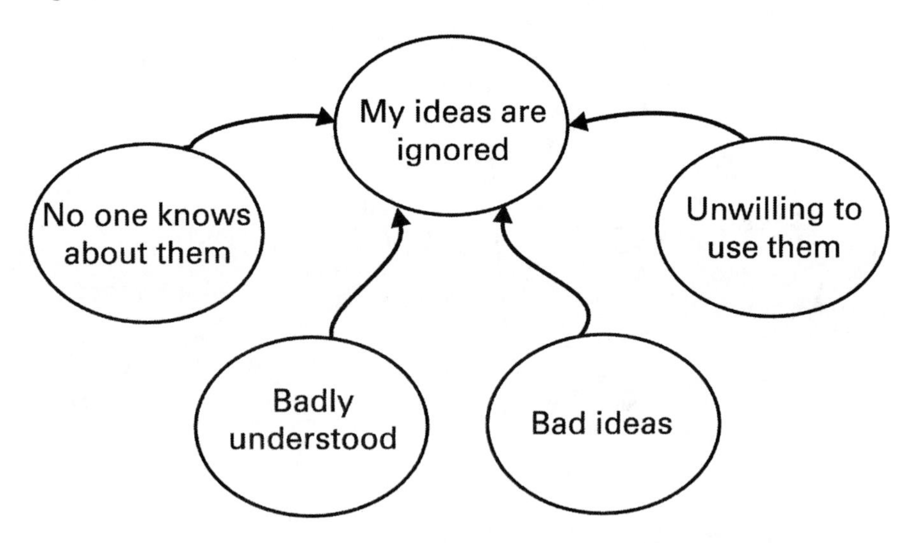


The next step is different from the Ishikawa diagram: some of the causes can be eliminated as you have carefully worked through several of your proposals with decision makers (figure 5.10).

**Figure 5.10:** Eliminating possible causes

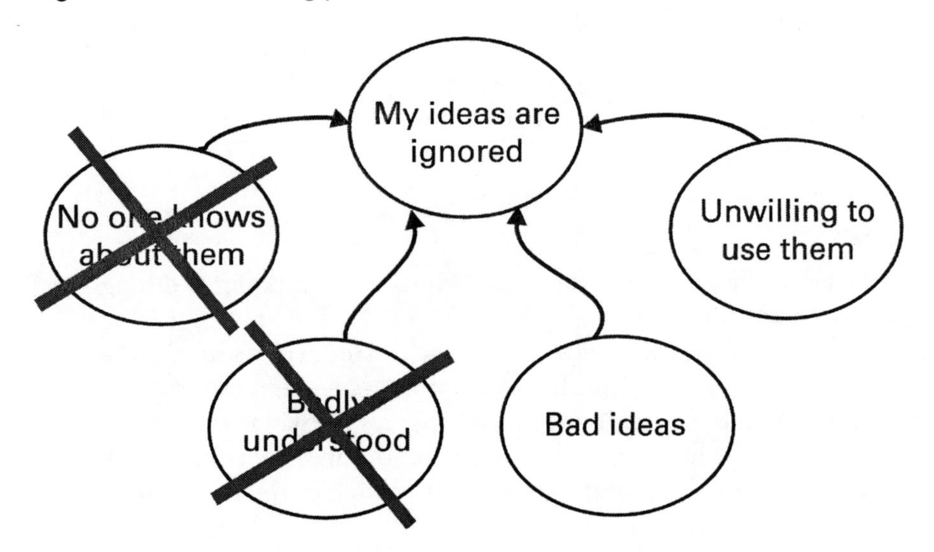


The next step is to work back in stages to identify root causes (there may be several) which underlie this problem.

**Figure 5.11:** The diagram complete

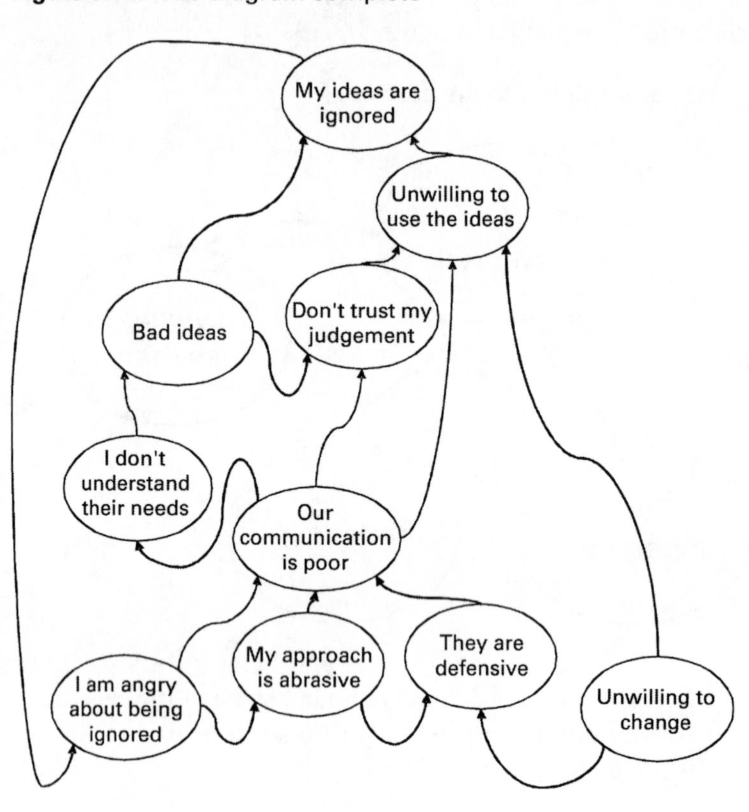


Once the diagram is complete (figure 5.11), there may be several root causes, some may be easier to resolve than others. In addition, there is often some feedback from parts of the causes or effects, reinforcing or making the problem worse.

## Using the cause-effect-cause analysis

Developing the diagram forces some structure onto thinking. Working back to root causes is similar in approach to the '5 Why' technique. The important part follows the analysis: to tackle the root causes in order to reduce or remove the problem. In the example, a combination of actions is probably necessary. Breaking the unwillingness to change through small action steps may be fundamental; working on the approach, anger and communication may help, but these are not enough in themselves to eliminate the problem.

The cause-effect-cause method can be used for problems such as machine failure, but is really valuable for more complex systems, involving people and attitudes as in the example. It is effectively a very basic form of system dynamics. The more complex and hard to measure the system becomes, the more subjective the diagram can become: other people may have a very different view. While using this it is worth trying to use other people's perspectives and once complete, work through it, challenging your logic at every stage to make sure you have not just reinforced your assumptions.

### Learning activity 5.3

Compare the cause-effect-cause approach to the Ishikawa approach to problem solving. Identify similarities and differences and suggest applications where each might be more appropriate.

*Feedback on page 85*



## Moving from the root to the fruit: decision trees

The first two tools in this section focus on finding out the root causes of problems. Decision trees look in the other direction: what problems or successes will this decision cause?

Take a simple example. You are setting the budget for your project and, unusually, you have the option to set the budget generously or conservatively. Which is better? One way of dealing with this is to use a decision tree and set up a series of scenarios. The budget could be high or low, the spend could be high or low (see figure 5.12).

**Figure 5.12:** Decision tree for budget setting

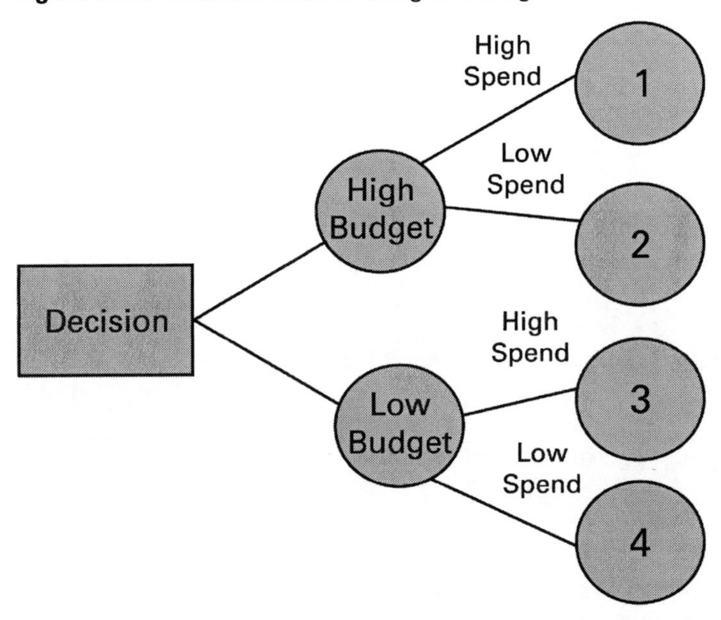


There are four outcomes. If the budget is high and the spend is high, no problem. If the spend is low and the budget is low, no problem. What happens for outcomes 2 and 3? If the budget is set and frozen, then option 3 is a disaster, so setting a high budget is far better. If expanding the budget later is not a problem, but underspends are, then setting a low budget is better.

## Adding numbers: expected value

The budget example is a very basic and simple form of decision tree. They can be used to make more complex decisions using quantifiable data. For example, there are two possible suppliers for some development work you need. A has bid £2 million, B has bid £3 million. Either can be used, but the cheap one is thought less likely to succeed. If one supplier fails, the other supplier will have to be used and the delay will cost about £1 million. After discussing the problem with your technical colleagues, the consensus is that A has around a 60% (0.6) chance of success, B has an 80% (0.8) chance of success. Which should you choose?

A decision tree for the supplier selection is shown in figure 5.13.

**Figure 5.13:** Decision tree for supplier selection

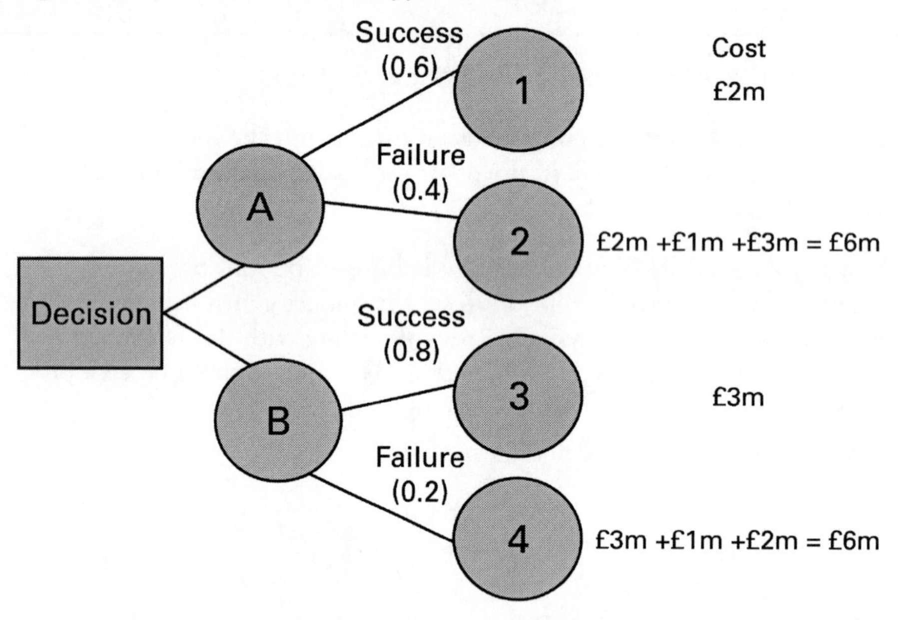


The decision tree identifies the four potential outcomes and the cost of each. Using some mathematics developed by the Rev. Bayes, a priest with a gambling interest, the two choices can be compared using *expected value*. This involves multiplying the probabilities by the cost for each outcome.

For supplier A the cost measured by expected value = 0.6 × £2m + 0.4 × £6m = £3.6m

For supplier B the cost measured by expected value = 0.8 × £2m + 0.2 × £6m = £2.8m

This measure of *expected value* makes supplier B look far more attractive overall and helps support the choice. Unless some other factor is overwhelming, Supplier B looks far better. As a note, expected value is just a measure of attractiveness of each choice, not a prediction of outcome. Whichever choice you make, the outcome will not be £3.6m or £2.8m.

### Using decision trees

Whether or not you use expected value calculations decision trees can be useful to give a clear comparison of different outcomes from different decisions. They rely on two simplifications: that the decisions and outcomes can be described in separate states, for this example high and low, supplier A and Supplier B, and that the likelihood and results of different scenarios can be predicted. These are not always true, for example in the budget example, the budget can be set at a wide range of figures, not just high and low, and if it is set high, spend is almost certainly going to be high as well: setting the budget effects the outcome.

### Self-assessment question 5.3

How can the decision tree approach be used to help the project manager make decisions?

*Feedback on page 85*



## Revision question

Now try the revision question for this session on page 319.

## Summary

The approach taken to solving problems determines the results. A rational approach, using a toolkit of problem-solving approaches, can help to move project management away from frantic firefighting of seemingly insoluble problems which keep coming back towards a more effective approach.

Each of the tools here has different applications. Brainstorming and Ishikawa diagrams can be used to attack linear problems, while cause-effect-cause diagrams can accommodate more complex systems. Lewin's force field can map forces for and against change, while decision trees focus on outcomes. An effective tradesman has a good toolkit and the ability to use the different tools for different jobs. Effective problem solving relies on exactly the same things.

## Suggested further reading

- Maylor (1996); Chapter 13.
- Meredith and Mantel (2006); Chapter 6.
- Pareto Analysis, CIPS 2003.
- Pender (2001).
- Thamhain and Wilemon (1975).
- Weiss and Wysocki (1992); Chapter 8.
- Williams (1999).

## Feedback on learning activities and self-assessment questions

### Feedback on learning activity 5.1

This question is about the application of the approaches more than how they work. Your answer should focus on the outcome and usefulness rather than the nature of each approach. Potential answers might include:

- Pareto analysis: This analysis could be developed with the team to focus effort on the right activities and problems. The dangers are fairly limited.
- 5 Whys: This is more complex to apply and requires sensitive use with stakeholders as there is a danger of alienating them. It could be used

to structure group discussions and encourage team members to drive towards root causes rather than accepting superficial answers.
- Brainstorming: This needs a group and could incorporate people beyond the team into brainstorming sessions. Brainstorming becomes easier with repetition, so starting at this stage can be useful. It also encourages creativity in problem solving. The dangers are mainly cultural: team members may resist using it and early failures are hard to recover from.



## Feedback on self-assessment question 5.1

These are some suggested ideas.

**Table 5.1**

| | **Likely to be useful...** | **Not useful for...** | **What is needed to make this work** |
|---|---|---|---|
| Pareto analysis | At the start of a project or for getting an overview, where there are many problems competing for attention | Finding a solution, where one problem dominates | Data on frequency or impact of the problems |
| 5 Whys | Where there is one key problem, where the root cause is not known, as a structure for discussing problems with stakeholders | Where stakeholders are confrontational, where the root cause is clear | Patience |
| Brainstorming | In a group, where innovation is needed | Where the solution is clear, where the solution relies on detailed analysis | Preparation and careful management |
| Fuzzy numbers and options | Complex situations with no clearly defined states, where unavailability in the future could be a problem | Simple solutions, where understanding is limited | An understanding of the mathematics behind options/fuzzy logic |
| Lewin's force field | Where change is needed | Finding one single solution | An understanding of the forces involved |

## Feedback on learning activity 5.2

In brief, schedule conflict increases as the project continues and time runs out, conflict over priorities decreases over the same time and flexibility to change priorities decreases.

A series of conflict resolution methods are outlined below in this section, your suggestions may fall into these categories or may go beyond.

## Feedback on self-assessment question 5.2

You may have chosen any combination of the five conflict modes described above. If identifying the mode is difficult, work on each axis in turn: was assertiveness high? Was cooperativeness high?

To answer (1) you can refer to the description. For an unimportant decision with entrenched views, avoiding may be appropriate. Where time is short and the impact is high, it is less useful.

To answer (2), it may be necessary to step back from the conflict and the results and decide what success means. Getting your own way but alienating an important person by using assertiveness is limited success. Compromising on an important point limits success. Judging successful conflict resolution is not just about whether the parties felt good afterwards or accepted the solution or whether the project aims were met, but a combination of all three.



## Feedback on learning activity 5.3

The similarities centre on linking a problem to a series of causes by diagram and both can use a number of layers or steps. The key difference is that the Ishikawa approach is linear: it assumes no feedback and ignores cross links, for example bad ideas can lead to a lack of trust in judgement as well as leading to individual ideas being ignored.

In application, Ishikawa diagrams were developed for manufacturing processes, so systems which are of a similar type will work well. It is generally used where a lot of potential causes are known, for example to bring structure to brainstorming outputs, but could potentially be used to work back from the problem to identify causes.

Cause-effect-cause diagrams are designed to accommodate any combination of links between causes, although the more complex, the more the diagram grows. They are commonly used to work back from a problem to generate causes and causal links in a more complex way. While using them in a group can be successful, developing a complex understanding of a complex system, given the potential differences of opinion, is difficult.

## Feedback on self-assessment question 5.3

Where the decision can be broken down into choices and the outcomes can be predicted and described, it gives a quick and clear rational comparison of choices. It can be developed to incorporate probability and other numerical factors to give clear direction on choices.

## Study session 6

# Contemporary approaches to managing projects

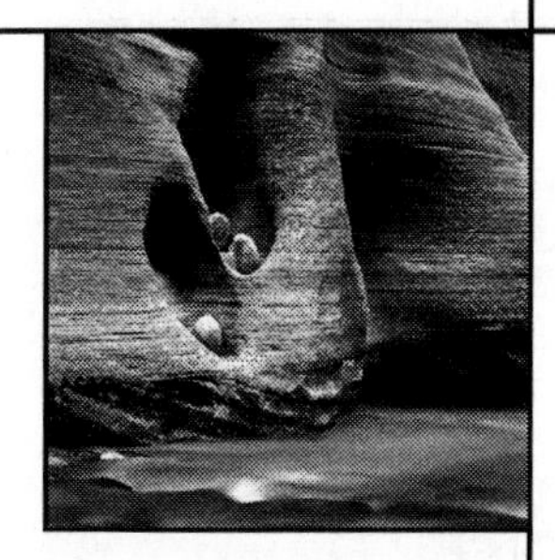

There has to be a better way: very different ways of managing projects.

### Introduction

At the start of this book, the variety of projects and the difficulty of managing them was discussed. As humans always do, many have tried to improve the way projects are managed, challenge established practice and reduce the worryingly high chance of failure. This session looks at three different current approaches to project management, from three very different sources. Six-Sigma was born out of the success of the quality movement and developed by Motorola, PRINCE2 was developed to reduce the failure of UK government projects, and Critical Chain is a concept to improve project management radically using ideas transferred from production management.

There may be no 'holy grail' of perfect project management, but each of these approaches has something fresh and challenging to offer.

### Session learning objectives

After completing this session you should be able to:

6.1 Explain the six-sigma approach and what it seeks to achieve.
6.2 Identify the eight key processes and requirements of PRINCE2 (Projects In Controlled Environments) and evaluate the effectiveness of this approach to project management.
6.3 Analyse the key requirements of CCPM (Critical Chain Project Management).
6.4 Explain how projects that use CCPM can achieve better results than other project management methods.

### Unit content coverage

This study session covers the following topic from the official CIPS unit content document.

#### Learning objective

2.0 Assess and justify the approach to managing projects using a variety of methodologies.
2.4 Critically evaluate Six-Sigma, DMAIC, PRINCE2, Critical Chains and other contemporary project approaches.
- Six-sigma methodology, General Electric and Motorola
- DMAIC, product/service improvement
- PRINCE2, Projects in Controlled Environments
- Critical Chain, Goldratt (1997)

## Prior knowledge

Study sessions 1 – 4. Operations Management in the Supply Chain would provide a good foundation.

## Timing

You should set aside about 8 hours to read and complete this session, including learning activities, self-assessment questions, the suggested reading (if any) from the essential textbook for this unit and the revision question.



## 6.1 Six-Sigma: projects to drive quality performance improvement

Projects are very often used to drive change in an organisation and one example of a structured, project-based change process is Six-Sigma, developed by Motorola. This has its roots in the quality movement developed in Japan and spread through Total Quality Management, but now extends across companies producing a huge range of goods and services. Six-Sigma 'black belts' (experts) can be found from aerospace companies to high street banks.

### Learning activity 6.1

Review the Motorola website (Motorola: http://www.motorola.com) and identify what is required in order to become:

1 a Six-Sigma black belt
2 a Six-Sigma green belt.

*Feedback on page 99*

### What is Six-Sigma?

The name comes from a statistical term linked to quality and reduced failure. Six-Sigma implies a target of just 3.4 failures per million, or 99.9997% perfect, a very demanding goal. In addition to that goal, Six-Sigma involves a system of managing projects leading to structured improvement and measure of success.

### The Six-Sigma basics

Before improvement can be started, it needs to take into account what is important to customers and this leads to some basic elements:

- Voice of the Customer (VOC): some way of finding out what the customer wants

- Requirements: the VOC translated into specifics: aspects of the product that can be measured
- Critical to Quality (CTQ): requirements that are most important to customers
- Defect: failing on a CTQ requirement
- Design for Six-Sigma: designing goods and services according to customer requirements.

### The DMAIC cycle

Building on total quality management (TQM) practice, Six-Sigma uses a defined cycle of improvement:

- Define: clarify goals, establish what the project is and what it will achieve
- Measure: gather data on the project from a variety of sources including process mapping and value analysis, statistical and failure charts, brainstorming
- Analyse: use statistical methods such as regression, ANOVA, capability analysis, plots and opportunity maps to understand the problem or opportunity
- Improve: identify and implement desired improvements using the analysis, benchmarking, experiments
- Control: ensure those improvements work through measuring performance continuously afterwards.

### The Six-Sigma project environment

One-off improvement projects may succeed in any environment, showing benefits which often decay away, but if the intention is to change an organisation radically, the environment for projects must be right. Experience in programmes at Motorola and other organisations as well as the wealth of information on TQM allows identification of the environment needed to make Six-Sigma projects work:

- A focus on what the customer wants.
- A focus on translating improvement into money: savings or increased sales.
- A lot of resources: up to 3% of *all* staff working full-time on Six-Sigma projects.
- Knowledge support: Training and education to ensure the people active in the projects have a strong understanding of the requirements and methodology.
- The right structure: Good project managers and effective project teams are not enough, there must be management coordination of the different projects up to the top of the organisation or business unit, full time. In addition, the projects should have lateral communication with each other to share enthusiasm, experience, solutions and best practice.
- Management support: Most importantly, visible, active sustained commitment from senior management is needed, first to provide resources, and second to lead the programme, demonstrating its importance.

### Self-assessment question 6.1

Six-Sigma projects are aimed at improving processes. In 400 words identify which aspects of Six-Sigma could be of value more generally to project management.

*Feedback on page 100*



## 6.2 Stopping those disasters: PRINCE2

The failure of many projects has been identified and discussed earlier in this course book, and the blame for these failures must lie not just with the project manager or team, not just with the management of the project, but with the environment the project must operate in. Part of Six-Sigma described in section 6.1 above involved a definition of the project management environment, PRINCE2 takes that one step further and outlines a project management methodology that integrates the management of the project with the environment.

### Learning activity 6.2

PRINCE2 includes a specification of how the project is overseen by a Project Board and review points. Examine a project with which you are familiar, whether through experience or research, and identify:

- Who oversaw the initiation, start-up, management and closure of the project?
- What were the formal review points?
- What was presented, discussed and decided at those points and what were the options open to the people reviewing?

*Feedback on page 100*

### What is PRINCE2?

PRINCE2 (P**r**ojects in Controlled Environments) is a structured method for effective project management. It has been adopted by many government bodies in an attempt to move from a string of failures to an environment for success and has wide adoption in the private sector. The basic ideas are public domain although training, software and the name are proprietary.

The methodology divides and specifies activities involved at the beginning, middle and end of a project as well as the roles within the project team and outside, coordinating the project. There are eight activities at different levels.

*Starting up a project (SU)*

This is the first process in PRINCE2 and should be very short but, like all the processes, it is essential. It occurs before the start to ensure that the prerequisites for initiating the project are in place. It requires a project mandate which defines the justification and intended outcome in high-level terms.

There are three elements:

- ensuring that the information required for the project team is available
- designing and appointing the project management team
- creating the initiation stage plan.



*Initiating a project (IP)*

This is aimed at setting a firm foundation for the project:

- ensure the project is justified
- establish a stable management basis
- document and confirm the business case
- ensure that the investment of time and effort required by the project is made wisely, taking account of the risks to the project
- gain commitment of resources for the first stage of the project
- enable and encourage the project board to take ownership of the project
- provide a baseline for the decisions required during the project's life.

*Controlling a stage (CS)*

This starts with the first stage and defines what the project manager should do for each stage to manage progress and any problems. It is a cycle of:

- authorising work
- monitoring progress of that work
- watching for changes, reviewing and reporting
- taking any necessary corrective action.

In addition there is ongoing work of risk management and change control.

*Managing stage boundaries (SB) (Projects in Controlled Environments)*

As the project progresses it moves between stages and these transitions are the key decision points on whether to continue with the project or not. The project board needs to control this and it involves:

- ensuring all deliverables planned in the current Stage Plan have been completed as defined
- providing the information needed for the project board to assess the continuing viability of the project
- providing the project board with information needed to approve the current stage's completion and authorising the start of the next stage, together with its delegated tolerance level
- recording any measurements or lessons which can help later stages or other projects.

*Closing a project (CP)*

This covers the project manager's work to wrap up the project, whether complete or terminated. The main tasks are to:

- inform the project board to obtain confirmation that the project may close
- check the extent to which the objectives or aims have been met
- confirm the customer's satisfaction with the deliverables and gain formal acceptance of the deliverables
- identify how much of the expected products have been handed over and accepted by the customer
- ensure maintenance and operation arrangements are in place
- make any recommendations for follow-on actions
- capture lessons resulting from the project
- prepare an End of Project Report
- notify the host organisation of the intention to disband the project organisation and resources.



*Managing product delivery (MP)*

Alongside the project management is the activity of making sure the product, the output is delivered:

- make certain that work on products is effectively authorised and agreed
- ensure that work conforms to the requirements identified in the work package
- ensure that the work is done
- assess work progress and forecasts regularly
- ensure that completed products meet quality criteria
- obtain approval for the completed products.

*Directing a project (DP)*

Directing a project is the control activity overseeing the project management throughout and is largely carried out by the project board. It focuses on decision points and management by exception.

*Planning (PL)*

Planning is a defined process which happens at several levels: planning an initiation stage, planning a project, planning a stage, producing an exception plan.

### Intended benefits of PRINCE2

- The clear definition of different parts of the project, the different roles and the different management activities help to ensure the project management is comprehensively carried out.
- The separation of project from product ensures a focus on product delivery.
- The stage separation and decision points ensure the project is on track and that continuing is a considered choice. The project cannot become a runaway train with its own momentum.

- The consistent effective review structure ensures everyone carries out their roles.

## Summary

PRINCE2 (Projects in Controlled Environments) is a structured, comprehensive project management methodology which breaks down the tasks, roles and control of project management and identifies in detail how these fit together. It was developed for public sector projects prompted by failures but has migrated to the private sector.



## Self-assessment question 6.2

In 300 words, use your analysis or any sources you can find to identify and explain the main criticisms of the PRINCE2 approach to project management.

*Feedback on page 101*

## 6.3 Challenging the way we work: the basis for critical chain project management

In spite of complex planning tools and management experience built on projects stretching back into history, projects all too often run late. It seems a rarity that projects are delivered earlier than their first due date. As was mentioned in study session 1, in civil engineering in the UK, many people believed it was impossible to deliver a major project on time. Set against this are examples of almost superhuman success. In shipbuilding, during World War I, the time taken to build each ship was reduced by 70% through effective project management, involving Henry Gantt. In World War II, the record for building 'liberty ships' was driven down to one day.

## Learning activity 6.3

Explain some key factors that commonly make projects substantially late.

*Feedback on page 101*

Classical time planning techniques such as network analysis (Critical Path Methods (CPM), Project Evaluation Review Techniques (PERT)) and Gantt are well known and widely applied. Using software such as the dominant Microsoft Project, complex charts can be constructed easily. Using statistical methods such as those in PERT and developed by Meredith and Mantel (2006: Chapter 8), complex probability calculations can be used to predict the probability of different finish times. Projects are still late and probabilistic estimates do not seem to prevent this.

Some writers attack the basic ideas of network planning and Gantt charts. Obeng (1996) dismisses the ideas behind the time plans and recommends focusing on managing resources rather than time. He recommends: get people working early in the project, get delivery dates in people's diaries rather than on a Gantt chart, and add time buffers between any two activities which feed a third. This radical, almost iconoclastic approach seems to sweep away any benefits from 100 years' experience in time planning but perhaps offers insight as well. The key to time planning may be with the people doing the activities rather than a complex chart. In many cases, discussing and negotiating with the people involved when they will do the work is more important than theoretical precedence and circulating a hard-to-read plan.



Some delays can be caused by 'acts of God' and unforeseeable factors, but flood and famine are rarely key to delays in software projects in the UK. In addition, if unforeseen problems delay some projects, unforeseen simplicity should speed some up, leading to early completion. Unfortunately, few projects seem to be delivered early, with the claim that 'the programming turned out to be far easier than we thought' or 'the rock layers we were drilling through were softer than predicted'. If estimating were working well, then for roughly half of all projects, we could expect to hear 'there were fewer unforeseen problems than we had allowed for, so completion is early'.

This problem of delay and late completion opens up a challenge. It would seem to be human factors – planning and managing – which make the difference. Any new project management technique which seeks breakthrough must deal with these factors rather than improving the mathematics of PERT or increasing the detail of probability.

### Goldratt's view of the problems of time planning

Goldratt (1997) delivered an analysis of the problems of time planning from a human and cultural viewpoint.

#### *Time estimates lead to problems*

- When asked 'how long will that take you', most people build in a safety margin, 'just in case'. Effectively, people tend to give times by which they are pretty sure they can finish. PERT uses 'pessimistic' times by which there is 99% confidence an activity can finish.
- The activity generally takes *at least* as long as the time estimate. Given ten days, most people will take ten days (this is sometimes called Parkinson's Law). Many activities suffer from 'Student Syndrome' as Goldratt calls it. Some students, given three months for an assignment which will take two days, leave the assignment until they have just two days left, wasting any 'safety buffer' they had.
- A late finish is always passed on, an early finish is not. If one person finishes their activity early, it is very unlikely the next activity will start early. The first person will tend to hang on before passing the results on, to ensure their job does not look too easy. Even if they pass on the results early, the second activity may not be ready or simply waits until their start date.

- Activities with any slack, or spare time will generally be postponed until the latest start date. Why spend time and money before you have to? This means there is no allowance for overrun without affecting the next activity.

*Resource scheduling is complex*

- Projects will frequently need people or other resources who have other work to do, frequently plenty of other work. Competition between projects and other work raises the risk some people will be overloaded. In order to counter this, resource planning can be carried out, but this relies on good information not only about the project work, but any other work those people will undertake.
- As people are working on many different activities at the same time, they tend to 'salami slice': do a little of one activity, then a little of the next and so on. This leads to two problems: time wasted swapping between activities, but more fundamentally, every activity takes longer. To try and explain this, figure 6.1 shows two schedules (A and B) for completing three activities. Each activity takes one day. In schedule A, each activity is carried out in turn. In schedule B, each activity is salami-sliced into three parts. If you consider activity 3, there is no change to completion: it is finished on the third day. Activity 1, however, suffers enormously: it now takes 3 days to complete. In fact, although the work is completed in the same time overall, the *lead time* for each activity increases from one to three days.

**Figure 6.1:** The source of these problems

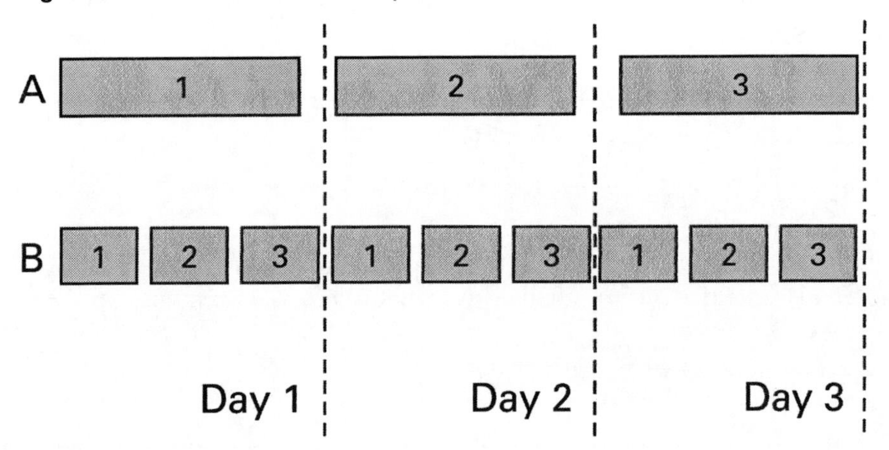


The problems highlighted by Goldratt do not challenge the need for time planning, or the logic behind established time-planning tools. They do highlight problems which happen in practice. If this is right, what are the causes of the behaviour which leads to the problems? Why would people give over-long time estimates? Why are activities so rarely finished early? Why do people postpone work to the last minute? Why do projects that are going well suffer from scope changes?

The answers lie in the management environment or culture. If there is no incentive to give accurate or challenging time estimates and blame waiting for anyone who overruns, estimates will be high. If an early finish means you will have less time allowed for the same activity next time, you will not finish early. If rushing to finish, firefighting and lateness are normal, people will conform to this. It is often far more exciting to rush to finish for a deadline than to plan and work effectively.

A study in a company making railway equipment tried to find out why every project was late, in one case over a year late for a ten-month project. The study found varied causes at different stages: machine malfunction, changing specification, illness, supplier failure. Different departments had some different problems, but in each department the list of reasons was long, yet it did not add up to the substantial delays in every project. The fundamental reason was discovered when projects were tracked and it was found that while projects were on time all efforts were made to maintain that. Once late, the delay increased and increased. One project had entered a department one week late but left six weeks late and there was no obvious reason. The department head explained the delay and the fundamental problem: 'That project was late to us so we already had an excuse. We put it to the bottom of the pile.'



Goldratt's analysis of the common project management problems shifts the focus from the technical to the application of time planning and seems to fit some observed behaviour. The next stage is identifying what can challenge this way of working.

### Summary

There appear to be some basic problems with time planning for projects, and if Goldratt and Obeng are right, most of these are fundamentally placed in the human use of time-planning tools rather than technical problems of the tools themselves.

### Self-assessment question 6.3

From your knowledge of projects, this section and other reading (for example Meredith and Mantel (1996) Chapters 8 and 9 or Maylor (1996) Chapter 11), identify the key challenges for a project management approach such as CCPM.

*Feedback on page 102*

## 6.4 Breakthrough? Critical Chain

Goldratt's analysis of the problems with project management (see section 6.3 above) form the foundation of his new project management approach: Critical Chain, explored in his business novel of the same name. This combines the application of Theory of Constraints, an idea already applied to production management: with other principles.

### Theory of Constraints (TOC)

This relies on the idea that there will be bottlenecks or constraints in the progress of the project, resources which will be overloaded. The whole project cannot progress faster than that resource allows. Goldratt uses the analogy of people walking together: the group can only walk at the pace of the slowest, so all should be matched to that pace. This gives the name: the weakest link in the chain defines the strength. In project or production management this leads to a series of steps:

- *Identify the constraint*: In production, the bottleneck will typically be a machine working non stop and surrounded by work waiting to be done. Maylor (1996) suggests that for a project, the constraint might be dates that cannot be moved, the activities on the critical path, or resources. It is probably more effective to look at resources or processes which carry out the activities as constraints.
- *Exploit the constraint*: This means ensure it works to the maximum: no interruptions, no unnecessary work etc.
- *Subordinate all other activities to the constraint*: Change the scheduling of all activities so that they fit the constraint. There is no point speeding up or moving other activities if this one cannot move. As an example, a sourcing project might rely on legal review of the new contract and this is commonly a delay because the legal team are very busy: a constraint. If the legal team can fit review into their schedule only on fixed dates, the project should be scheduled around those dates, even if it means moving activities. Any problems with activities preparing the contract must be dealt with quickly and effectively.
- *Elevate the constraint*: This means remove it as a constraint: expand the legal team, pre-check contracts before submission, move to standard contracts, etc.
- *Go back to find the next constraint*: Once the weakest link is fixed, the next weakest link should be tackled.

### Changing estimates

With all the problems identified, the way estimates are made and used need to change. Rather than estimates with safety time, down time and anything else included, Goldratt recommends 50:50 estimates. These are an estimate of the work involved to give an estimate on the median time: there is a 50% chance it will be finished by then, but a 50% chance it will take longer. This relies on a series of changes. Blame for lateness must be removed, as half of activities will be late. Giving up that safety buffer of 'what if' time is not easy.

### Move safety time to the end

The safety time is now managed centrally. As the activities are now likely to overrun, some time allowance for this is necessary. The first big change is that the safety time is added at the end of the project. The activities are scheduled using the new shorter times, then a safety buffer of 50–200% is allowed. This safety buffer can then be used for any overrun by any activity. This leads to a very different project plan: all activities are clustered at the front end, with the expectation that some will overrun and the timings will change. The predicted end date is well after the last scheduled activity, as some or all of that safety buffer will be needed. There is a danger here: the temptation to cut back on the safety buffer after the project is started will be strong. The idea of an empty safety buffer conflicts with established practice.

### Protecting 'critical' activities and constraints

Network time planning (see study session 10) identifies a 'critical' path: activities which, if delayed, will delay the whole project. This approach is accepted in Critical Chain, and there is a need to protect these activities from delays of other activities which feed them (must be done before). This is overcome by putting a time buffer between the feeding activities and the critical activities: any delay can be absorbed by the buffer. Constraints such as resource constraints can be protected by ensuring they always have work, through time buffers just before, or a stock of work waiting.



### Learning activity 6.4

Using a project from your experience or a case from any source, take around 200 words to:

1. Identify whether Critical Chain could have improved the time and resource planning.
2. Explain what barriers there may be to introducing Critical Chain.

*Feedback on page 102*

### How does Critical Chain meet the challenges?

Unsurprisingly, Critical Chain meets the challenges of time estimates head on. It encourages and relies on good, rational time estimates. By stripping safety time out of the activities and collecting it where needed, it allows the project to gain from early finishes and to cope with delays. It also simplifies the management of resources by using the TOC assumptions that bottlenecks can be tackled one by one.

### Drawbacks and obstacles

The method is relatively new and uptake has not been dramatic, so it is hard to assess the benefits of Critical Chain empirically. Goldratt's website offers some cases and Maylor cautiously reported success as far back as 2000. By its nature, changing the way people estimate and plan is a substantial cultural obstacle which requires a large change in all involved in managing and overseeing the project. The relative novelty of Critical Chain means that books and software are far less freely available than, for example Gantt, PERT and CPM methods.

### Self-assessment question 6.4

Write a memo to a senior manager making a case for the introduction of CCPM.

*Feedback on page 102*

## Revision question

Now try the revision question for this session on page 320.

## Summary

The three different approaches each offer some insight into effective project management, and there is some overlap:

- Six-Sigma demonstrates how relatively small projects can add up to a programme of substantial change. Six-Sigma projects are widespread and the methodology has proven successes. The more general learning is that it is the project environment as much as the individual project management which makes the difference.
- PRINCE2 tackles the environment and management head-on with a detailed structure and process, focused on product delivery. Again it highlights the importance of environment, but perhaps the general point is the need for structure and process to be balanced against the cost and overhead of applying it.
- Critical Chain takes a radical approach to time and resource management, facing the challenges identified by Goldratt head-on. It requires a very different way of estimating and planning, which appears to offer enormous benefits. It is early to judge the true value, but successes have been reported from a range of projects.

## Suggested further reading

- Goldratt: http://www.goldratt.co.uk
- Goldratt (1997)
- IT Service Management Forum (2004)
- Maylor (1996)
- Motorola: http://www.motorola.com
- Newbold (1998)
- Office of Government Commerce (2005)
- Pande and Holpp (2001)
- PRINCE2 training: http://www.prince2.com

## Feedback on learning activities and self-assessment questions

### Feedback on learning activity 6.1

There are key parts to both:

- A structured approach to problem solving and project management
- The DMAIC cycle (see below)
- A set of statistical and other tools to make 'fact-based decisions'.

These form the backbone of Six-Sigma practice.

1 Black Belts are expected to lead project teams, so the understanding should be thorough in the technical areas but also in managing those

projects: 'the skills and knowledge they need for the exceptional leadership of business improvement projects'.

2 'Green Belts receive a subset of the more comprehensive Black Belt curriculum.' Green Belts are expected to be led, hence need an overview and the 'intermediate level' tools and techniques.

It should not be ignored that the required commitment is substantial: Black Belt training costs around $14,000 and takes four weeks over four months, while Green Belt training costs around $3,000 and takes five days.

## Feedback on self-assessment question 6.1



Some of the technical aspects, the statistical tools, for example may not be generally applicable but much of the rest is useful.

### *The basics*

The focus on the customer and the customer's requirements is very valuable and the idea of failure relating directly to customers' CTQ requirements is a valuable reminder.

### *DMAIC*

Define; clarifying goals and focus is strong project management practice, while stages which focus on measuring and analysing the opportunity fit with re-sourcing or category management projects. The addition of Control is useful: putting in place measures to ensure the changes work and are sustained. This is often neglected in the rush to complete and close a project.

### *The project environment*

This holds a mass of guidance for project management generally. In order to have a programme of successful projects driving change, experience suggests the organisation needs an environment as described in the information on Six-Sigma. A focus on what the customer wants, on translating improvement into money, resources of up to 3% of *all* staff, knowledge support, the right structure: management coordination and lateral communication. Most importantly, management support.

## Feedback on learning activity 6.2

In terms of overseeing the project, was there one group of people, or one person in place from beginning to end? What was their role? Many projects have limited or haphazard oversight, with the role passing from person to person. A group or board can provide a much stronger, more balanced and stable oversight.

Were there formal review points? At which stages of the project? There is normally some review at the start, less commonly towards the end, and regular review is important but often overlooked.

The nature of review is central to its effectiveness. An informal chat which 'Nods the project through' can be useful in certain circumstances, but unless the review has strong information, open dispassionate discussion and the option to change or stop the project, it has limited value.

### Feedback on self-assessment question 6.2

The main criticisms centre on the amount of work needed to follow the process and the training needed to support that. This work must be offset by performance improvements hence many suggest it is best suited to larger projects, with £10 million being a typical watershed.

It is also abstract in structure and some people struggle to grasp it: what are the stages? Some activities are simultaneous, some successive. This can cause problems where the client is not familiar with the process.



It is not well adapted to change. For a project delivering stable technology, it may fit well, but it focuses on a rational, but not always appropriate, approach to setting clear goals and objectives then meeting them. This may not be the best approach, for example for a predominantly 'soft' project.

It does little to change the problems of excessive estimates and overruns highlighted in section 6.3.

Finally, it is rules-based and heavily structured. This may be appropriate in the public sector but may conflict with agile, entrepreneurial environments.

There are other criticisms, but it should be remembered that PRINCE2 has adherents and many successes.

### Feedback on learning activity 6.3

There are of course many reasons for different projects, here are some common groups:

- Starting from outside the project, acts of God/dramatic changes which slow progress could occur. Floods, fire or changes in regulation.
- The demands on the project, the scope of work, could change, for example having to implement on three sites instead of two. This would mean some work would need to be done again or new activities will be added to the plan.
- The original time estimates for each activity could be too low, through poor estimating or due to the uncertainty inherent at the planning stage, for example a technical problem in an R&D project could become far more complex than first thought.
- People completing activities may take longer than planned.
- The resources needed for activities could be unavailable through competition with other projects.

They can be divided into two basic areas:

- unforeseeable changes: acts of god, illness, unforeseen technical difficulties
- human/system problems: poor planning, low estimates, conflicting resources, adding to the workload, failure to deliver activities.

Of these, the human factors tend to be more common and more powerful.

### Feedback on self-assessment question 6.3

Your answer should focus on specifying the changes needed in the way time planning and resource contention are dealt with.

Looking at the criticism Goldratt and Obeng level at project management practice, any new approach must meet that criticism, or other challenges you have identified. As examples:

- How can people be persuaded to give challenging time estimates?
- What happens to the buffer times if people do?
- How can people be persuaded to try and finish on time?
- How can early finishes be captured rather than lost?
- How can the problems of competing for resources and resource overload be overcome?

These come directly from Goldratt's criticism and should form part of your answer. Challenges beyond these will give a more complete answer. As examples:

- How can the strongest parts of current practice be retained?
- Any new approach must be simple and effective.
- To persuade people to change, a new approach must show radical improvement.

### Feedback on learning activity 6.4

1. The relevance of Critical Chain may depend on context but there are three central issues: were estimating, time planning, time management and resource management done badly? Are the challenges as Goldratt has described them? Would this approach have overcome the problems? If the answer to these is yes, in one form or another, then Critical Chain makes sense. If in your analysis of the project you can identify areas where those issues do not fit, it challenges the idea that Critical Chain could have helped. This then opens up further discussion: are there projects where it would be useful and what would characterise those?
2. Some barriers are identified below, but in summary:
   - it challenges established practice
   - it involves a huge and potentially difficult change in behaviour
   - it is difficult to implement from existing material: there is far more guidance available for other methods.

### Feedback on self-assessment question 6.4

The core argument for Critical Chain rests largely on the current problems with time planning. A comparison of Critical Chain with the problems outlined in the previous section can be a starting point.

A second part of the benefit for Critical Chain is the potential to benefit from improvements driven by the Theory of Constraints approach. These can have an impact on capacity in themselves.

The case might look at the cost. Critical chain is relatively new and most software, training and materials in project management is based on other methods. It is possible to adapt them, but this is complex and to adopt Goldratt's own materials carries a cost.

Finally, the change in the management of projects will be substantial. The shift from fear of failure, blame and safety time in every activity to the approach of 50:50 estimates and carefully and centrally managed buffers is challenging.

Study session 7

# Selecting the best approach for a purchasing and logistics project

Purchasing leading the way: different approaches for different purchasing projects.

## Introduction

There is no 'one best way' to manage projects and there is no 'one best way' for purchasing projects. A project to source suppliers for a new product has a very different set of needs from the introduction of a contract management system. This session looks at current practice in purchasing and logistics and identifies three general types of project with very different needs and challenges. To match these, different approaches are needed, approaches which can meet the demands of success in the current purchasing environment.



## Session learning objectives

After completing this session you should be able to:

7.1 Identify and analyse the most common types of purchasing and logistics project in manufacturing, service and not-for-profit sectors.
7.2 Evaluate the advantages and disadvantages of the various approaches to project management to the types of purchasing and logistics projects identified in section 7.1.
7.3 Explain and substantiate using examples which approaches to project management are most likely to be of benefit to purchasing and logistics projects.

## Unit content coverage

This study session covers the following topic from the official CIPS unit content document.

### Learning objective

2.0 Assess and justify the approach to managing projects using a variety of methodologies.
2.5 Synthesise various approaches and be prepared to justify an approach which is suitable for purchasing and logistics projects in various industry sectors.
- Explore the pros and cons of each approach
- Examine each approach in the context of different industry/market conditions
- Assess each approach in the context of a purchasing and logistics project

## Prior knowledge

Study sessions 1 – 6.

## Timing

You should set aside about 6 hours to read and complete this session, including learning activities, self-assessment questions, the suggested reading (if any) from the essential textbook for this unit and the revision question.

## 7.1 What does purchasing do: an analysis of purchasing led projects



### Learning activity 7.1

Appraise three supply chain management projects from newspaper or professional journal articles. Characterise them in terms of, for example:

- mainly hard or soft (see study session 1)
- cross-functional or restricted to the purchasing function
- involving change for many stakeholders or small changes for few
- high or low impact on the organisation
- clear detailed objectives from the outset or aims with objectives developing later.

*Feedback on page 114*

Looking through articles in professional magazines, lists of job vacancies and talking to supply and logistics professionals, it is possible to find information on purchasing led projects. Similar projects sometimes crop up. A review of these sources looking back one year identified a series of common themes:

- Supplier Relationship Management or collaboration (39%)
- outsourcing (22%)
- moving supply to low-cost countries (includes some outsourcing to low-cost countries hence the total is not 100%) (20%)
- category management (18%)
- restructuring or redesigning the purchasing organisation (6%)
- developing purchasing talent: training and development (3%)
- developing risk and problem management (3%).

### Hard or soft?

Some may involve hard skills, for example outsourcing part of production or a key service will show any deficiency in the switchover. Careful time management, a strong task plan and monitoring and risk management will be important. All have a strong requirement for soft skills; looking at outsourcing again, the human element is likely to be large.

### Cross-functional or purchasing?

All of these require involvement across different functions and departments, even training and development is likely to involve Human Resources. For success with the others, many departments are likely to be involved. For outsourcing, there may be redundancies or transfer of staff; for developing risk management approaches, operations and perhaps even marketing functions will be needed.

### Stakeholder impact

The cross-functional nature suggests there will be a wealth of stakeholders. The impact varies from project to project.



### Impact on the business

Once again, the higher the impact, generally the wider the spread of stakeholders, the more functions are involved.

### Clear or fuzzy objectives

All the projects have aims of some sort, but the more novel the project, the more complex and the less specific the early objectives may be. Category management, Lean Six-Sigma and outsourcing are projects similar to many that have been done before so objectives can be fairly specific and detailed. Developing a risk management process or the first supplier collaboration may be new to the organisation, with long-term benefits. In these cases the objectives may be more varied.

### Three example supply chain projects

> 'The Supply Chain project enforced our commitment for internal process improvement and helped to strengthen the relationship with the customer.'
>
> From an automotive supplier
>
> 'To improve customer service and information, and to reduce products' time to market,... decided to develop a single supply chain system to integrate all its activities for every supply chain step across its core businesses, as part of a unified and logical data stream.'
>
> From a chemical company
>
> 'Pharmacy supply chain project
>
> The Agency, in conjunction with pharmacy colleagues and NHS Logistics, is currently leading a project to improve the pharmaceutical

supply chain into (and within) the NHS, with particular focus on the interface between trusts and wholesalers.

The project has been conducted in a number of phases:

Phase one – information gathering and identification of options

Phase two – detailed work around priority areas and piloting the recommendations [including] specific guidance on the acquisition of robots for dispensing.

Phase three – piloting the recommendations

Phase four – rolling out learning/best practice outputs.'

From part of the NHS (http://www.pasa.doh.gov.uk/pharma/pharma_supplychain.stm)



Again, far-reaching, high-impact projects involve change for many stakeholders and functions. The objectives may develop as time passes and the ability and flexibility to manage the stakeholders, the change of the project in the changing environment is crucial.

## Forgotten projects

All the projects described above have common themes, but there is another type of project unlikely to be found by searching in this way. What about a straightforward project to re-source power for the company? This will have very few stakeholders and as long as the supply is stable, the objective can be clearly set on price. The project then needs 'hard' skills to make sure it works well. What about the project to buy in a new piece of process equipment for production? There is not much 'change' for stakeholders, it is more about careful planning to ensure the specification is right and the purchase and commissioning are smooth and effective. These projects may not have the novelty of those described above, but they are still valuable purchasing led projects.

## Three general types of purchasing led project

This leads to three general types into which projects can loosely be grouped:

- Traditional purchasing: The 'forgotten' projects above are the sort of activities traditionally associated with purchasing. The technology is stable, the specifications clear, the objectives well defined and generally focused on getting the right thing at the lowest cost. The impact on the business tends to be low.
- Repeated change: Six-Sigma or category management involve a series or programme of projects which tend to do different things, but in a similar way. They will typically involve change, many stakeholders, cross-functional involvement and the objectives may well develop through the project.
- Radical: Creating a new procurement department or developing a process for supplier collaboration where nothing exists. Setting up a

pipeline of new purchasing talent. These are typically cross-functional, with complex stakeholder relationships and fuzzy, long-term objectives. They focus on longer-term value to the business and perhaps will involve a different management approach.

### Self-assessment question 7.1

You are given the management of a project to introduce environmentally sound purchasing to a company. How would you characterise it using the descriptions above, and why?

*Feedback on page 114*

7

## 7.2 The right approach: do not get kicked or thrown off

### Learning activity 7.2

Choose a project with which you are familiar.

- Compare it with the three general types of purchasing led projects from section 7.1 above.
- Suggest what would be important in setting an approach to managing it.

*Feedback on page 115*

Dealing with a new project is a little like dealing with a strange animal: the right approach can pay off, the wrong approach can lead to problems: bites, scratches, kicks or worse.

If you had to tackle an animal, you might first identify what type it was – horse, cat, bird, hedgehog – then find out what the dangers were. A kick from a horse, scratch from a cat, the shock of handling might harm the bird, while a hedgehog offers little worse than a prick from its spines or a lot of fleas. You might then take an approach which suited the animal: some recommend gloves for a hedgehog, wrapping a cat in a towel, not walking behind a horse, minimum interference with a wild bird and so on. If the animal turns out to be a tiger, however, professional help might be needed, just as with a really complex project.

Similarly with projects, the first step is to identify the type, then the requirements and dangers, and plan an approach which matches these.

### Needs, risks and approaches.

Taking the three general types from section 7.1 above, what are the needs and challenges? What approach might be appropriate?

### Traditional purchasing projects

Projects such as sourcing new production machinery, renegotiating a contract for energy or maintenance services have traditionally been well within the capability of purchasing. Clear and simple objectives can be set and the way to do this is well established.

A comparison would be building projects and this type of project typically needs strong control and a clear process. The requirements are mainly hard, and the tried and tested project management techniques such as network analysis and Gantt charts work well.

Common challenges come from familiarity: similar projects have been done before so there is a temptation to think it should be easy and that this one should be quicker, cheaper and better. At the same time, less effort and attention are devoted to projects which have been done before.



A strong approach would involve clear direction and control from one person or a small team, with input from some others. Responsibilities need to be clear and adhered to. Timing, resources and so on need to be carefully planned, but as the outputs are tangible and identifiable, this is not too difficult. Established methods of project planning and control such as Gantt charts, network analysis and responsibility charts, work well. Stakeholders and soft factors should not be neglected, but take second place. A fairly standard project management process can be used, even something like PRINCE2, perhaps simplified for smaller projects.

### Repeated change projects

These are the projects where purchasing can lead or assist substantial change for the organisation, leading to competitive advantage or large efficiency or cost gains. They have become increasingly important to organisations for all the reasons outlined in study session 1.

Category management and Six-Sigma are examples, where a range of projects focused on different areas or subjects follow a very similar process. The requirements include a strong project management process, flexible enough to be adapted to different areas, with good stakeholder management incorporated. Although similar projects may be working in parallel, many stakeholders may resist change and struggle to accept the project.

Challenges will change as more projects are carried out. When the first project starts, there will be little experience on which to base the process. There is a danger of having clear objectives but a team unable to find the way to achieve them. Once experience builds, the process becomes more familiar and the same things happen as with traditional projects: less focus and effort with higher expectations. Finally, teams become entrenched in the process and there is a danger that they keep on carrying out the projects when the objectives are no longer clear or necessary.

The best approach is exemplified by the Six-Sigma experience. As a basis a very supportive environment with senior management buy-in is central. The process can then be established, with stakeholder and change management as a part of it. Embedded within that process are the specific tools for that type of project: the DMAIC cycle and tools for Six-Sigma, market and requirements analysis tools for category management.

### Radical projects

These will include projects like developing a Supplier Relationship Management process from scratch, e-enabling purchasing, implementing an 'environmentally sound' purchasing policy. The projects are very new and the objectives are unclear. At the same time, change is likely to be substantial and stakeholders varied and important.

The fixed processes of the other two types are not appropriate, there is no experience to build on. These projects need an approach which can accommodate uncertainty and flexibility. At the same time, progress and success are needed and the requirement to control cost and deliver valuable outcomes remains.

The challenges are widespread. It is easy to do something: buy some e-purchasing software, draw up an SRM process, write a simple policy, but these are only a small part of successful projects in these areas. All the risks of projects come together here: the project could wander off course, delivering little, it could lose momentum and die away, it could divert resources from other more important activity, and finally, it could deliver something useless to the organisation or worse, based on objectives which are out of date, misunderstood or just plain wrong.

The approach must involve a drive to understand objectives, strong but flexible control and effective change management. It must be able to cope with uncertainty and change in the objectives and the requirements of the project. Typically the project will be broken down into phases, the first having a clear goal and work can be planned for each phase as it is approached. As an example, the first phase is often focused on building agreement on the need for and goal of the project, combined with gathering data on what is available or has been done by others.

### Self-assessment question 7.2

Write an outline description of the approach you would take for two Six-Sigma projects, the first within a company and the tenth within that same company. Highlight differences between the two.

*Feedback on page 115*

## 7.3 Case-based learning: which approach for e-auctions?

This section is case-based. The first element of managing the project – understanding the challenges and selecting an approach – sets the scene for the whole project. A mistake here is likely to cause lingering problems throughout.

The extended learning activity looks at one company moving towards e-auctions. By working through the five questions and scenarios, you should be able to identify different types and approaches, tailored to the individual project.

## Learning activity 7.3

Case Study

Wazzcorp is a large manufacturer of low-technology consumer products in the US supplying major retailing chains such as WalMart with branded and own-brand product. In their markets, they are the largest player and have been protected until recently by the customers' preference to 'buy domestic', to source from within the US or its neighbours. Wazzcorp has a few plants in South America, but most production is still in the US with a well-established supply base.

Over the past year, Wazzcorp has found that its cost base is being challenged by customers who are looking with interest to low-cost competition, particularly from low-cost countries.

In the long term, the company may shift production to low-cost countries, but there is strong resistance. That 'buy domestic' attitude is strong. The strategy for the next two years is to take aggressive 'cost out' measures across the supply base.

A central part of this strategy is to standardise specifications and open up competition for raw materials, packaging, etc through e-auctions: online reverse auctions. The software is in place, the next stage is to run effective auctions.

1. Looking at the first auction, code-named 'auction zero', what sort of project is it? What sort of challenges and needs would you expect?
2. Alongside the first auction, a small team of three has been given the task of capturing the learning from the first auction for others. This project is code-named 'move to BAN' (business as normal). What sort of project is this? Are there different challenges?
3. Both of these auctions are really sub-projects of this move to e-auctions to drive out cost and introduce competition. This overall project is called '2020 Challenge': what are the challenges and dangers?
4. The first five auctions were successful, averaging 38% price reductions, with one packaging auction reducing price from around $1 million to $92,000, over 90% reduction. What sort of project is the next auction? (It will be called #5.)
5. The dramatic results of the first auctions have scared many of the established purchasing team. They feel the auctions show them in a bad light, that they have been doing their job badly in the past. As a result, they are not coming forward with new opportunities and are resisting

*(continued on next page)*

Learning activity 7.3 *(continued)*

the move to standardise specifications, the first step in the auction process. Has 2020 Challenge changed? Is it a different type of project?

*Feedback on page 115*

Now answer the self-assessment question 7.3 below.

Self-assessment question 7.3

You work for a branch of the Ministry of Defence. Historically cost has been of limited impact on sourcing, but commercial pressures are becoming much stronger and the cost of sourcing will be driven down in a range of areas, through a range of projects. These will include sale of some facilities to private partners who will run them, e-auctions and competitive tendering, and reducing stock costs by eliminating obsolete stock.

Your director has suggested that a standard, fixed project management approach will be used across the board to help these projects succeed.

Write a 150 word memo in response to the suggestion.

*Feedback on page 117*



### Revision question

Now try the revision question for this session on page 320.

### Summary

Projects in purchasing and logistics cover a wide range of areas. A search of reported projects will show different types from automating ordering and delivery through to developing new purchasing talent within an organisation. Developing a 'one size fits all' approach to purchasing projects is difficult as each has different needs and challenges.

In order to identify a project type and predict the challenges, looking at a range of features is useful. The example used here is:

- mainly hard or soft
- cross-functional or restricted to the purchasing function
- involving change for many stakeholders or small changes for few
- high or low impact on the organisation
- one with clear detailed objectives from the outset or aims with objectives developing later.

From this, it is possible to identify different types, such as the split between radical, repeated change and traditional purchasing. If purchasing and logistics projects are to deliver real value to the organisation, they must embrace all three types.

## Suggested further reading

- Ayers (2004); Chapter 2.
- Meredith and Mantel (2006); Chapter 2.
- Obeng (1996); Chapter 1.

Journals and periodicals such as

- *Supply Chain Management Review*
- *CPO Agenda*
- *Journal of Supply Chain Management*



## Feedback on learning activities and self-assessment questions

### Feedback on learning activity 7.1

The range of projects is wide (see below) but there tend to be some links and common project areas. As common examples, you may have found category management or Lean Six-Sigma projects. These tend to use a standard approach, fairly similar with fairly well-defined goals; they may be led by purchasing. The impact may be high, particularly when a series of projects is looked at together. There may be 'hard' changes but the majority of work and risk is in the data gathering and change management. The projects which have a high impact tend to be cross-functional, even reaching beyond the organisation and across the supply chain.

### Feedback on self-assessment question 7.1

If you struggle to characterise it, use the five questions from learning activity 7.1:

- Mainly hard or soft? There will be a need to change employees' buying behaviour and to encourage compliance, perhaps persuading the CEO to mandate use of a new policy. This involves soft skills.
- Cross-functional or restricted to the purchasing function? This has an impact on anyone who makes purchasing decisions. This generally means many functions for example including IT, production and engineering.
- Involving change for many stakeholders or small changes for few? As above, many stakeholders.
- High or low impact on the organisation: there is the potential for a high impact in terms of cost and other factors from success or failure.
- Clear detailed objectives from the outset or aims with objectives developing later? From the information you have, the objectives are woolly. It will be hard even to define environmentally sound purchasing, let alone to clarify costs and impact.

This is probably a radical project.

### Feedback on learning activity 7.2

Comparing it with the three types it helps to see what sort of project it might be similar to, hence what is important and what problems are likely and should be prevented.

For a traditional project, the process and dangers should be well known. An approach which takes strong control over key factors such as time, cost and business requirements would probably work well. A well-developed time plan for activities, with clear fixed dates and risk analysis would fit. The overall approach might be similar to that for a building project.

For a repeated change project, a fairly standard process may have developed. The difference will be that the change will demand strong cross-functional stakeholder management. Circulating a fixed project plan and expecting people to fall into line is unlikely to work.

For a radical project, all aspects are difficult to pin down and the approach will need plenty of drive, flexibility around exactly what the timings and activities are, even better stakeholder management than the other types. Perhaps most important will be strong management of the aims and objectives: guiding the project into a position where each stage of it can be planned and carried out more effectively.

### Feedback on self-assessment question 7.2

The first: This is more like a radical project in that it is new and unfamiliar and the methods are little known. In addition to top-line objectives such as savings or solving defined problems, it will be important to act as a pathfinder for the other projects.

The approach you describe should incorporate getting and maintaining strong commitment. Building a process from other experience, other companies, etc, using the step-wise approach of radical projects and dealing with the change management and stakeholder challenges.

The tenth: This is more like a traditional purchasing project and can use a standard format. Commitment and support are still important and interest may have dropped away with the nine similar projects.

Your approach should use a stable and well-developed process, as described in the text. In addition, there should be activity at the start of the project to overcome the dangers of repeated projects. One aspect is to manage stakeholders' expectations, ensure resources are sufficient and focus is maintained. The second aspect is to set objectives and timing well to avoid drift or the development of the project because 'this is what we always do'.

### Feedback on learning activity 7.3

The best place to start is to consider a range of factors for each project, as used before:

- mainly hard or soft
- cross-functional or restricted to the purchasing function

- involving change for many stakeholders or small changes for few
- high or low impact on the organisation
- clear detailed objectives from the outset or aims with objectives developing later.

Looking at each one in turn, different types emerge, but of course each one has individual needs and challenges.

1. The challenges are a mix of hard and soft: getting internal stakeholders and suppliers to participate alongside the technical challenge of understanding and standardising specifications. The cross-functional links and changes for stakeholders depend on the complexity of the products to be sourced: simple commodities will involve limited cross-functional requirements. Selecting products which are currently single sourced with a strong relationship will increase the challenge and size of change. The impact should be high. Although the savings may be minor as a proportion of total turnover, as this is the first auction and a lot of attention will be focused on it, if it fails, the strategy for cost reduction could be harmed. The objective seems clear: reduce cost through an auction, so this project can be used as an example.
   In summary, although this is the first project and involves some change and soft elements, the main challenge comes from the project's prominence: being the first. The project type will be affected by the product selected. By selecting a commodity type product, the complexity, change and cross-functional elements can be reduced, making the project more like the 'traditional purchasing' or 'repeated change' types, with limited risk and simpler project management.
2. The project type depends on what the objectives are and when the project ends. If the aim is to make auctions business as normal, it is a radical project, with a lot of cross-functional engagement and change, focused on soft activities, with a high impact.
   If the project aim is defined as 'to capture learning', the project becomes much simpler and can use an approach from traditional purchasing: strong time planning to link with the auction, clear activities, a fairly short timescale and a clear output: a report or process captured.
   It is probably wiser to keep the objectives restricted, as the whole '2020 challenge' project is really aimed at making auctions business as normal, this is only a small part.
3. The overall project has almost all the features of a radical project: high impact, cross-functional change with many stakeholders, mainly soft activities. Although the headline objective is fairly clear (reduce cost), this needs to be done in a radical but sustainable way: large one-off savings are of limited value in the strategy of driving out cost. You can list the dangers and challenges across the project, from technical risks (software and provider failure) through resistance from stakeholders (including suppliers) to specification error: the savings may not be available. Most of these risks are manageable, but making sure each sub-project is as well defined and managed and low risk as possible will help.
4. This is a slightly unfair question. A definition as repeated change or even traditional purchasing would make sense, as there have been five successes. There is a strong risk, however, that the first five auctions were the easy ones, 'low hanging fruit', to help overcome some of the

internal resistance when people see that the project is working and providing benefits. If so, this could be the first auction to involve a lot of cross-functional engagement and specification challenge. To treat it as traditional purchasing would in this case be very dangerous.
The type of project and its challenges depend not just on whether something similar has been done before, but whether it has been done in this area.

5 Put simply, no. The factors are still largely the same, although some success has been gained and the risks are reducing in some areas. Technical risk is lower, for example. Other risks have increased: there is a danger of complacency with success, while this success has threatened important stakeholders. The challenges have shifted, but the project is still radical and substantial long-term sustainable savings are not assured yet.

## Feedback on self-assessment question 7.3

This example has similarities with Wazzcorp in learning activity 7.1: increased commercial pressures, a range of different projects.

You will by now be familiar with different types of project and you should highlight these differences, perhaps with examples or a reflection on the projects listed.

Standardising some elements of project management can be valuable, but a rigid process is likely to cause problems. You may have reflected that a government organisation is likely to have strong adherence to processes, so standardising project management could fit the culture, but restrict the types of likely project.

If you wanted to go into more detail, you could suggest, for example, that tools, such as time planning and risk management might be standardised. The governance structure could be similar and formalised, and perhaps three or so project types could be identified. A set of flexible processes might be appropriate, or one process for common project types and 'exceptional' processes for others.

Study session 8

# Sorting out the project: initiation and definition

'It's not always a bed of roses, but the blend of characters makes the strength of the team.'
**Steve Redgrave**

## Introduction

So far in this course we have looked at defining project management using life cycles and various problem-solving approaches. In this section we deal with the critical aspects of managing the project planning activity itself including deciding what activities are needed, how they relate to each other and also how to manage the project scheduling. Successful projects must begin with and maintain a clear definition of their aims and objectives.

## Session learning objectives

After completing this session you should be able to:

8.1 Identify and explain key stages in the project initiation and planning process.
8.2 Articulate the benefits of coordination and systems integration in managing a large project.
8.3 Explain how work breakdown structure and linear responsibility charts are produced and their importance in planning and managing a project.
8.4 Evaluate several approaches to interface management.

## Unit content coverage

This study session covers the following topic from the official CIPS unit content document.

### Learning objective

3.0 Develop and apply project management concepts, models, tools and techniques to create solutions to a range of practical project management problems.
3.1 Develop a project plan, working through the various phases of a project, and the activities to be considered in each phase.
4.1 Initiation and definition. State the problem
- Identify project goals
- List the objectives
- Determine preliminary resources
- Identify assumptions and risks

5.1 Appraise the range of tools and techniques available to the project team in terms of appropriateness, selection and implementation.
- Appropriateness. Pick the right tools for the task
- Selection. Be aware of the limitations of tools and techniques
- Implementation. Be able to use the tools correctly

## Prior knowledge

Study sessions 1 – 7.

## Resources

If you have access to it, the recommended textbook (Meredith and Mantel, 2006: Chapter 5) offers more detail on the topics covered in this section.

## Timing

You should set aside about 5 hours to read and complete this session, including learning activities, self-assessment questions, the suggested reading (if any) from the essential textbook for this unit and the revision question.



## 8.1 Defining and organising projects

### The project definition

A thorough statement of the project scope, timing and resources is central to managing a project. While this project definition is likely to develop as the understanding of scope, timing and resources grows, it is important to set as a benchmark early on.

**Scope** captures the outcomes of the project in terms of major deliverables which become the focus of management efforts during the project implementation phase. How much will be done, which departments will be covered, what systems will be included and integrated, and just as importantly, what is excluded.

The **timing** describes the duration of the project and its elements, and should be as specific and realistic as possible. An approximate time for completion is frequently not accurate enough as the tools which managers adopt (and as explained in the next few sessions of the course) deal with very small elements of time. The time frame should be a statement of completion, specific to the date where necessary, for example engaging suppliers ready for a product launch. Where the project is more flexible or hard to define, a more general statement such as 'early spring 2009' is sufficient.

The last element of the project definition is **resources**. This may be difficult to do at the planning stage, but it normally involves a budget for direct costs, staffing and other resources such as land, office space or equipment. This can then be used to specify the detailed costs and resource issues for the project. Again this needs to be as specific as possible, such as £2.5 million rather than a vague idea of the resources available. For example, many of the biggest failures in projects can be attributed partly to failure in identifying the resources required early on.

As discussed elsewhere, it is unreasonable to expect that these definitions need to be made early and held rigid. A project lasting two years will see changes in the environment and may well need to be flexible to incorporate these. A clear definition of scope, timing and resources allows any changes to be managed and helps to reduce drift and scope creep, while helping the project management to assess the impact of any changes.

## Learning activity 8.1

Review the initiation and planning process of your last project. Begin by defining the situation at the start. Review the outputs at the end of the planning stage. Analyse and identify the different activities involved in initiation and planning.

*Feedback on page 130*

### Project plan elements



The actual process of developing project plans is not fixed and different firms have their own approaches while different projects have very different needs. Meredith and Mantel (2006: 41) give their definition of the elements of a project plan.

- *Overview:* Summary of objectives and scope of the project linked to the firm's goals and objectives.
- *Objectives*: A more detailed statement of the goals along with quantification of how we know if they are met.
- *General approach*: Descries the approaches to the work and should be both technical and managerial in nature.
- *Contractual aspects*: A critical part of the plan, which covers the formal relationships of the elements and outside involvement.
- *Schedules*: A list of milestone events which will eventually be broken down into a detailed plan. This must be agreed by the senior management in the organisation as it represents the monitoring of the project progress. We will look in more detail at the development of work breakdown structures in the next section.
- *Resources*: The lists of activities or milestone events need to be accompanied with a list of the resources required, both capital and running. This is essential for monitoring the budget progress of the project.
- *Personnel*: What are the staff requirements of the project including the level of expertise and skills needed.
- *Risk management plans*: What are the major possible problems which might occur and how might they be addressed? There are some very advanced techniques for quantifying the risk levels and firms need to be sure they have an appreciation of the potential disasters.
- *Evaluation methods*: How will we know if the project went well? What steps will be taken to learn from the project itself?

This has been generated from long experience within companies, particularly with new product development or new facilities development projects. It probably fits these well, but other factors may need to be included and different areas stressed for different projects.

## Self-assessment question 8.1

Why should the project plan be viewed as a value adding activity?

*Feedback on page 131*

## 8.2 Developing coordinated plans: integration

Developing project plans is a continuous process of opening up boxes to give more and more detail until we have sufficient to map the steps needed to complete the project. Whilst there is much theory on how this might be achieved, it is rarely a straightforward exercise as there are many individuals and parties involved. When we start thinking about large projects which can span many different organisations, then the process becomes more complex and probably less structured as better plans emerge from existing ones and the iterations continue with contributions from both formal and informal meetings of groups and individuals.



The issues of how to manage these project planning activities become issues when there are many stakeholders with conflicting aims to accommodate, as often found in projects and of course in multidisciplinary teams. Here the project manager's task becomes one of coordination through integration management.

### Integration management

One successful way of involving cross-functional teams in project planning is by imposing a structure on the planning process by defining the task of the group as generating a plan to accomplish the project scope. This can lead to conflict as the different groups seek to develop plans which optimise their own concerns. As a result there are many approaches to trying to either remove conflict by planning or ways of dealing with plan conflict when it emerges.

Much of understanding how to manage conflict depends on the nature of the project and its manager. Wheelwright and Clark (1995) have investigated the role of project teams and found four different types:

- functional
- lightweight
- heavyweight
- autonomous.

These are described, along with strengths and weaknesses, in table 8.1.

**Table 8.1** Wheelwright and Clark's different project team types

| Project structure and associated characteristics | Strengths | Weaknesses |
|---|---|---|
| *Functional team* | Brings functional expertise to problem solving. | Judged on adherence to functional processes rather than overall results. |

*(continued on next page)*

Table 8.1 *(continued)*

| **Project structure and associated characteristics** | **Strengths** | **Weaknesses** |
|---|---|---|
| Members are answerable to their respective functional heads; team is abandoned on completion; projects evolve in a serial fashion as tasks pass from one function to the next; assessment not as team but by functional managers. | Function managers control resources for the tasks they own.<br><br>Clear career path.<br><br>Clear control, functional accountability. | Cookie-cutter approach to solving varied problems.<br><br>Team does not own business results.<br><br>Narrow levels of expertise.<br><br>Disjointed development.<br><br>Turf battles possible. |
| *Lightweight* | Same as functional. | Same as functional. |
| Most common; heightened degree of coordination due to administrative oversight; individuals continue to be focused primarily on their function, not on overall project results; improved communications. | Oversight of collective functional responsibilities helps to ensure timely project completion. | The lightweight manager has little organisational clout and little power to affect critical decisions. |
| *Heavyweight*<br><br>Core team members are representatives of their functions on an integrated development team; heavyweight manager is the heavyweight in the organisation. | Heavyweight manager has broad control over decision-making processes, resources used and targets established. | Team members still report to functional heads; rewards and responsibilities are disconnected from project deliverables.<br><br>Political tightrope – project manager has about the same stature as functional heads. |
| *Autonomous*<br><br>Team members are co-located and answer only to the heavyweight project manager; the team has extreme latitude to devise solutions to the problems it has responsibility for; sets own objectives; truly integrated cross-functional structure. | Focus on results.<br><br>No conflicting sources pulling at team members.<br><br>Speed and ability in solving challenging, novel problems.<br><br>Complete functional integration, the broadly skilled team is independent. | Less control; team tends to expand on original project description.<br><br>Little use of existing process solutions.<br><br>Independent/lack of integration with others.<br><br>Unique product and process solutions may be difficult to integrate into existing business. |

*Source: Adapted from Wheelwright and Clark (1995)*

## Learning activity 8.2

Think of a recent project you have been involved with. Which of the four types of project team identified by Wheelwright and Clark best describe the

*(continued on next page)*

### Learning activity 8.2 *(continued)*

organisation of your project and what were the benefits and disadvantages over the other types?

*Feedback on page 131*

Now try the case in self-assessment question 8.2 below.

### Self-assessment question 8.2

Read the following case on Stacee Labs, which was adapted from Meredith and Mantel (2005: 269), and answer the questions which follow.

**Stacee Laboratories**

8

Stacee Labs is the research and development subsidiary of a large medical drugs manufacturer. They operate using individual projects consisting of teams of scientists that operate largely without schedules, budgets and precisely predefined objectives. The parent company do not want the creativity to be encumbered with bureaucratic record-keeping chores, and so they want the scientists to determine their own directions.

A study of Stacee Labs for the parent firm found that, on average, the projects require much longer to complete and at higher cost than others in the industry. Such projects need in the region of 10–15 years before drugs are released to the market. However, Stacee Labs projects have a better success rate.

As a result of the study, a management consultant, Ms Millie Tasha, was approached and asked to recommend ways to speed up the completion of projects and save money. The managers were not seeking nit-picking, cost-cutting, or time-saving recommendations that might lower the quality of Stacee Labs' results.

After her study, which included many interviews with almost all the staff in the laboratories, Ms Tasha began with the observation that the scientists avoided contact with Marketing and Governmental Relations until they had accomplished most of their drug development work. When asked why they waited so long, they replied that they did not know what specific products they would recommend for sale until they had completed and tested the results of their work. There was a belief that the marketing department had a record of interfering with drug design and sought exaggerated claims or asked the scientists to design drugs which maximise sales rather than allowing innovation based on scientific development.

The consultant also showed that the scientists failed to contact the toxicity or efficacy testing groups until scientific work was completed and there was

*(continued on next page)*

Self-assessment question 8.2 *(continued)*

a drug to test. This resulted in long delays, as testing groups were usually involved in other projects and could not develop the tests immediately. It usually took months for testing to be organised.

In her opinion, the only way cut time and costs significantly for the drug projects was to form an integrated team composed of representatives of all the stakeholder groups and involve them from the beginning of the project. All parties could then monitor drug development and be prepared to contribute to the projects at the appropriate time. If Stacee did this, then delays and cost inflation could be significantly reduced she concluded.

Questions: Do you think Millie Tasha is right? If so, how should new drug projects be planned and organized? If Stacee Labs goes ahead with a reorganisation of lab projects, what are the potential problems? How would you deal with them? Could scope creep become more of a problem with the new integrated teams? If so, how should it be controlled?

*Feedback on page 131*



## 8.3 Developing detailed project plans

### The work breakdown structure (WBS)

The work breakdown structure (WBS) is a statement of all the work that has to be completed. Perhaps the most important contributor to delay is the omission of work that is essential to the successful completion of the project. The project manager must work closely with the project team to identify all work tasks. Typically, in the process of accumulating work tasks, the team generates a hierarchy to the work breakdown. Major work elements are broken down into smaller components by the project team and another level of detail is added. An example is shown in figure 8.1. There is no perfect way of developing a WBS, but two methods are discussed in section 14.2.

How far to break down tasks is not an easy question to answer. As a guide, an activity, the smallest level, is the smallest unit of work that a project manager can usefully schedule and control. It may be a task with long duration but low input or a very rapid task but with high risk. The WBS should be developed according to planning needs.

One valuable application of the WBS is to help assign ownership to ensure every activity is completed. Each activity should have an owner who is responsible for the work, whether they do it themselves or oversee it. Task ownership avoids confusion in the execution of activities and assigns responsibility for timely completion. The team should define a procedure for assigning tasks to team members, which could be democratic or autocratic.

**Figure 8.1:** A work breakdown structure

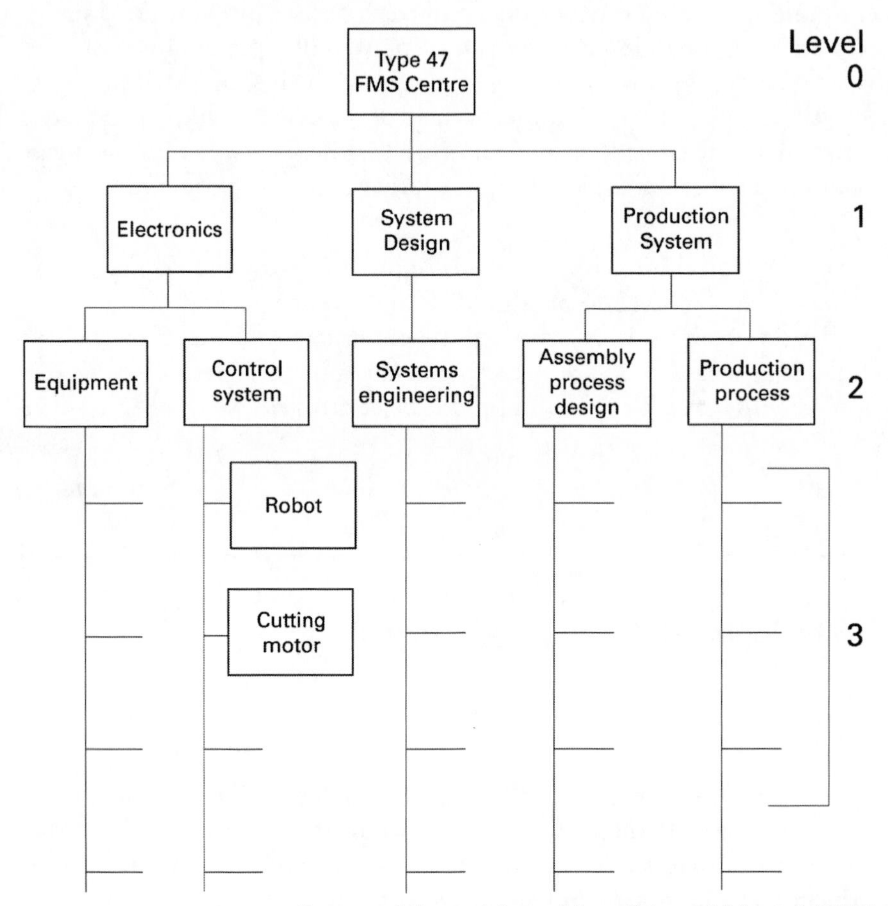


*Source: Adapted from Meredith and Mantel (2005: 258)*

## Linear responsibility charts

Assigning responsibility for each activity in the WBS is important, as mentioned above. If an activity is without an owner, it is unlikely to get done and ownership helps the project manager in coordinating activities. One tool for recording ownership is the linear responsibility chart (see figure 8.2). Using standard format and symbols helps to identify clearly the different ownership. This also highlights some of the interfaces between different organisations or functional groups which may require coordination or could even be the source of conflict. Once identified, these interfaces can be managed more effectively.

**Figure 8.2:** Linear responsibility chart

| Task | Responsibility: John | Mark | Edith | Beryl |
|---|---|---|---|---|
| Develop budget | | | X | |
| Cross reference commitments | | X | | |
| Prepare draft specification | | | | X |
| Develop contract specimen | X | | | |
| Conduct customer interviews | | X | | |

## Learning activity 8.3

Produce a linear responsibility chart for a private project such as organising a holiday.

*Feedback on page 132*

Now let us try a question to address the importance of the WBS.

## Self-assessment question 8.3

Why is the use of WBS important to project managers?

*Feedback on page 132*

## 8.4 Avoiding and resolving disputes

This section focuses on ways of avoiding disputes through effective communication and means of resolving disputes that can occur between contracting parties.

### Types of dispute

Clearly there are many different types of dispute. These may be about the desired outcomes within a contract, or the way in which these outcomes have been delivered. In the case of construction contracts, disputes may range from projects overrunning time or budget, through poor health and safety records, to sloppy administrative work. In the case of an IT project, disputes could arise over software suitability, hardware warranties or cost overruns.

Disputes may be minor, major or intractable, and it can be useful to have a method of categorising these and a standard set of responses as a first step to resolution. The clearer such conflict and dispute handling mechanisms are, the less likely disputes are to remain unresolved – and possibly escalate from minor to major, or even intractable disputes.

Conflict is the heart of a dispute, but does not need to be destructive. It is possible to identify two types of conflict: constructive and destructive conflict.

Constructive conflicts:

- tend to be centred on interests rather than needs
- tend to be open and dealt with openly
- are capable of helping a relationship develop
- focus on flexible methods for solving disputes
- help both parties reach their objectives.

Destructive conflicts:

- often centred on people's needs rather than interests or issues of fact
- focus on personalities, not action or behaviours – typified by 'You are awkward' rather than 'You've been awkward recently; what has been wrong?'
- involve face-saving and preservation of power
- attack relationships
- concentrate on quick-fix, short-term solutions
- tend to repeat themselves.



### Communications planning to reduce conflict

Many cases of conflict arise not because of insurmountable problems of different work groups or stakeholders, but often because of poor communication. A formal plan for communication is an important part of stakeholder management and central to the project plan. It is a description of who is responsible for communicating, what should be passed on, to whom, how and when.

This not only provides the people involved in the project with a clear description of their communication activities, but can also prompt them to think about areas of possible conflict in advance. In drawing up the communication plan, like the one shown in table 8.2, the stakeholders have to go through their own links and understand what they are trying to communicate. Such exercises often remove many of the possible problems which can happen in times of stress during the project as a result of some mutual appreciation of each other's concerns.

**Table 8.2** A simple communication plan

| Stakeholder | Communication | Timing | Format | Distribution | Person responsible |
|---|---|---|---|---|---|
| Project sponsor | Monthly | Week 1 each month | Short report | E-mail | Project manager |
| Accounts dept | Monthly spend schedule | 2 weeks before start of month | Short budget | E-mail | Administrator |
| Client dept | Monthly | Week 1 of each month | 1-page report | E-mail and notice board | Liaison officer |

## Avoiding litigation in resolving disputes

As anyone who has ever been involved in the process of resolving a dispute through litigation can tell you, it is a long, drawn-out, stressful, draining and costly experience. According to an American study of civil litigation by the Rand Corporation, the average lawsuit in America usually takes over three years to reach trial or settlement. In Japan, this period can be even longer.

Other methods are available for resolving disputes and are under-used, with negotiation being the most common. The objective of sensible dispute management should be to negotiate a settlement as soon as possible. Each of us negotiates every day, whether we negotiate the terms of a business contract, haggle over the lunch bill or discuss what we will do tonight with friends or family. When a dispute arises, direct negotiations between parties more often than not lead to a resolution. In negotiation, each side retains two important things: control over the process and control over the outcome. However, if you cannot resolve the dispute by direct negotiation, then you need to call in a third party to settle the dispute for you.



There are a number of informal types of dispute resolution, without recourse to law:

- Mediation: A private and structured form of negotiation assisted by a third party; it is initially non-binding. If settlement is reached, as with any agreement it can become a legally binding contract with the consent of the parties involved.
- Conciliation: Similar to mediation, but a conciliator can propose and recommend solutions rather than just facilitating negotiations.
- Expert determination: A private process involving an independent expert who provides a decision. Again, this can be binding with the consent of the parties.
- Adjudication: An expert is instructed to rule, with a binding outcome. This is commonly used in disputes relating to construction contracts. The Housing Grants, Construction and Regeneration Act 1996 made adjudication a compulsory form of dispute procedure for construction contracts.

These are valuable and low-cost means of resolving disputes. Before selecting one of these, you should consider to what extent you are willing to:

- play a direct role in the resolution of the dispute
- surrender control of the process to others
- empower third parties to make decisions for you
- have the final outcome determined by the process.

### Learning activity 8.4

Conduct assessment of your own communication effectiveness and reflect upon methods of improvement. You may wish to examine feedback from colleagues and stakeholders on a previous project.

*Feedback on page 132*

Now let us try a question to examine different approaches to conflict resolution.

### Self-assessment question 8.4

Outline three approaches you could consider in dealing with a conflict between members of a project team and non-project functional managers whose cooperation is essential for the success of the project.

*Feedback on page 133*

## Revision question

Now try the revision question for this session on page 320.



## Summary

In this section, we have looked at the crucial stage of developing project plans. The detailed plans are important and the WBS can form a basis for these. Just as important is the process of development and the resulting engagement of stakeholders: the team understands and agrees their responsibility for activities, the stakeholders agree the objectives of the project and the commitment of time, resources and people. Finally, avoiding and resolving disputes is part of managing through to success.

Now we have the detail of the activities, we can look at how we decide whether projects get the go ahead or not, and how risky each project might prove.

## Suggested further reading

A good place to find more information is to look at Frigenti and Comninos (2002), Turner (1993) and Lock (2003).

## Feedback on learning activities and self-assessment questions

### Feedback on learning activity 8.1

The initiation and planning process was touched on in study session 4 in the discussions on the project life cycle.

The first challenge to this question is to define the start and end of the initiation and planning process. There is no perfect answer, but if you are stuck, begin with the first time the project is identified, and stop when the project work itself starts in earnest.

At the start, the project is likely to be ill-defined, cost and timings are either hard to assess or possibly defined externally (it *must* be finished by 1 June, we have a budget of *just* £127,000).

At the end, there should be a written and agreed project definition in some form, clear plans in terms of risk, timing, cost and outputs according to what is important to the project. In this section, Meredith and Mantel's list for a project plan is given and that can be a good comparison,

The activities in between start and finish must incorporate developing these plans, and you will probably identified these as part of planning. You may well have found that planning is an iterative process: the first time plan conflicts with the budget, the first proposed definition is not agreed by stakeholders, the budget is increased by negotiation. This is normal and part of an activity which is less tangible than creating plans: defining and agreeing the project with stakeholders. This iterative cycle of developing a clearer vision of the project and an understanding of what is involved is as important as the detail of the time plan or the exact budget.

### Feedback on self-assessment question 8.1

First, project plans can often be too brief and informal. There are many cases where the carrying out of the project was not at fault, but the definition stage was. If the organisation is serious about the project, then it needs to have a serious plan with as much detail as is possible. They should also be very careful about scope creep where the specifications are constantly changed as the project is progressing. Examples where the plans appear not to have been as detailed as they should and the scope kept evolving include Wembley Stadium and the Millennium Dome.

Secondly, as discussed in learning activity 8.1, the planning process is a vital part of developing and agreeing a vision of what the project is and will involve with stakeholders. Detailed plans are not, in themselves, value-adding. They need to be coherent and agreed. It is the research done to create them and the discussion of those plans which have such a high impact in setting direction and preparing the ground for success.

### Feedback on learning activity 8.2

The answer will depend on the case selected, but it is important to stress that there is no one best way of managing projects. Some approaches can limit conflict between groups in the project, such as the autonomous group, but this generates its own issues of finding someone in the organisation who can carry off the project. The leader has to be very senior and charismatic to pull the project together, and these people are few and far between.

### Feedback on self-assessment question 8.2

The case shows the need for integration management and the benefits of cross-functional teams. However, the problems which may be generated result from the existing differences between the groups and their focus on working to produce the best solution to their own set of issues. The adoption of a heavyweight project manager would be a good approach to use to address this difference in focus in the groups where each becomes identified with the project team rather than their original functional part of the firm. A problem with this is that when the project team builds its own identity and authority, it can lose the checks and balances of having to work with other groups and so can be subjected to scope creep. This needs the strong supervision of the senior managers and strict adherence to authority and sign-off controls to ensure that the project is not redefined as it develops.

### Feedback on learning activity 8.3

The first step is to develop a WBS giving all the tasks such as booking flights, car hire, accommodation, buying insurance, arranging pet care, etc. Then a linear responsibility chart can be produced, identifying one owner for each activity. This may demonstrate an overload on one person or lack of consultation in some areas. As with any responsibility chart, it is important that all the people involved 'sign up' to it and are aware of their responsibilities and accept them.



### Feedback on self-assessment question 8.3

The WBS is important for the project as it lists the activities which are needed for the project to be completed. It is not a plan in itself, but is the basis for many of the core elements of project planning – ownership, scheduling, budgeting, for example – so needs to be very accurate as any errors or omissions can have serious knock-on effects.

As an example, if the project costs are unreliable, then the impact on the contracting organisation or the sponsor can be catastrophic and far reaching. In the construction of Wembley stadium, the main contractor and subcontractor for the steelwork have both suffered greatly through cost overruns. It is still unclear who is at fault and the affair has degenerated into a series of claims and counterclaims in the courts.

### Feedback on learning activity 8.4

This answer will depend on the example selected. However, try and be honest with yourself and think about how you really communicate with people in your project team. You may find you feel you are too abrupt and might want to think about how to approach conflict in a more constructive manner, or you may think you need to undergo some improvement in assertiveness training.

If you were particularly brave, you may have asked for comments from colleagues and stakeholders from past projects. This is a very useful practice to develop, but can be quite a rollercoaster ride as criticism can be hard to take.

As you meet various people throughout the day, try to determine whether your current feelings reflect a dominant pattern in your relationship with them. Are you happy with your findings? How could you improve things? Did you notice any pattern in your responses to difficult people? Could you change this response – and what else could you do if you encountered this type of situation again?

## Feedback on self-assessment question 8.4

This answer will depend on the example selected.

There will be differences between how you deal with internal and external people as the chain of command and influence is very different.

Study session 9

# Project evaluation and managing the risk

'Uncertain ways unsafest are,
And doubt a greater mischief than despair.'

**Sir John Denham**

## Introduction

So far in this course, we have examined the planning stages in establishing projects. At some point the organisation needs to decide whether the project in question is given the formal green light. As there may well be any number of projects vying for the limited resources in the organisation, a number of different approaches to selecting projects have been developed. These can be classified as either non-numeric or numeric, and we will look at some of each in the next few pages.

## Session learning objectives

After completing this session you should be able to:

9.1 Appraise the application of non-financial project selection models.
9.2 Identify the advantages and disadvantages of numerical models of project selection and evaluation.
9.3 Outline the application and effectiveness of methods of evaluating risk in a project.
9.4 Outline common approaches to project budgeting.

## Unit content coverage

This study session covers the following topic from the official CIPS unit content document.

### Learning objective

3.0 Develop and apply project management concepts, models, tools and techniques to create solutions to a range of practical project management problems.
4.0 Initiation and definition. State the problem
- Identify project goals
- List the objectives
- Determine preliminary resources
- Identify assumptions and risks

5.0 Appraise the range of tools and techniques available to the project team in terms of appropriateness, selection and implementation.
- Appropriateness. Pick the right tools for the task
- Selection. Be aware of the limitations of tools and techniques
- Implementation. Be able to use the tools correctly

3.3 Utilise a range of tools and techniques to assist in robust and systematic data collection, analysis of options and decision-making.
- SIPOC
- 7 tools of quality control

- Financial appraisal
- Voice of the customer
- Quality function deployment
- Project initiation document (PID)
- Moments of truth
- Work breakdown structure
- Critical path analysis. Network diagrams
- Risk analysis and assessment. Mitigating risks
- Risk/Impact matrix
- Suitability/feasibility/vulnerability

### Prior knowledge

Study sessions 1 – 8. The Risk Management and Supply Chain Vulnerability and the Finance for Purchasers modules would provide a good foundation, particularly in understanding discounted cash flow and risk appraisal techniques. Operations management should also provide some foundation in evaluation.



### Resources

If you have access to it, the recommended textbook Meredith and Mantel (2006: Chapter 2) offers more detail on the topics covered in this section.

### Timing

You should set aside about 4 hours to read and complete this session, including learning activities, self-assessment questions, the suggested reading (if any) from the essential textbook for this unit and the revision question.

## 9.1 It is not just about money: non-financial project selection

### Learning activity 9.1

Review three to five projects with which you are familiar which were not selected purely on a financial basis. Analyse the selection to identify the basis for selection: why did they get the go-ahead?

*Feedback on page 142*

Financial analysis of projects can be very useful and forms a part of many project selection processes. Investment analysis uses one measure – money – to provide 'like for like' comparison. Finance is limited, however. As an example, some projects are necessary for the company to stay alive, such as responding to price competition. Some projects are very hard to quantify: advertising and branding can be long term with benefits which are elusive to measure. Non-financial techniques are necessary in some circumstances and can be simpler to use. Here are a few of the options:

- *Operating necessity*: Some projects are generated by the need to maintain some other element of the business. As such these projects also do not require much formal justification, only an assessment that the costs of the project do not overshadow the returns of whatever process they support.
- *Competitive necessity*: In many cases, the need to compete with others forces the hand of firms when it comes to deciding which projects to adopt. If it is likely that your firm will fail to be competitive without, say, a new plant or redesign of the product, then to some extent you must carry out such a project or face closure.
- *Product line extension*: Some new products seem obvious as firms look to exploit gaps in existing offerings. These may demand some casual figures to show that the new product does not impact the profitability of the existing line-ups.
- *Comparative benefit model*: A common way of distinguishing between rival projects in a possible portfolio is by comparing the advantages of the projects to rank them. After several iterations, the projects become sorted by benefit to the firm and the top ones can then be selected to be pursued, depending on the resources available.
- *Sacred cow*: Some projects do not need any formal justification or selection process, as they are suggested by very powerful people in the organisation and as such have a massive weight of support behind them. It is only when the champion decides to try something else that the project can be dropped from the organisation.



### Self-assessment question 9.1

Identify faults with each non-financial approach to project evaluation.

*Feedback on page 143*

## 9.2 Numerical project selection methods

### Learning activity 9.2

Think of three projects with which you are familiar, and apply one scoring method and one financial tool to rank the projects.

*Feedback on page 143*

### Scoring methods

There are many ways of trying to differentiate possible alternative projects based on pseudo-numerical methods which try and assign values to features and then calculate some statistic based on the data. We now list a few of these and show how they get more complex as the methods try and assign different scores to factors.

*Unweighted factor model*

At its simplest this just has an unweighted identification by a number of senior managers of whether a factor applies or not. Their scores are then added up to rate the projects.

*Unweighted factor scoring*

An advance on the basic approach is to rate the degree of fit to the factor being judged, such as a Likert type 5 point scale. Again the final scores are added together to rate the projects for comparison.

*Weighted factor scores*

Here each factor is rated as above, but instead of the simple summing of the scores, each factor is assigned a weighting based on the importance as judged by the managers. This weighted score is then used to rate the projects for selection.

The development of these factor scoring models can be as simple or complex as the organisation demands; however, they are often based on judgement of the managers and those giving the scores. As such they may appear to be objective, but this may not be the case.



### Financial methods

Many firms select their projects based purely on profitability measures. You will have covered these elsewhere in your studies, such as payback period, average rate of return, and discounted cash flow such as net present value and internal rate of return. If you are unfamiliar with these techniques, you can read about them in Meredith and Mantel (2005) or any finance textbook you can find.

### Self-assessment question 9.2

Identify the problems and particular benefits associated with four different numerical and non-numerical models of project evaluation.

*Feedback on page 143*

## 9.3 Evaluating risk in project environments

### Learning activity 9.3

Identify two recent projects from your own work experience or from the media and describe their methods of managing risk.

*Feedback on page 143*

Maylor (2005) talks of two basic approaches to handling uncertainty and risk in project management: the mathematical and the managerial.

Treatment of the mathematical side is vast, and usually relies on developing ways of quantifying the risk and uncertainty to allow some decision to be made. Examples include financial tools, simulation, network analysis, decision trees (which were discussed in section 5.3), fuzzy logic and Markov chains. On the managerial side, the approach is to develop ways of handling the effects of uncertainty and the risks this implies.

### Risk management

Identifying possible risks is a relatively easy thing for managers to do and there are some well-developed procedures, particularly in industries where the penalties can be large such as heavy engineering and aerospace. The next step is to quantify it so that proper attention can be given to the most significant. Some areas to help with risk identification include:

- *Key risk symptoms*: those elements which will indicate that something is going wrong. The project plan and milestones are a good way of designing a system to show up when problems are happening.
- *External sources*: there may be opportunities to employ external people from outside the organisation to review the project plans and see if they spot anything inherently risky. In the academic world, peer review is used to ensure the quality of the work before being published.
- *Project performance reviews*: the 'iron triangle' – time, cost and quality – can be used. Time – checked using tools such as critical path analysis and programme review technique (see study session 9 for details) which examine and highlight the activities which may cause possible problems if they are delayed. Cost – the values of cost in project proposals and plans are only estimates and it is important to be realistic about how much experience the individuals making the guesses have to draw upon. Quality – are there adequate procedures in place to ensure that we can meet the quality criteria for all the elements of the project?
- *Assumptions*: there will always be assumptions in the project proposals and plans, and it is important that we have revisited them to be sure they are not false.

### Response control/mitigation strategies

Having identified the risk elements that need to be managed, we need a procedure for dealing with the eventualities. Two main types of risk mitigation strategies exist:

1. *Preventative*: develop actions to reduce the likelihood a risk will occur.
2. *Contingency*: develop actions to reduce the seriousness if the issue occurs.

If a risk occurs, it is important that firms have some form of recovery action and these can be built into the work breakdown structure for the project.

Some firms have formalised risk registers which specify:

1. who is responsible for implementing the contingency
2. the times of the action to implement
3. the costs associated with the mediating action.

### Decision trees

A useful tool in trying to compare the risks of different projects is to use decision trees (see section 5.3). When it is possible to estimate the probability of success and the expected benefits or costs resulting from certain projects, a decision tree can help select the best solution.

Decision trees look at project choices, typically which project to choose from a selection. They use estimates of possible outcomes (could return £1 million, could lose £3 million) and estimates of probability (0.3 chance of losses, 0.7 chance of success). Using calculations, it is possible to express the 'expected value' of a choice: a financial expression of the 'average' benefit.

### Self-assessment question 9.3

What are the main drawbacks of using the decision tree approach combined with expected value to identify and manage risk?

*Feedback on page 143*



## 9.4 Common approaches to project budgeting

### Learning activity 9.4

Reflect upon different budgeting approaches required for one-off and multiple projects.

*Feedback on page 144*

Money is frequently a central part of planning for projects, yet over and over again, projects suffer from cost overruns of 50, 100, 300 or even 1,000%. The Scottish parliament building was originally budgeted at £62 million but costs are currently estimated at £431 million. This increase of almost 600% in cost may represent excellent value for a landmark building for the important Scottish assembly to meet in, but it does suggest poor cost management. It also highlights two aspects of project budgeting: it is difficult to do well, and budgets are likely to change as the project develops. That change is almost always upwards, of course.

The process of developing budgets is more than just estimating the possible total cost of the project, a budget provides a breakdown of costs to help monitoring and control and provides the basis for earned value calculations (see section 12.3). As a result, the budgeting process is very important to ensuring not only that the project is completed within cost boundaries, but also for its smooth completion.

Some firms and projects have highly developed methods for estimating budgets depending on their experience and the nature of what needs estimating. Architects, for example, can take the area of the building and multiply by a figure to give a good approximation of the construction costs of a normally constructed building. They can then break down the detailed design of the building to provide a detailed cost estimate. Similarly, software estimates are based on the lines of code required, and standard values are available in manuals. However, in some unusual cases, estimates based on experience may need some manipulation or may have inappropriate assumptions. Either way, there are set ways for developing budgets.

### Top-down budgeting

Top-down budgeting involves fixing an overall cost then dividing it between the different areas or activities of the project. This is often a reliable approach in terms of estimating the budgets for whole projects and multiple projects by predicting the total budget based on experience or comparison with similar projects. By using similar projects or a combination of projects, an accuracy typically of 10–50% can be achieved in overall cost. This can then be given to others to explode the detail and divide the amalgamated amounts into views of ever finer detail.

A problem with this approach is that even though there is evidence that the overall budget totals for the project may be quite accurate, there is an opportunity for major errors to enter the system as the detail is added as certain things may have been overlooked: too much money may be devoted to programming rather than implementation of a system, for example, and once allocated, the money is hard to claw back.

### Bottom-up budgeting

Bottom-up budgeting involves estimating costs for individual activities or parts of the project, then adding these up to form a whole. One common route is to use the individual elements of the work breakdown structure as a basis, then add them to develop a budget at several levels. The overall project budget is then calculated by adding up the different parts. These budgets can potentially be very accurate as each element represents a well-defined piece of work to estimate. Another benefit is that there are many people involved in developing these budgets and so the climate of inclusion can have serious benefits to the future running of the project itself. The core problem with this is similar to the problems with time estimates identified in section 6.3. People tend to be generous when estimating costs, then add a buffer in case of problems, then use all that money and more. Bottom-up budgets without careful management can swell to outsize proportions.

A second problem is that, developing complete lists of the tasks involved and estimating in minute detail can be difficult and very time-consuming. This is compounded by a temptation to cut budgets as part of efficiency drives and this can cause problems in delivering the project at a later stage.

### Top down vs. bottom up

Neither method can claim better accuracy and both are subject to bias and incomplete information. They use different bases and information so one of the most effective methods of budget setting is to do both: estimate costs from the bottom up and top down, working through to eliminate discrepancies.

Top down is more common than bottom up for two simple reasons: senior managers tend to set budgets and the top-down approach reflects the money available rather than a figure based on a scope which may not be affordable.

### Self-assessment question 9.4

How would you go about budgeting for a new project which is totally unfamiliar and a project that is very similar to projects that you have managed in the past?

*Feedback on page 144*



## Revision question

Now try the revision question for this session on page 320.

## Summary

In this session we have looked at some of the techniques available for helping firms identify which projects to select when they have many vying for funding. Many of these decisions involve trying to quantify risk as this impacts how certain we might be about possible future returns.

An extension of the ideas concerning risk is the issue of appreciating the uncertainty of developing budgets. These processes can be critical to returning the cost aims of the project.

## Suggested further reading

If you have access to it, a good place to find more information on these topics is to look at the recommended list at the end of the relevant chapter of Meredith and Mantel (2006).

## Feedback on learning activities and self-assessment questions

### Feedback on learning activity 9.1

The answer will depend on the projects identified, of course, but typical reasons might be:

- 'we had to because our competitors…'
- 'the director of operations wanted it and that was that'
- 'we needed it to make the production line run smoothly'
- 'it is the sort of thing we *should* be doing: developing new products'

- 'we tackled that category because it would be high profile and show we were serious'.

## Feedback on self-assessment question 9.1

All the selection approaches above depend on subjective judgements and so may be subject to bias based on whoever is performing the choice. Even ranking projects is based on subjective comparisons and so may not always make the optimum decision. This is why a range of numerical methods have been developed which purport to be less biased.

Many managers and firms require financial or at least numerical justification of projects, as this instils an aura of scientific detachment which may not be true.

## Feedback on learning activity 9.2

The answer will depend on the projects selected, but it is possible that different results will be generated. Try to think whether the scale of the projects would justify the extra demands in time and energy in refining the data needed for the different scoring methods, or the more advanced discounted cash flow approaches.

It is important to note that many qualitative aspects cannot be effectively or easily measured with scoring methods. As such the justification techniques will be different.

## Feedback on self-assessment question 9.2

Each method has its own strengths and weaknesses, some of which are discussed in the section. It is worth noting the complexity and cost of each method: some are simple but inaccurate, some require more effort both in data and analysis. Where the project is more expensive or higher impact the more complex methods may offer greater accuracy or confidence.

## Feedback on learning activity 9.3

The answer will depend on the cases chosen, but it is likely that you can spot evidence of both prevention and contingency. If you only see one (or neither), revisit the projects and think about how risks could have been managed better. The description of risk management in this section may help you analyse the risk management used.

## Feedback on self-assessment question 9.3

There are fundamental drawbacks:

- They rely on financial and probability estimates which are hard to make accurately.
- They focus on finance, hence disadvantage any projects where the benefits are hard to express financially.

- They rely on discrete outcomes: either A or B will happen, while project success is often a complex and continuous phenomenon.
- It is really a project selection technique and offers almost no value to the management of risk within a project.

There are some resultant drawbacks:

- It favours projects which are risky: a small chance of a huge payoff will outweigh a high probability of failure.
- The result is not an indication of any possible outcome, but an average which is often misunderstood.

As a note, decision trees can be used without expected value calculations to offer only a visual representation of outcomes. This overcomes some problems, such as favouring risky projects, but removes the benefit of a single figure for comparison.

### Feedback on learning activity 9.4

The issues with single projects are on the lack of experience which firms can gather. If the project is similar to others which have been developed in the past, then there is much knowledge to draw upon, whereas unique activities carry much more risk.

### Feedback on self-assessment question 9.4

In many cases, a combined top-down and bottom-up approach is normally adopted in such a situation. Senior managers are best placed to estimate the headline costs for the project based on their own experiences and as they must take the responsibility for the risky exercise itself. Then it becomes a detailed task for members of the project planning team to investigate the work elements which contain unfamiliar activities and report back to their superiors. This then becomes as iterative process whereby estimates are made and then refined.

## Study session 10
# Planning, scheduling and managing resources

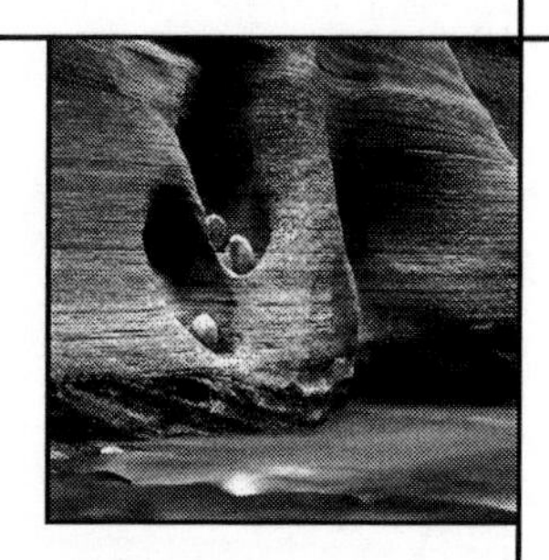

'My timing has been perfect all game. Test cricket is about playing the situation, not being an individual.'
**Nasser Hussain**

### Introduction

At the heart of project planning is the activity of scheduling: coordinating activities in terms of timing and the costs associated. Many techniques have been developed to help with this complicated task and the use of computers has brought great power to the non-specialised project manager's fingertips.

Summarised below are some of the more popular approaches to project scheduling and the tools they use. Scheduling deals with both the timing of activities and the costs or usage of resources. Developing a schedule is of course only a first step and part of planning, it should form the basis for the measurement, monitoring, control and management which ensure the project achieves the planned work.

### Session learning objectives

After completing this session you should be able to:

10.1 Explain the relationships between scheduling and network techniques.
10.2 Evaluate the application of PERT/CPM and Gantt charting to project scheduling and resource allocation.
10.3 Explain the advantages of precedence charting techniques and GERT in project scheduling.
10.4 Evaluate basic approaches to resource management; the CPM, resource loading, resource levelling and constrained resource scheduling.

### Unit content coverage

This study session covers the following topic from the official CIPS unit content document.

#### Learning objective

3.0 Develop and apply project management concepts, models, tools and techniques to create solutions to a range of practical project management problems.
  3.1.2 Planning
  - Identify activities
  - Estimate time and cost
  - Sequence activities
  - Identify critical activities
  - Write project proposal

3.2 Appraise the range of tools and techniques available to the project team in terms of appropriateness, selection and implementation.

- Appropriateness. Pick the right tools for the task
- Selection. Be aware of the limitations of tools and techniques
- Implementation. Be able to use the tools correctly

3.3 Utilise a range of tools and techniques to assist in robust and systematic data collection, analysis of options and decision making.
- SIPOC
- 7 tools of quality control
- Financial appraisal
- Voice of the customer
- Quality function deployment
- Project initiation document (PID)
- Moments of truth
- Work breakdown structure
- Critical path analysis. Network diagrams
- Risk analysis and assessment. Mitigating risks
- Risk/Impact matrix
- Suitability/feasibility/vulnerability

## Prior knowledge

Study sessions 1 – 10. Operations Management in the Supply Chain will provide some background here.



## Resources

If you have access to it, a good place to find more information is to look at the recommended textbook: Meredith and Mantel, 2006. You might read Chapters 8 and 9 for more detail on the topics covered in this section.

## Timing

You should set aside about 6 hours to read and complete this session, including learning activities, self-assessment questions, the suggested reading (if any) from the essential textbook for this unit and the revision question.

## 10.1 Project scheduling techniques

Schedules are central to project planning and frequently scheduling is the main element of the plan, the only part to be completed comprehensively and kept up to date.

Schedules are often tight and the pressure to deliver is heavy. If the tasks are simple, or focused on one output, time management is simple: focus all work on achieving that output. For more complex projects such as category management, there are frequently many outputs required and a series of activities happening at the same time. In such a complex situation there is a risk that some activities are forgotten, some run late, some never happen at all.

There is a tendency to respond to this with complex planning and to assume that effective scheduling relies on complex network analysis or charts generated by software such as Microsoft Project. Once the schedule is complete and agreed, it is assumed that everyone has understood it and will stick to it – a fatal error. This can be very useful for understanding the detail of complex interwoven activities but can also be a barrier to seeing the schedule as a whole or communicating it.

Obeng (1996) dismisses network charts and Gantt charts entirely, suggesting that getting the schedule into people's diaries is more important. Some projects work between milestones: key review points or achievements with no detailed Gantt or network charts. A complex situation does not necessarily need a complex tool. The more complex the tool, the more time it takes and the less it is likely to be used.

There is a need for balance in creating the schedules: using the tools and methods appropriate to the situation and the level of detail needed.

### Different levels of schedule

Just as a Work Breakdown Structure has many levels, schedules can be at a series of levels, ranging from an overview to detail of each activity.

1. At the top level there is a need for a simple overview of the project from start to finish. This could use a Gantt chart, milestones, or any other method, provided it:
   - is simple and quick to use
   - is easy to understand: good for communicating
   - helps identify potential problems: overruns, too many tasks at one time
   - is easy to compare with progress during the process
   - is easy to update.
2. Below this the project will be split up: a long project might be have a schedule for each six-month milestone, a large project could have a schedule for each region, country or site. These schedules could incorporate every activity, but more often combine activities into larger tasks. Where a long project is broken down between milestones, it is common to plan in detail only to the next milestone, leaving the detail beyond that to allow for changes and developments.
3. At the level of groups or individuals, there could be a more detailed schedule showing individual activities for a small element of the project.

In some cases, all the individual activities are combined into one complex plan for the project manager. This can be useful to keep all the information in one place and to demonstrate the complexity, but it is rarely a useful tool to communicate the schedule or to ensure individuals understand their start or finish dates.

### Network diagrams

One method developed to help create schedules is network analysis. This is based on the idea that of all the activities, some cannot be started before others are finished (precedence) and that if there are many of these, as in a building project, there is a need to understand the complex network of precedences.

There are many slightly different approaches which use precedence relationships grouped together as network approaches. Critical Path

Method (CPM) will be discussed in this section, and in section 10.2 below the Program Evaluation and Review Technique (PERT) will be covered in detail, and section 10.3 below covers Precedence Diagrams and the complicated Graphical Evaluation and Review Technique (GERT) in outline.

### Scheduling with fixed times: Critical Path Method (CPM)

The critical path approach uses a network diagram to represent the project with the precedences indicated by a flow of arrows from left to right on the diagram (see figure 10.1). The longest path through the project is the 'critical path': the project can be finished no more quickly than these activities allow. Any delays on the critical path mean a delay for the whole project, while the other activities have some 'slack' or room for delay or movement.

The first use for the CPM technique is to identify the activities on the critical path and allow time and effort to be focused on them to make sure there are no delays.

The second use is to discover where the other activities have to be in the schedule.

**Figure 10.1:** Critical path method

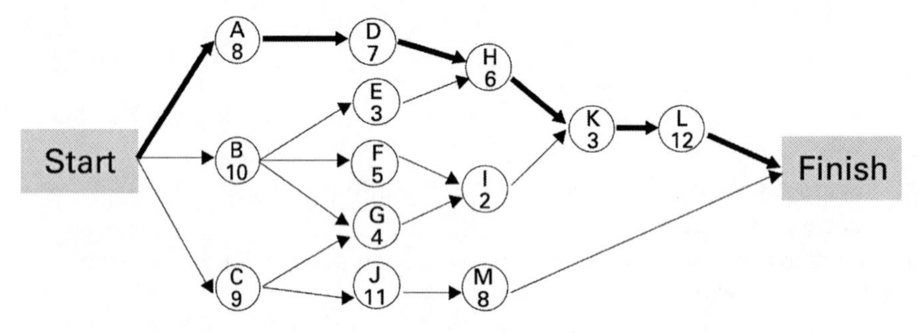


**Table 10.1** Estimating time of completion

| | Path | Length |
|---|---|---|
| 1 | A-D-H-K-L | 36** |
| 2 | B-E-H-K-L | 34 |
| 3 | B-F-I-K-L | 32 |
| 4 | B-G-I-K-L | 31 |
| 5 | C-G-I-K-L | 30 |
| 6 | C-J-M | 28 |

** The critical path is the longest path in the project

First the earliest start time (EST) for each activity is calculated through the network. From the first activity, work forwards adding the times for the activities. This gives the earliest possible start times (see figure 10.2). By working from the back and subtracting the times, the action is then repeated starting with the completion time of the last activity to give the latest start times (LST) of all the others. You may have noticed or realised that activities on the critical path have matching LST and EST times.

The approach can also be used to determine the 'float' of activities: the amount of slack time between having to start the activity and getting the project finished on time and the earliest possible time the activity could be started. This is useful for balancing the demand on resources without disturbing the total project time. Another useful piece of information which can be calculated using the CPM method is the early finish time (EFT), showing quickly if the activity is running late.

**Figure 10.2:** CPA: start and finish times

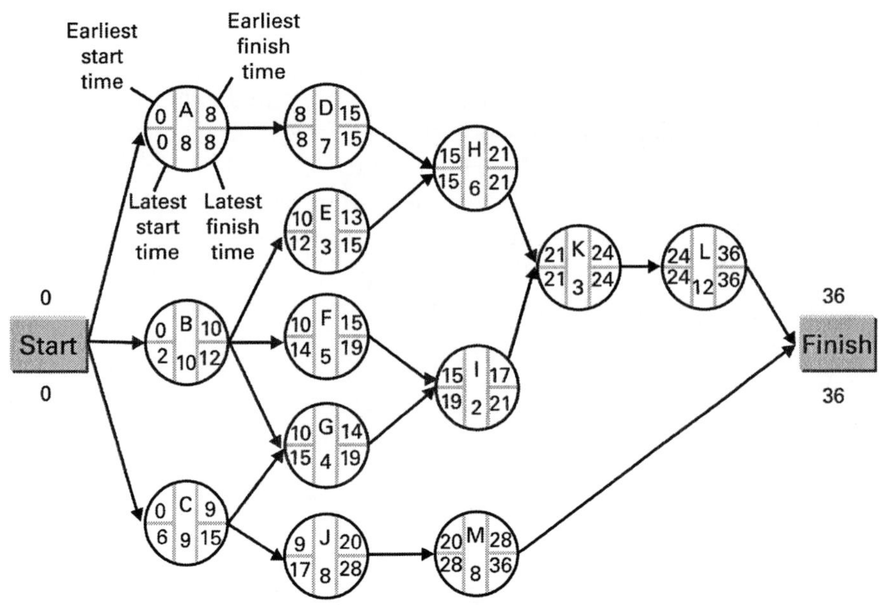


*Source: Adapted from Meredith and Mantel (2005)*

## Learning activity 10.1

To practice your skills in networking and understanding CPM, try the following question:

The AoA network in figure 10.3 was prepared at the beginning of a small construction project.

**Figure 10.3:** Sample network

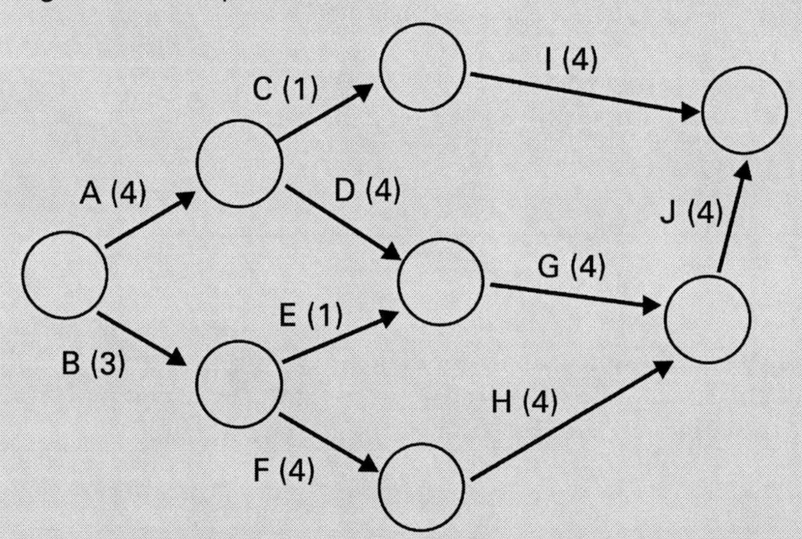


*(continued on next page)*

### Learning activity 10.1 *(continued)*

The duration, in days, follows the letter of each activity. What is the critical path? Which activities should be monitored most closely?

At the end of the first week of construction, it was noted that activity A was completed in 2.5 days, but activity B required 4.5 days. What impact does this have on the project? Are the same activities critical?

*Feedback on page 162*

## AOA and AON

An aspect of network approaches which is often presented is the nomenclature and rules of the network diagram. Essentially there are two approaches – activity on arrow (AOA) (see figure 10.4) and activity on node (AON) (see figure 10.5). These differ in the way the work element is represented, but all show the interaction or dependency of events with distinctions made between activities (things which need to be done), events (things which happen) and milestones (project tracking points or go-no go control points). There are some differences in use but these are small.

**Figure 10.4:** Activity on arrow network

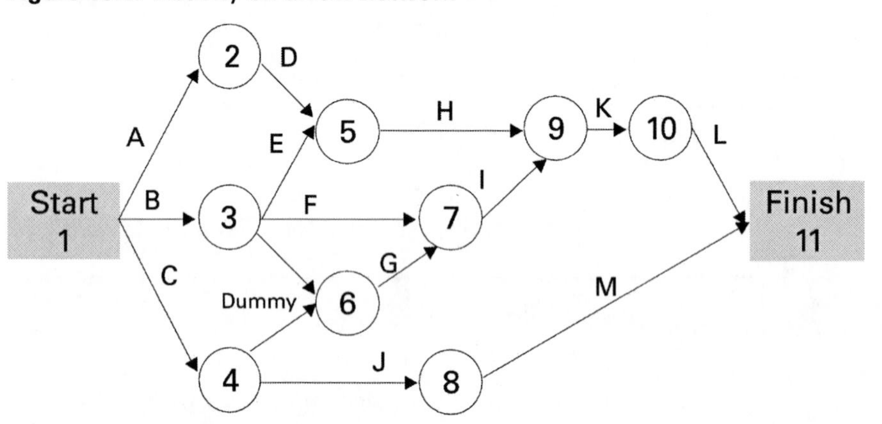


**Figure 10.5:** Activity on node network

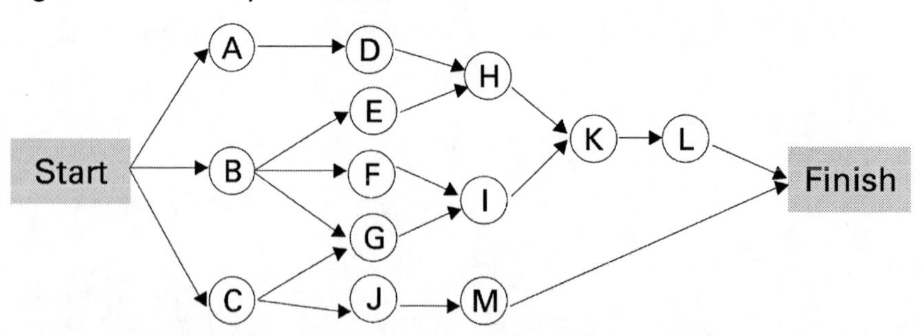


### Self-assessment question 10.1

How does the use of network analysis, for example CPA, help with the formation of project schedules? Write a 100-word recommendation for when to use them (in what situation) and what they should deliver.

*Feedback on page 162*

## 10.2 More complex time planning: Gantt, resources and uncertainty

Section 10.1 above introduced schedules and CPA as a form of network analysis. In this section, the use of Gantt charts and Project Evaluation Review Technique (PERT) is discussed.

### Gantt charts

Sometimes known as bar charts, Gantt charts are the simplest form of representing project timing and contain much information (see figure 10.6). With the great virtue of being easy to follow, they are useful as schedules, communication tools and for resource planning. They do not normally show precedence between activities, but that can be added (as in Microsoft Project) and are probably the single biggest aid to scheduling projects.

**Figure 10.6:** A very basic Gantt chart

| | Jan | Feb | Mar | Apr |
|---|---|---|---|---|
| Build the team | ■ | | | |
| Initial analysis | | ■ | | |
| Strategic analysis | | | ■ | |
| Agreed source plan | | | | ■ |

By introducing different colours and shading the critical path of the project, progress to date and criticality can also be clearly shown on a Gantt chart. Their big strength is that they can easily be extended to show the loading of resources – normally a table at the foot of the bar chart which uses the same time axis to show the demand on each type of resource available (see figure 10.7).

**Figure 10.7:** A Gantt chart with simple resource planning

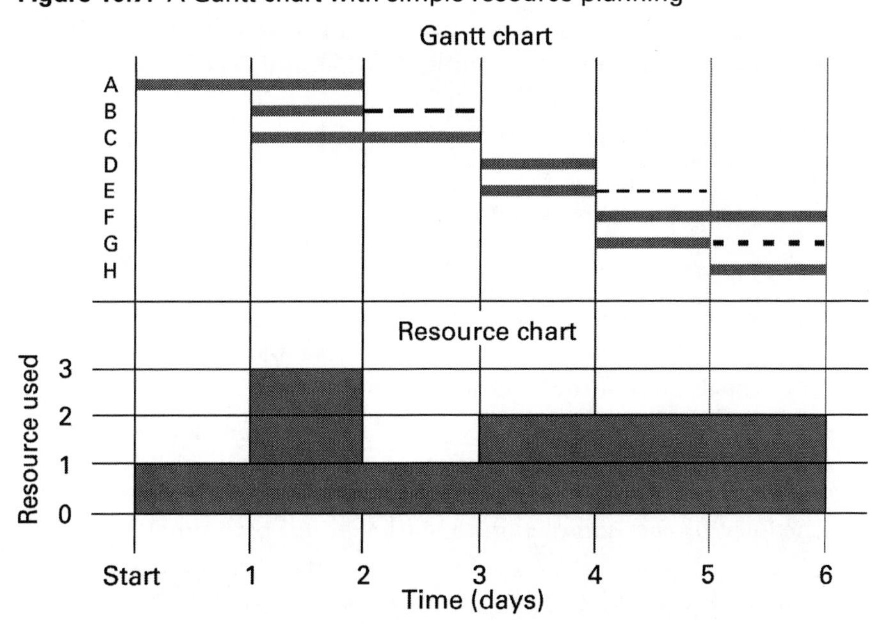

## PERT: adding uncertainty and complexity

PERT is similar to CPM in its approach – using a network and critical path. The key difference is that it incorporates uncertainty in how long an activity will take. Instead of using a fixed duration it relies on estimates of optimistic, most likely and pessimistic times. These are typically prepared by quantity surveyors in the building industry and by sampling the opinions of experienced managers or operators in other kinds of projects. The result is a richer picture of potential project timing and an assessment of how sure we can be about project timings.

The key approach uses a little statistics to predict what will happen and how likely this is, based on those estimates of likely, optimistic and pessimistic times. The important formulae to know are:

$$\text{Expected time} = \frac{\text{Optimistic Time} + 4 \times \text{Most Likely Time} + \text{PessimisticTime}}{6}$$

$$\text{Variance} = \left(\frac{\text{Pessimistic time - Optimistic time}}{6}\right)^2$$

The first is used to work out the expected times of the project elements and the project itself. The expected time of the critical path is just the sum of the expected times for the activities on it.



The second is used as a measure of how likely the calculated timings are. The variance of the whole project is the sum of the variances along the critical path.

Once the estimated time and variance have been found these measures can be used, in conjunction with simple normal distribution tables to answer some important questions. These questions include things like: how sure are we that the project will be finished in six months? By what date can we be 99% sure that the project will be completed?

Note: normal distribution information can be gained from Z tables or by using the Microsoft Excel functions NORMSDIST and NORMSINV.

To answer these questions we use one more formula:

$$Z = \frac{D - S}{\sqrt{V}}$$

Z = the number of standard deviations represented by the percentage probability we use (the figure found in the statistics table in the textbook: Cumulative Probabilities of the Normal Distribution)

D = desired project completion time

S = the scheduled project completion time (the critical path time)

V = the variance of the critical path

So, for example if we have a project with expected time of 43 days (S) and variance of the CP of 33 (V) and want to know how likely the project is to be finished in 50 days (D):

$$Z = \frac{50-43}{5.745} = 1.22\ s.d.$$

Using the table this is equivalent to a probability of 88.88% (or you can find the value using the Excel function NORMDIST. To identify the probability of getting a Z value of 1.22, use the function: '=NORMSDIST(1.22)' and you get the answer 0.888767562552165).

Similarly, if we want to know with 99% confidence the time to complete our project, then we apply the same formula in reverse. The Z value associated with 99% is 2.33 (from standard Z tables or using the Excel function: '=NORMSINV(0.99)', which gives the answer 2.32634787404084) then the formula becomes:

$$2.33 = \frac{x-43}{5.745}$$

$$\Rightarrow x = 43 + (2.33 \times 5.745) = 56.4\ days$$

## Learning activity 10.2

Given the estimated activity times and the network in table 10.2, what is the probability that the project will be completed within 21 days?

**Table 10.2**

| Activity | Optimistic time | Most likely time | Pessimistic time |
|---|---|---|---|
| A | 6 | 7 | 14 |
| B | 8 | 10 | 12 |
| C | 2 | 3 | 4 |
| D | 6 | 7 | 8 |
| E | 5 | 5.5 | 9 |
| F | 5 | 7 | 9 |
| G | 4 | 6 | 8 |
| H | 2.5 | 3 | 3.5 |

*Feedback on page 163*

## Using PERT

The various problems of time estimates were discussed in study session 6 while looking at Critical Chain. Time estimates are predictions and therefore inherently involve uncertainty. PERT introduces probability statistics to cope with this problem. By asking for estimates of optimistic and most likely as well as pessimistic, it is possible to make some assumptions and answer the questions discussed.

PERT can be useful where accurate assessments of likely times are available, but does not tackle the problems highlighted by Goldratt of buffered estimates and the tendency to take all the time available and more. If this tendency occurs in practice, a '99% certain' schedule used to reduce the chance of overrun would encourage each activity to take more time and extend the project, rather than reducing risk.

PERT is widely explained in project management texts, although use in practice may not be so widespread. There are few studies demonstrating emphatically that it is a major advance on CPA. Winch (1996) suggested that PERT was developed for the Polaris project not as a valuable project planning tool, but to provide an impressive time plan for the various clients. This may or may not be a fair analysis, but PERT has certainly lived on well beyond that beginning.

### Self-assessment question 10.2

Referring to the learning activity 10.2 above, what are the probabilities of completing the project within 22 and 25 days?

*Feedback on page 164*



## 10.3 Combining tools: GERT

### Learning activity 10.3

Consider a project with which you are familiar and determine which approach was used to scheduling and planning and why.

*Feedback on page 164*

There are many developments to improve Gantt and network techniques. Some of these reflect adaptations to deal with specific situations or contexts, many involve more flexibility in the scheduling approach to combat uncertainty. A good example is the application of fuzzy-set logic by McCahon (1993). Most focus on the uncertainty related to timing, few adapt to the more complex uncertainty: that different activities may or may not happen at all.

### Graphical Evaluation and Review Technique (GERT)

GERT follows the network approach of CPA and PERT but accepts that at certain points in a project there might be alternative ways of getting the job done. Different activities may be needed, for example a simple or a complex testing regime may be required and which is not certain at the start of the project. It can also accommodate loops, where some stages may have to be repeated.

The likelihood of each path or resource loading of activities being taken can be represented in the model. This means GERT combines signal flowgraph theory, probabilistic networks and CPM and decision trees into one framework.

The GERT contains logical nodes (decision points) and branches (with their probability of happening and associated duration).

The following example is adapted from Meredith and Mantel (2006) Chapter 8.

A part is manufactured on a production line in four hours. Following manufacture, parts are inspected. There is a 25% failure rate and failed parts must be reworked. Inspection time is one hour. Rework takes three hours and 30% of the reworked parts fail the next inspection and must be scrapped. The good parts are then subjected to finishing, after which an inspection determines that 80% are still good, and the rest must be scrapped.

The GERT diagram is shown and can be used to find out how many parts fail the system (figure 10.).

**Figure 10.8:** The GERT diagram

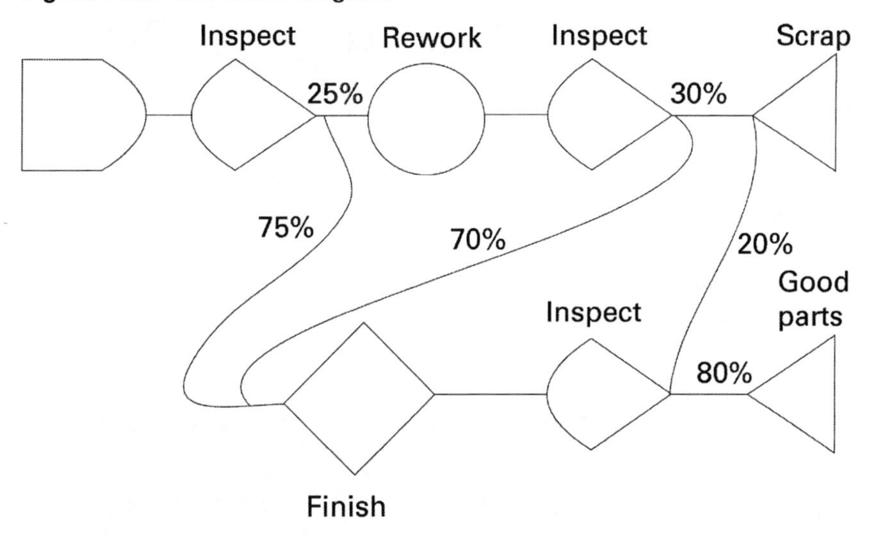


You can see that by working through the logic and probabilities, it is possible to find the total number of parts which go through the system as good and how long they take to make. Similarly, the same logic can help us determine the scrap rates and how long each piece of scrap takes to produce (how much we have spent on it).

## Using GERT analysis

GERT was developed for system design and typically used as in the example above, for repetitive activities such as production or processing orders, requests and service products. Branches and particularly feedback loops are very sensitive to the percentages used and those percentages are far easier to estimate for repetitive processes than projects with just one occurrence well in the future.

Where branches and probabilities are well understood and important to the timing, resourcing or cost of the project, GERT can offer a method of combining several factors into one analysis.

### Self-assessment question 10.3

Read the case called Yankee Chair Co. (adapted from Meredith and Mantel, 2005:429) and answer the question at the end.

Yankee Chair Company

The Yankee Chair Company is developing a new model rocking chair but new model introduction is not something which they had managed successfully. Bret Ricks, president of Yankee Chair, did not want the same disasters to happen again. Lacking confidence in his current management team, he recruited Jan Dymore, a local management consultant, to supervise the project. Tom Gort, a manager with Yankee, was set to work with Dymore to develop some project management skills in the company. Dymore set up a PERT network and taught Gort the steps of listing activities, assigning precedence and estimating completion times. She also showed the value of critical path analysis to Gort, who felt he knew now the project direction. At a review with Mr Ricks, the PERT approach was accepted keenly, but Dymore had made critical comments about the product design and so it was decide that she should leave the organisation.

Ricks had little option but to see if Gort could carry on the PERT study alone. Gort leapt at the chance, but later started questioning if he really could use PERT properly. Dymore had already identified what the critical path might be and the duration of the project, but Gort knew that other calculations were needed in order to calculate the exact time estimates for each activity and their variances. Gort felt that he really did not understand the maths involved and was worried he would appear incompetent to Ricks, so he decided to use Dymore's critical path guess and concentrate his attention on the duration of the critical path activities whilst ignoring their variance. Gort thought that was the only chance he had to deliver the project.

Questions: Will Gort's approach work? How much more of a gamble is Gort taking than any project manager normally takes? What should Gort watch out for?

*Feedback on page 164*

## 10.4 Resource planning with project networks

### Learning activity 10.4

Why are large fluctuations in the demands for particular resources undesirable?

*Feedback on page 164*

This section examines using network methods and Gantt charts in the management of time and resources to smooth loading and schedule to best effect.

### Crashing times and costs using CPM

One main development of using the CPM method is in determining trade-offs between total project time and the costs associated with project duration. If the cost and duration of an activity can be reduced by extra investment (either in labour, machines or other resource), and the cost of speeding up that activity is known, the CPM method allows the project manager to find the best balance between cost and total project time. This reduction in time is called 'crashing' and it is assumed that there is a clear relationship between doing an activity quicker and increasing costs.

Some terms used in this approach include the crash cost and crash time, crash being when the activity has been reduced to its minimum time and hence most expensive and so cannot be speeded up, no matter how much extra money is spent.

A common example is when cost penalties arise as projects exceed certain dates and the manager has to determine whether it is worth spending money on crashing the project or taking the penalty. Another example is in calculating the best use of the available resource to finish the project in a certain time.

As an example, Chapter 9 in the textbook has the following worked example.

Given the following network (time in days) (see figure 10.9 and table 10.5), find the lowest cost to complete the project in ten days.

**Figure 10.9:** Crash network example part 1

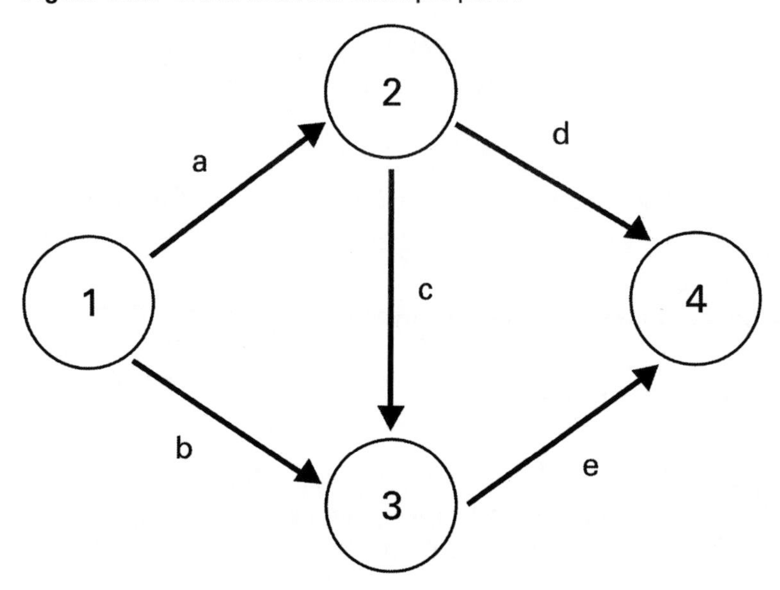


**Table 10.5** Crash network example table

| Activity | Crash time, cost | Normal time, cost | Partial crashing? |
|---|---|---|---|
| A | 3, $60 | 3, $60 | No |
| B | 6, $80 | 7, $30 | Yes |
| C | 2, $90 | 5, $50 | No |
| D | 5, $50 | 6, $30 | No |
| E | 2, $100 | 4, $40 | Yes |

Current time and cost: 12 days, $150.

**Figure 10.10:** Crash network example part 2

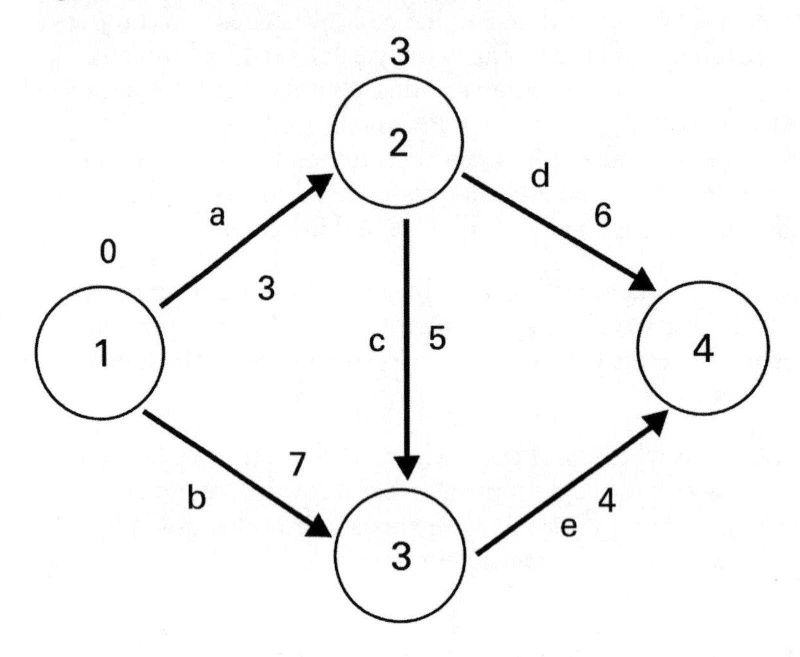




Since the critical path is A-C-E, we only initially need to consider these three activities:

A: Cannot be crashed

C: Can cut three days at an extra cost of $40 but only results in project completion by day 11, due to B. To reach ten days, cut B by one day, total extra cost $90.

E: Can cut E by two days for an extra cost of $60 and results in project completion by day 10.

Thus, the best solution is to cut E by two days at a cost of $60.

## Resource allocation with networks

We can modify the CPM and PERT networks to add information on the resources used in each activity, then we develop a means of showing and then balancing the resources across the projects. For example, figure 10.11 shows the PERT AoA diagram for a project. Underneath each activity arrow are the resources used of type A and B. As an example, activity A has a duration of four days, and uses four type A resource and 0 of type B.

**Figure 10.11:** PERT AoA diagram showing resources

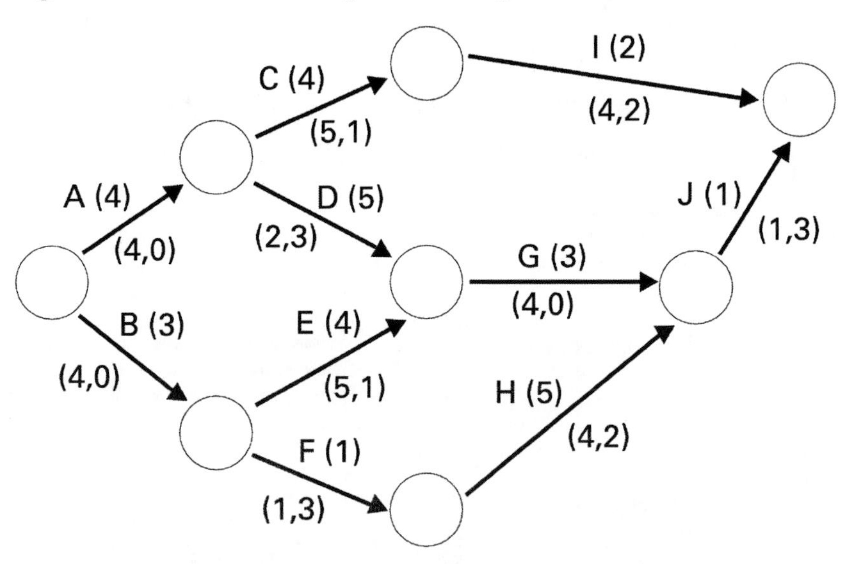


This can also be shown as a GANTT chart and a summary of the resource used on the same time scale (figure 10.12).

**Figure 10.12:** GANTT chart showing slack times and resource utilisation

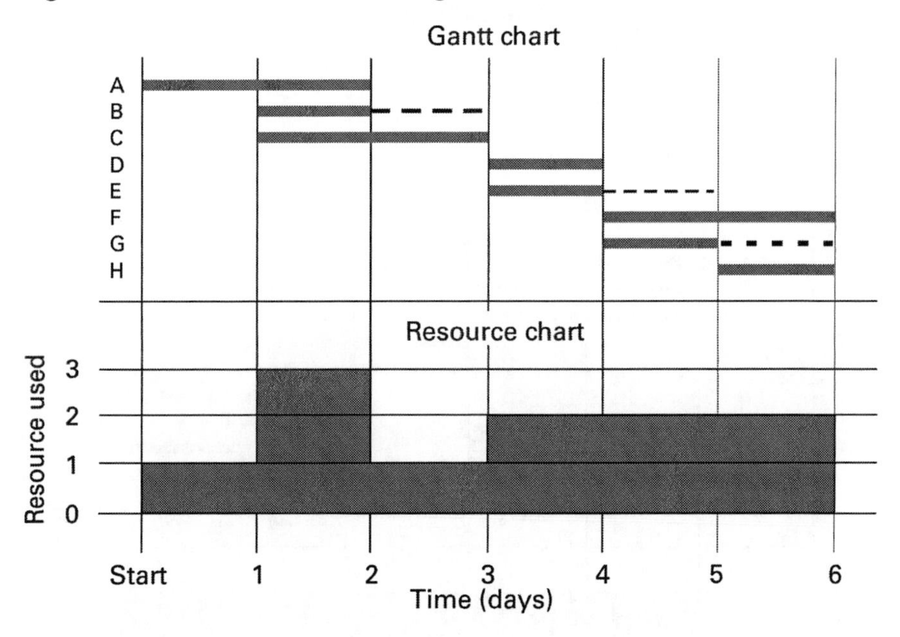


The load diagrams show the usage of the resources as the project develops, and some constraints can be easily identified.

## Resource levelling

The above example is based on resource allocation against earliest start times and so by examining the slack in the network, it may be possible to schedule the project activities so as to smooth the resource demand.

The following diagram (figure 10.13) shows the effect of this resource levelling on a simple project. By delaying the start time of activity B, the project can now be completed with a level resource usage with all the advantages this generates in terms of complex hiring and firing patterns of staff, problems with learning curves, and in this case we can actually manage the project with a fixed number of staff for its duration.

**Figure 10.13:** Resource levelling by moving activities within slack

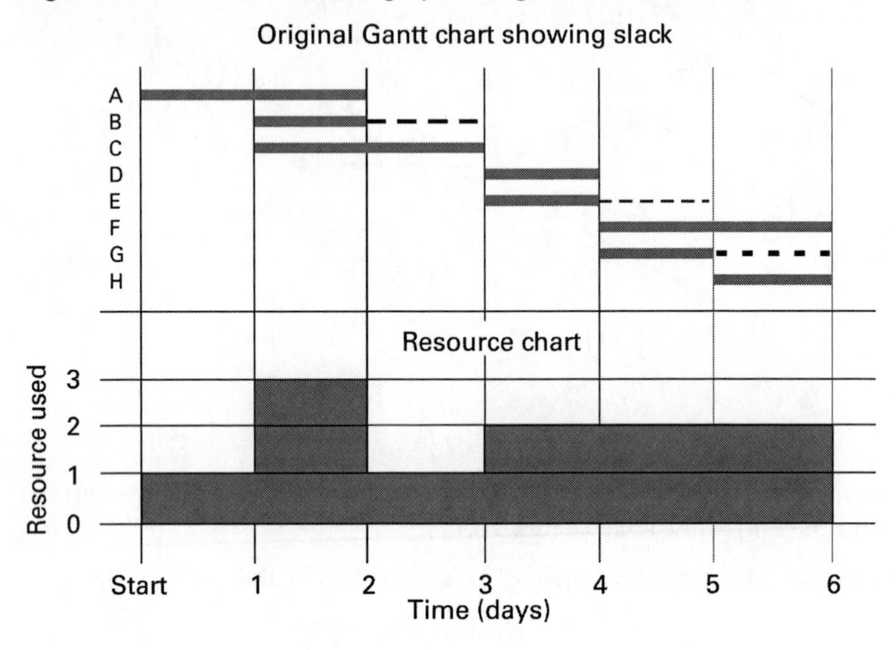


Gantt chart with balanced resources

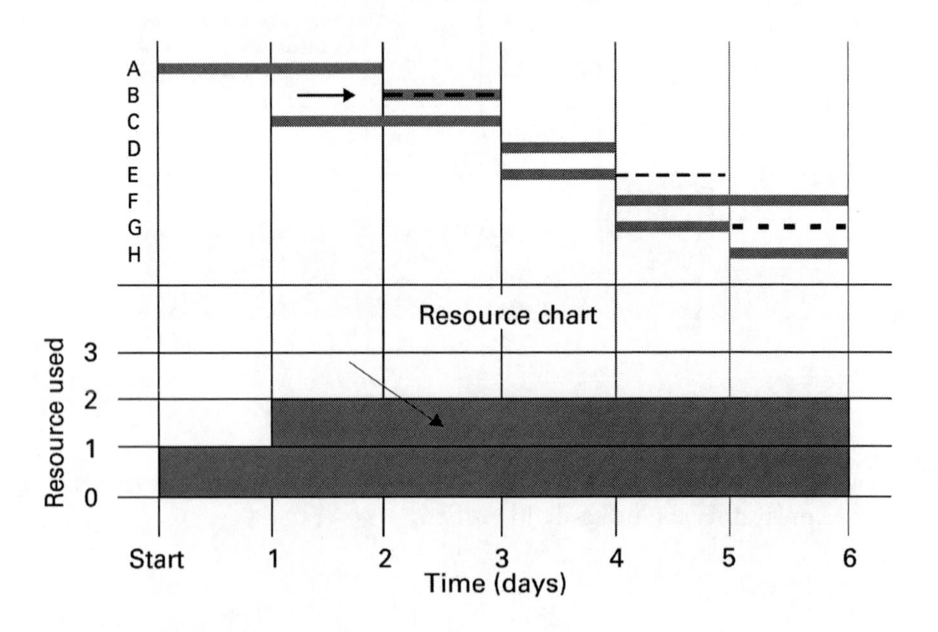




## Resource management

Managing resources and staffing is complex with many variables and potential solutions. Unfortunately the solutions rarely seem to align with the best use of resources in practice. Creating a schedule which offers the best trade-off between time, cost and other resources often takes several iterations and questioning some of the activities, precedences and requirements.

Network analysis and Gantt charts can help by demonstrating the impact on resources and timing simultaneously.

## Self-assessment question 10.4

If you have access to a copy, try to complete the sections of the following question using MS Project (a trial copy comes with the text book) or another software tool. If you are unable to gain access to software, you can work through the sections using the figures in the feedback sections below.

This question is taken from the set text, Meredith and Mantel (2006: 482).

The WBS and resources for a project to landscape a new building site are shown in table 10.6.

**Table 10.6** Landscape project details

| Activity | Immediate predecessor | Activity duration (days) | Resource used |
|---|---|---|---|
| A | – | 2 | X, Y |
| B | A | 2 | X |
| C | A | 3 | X |
| D | B, C | 4 | X, Y |
| E | D | 3 | W, X |
| F | D | 1 | W, X, Y |
| G | E, F | 2 | X, Y |

1 Draw a Gantt chart.
2 Find the critical path and project duration in days.
3 Given that each resource is assigned 100% to each task, identify the resource constraints.
4 Level the resources and determine the new project duration and critical path.
5 Identify what alternative solutions can be used to shorten the project duration and not over-allocate the resources.

*Feedback on page 165*

### Revision question

Now try the revision question for this session on page 320.

### Summary

This section looks at the issues around scheduling within project management. It is often a complex task and calls for intelligent use of different tools: CPA for complex networks of precedences, PERT where time uncertainty is key and possible to estimate, GERT where probabilities of different paths are important. Network analysis is not a scheduling tool, however, in that schedules are not the output. These will be expressed in a different form, lists of dates, milestones and deadlines or possibly the most useful, versatile and simplest scheduling tool: Gantt charts.

## Suggested further reading

A good place to read more on these techniques is Maylor (2005), which covers scheduling in Chapters 5 and 6.

For a further guide to more readings on these subjects, look at the recommended list at the end of the relevant chapter of Meredith and Mantel (2006).

Winch (1996).

## Feedback on learning activities and self-assessment questions

### Feedback on learning activity 10.1

The paths are:



ACI = 7 days

ADGJ = 13 days

BEGJ = 11 days

BFHJ = 10 days

Slack: Latest start – Earliest start, H = 3, and I = 6.

And so the critical path is ADGJ. These should be monitored closely, with special attention paid to GJ as these are the latter stages and may need to be coordinated as they form part of the other long path BEGJ. Any delay in starting G will delay the entire project.

In the second part, the critical path becomes BEGJ at 12.5 days as ADGJ is now expected to take 11.5 days.

### Feedback on self-assessment question 10.1

*What situation?*

Network analysis is based on the idea that with a lot (more than five, for example) of activities with precedence between them, it is useful to establish a network, so those are the criteria for when they could be useful.

Examples would be building projects, office moves, complex contract signing processes. Network analysis was developed for ‘hard’ projects and that is where it is most appropriate.

*Output/what it delivers*

In terms of output, the first thing to note is that network analysis does not produce a schedule.

- It identifies 'critical' activities: those that determine how fast the project can be done.
- It gives start and finish times for critical path activities, although a 'buffer' time could be added in the schedule which would change this.
- It gives earliest and latest dates for non-critical activities.
- It gives a visual impression of the order of activities, understandable to those familiar with network methods.

From this it is necessary to draw up a schedule: will buffers be added to the critical path? Which activities will be started as early as possible to reduce risk of overrun? Which activities will be started later to delay cash flow or manage resources?

## Feedback on learning activity 10.2

Calculate the expected time and variance of each activity (table 10.3).

**Table 10.3**

| | to | tm | tp | te | Variance |
|---|---|---|---|---|---|
| A | 6 | 7 | 14 | 8 | 1.778 |
| B | 8 | 10 | 12 | 10 | 0.444 |
| C | 2 | 3 | 4 | 3 | 0.111 |
| D | 6 | 7 | 8 | 7 | 0.111 |
| E | 5 | 5.5 | 9 | 6 | 0.444 |
| F | 5 | 7 | 9 | 7 | 0.444 |
| G | 4 | 6 | 8 | 6 | 0.444 |
| H | 2.5 | 3 | 3.5 | 3 | 0.028 |

Then apply these to the network to give the critical path time and variance (table 10.4).

**Table 10.4**

| | Exp | Variance | |
|---|---|---|---|
| a-d-g | 21 | 2.333 | |
| a-c-e-g | 23 | 2.778 | Critical path |
| a-c-f-h | 21 | 2.361 | |
| b-e-g | 22 | 1.333 | |
| b-f-h | 20 | 0.917 | |

$$Z=\frac{21-23}{\sqrt{2.778}}=\frac{-2}{1.667}=-1.199$$

From Z tables (or using excel =NORMSDIST(-1.1999)), the probability of the Z value -1.199 is 11%.

Note a zero value for Z has a probability of 0.5, and a negative value for Z shows that it has a probability of less than 0.5. Hence to find the answer above using tables, look up 1.19 in the table, and read off the value of 0.8830, but we require -1.199 and so this is given by 1-0.883 = 11.7%.

### Feedback on self-assessment question 10.2

$$Z = \frac{22-23}{\sqrt{2.778}} = \frac{-1}{1.667} = -0.599$$

From Z tables (or using excel =NORMSDIST(-0.599)), the probability of the Z value -0.599 is 27%.

$$Z = \frac{25-23}{\sqrt{2.778}} = \frac{2}{1.667} = 1.199$$

From Z tables (or using excel =NORMSDIST(1.199)), the probability of the Z value 1.199 is 88.5%.

### Feedback on learning activity 10.3

You will almost certainly have seen Gantt charts, and possibly CPM. Were these used because they are the best tools or because they are familiar? It is unlikely that you have come across GERT or even PERT unless you work in some specific aspect of supply industries, as these tools can be quite specialised and not normally in the project manager's tool kit. GERT combines different aspects of the project into one analysis and this session aims to give an overview of the potential benefits

### Feedback on self-assessment question 10.3

Gort seems to have missed the essential benefit of PERT – being able to assess the variability in finishing a project by a particular date. By ignoring the variance, he cannot assess how definite the estimate will be.

In answer to the direct questions, his approach might work but the likelihood is lower than if he were using PERT well. His gamble is potentially higher than if he had used the variance and there is a stronger potential for overruns.

Another worry could be the accuracy of the estimates. In many cases the estimation of the times for the PERT input is the most critical and takes much experience to get right to a degree which gives an appropriate and accurate answer, this experience is lacking.

### Feedback on learning activity 10.4

They generate variability for the project manager and make the managing of the project much more complex. Peak demands often need more staff than are available and so external sources are needed, and this creates its own set of problems and costs in terms of contract staff which cost more and require some extra training to get up to speed. The converse also applies in that if there are periods of little resource demand, the firm may still need to keep the staff employed, but is getting no return for the outlay.

## Feedback on self-assessment question 10.4

**Figure 10.14:** Gantt view from MS Project

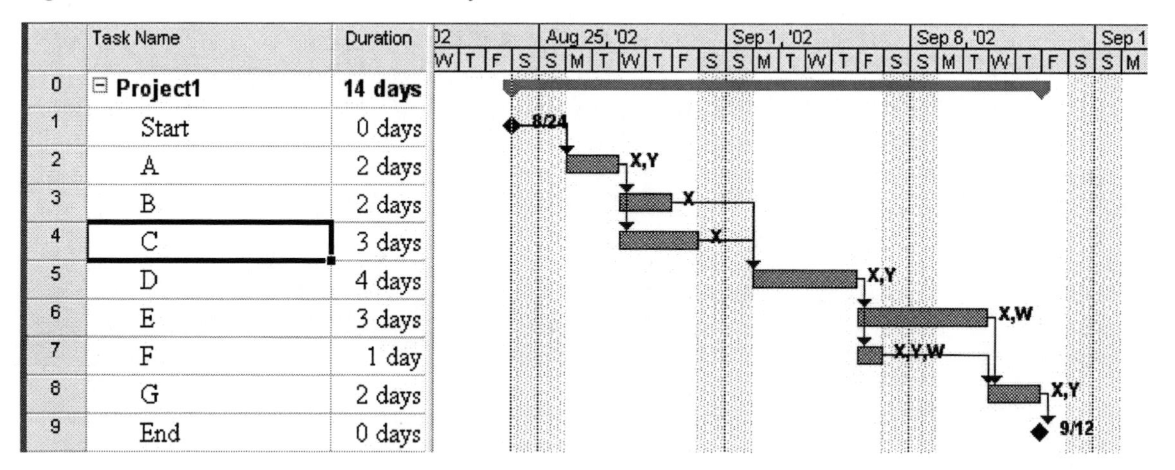


**Figure 10.15:** Tracking Gantt view from MS Project

| | Task Name | Duration |
|---|---|---|
| 0 | Project1 | **14 days** |
| 1 | Start | 0 days |
| 2 | A | 2 days |
| 3 | B | 2 days |
| 4 | C | 3 days |
| 5 | D | 4 days |
| 6 | E | 3 days |
| 7 | F | 1 day |
| 8 | G | 2 days |
| 9 | End | 0 days |

**Figure 10.16:** Resource usage view from MS Project

| | | Resource Name | Work | Details | M | T | W | T | F | S | S |
|---|---|---|---|---|---|---|---|---|---|---|---|
| | | Unassigned | 0 hrs | Work | | | | | | | |
| | | *Start* | *0 hrs* | Work | | | | | | | |
| | | *End* | *0 hrs* | Work | | | | | | | |
| 1 | ◈ | **X** | **136 hrs** | Work | 8h | 8h | 16h | 16h | 8h | | |
| | | *A* | *16 hrs* | Work | 8h | 8h | | | | | |
| | | *B* | *16 hrs* | Work | | | 8h | 8h | | | |
| | | *C* | *24 hrs* | Work | | | 8h | 8h | 8h | | |
| | | *D* | *32 hrs* | Work | | | | | | | |
| | | *E* | *24 hrs* | Work | | | | | | | |
| | | *F* | *8 hrs* | Work | | | | | | | |
| | | *G* | *16 hrs* | Work | | | | | | | |
| 2 | | Y | 72 hrs | Work | 8h | 8h | | | | | |
| 3 | ◈ | **W** | **32 hrs** | Work | | | | | | | |
| | | *E* | *24 hrs* | Work | | | | | | | |
| | | *F* | *8 hrs* | Work | | | | | | | |
| | | | | Work | | | | | | | |

In figure 10.16, resources X and W are highlighted in bold and the information column displays a warning sign (represented as an exclamation mark in a diamond). This means that the resources are over-allocated.

For the week displayed, resource X is scheduled to work 16 hours on Wednesday and Thursday. Since it is usually not a good idea to kill project resources by overworking them, the schedule should be adjusted to work within the available resource constraints.

**Figure 10.17:** Split screen view of a customised Gantt chart showing the critical path and assigned resources (top pane) and the Resource Histogram for resource X (bottom pane)

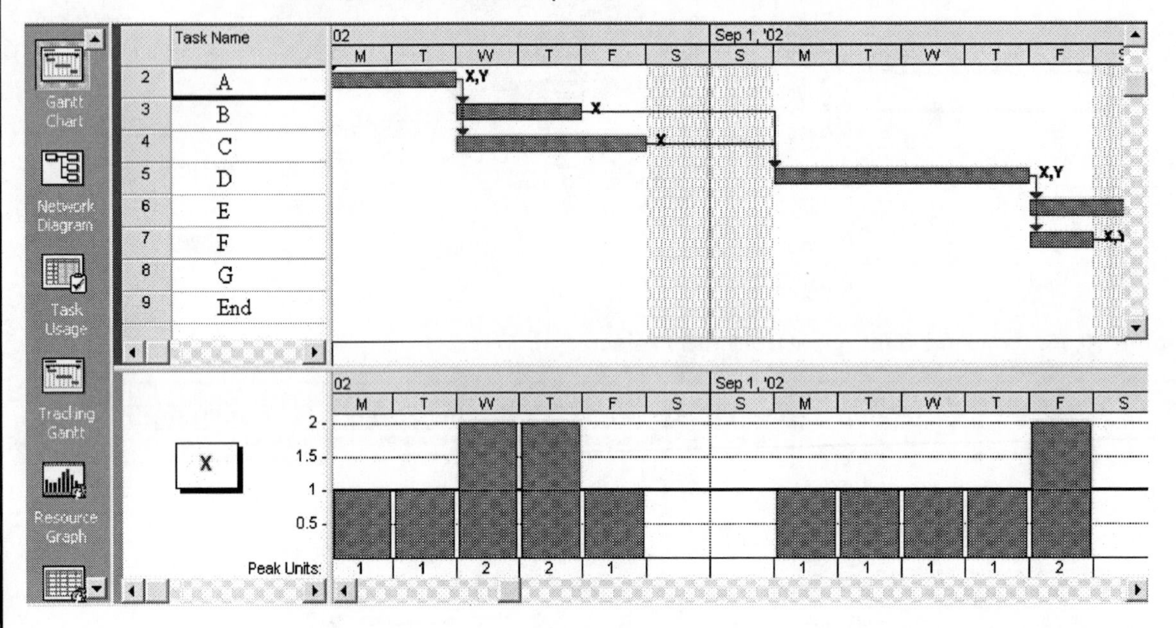




Using this view, we can see that resource X has been simultaneously assigned to critical task C and non-critical task B on Wednesday and Thursday. If another resource equivalent to resource X cannot be obtained, then Task B should be delayed to level the load on X to a normal workday. However, doing so will make task B delay critical path task D, which uses both X and Y as resources. Therefore, it may make more sense to perform task B prior to doing task C since task B is shorter. There are varieties of assumptions that can be used to level the load on a resource, so submitted answers may differ from the answer provided here.

Study session 11

# Organising the project for successful implementation

'Hell is other people.'
**Jean-Paul Sartre**
'Well, our task in life is to make it heaven. Or at least earth.'
**Alan Alda**

## Introduction

From the level of individual types and preferences, through team dynamics to the whole organisation, the people involved in the project hold sway over what works and what does not.

This session works from the organisation down to the individual looking at some of the factors that make a difference and the impact on project management. The first section looks at the impact of different organisational structures, the second at the way teams develop, the third at building teams from individuals.

Included here: how a project-based organisation structure can be a barrier to project success, how being invisible can make you a good leader and how the best people frequently do not make the best team.

## Session learning objectives

After completing this session you should be able to:

11.1 Evaluate the importance of structure on project management.
11.2 Explain life cycle of the team and how teams can be managed effectively.
11.3 Define team roles and assess their importance.

## Unit content coverage

This study session covers the following topic from the official CIPS unit content document.

### Learning objective

3.0 Develop and apply project management concepts, models, tools and techniques to create solutions to a range of practical project management problems.

3.1.3 Organisation and implementation
- Determine personnel needs
- Recruit project manager
- Recruit project team
- Organise team
- Assign work packages

3.2 Appraise the range of tools and techniques available to the project team in terms of appropriateness, selection and implementation.

- Appropriateness. Pick the right tools for the task
- Selection. Be aware of the limitations of tools and techniques
- Implementation. Be able to use the tools correctly

## Prior knowledge

Study sessions 1 – 10. The Management in the Purchasing Function module will provide a useful foundation to this session.

## Timing

You should set aside about 6 hours to read and complete this session, including learning activities, self-assessment questions, the suggested reading (if any) from the essential textbook for this unit and the revision question.

## 11.1 The big picture: structure

### Scenario A

Imagine an organisation where every employee has a clear and comprehensive functional role. Every day the finance people have a full day of work dealing with the financial management and control of the business, the marketing staff have a full day of work fulfilling customers' needs, and operations staff have a full day of work managing the delivery of products to those customers. Every employee reports solely to their functional manager: finance to head of finance, marketing to head of marketing. The roles and responsibilities are clear, loyalty and routes to promotion are likely to be well defined. This is perhaps the ideal bureaucracy identified by Weber (1947). A project trying to drive change in this organisation, relying on work by staff from those functions, may struggle.



### Scenario B

Imagine a different organisation, in which projects are all the work people do. Every employee reports to their project manager and their day's work is devoted to the project. There is no direct reporting to the head of marketing by marketing specialists, in fact the head of marketing's role will focus on policies and cross-project activities. In this scenario, a project will fit very neatly, alongside all the others. Unfortunately the loyalty, routes to promotion and other factors so clear in the first scenario now seem more blurred.

### Learning activity 11.1

Identify which of the above structures your current organisation, or one with which you are familiar, most closely resembles. Discuss whether the structure forms a barrier or support to project success.

*Feedback on page 178*

The structure of an organisation has a very strong effect on how individuals behave and how the organisation as a whole behaves. This has been studied at length and in some depth. The most important division to be examined here is the split between project and functional organisations and structures in between.

Scenario A describes the functional organisation: each member of staff in a functional group. This gives great flexibility in theory (staff can work on any activity without being reassigned) and helps to foster strong functional development (policy and best practice can be spread quickly). A project must cut across these boundaries, drawing some resource from each area (see figure 11.1). This becomes particularly problematic where the project passes from function to function: first marketing, then development then production, for example. At each boundary there is likely to be friction and loss of clarity, while the whole functional 'pass the parcel' where the project is passed on to the next department introduces delays and time lags.

**Figure 11.1:** A stylised diagram of a functional organisation

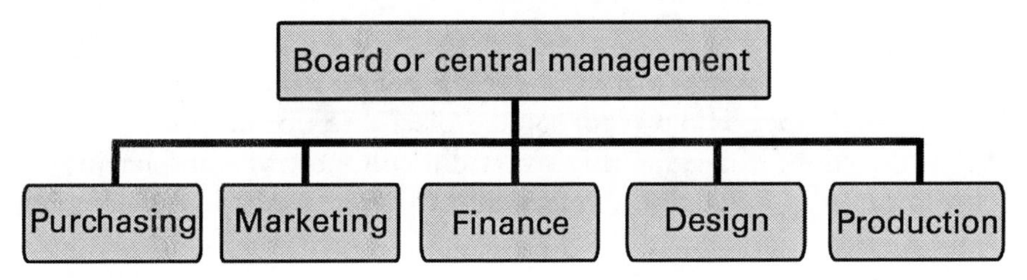


Scenario B describes the 'pure project' organisation: each member of staff in a project. This gives far better alignment with the project, but naturally loses some of the functional advantages of strength and theoretical flexibility compared to A. Projects which follow the standard type do not have the problem of cutting across functional boundaries. There are of course problems with this, not least the mobility of staff: having to switch from project to project, and the difficulty of managing workloads of individuals. The last and most surprising drawback is that projects which do not follow the standard type still have boundary problems: a project to improve procurement in a project engineering company has to work across many projects (see figure 11.2).

**Figure 11.2:** The pure project organisation

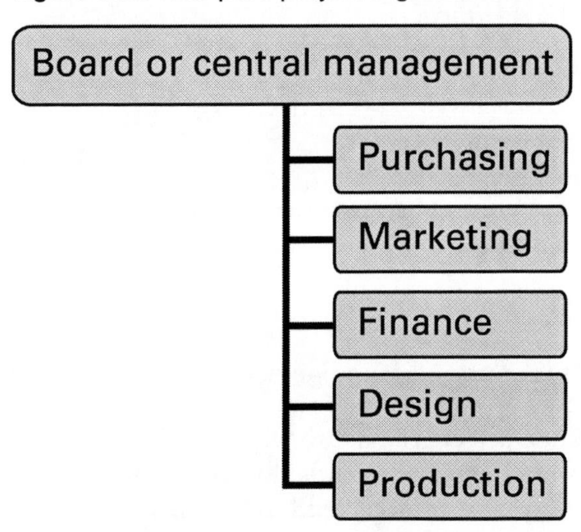

In reality, most organisations use a mix of the two. A matrix of some sort (see figure 11.3) or a project function next to the other functions (see figure 11.3).

**Figure 11.3:** The matrix organisation

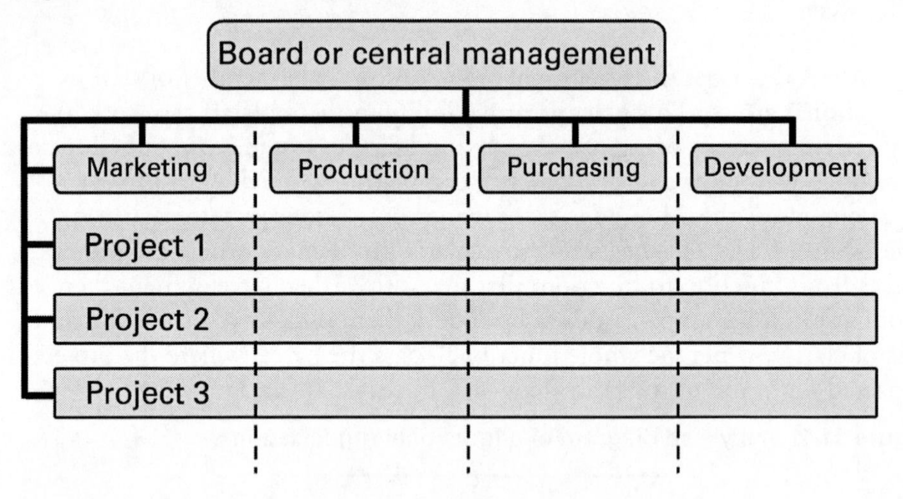


The matrix organisation can offer a mix of the benefits and problems of the two 'pure' types. It allows for some project direction with some functional direction. Managing this is very difficult, however, and having multiple loyalties and direction can lead to confusion in decision making for individuals or groups.

**Figure 11.4:** The mixed organisation

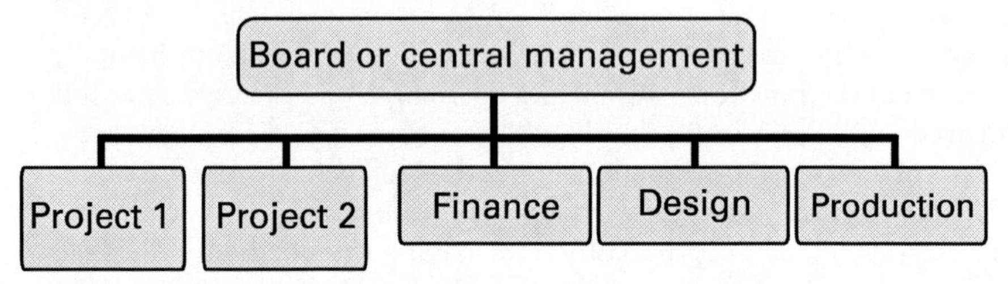


The mixed organisation separates a project from the functional departments. This again mixes the benefits with one further aspect: being selected for the project can be seen as 'a place in the sun' or a punishment. Those selected to lead special projects can be a mix of the unmanageable, the rising stars and the incompetents who need to be sidelined.

## The structure of the project

Projects can be defined as temporary organisations:

> 'a combination of human and non human resources pulled together into a temporary organisation to achieve a specified purpose'.
>
> Cleland and Kerzner (1985)

This gives three useful viewpoints on the organisation needed:

1 As a temporary organisation, a project can use the same structures as any other organisation and has the same potential for the problems described above. By definition most projects tend to be small

organisations and frequently use a fairly flat structure by default or design. A tall hierarchy takes resources and time to develop. This helps to enhance delegation, empowerment and teamwork.

2 Developing a new organisation within another is likely to be painful and occasionally difficult. This helps to explain some of the problems of developing a project team.

3 The project manager is effectively the chief executive of the new organisation. This extends the role beyond simply managing time plans and directing activities to one of active, strategic, leadership (Turner 2003).

### Self-assessment question 11.1

Using two different structures taken from those described in this section, evaluate benefits and problems of applying them to a project.

*Feedback on page 179*

## 11.2 Teams: the way to win or lose

For the vast majority of projects, success results from team work. Teams of apparently mismatched and under-skilled people with indifferent project planning can outshine teams of high fliers. Even projects which seem to rely on one person generally involve teams: when Ellen MacArthur broke the solo record for sailing round the world, she claimed it was entirely a team effort. Graham Wylie, founder of Sage software, added to the list of successful leaders when he explained that his achievements were due to 'a great team around me' (*Northern Echo*, 7 June 2005). Teams can work beyond anything that seems possible, or obstruct and slow progress until the project fails.

Within projects, the challenge of team building is even greater than in line management. Teams are temporary and must be created and disbanded, team members are frequently part time and difficult to bond. Strangely, books on project management tend to deal with teams briefly and superficially, but there are a few books which centre on the team (Obeng, 1996; Boddy, 2001). There is a wealth of more general information available on the development of teams. From the inspirational (Adair, 1987) through the minimally practical (Blanchard, 2000) to the theoretically centred (Salas and Fiore, 2004).

The team in a project can extend to many hundreds of people involved, the whole organisation of the project. Some sources divide up the visible or core team: those working for the project from the invisible team, those involved and supporting but not part of the core team.

This section and section 11.3 below will focus on the core team of the project, the small group of people who drive the activity of the project. Usually between three and ten people, they will meet regularly and be responsible for the project overall, with different roles and areas of the project split between them. They can be full time on the project, but for many purchasing projects most will be part time.

### Learning activity 11.2

Keep a log of the next team you are involved in. Record behaviour and attitude, including your own, as reliably and independently as possible. Compare and evaluate the team development against a model of team life cycle or development.

*Feedback on page 179*

### Team development

One of the easiest ways to get to grips with team development is to look at their life cycle or stages of development. When a group of people come together for the first time for a project meeting, they can hardly be described as a team, perhaps excited or resentful, unlikely to know the other people in the room well. Looking at that team a few months later, bonded and linked by something invisible, their behaviour, attitudes and output will have radically changed. The stages between those two situations vary but seem to follow similar patterns. Through understanding those, it is easier to support and guide development.

### The 'orming' model

A simple and very accessible model was developed by Tuckman (1965) based on extensive research. This breaks down team development into four stages: *Forming Storming Norming* and *Performing*.

- *Forming* is the stage when the group first comes together, with mixed ideas, feelings such as fear excitement or resentment. They are dependent on a leader and each other to help identify the way ahead and test the boundaries and standards they need to work to and the other people in the group. By trying different tasks, methods and ways of working with each other, some basis for the team is built up. Little work is done.
- *Storming* follows, where people focus on interpersonal issues and position in the group. Emotions begin to come into the open and can dominate the work. Small groups or factions may form and work together only with friction and difficulty. Work output remains very low.
- When new roles and ways of working emerge and individuals develop more cohesion with each other, the stage is called *Norming*. People work together well understanding and adapting to each other with more flexibility. Confidence in each other increases and so does output.
- If the team continues to develop, *Performing* is reached. This is where the group structures itself around tasks and work together almost automatically, distributing tasks and collaborating without direction, channelling energy into the work. Output can be very high, team loyalty and cohesion are also likely to be strong. This is not always reached and is not necessary to get good output from a team.

Moving between stages is not automatic and teams can fall back to earlier stages, for example when membership changes. To encourage development, effective leadership is vital. Leadership also needs to be very different at each stage. At first, involving, inspiring and informing are important. Once development moves into storming, the team needs are different. Conflict resolution, direction and commitment are far more important. Once the team reaches norming, a lighter touch is more useful. At this stage, leadership becomes more about coordination and direction setting than management of the team. This is even more apparent if the team reaches performing. Strong leadership would interfere in the team dynamic and probably cause resentment and a move towards forming. Leadership here can be almost invisible, working more by exception and focusing on the direction-setting role.

### Does Tuckman's model work?

This is a very accessible model and 'feels' right to many people. On the other hand, horoscopes fulfil those criteria, so the question remains: does it work? This model and the idea of stages in team development have been criticised, for example there is no clear division between stages and the variety of possible stages is nearly infinite. Perhaps the best measures are that the model is still very widely used and many have developed and built on it, frequently using very similar stages with different names. For all the criticism, the model and the idea of stages seem a valuable way of understanding, predicting and dealing with team development.

### Maylor's model



Maylor (2003) follows Tuckman with a model for the life cycle of teams, involving six stages. This is apparently not based on research or other work, but is aimed at teams within projects. The first four stages are similar to Tuckman's with the addition of *Decline* and *Break-up* as the fifth and sixth (see table 11.1).

**Table 11.1** Maylor's team life cycle

| Stage | Characteristics |
|---|---|
| Collection | The team come together with eagerness and enthusiasm and rely on the authority and hierarchy to define what is expected of them. |
| Entrenchment | Due to preconceived ideas and inflexibility on the way to proceed, agreement is difficult. Disillusionment with the project goals, competition for power and attention and confusion mean little work is done. |
| Resolution/ Accommodation | Negative social effects are put aside, disagreements are resolved, the team starts to work together. |
| Synergy | This is where the output of the whole is greater than the sum of the parts. (Here Maylor refers back to the idea of strategic organisational synergy but there are many other descriptions of this phenomenon in teams, where the team works together so effectively it far surpasses what the individuals could achieve separately.) |
| Decline | 'At some point the team will meet an event when its effectiveness starts to decline – this can be through the nature of the task...not changing, or the focus...being allowed to move towards a social group.' Or perhaps people leaving, irreconcilable arguments or the end of the project. |
| Break-up | At some point, the team must end. |

While the focus on projects is useful, the additional stages appear simply to identify that teams can decline and will inevitably come to an end.

### Implications of the models.

The models cannot direct how teams should be managed, but perhaps their greatest value is in suggesting what behaviour might be expected, leaving the more complex role of managing that behaviour to you (see table 11.2).

**Table 11.2** Typical behaviour at different stages

| Stage | Typical behaviour |
|---|---|
| Forming/Collection | Attempting to define the project, current important tasks and what behaviour is acceptable. Discussions on abstract or overarching aspects of the project by some, while others resist this and focus on the immediate. Irrelevant discussions are common. Complaints about all the things that will obstruct or stop the project are likely. |
| Storming/Entrenchment | Competition and friction between people or small groups or factions. Arguments which have no core: the sides agree on the essentials, but argue apparently for the sake of it. Increasing questioning of the project, the leaders and the organisation. Complaints about workload with little useful output. |
| Norming/Resolution/ Accommodation | People use clear 'norms' or ways of working, whether stated or not. There is an effort to avoid conflict. Interpersonal behaviour is friendlier and more open, sharing personal confidences. A common view of goals, more cohesion and 'team spirit'. |
| Performing/Synergy | A really close attachment to the team, it is part of the members' identity. Friction or conflict is used constructively, with group problems avoided almost without effort or unconsciously. The team behaves as a unit in approaching new work, dividing and absorbing it very effectively. |
| Decline | This is effectively a return to storming, with the potential that new norms may not be reached. Friction, lack of commitment and competition will resurface. |
| Break-up | If the team is close and performing, anger, discomfort and uncertainty may provoke resistance and irrational behaviour. Otherwise team members focus on new roles and neglect any outstanding work. Some working or social relationships are maintained but most disappear. |



### Self-assessment question 11.2

Use your experience of teams and any research material to create your own list of 'Dos and Don'ts' for managing the forming and norming stages.

*Feedback on page 179*

## 11.3 People: the perfect mix

Understanding the development of teams is valuable, but each team is built up from a group of individuals. Another way of approaching the problem of building successful teams is to look at the make up or balance of people involved, their skills, strengths, weaknesses and knowledge.

It is very rare that a project manager has a free hand in selecting team members, so never expect a perfectly balanced team with exactly the right skills or attributes. The ideas in this section are intended to suggest ways of looking at team make-up so that mild problems can be allowed for, and severe imbalances can be corrected.

### Learning activity 11.3

You are about to lead a project in your organisation developing the relationship with your most important supplier. Without identifying individuals, suggest what skills, knowledge and types of people you need in your team to make it work well for this project.

*Feedback on page 179*

### Mixed backgrounds

Different departments or functions are a good way to identify team needs. Bringing different functions into the teams is one way of involving the core stakeholders and in learning activity 11.3 above the supplier is an example of this. The backgrounds of the people involved will have a strong impact on the way the project is seen. Winch (1996) uses the example of the Channel Tunnel. The project team for this transport link was dominated by civil engineers and had no one with experience of commissioning and running a railway system. As a result, the focus of the project became the civil engineering challenges of tunnelling, building, services, etc, neglecting the commissioning and handover of a working rail link.

### Mixed knowledge

It is useful to have knowledge and experience on the team. There are dangers that come with this. First, experience tends to mean the project will be done the same way as the last, using established practice. More damaging is where some of the project team with experience of partly similar projects drive the project and solutions in the same way: an expert in Supplier Relationship Management (SRM) will tend to drive towards a SRM solution, someone who has succeeded with e-auctions will lean towards using them each time. Team members with less experience are more open to different approaches and more ready to challenge accepted practice. The extreme of this is the 'useful idiot': someone who asks very basic questions and assumes nothing. In moderation this is very valuable as it will uncover large gaps in thinking or reasoning.

### Mixed power

While it is useful to have people from different levels in the organisation, this has to be carefully managed. The inclusion of a senior manager can lead to team members deferring in decision making and keeping quiet about problems or ideas. The aim should be to manage the team dynamic so that each member feels the value of their ideas, comments and input is as great as other team members.

### Mixed types

Different people have different strengths and weaknesses in their personality in the way they work in a team. Eleven star strikers does not make a good football team, in fact 11 stars can be very difficult to mould into a team at all. A team made up of excellent leaders is unlikely to have good leadership. Luckily people vary and the different types can interlink well. Different ways of identifying types are available, one of the most widespread and long lasting was developed by Belbin (1996 and many previous works). He used extensive study of successful and unsuccessful teams to identify nine team roles. It is possible to identify a dominant and secondary role for each individual through questionnaire: how they are likely to behave, what are their likely strengths and weaknesses.

**Table 11.3** Belbin's team roles

| | | |
|---|---|---|
| Plant | Creative, imaginative, unorthodox. Solves difficult problems. | Ignores incidentals. Too preoccupied to communicate effectively. |
| Coordinator | Mature, confident, a good chairperson. Clarifies goals, promotes decision making, delegates well. | Can often be seen as manipulative. Offloads personal work. |
| Monitor Evaluator | Sober, strategic and discerning. Sees all options. Judges accurately. | Lacks drive and ability to inspire others. |
| Implementer | Disciplined, reliable, conservative and efficient. Turns ideas into practical actions. | Somewhat inflexible. Slow to respond to new possibilities. |
| Completer Finisher | Painstaking, conscientious, anxious. Searches out errors and omissions. Delivers on time. | Inclined to worry unduly. Reluctant to delegate. |
| Resource Investigator | Extrovert, enthusiastic, communicative. Explores opportunities. Develops contacts. | Over-optimistic. Loses interest once initial enthusiasm has passed. |
| Shaper | Challenging, dynamic, thrives on pressure. The drive and courage to overcome obstacles. | Prone to provocation. Offends people's feelings. |
| Teamworker | Cooperative, mild, perceptive and diplomatic. Listens, builds, averts friction. | Indecisive in crunch situations. |
| Specialist | Single minded, self starting, dedicated. Provides knowledge and skills in rare supply. | Contributes only on a narrow front. Dwells on technicalities. |

### Using team roles

Whether Belbin's team roles or another way of understanding individuals' strengths and weaknesses are used, it is important to allow for and manage the mix of types. More effective still is self management, where team members are aware of their own and others' types, and work around them.

As a final note, Belbin identified several factors why teams succeed and fail; role make-up was just one of them and perhaps not the most important.

### Self-assessment question 11.3

Suggest the likely strengths and possible problems of the two teams below, described by their Belbin team roles:

1. a team of two coordinators, two shapers and a plant
2. a team of three team workers, a company worker and a completer finisher.

*Feedback on page 180*

### Revision question

Now try the revision question for this session on page 320.

### Summary

Throughout this book, soft or human factors have been identified as extremely important to projects. This session looked at a few of those.

Organisation is important in two ways: the organisation of the project itself and the organisation the project has to work within. There are extremes of functional and project organisations, most fall somewhere inbetween.

Understanding team development is extremely valuable as a project manager or as a team member. What works at the start – or forming – will damage a performing team, while the turbulence of storming is something to expect, watch and manage through to norming. Getting stuck in a storm is likely to lead the team to fall apart around you.

Moving to individuals, understanding the people in a team should help in working with them. There are different balances needed for the ideal, and nine generalised team roles to help. Be reassured that the best teams are often not the most experienced, the most high-flying or the most creative people alone.

### Suggested further reading

- Adair (1987).
- Belbin (1996).
- Blanchard et al (2000).
- Boddy (2001).
- Maylor (1996); Chapter 6.
- Meredith and Mantel (2006); Chapter 4.
- Salas and Fiore (2004).
- Tuckman (1965).

- Weber (1947).
- Winch (1996).

Articles from the *International Journal of Project Management* such as:

- Burgess and Turner (2000).
- Gray (2001).
- Johns (1995).
- Turner (2003).

## Feedback on learning activities and self-assessment questions

### Feedback on learning activity 11.1

Most organisations are a mixture of the two scenarios, more similar to Scenario A.

*Scenario A*: people are organised functionally. Banks, universities, hospitals and factories are typically organised this way. Getting resource from functions to work on projects can be difficult, and loyalty will remain largely with the function, both of which are barriers to success. In addition, the success of the project is unlikely to have a very clear link to an individual's career. Prestige and promotion will not come from project success. This may be even worse, where functional staff join a project to 'fight their corner' and ensure the function's perspective dominates.



More positive aspects include staff availability: in theory staff from any function are available to help at any time, not tied up in other projects. There is no reliance on a pool of labour which becomes available as it is released from other projects. Also, for smaller projects which would need a small proportion of one person from each function, this structure offers the flexibility to do so.

Finally, once mandated, the compliance to any change is likely to be fast. If there is a change which impacts on finance policy, it will spread through the department quickly.

*Scenario B*: people are organised around projects. This is typically used by consultants, engineers, construction companies, where projects are the product. If your organisation is more like this scenario, getting people to commit to projects will be easier. Loyalty should be stronger and 'fighting the corner' will be greatly reduced.

There are barriers, however. Where resource is needed beyond the project team, there may be difficulties locating and obtaining it. While loyalty may be strong for much of the project, towards the end, employees must look for their next role. Finally, there is the more complex problem of change projects. In an engineering company where projects are organised around contracts, a project to change the way the business works will need to work across project boundaries. This is no easier than working across functional boundaries.

## Feedback on self-assessment question 11.1

This question is about applying the structures above to a project, for example organising the people involved in the project in a project, functional, matrix or mixed structure.

The advantages and drawbacks of each largely follow those described, however the balance of benefit tilts away from functional structures as the temporary nature means that the stability and flexibility given by a functional structure are no longer so valuable. At the same time, demands on the project will change. A mixed structure, with some fixed support functions such as finance, combined with project teams able to switch between activities can be very successful.

## Feedback on learning activity 11.2

Reflecting on how the team developed is the valuable part of this exercise. The first point is, did the team develop or did it remain roughly the same over the time period? If you saw development, did it follow the model of team development? Was there one stage which was particularly difficult or valuable? What seemed to prompt movement from one stage to the next? Finally the timing. How long did each stage take? Were there any reasons you saw for the speed or slowness of development?

## Feedback on self-assessment question 11.2

Management styles differ, so the lists will vary widely from person to person. It is important that your do's and don'ts:

- Reflect the stage: accepting and coping with typical behaviour. A statement like 'Do insist all team members accept and commit to goals' for forming is ambitious when full commitment is unlikely until norming.
- Change with the stage: good management of forming will be less effective in storming.
- Avoid simply saying the opposite. For storming, 'Do accept conflict' is valid, 'Do not prevent conflict' is less so. A better 'do not' would be 'Do not allow conflict to cause long-term friction'.

## Feedback on learning activity 11.3

A more detailed discussion follows, of course, but there are several areas to ensure there is a mix:

- Do you have the right functional or technical knowledge? This often involves team members from a range of departments who understand the project from a number of angles. Who is on the team from the supplier?
- Do you have the right mix of experience? Ideally there will be strong knowledge balanced with the ability to challenge accepted practice.
- Do you have a mix of types? Ten people who are all excellent at generating ideas and no one who can carry them out may cause an imbalance.

- Do you have a team where one or two people are far more powerful than others?

## Feedback on self-assessment question 11.3

1. These are all defined by Belbin as 'extrovert' types and tend to be dominating types. There are plenty of people there to direct and create ideas, to add dynamism and drive, but no one to carry through the work. Sparks are likely to fly and there will be a need for discipline to gain real progress.
2. These are all 'introvert' types and very focused on the task. Breakthroughs and creative solutions are unlikely, but the work that is done will be done well and effectively.

Study session 12

# Achieving your goals: monitoring and control

'You don't always get what you want, but if you try sometimes, you might just get what you need.' Measuring, monitoring and control: the ways of making sure you get what you need.

## Introduction

It is sometimes said that you get what you measure: if you measure output, that increases at the expense of quality, if you measure quality, cost rises. Measurement is critical in all management but has peculiar challenges in project management, with the temporary and undefined, changing requirements. This session looks at the need, the barriers and the practicalities of monitoring and control, from established practice to some suggestions for the future.

## Session learning objectives

After completing this session you should be able to:

12.1 Explain the role and importance of monitoring and information systems.
12.2 Outline the reporting process and identify the most common problems with reporting.
12.3 Explain key methods of measuring and controlling overall project performance; earned value charting.
12.4 Evaluate different types and purpose of control processes.

12

## Unit content coverage

This study session covers the following topic from the official CIPS unit content document.

### Learning objective

3.0 Develop and apply project management concepts, models, tools and techniques to create solutions to a range of practical project management problems.

3.1.4 Measurement, monitoring, control and improvement
- Define management style
- Establish control tools
- Prepare status report
- Review project schedule
- Issue change orders

3.2 Appraise the range of tools and techniques available to the project team in terms of appropriateness, selection and implementation.

- Appropriateness. Pick the right tools for the task
- Selection. Be aware of the limitations of tools and techniques
- Implementation. Be able to use the tools correctly

3.3 Utilise a range of tools and techniques to assist in robust and systematic data collection, analysis of options and decision making.
- SIPOC
- 7 tools of quality control
- Financial appraisal
- Voice of the customer
- Quality function deployment
- Project initiation document (PID)
- Moments of truth
- Work breakdown structure
- Critical path analysis. Network diagrams
- Risk analysis and assessment. Mitigating risks
- Risk/Impact matrix
- Suitability/feasibility/vulnerability

## Prior knowledge

Study sessions 1 – 11. Operations Management in the Supply Chain will also provide a useful foundation.

## Timing



You should set aside about 7 hours to read and complete this session, including learning activities, self-assessment questions, the suggested reading (if any) from the essential textbook for this unit and the revision question.

## 12.1 Measurements are difficult and inaccurate, so why bother?

Monitoring and information systems are about measuring aspects of the project and passing those measurements on in some way. There is an old saying that ' you can't manage what you can't measure', so comprehensive and effective measurement for the project seems beyond question. Most situations are not that simple, unfortunately.

### Reasons not to measure

The first problem with measurement is that it is expensive. Collecting and analysing data takes time and effort which could be spent on the activities of the project. The effort spent measuring how many people are using a new system could be diverted to training or other 'value add' activities. For the client, a simple view would be that all measurement activity is non-value-added activity.

The next problem is that getting effective measurement is frequently difficult. How do you monitor the number of people using a new system?

How many have logged on, how many use it every day, how many find it really useful or how many intend to use it in the future?

Finally, people can resent being monitored. Having to report what you have done or even worse, being watched as you do it, can be seen as a challenge to competence, loyalty and professionalism. Although almost everyone is monitored in some way at work, there are real dangers involved in measuring any activity, even more so for measuring the contribution to a project which is outside the main role.

### Learning activity 12.1

In around 200 words, suggest ways in which a monitoring system can impact on the motivation of project team members.

*Feedback on page 196*

In spite of the difficulties discussed, monitoring and reporting in different forms are a core part of project management. The feedback on the learning activity points towards the potential value for motivation, but there is also the need for measurement to direct action and to reassure. Meredith and Mantel (2006) suggest 'The job of the PM is to set controls that will encourage those behaviours and results that are deemed desirable and discourage those that are not.' This is easier said than done, of course, and driving behaviour through measurement is a complex and subtle subject. There are three main groups who benefit from monitoring and reporting: the clients, the project management and the people working on the project: the team and others.



### The clients

The obvious requirement the clients have is to monitor the project and make informed decisions on changes to schedule, output, activity or direction. The reports from the project should provide an overview alongside detailed information where decisions are needed. The second and perhaps more important requirement is to reassure the client (and other stakeholders) that the project is well managed and progressing satisfactorily. This reassurance can make the difference between a project seen as a running problem and a success, and could prevent an uncertain client taking dramatic action. The development of PERT was not driven by a need to manage projects better, but to reassure a demanding client that the very expensive and risky Polaris project was well managed (Winch 1996). Historically, clients often rely on the project management for information. The division between a client paying and the project manager delivering leads to a rather passive role. An active role in monitoring can be seen as interfering, but it is likely to support a successful outcome.

### The project management

The needs of the project manager are similar to the client: to be reassured that things are going well and to make decisions on work, schedule, resources and changes. The information needed is far more detailed, of course, while the responsibility for gathering data and analysing it generally rests here. Understanding current progress, costs, commitments and activity are key, then using that information to project forwards the impact on the project. In addition, some way of monitoring the 'soft' factors is very valuable but commensurately difficult. It may not be true that you cannot manage what you cannot measure, but measurements help decision making enormously.

### The people working on the project

Keeping the team and others in the dark is usually a recipe for disaster. The cathedral in Florence has a dome that was revolutionary when built and impressive even now. There is a story that while it was being built, no one could understand the plans of the architect Brunelleschi, so he gave the stonemasons instructions day by day, with only enough information to complete that day's work and no information on progress beyond what they could see. The results are stunning. Most purchasing and supply chain projects, however, do not involve such revolutionary ideas. Measurement, monitoring and feedback to the people involved are vital to motivation (as discussed in the learning activity) and direction. Unless there are compelling reasons, the people completing each part of the project are likely to work more effectively and with more commitment if they can see progress, momentum and their part in the whole. Their fundamental needs are just the same: to be reassured that progress is good (their own and the project as a whole) and to have information to make decisions. As a simple example, someone who can see their work is late and holding up the rest of the project can take action. The same person, with a full desk and no understanding except that the project work adds to their load, is less likely to act early.



### Summary

Monitoring and information systems must strike a balance between the cost of use and the benefit, and that balance is biased towards simple, acceptable, well-planned measures. There is a need for monitoring to be as accurate as is feasible and timely. The project manager should avoid being surprised by unexpected results and cannot afford senior management to be surprised in turn, by limited, slow or inaccurate reporting.

### Self-assessment question 12.1

Devise a checklist for assessing the suitability of a project management information systems software package for a particular project. Use the information in this section alongside the elements you think are important from your knowledge and judgement. There is further information in Meredith and Mantel (2006: 520–24).

*Feedback on page 197*

## 12.2 The challenge of reporting

Section 12.1 above looked at the need for monitoring and reporting, identifying three general groups who need the information: clients, project management and people working on the project. This section will look at how reporting can work between those groups and some of the barriers.

### Reporting structures 1

The idea of a project as the activity of delivering objectives for the client in terms of cost, quality and time, coordinated by the project manager, leads to a vision of the project as in figure 12.1. The project manager is responsible for planning and passing instructions to the team and others working on the project, then measuring progress in terms of timing, quality and cost against budget. From this data, the project manager can generate reports for the client. Accepting that there will almost always be changes, the project manager is responsible for identifying change needs from the project and negotiating them with clients, while the client presents changed needs to the project manager for discussion or inclusion.

**Figure 12.1:** A simple reporting structure

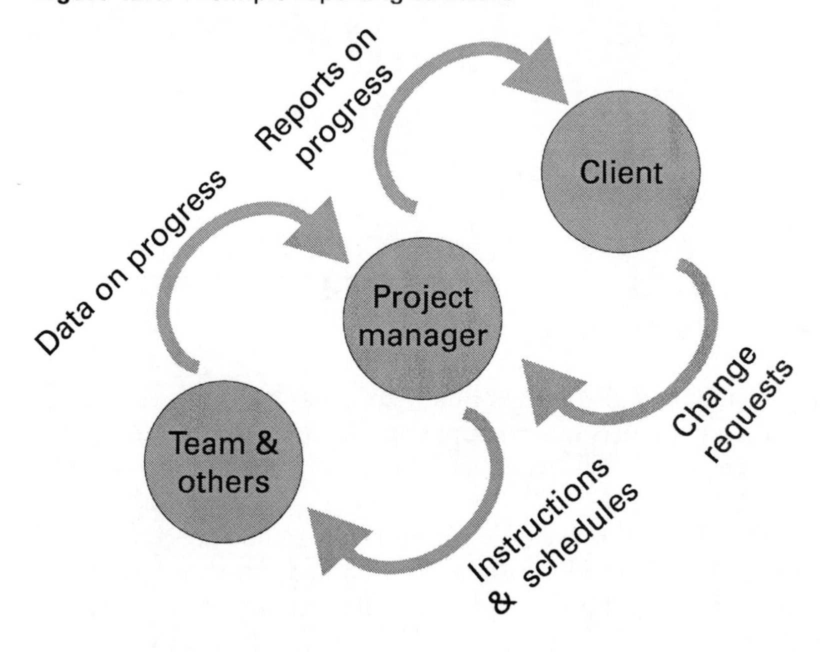


### Reporting structures 2

If the project is seen as a temporary organisation, the reporting structure and information needs are slightly different, as shown in figure 12.2. The responsibility of the project manager is longer term and leaning more towards leadership, hence the information needs to incorporate measures beyond the basic three, to look at organisational effectiveness, morale, etc. The roles also change: the team becomes more responsible for measurement and reporting, while the client responsibility shifts slightly from requiring reports on conformance of outputs to having oversight of an organisation – the direction and health of the organisation. The responsibility of the client extends at the same time, from passively requiring reports to a more active oversight role.

**Figure 12.2:** More complex reporting demands

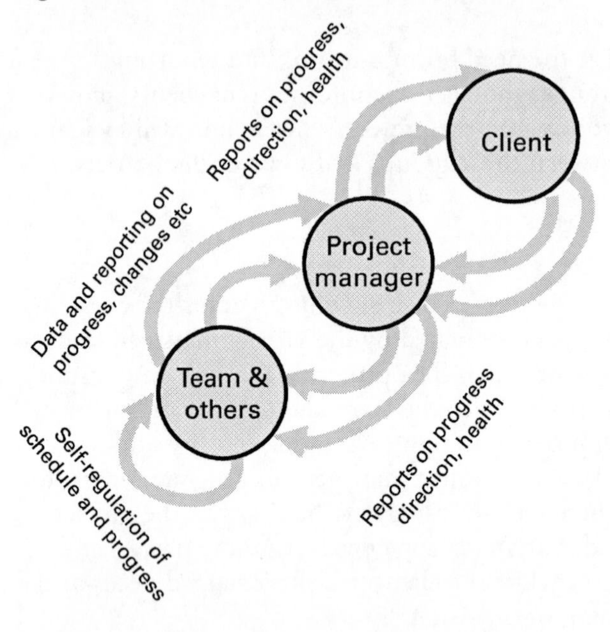


## Learning activity 12.2

List the potential problems of evaluating the quality of a supplier or subcontractor to a project.

*Feedback on page 197*



### The problems of measuring and reporting

The cost of collecting and distributing information has been discussed, but there are several other barriers touched upon in the feedback to learning activity 12.2 above.

Data is often difficult to obtain reliably. In most companies, the central systems such as SAP or other ERP systems have limited value with patchy or missing data and there is little confidence in the accuracy of some parts. Even where data is strong, it may not be possible to separate the elements relevant to the project and will only cover some of the measures required.

Financial data is frequently the strongest in the organisation, not least because it is the primary means of measuring organisations and money is the lifeblood of most. Even in this area, it is frequently difficult to separate the costs relevant to the project. Projects also require very up-to-date cost information, which many systems are unable to supply.

Biased information can cause problems. As an example, consider one of a project's team working on a long activity which is probably behind schedule. Asking the fundamental question on time: 'How complete is the work?' could produce different biased answers such as: 'It is going fine' to hide problems, or 'It is very hard work, it cannot be finished on time' to manage expectations. It is possible that neither answer is objectively true but they are hard to challenge or verify.

Finally, measuring changes things. This may seem a difficult idea when thinking about weighing fruit, and involves a shift from Newtonian to quantum physics (Palmer and Parker, 2001). More accessibly, any time you measure a human system, it changes. This becomes clearer if you think about why we measure people. Clock cards to measure timekeeping are there to make people turn up on time. Measuring people's work is there to drive output. Personal goals are set to drive achievement, not just as a basis to measure. This has an impact on measuring and reporting: measurement drives behaviour.

### Difficulties of reporting in projects

Measuring in a relatively stable organisation allows for refinement of the system and can be aligned with the organisational structure. In a project, the requirements are frequently unclear and changing, the timescales are shorter and people are working outside their normal roles in the hierarchy (see study session 11). These factors add to the problems of measurement and reporting.

As a very basic example, consider a member of the team working part time on the project. A fundamental reporting question could be progress on the work and the time taken to do it. This is formally the responsibility of the line manager who sits nearby, and the data may be reported in a timesheet and verbally: a measurement system embedded and aligned with the hierarchy. For the project manager, collecting that data involves either adding to the reporting burden, active collection of the data or waiting for the next project meeting to ask.



### Self-assessment question 12.2

Put yourself in the position of a project manager for a project relying heavily on the work of 5–8 subcontractors

1. What are the monitoring and reporting needs between you and the subcontractors?
2. List some of the potential problems in fulfilling those needs.
3. Suggest how you would limit the impact or work around some of those problems.

*Feedback on page 197*

## 12.3 How and what to measure

With a clear view of the barriers to monitoring and yet the need for it, the question turns to how and what to measure. The 'hard' factors are commonly measured and established, though imperfect methods are well developed. Soft factors prove more challenging.

### Measuring the hard factors

The factors of cost quality and time are at the core of the hard factors, as discussed. Time and cost are frequently combined into 'earned value' (see below).

### Quality

Quality presents something of a problem. The definitions such as 'fitness for purpose' can work well provided requirements are well expressed and unchanging, but quality management approaches such as TQM are designed and appropriate for repetitive work. There is plenty of research and writing on quality in projects, but two problems remain: projects are innovative, hence failure in some ways is inevitable, and time pressures mean that poor quality is frequently accepted, provided it can be rectified later. For example, time is allowed at the end of building projects for 'snagging': correcting all the things which were not quite right but were passed over in the rush for completion.

### Time measurement

The difficulties estimating percentage complete for activities have been discussed, but time is frequently a critical factor. The two most important elements in measuring progress are:

- Avoid blame for lateness, encouraging accurate estimates.
- Divide up activities into small, measurable chunks as far as possible. If team meetings or reviews are once a week, activities should be a maximum of one week long as far as possible. This way, percentage estimates are irrelevant, the activity is either not started, started or finished. Small activities also help with motivation and making progress visible.



### Time and cost combined: earned value

As mentioned in section 12.2 above, some measure of money spent is usually available, if imperfect, and time, or completion of the activities, is perhaps the most analysed element of projects. For many people, project management is solely time management: planning and control. If both cost and time are strong factors in the project, they should be monitored together.

Earned value combines time and cost into one measure. The principle is simple: compare the percentage completion of activities in the project against the planned spend and the actual spend.

Here is a simple example: a wall made of 100 bricks, to be completed in ten days with a total cost of £1,000. The earned value for each brick is £10.

Progress is reviewed at day 5:

1 If 50 bricks have been laid and £500 spent, time and cost are on target.

2 If 40 bricks have been laid and £400 spent, there is a 'negative time variance': it is one day behind time and likely to be late, but cost is on target.
3 If 60 bricks have been laid and £600 spent, there is a positive time variance. The cost is still on target, though.
4 If 50 bricks have been laid and £600 spent, there is a 'negative cost variance' of £100. It is, of course on time.
5 If 40 bricks have been laid and £500 has been spent, there is a time variance and a cost variance: it is behind and overspent.

This simple combination is quite powerful at exposing the real position of a project, where one or other measure alone will not show the true effect. More extensive examples of earned value calculations are available in Meredith and Mantel (2006), Maylor (1996), Lock (2000) and many more. There is a wealth of literature on the subject, frequently using contradictory terms and definitions, but the basic idea is the same.

## Learning activity 12.3

List the issues likely to be encountered in applying earned value to suppliers and subcontractors to a project.

*Feedback on page 198*

There are problems with the method, of course. Obeng (1996) dismisses it altogether, pointing out that a half-finished bridge is of no more value than no bridge at all, a point previously made by King Solomon, and that what is added throughout the project is cost. The value all comes in a rush when the results are handed over to a client. Earned value is of less use in valuing a project than probable future value to the organisation. This is partly true, but ignores the success of earned value as a monitoring tool and that many projects are handed over when not finished, either for snagging or because the client accepts the value of what is there.



The more severe problems with earned value are practical. How do you value an activity? How do you know how complete that activity is? The answer to the first is that earned value bases value on estimated cost in: if an activity is expected to cost £10, half of it has a *value* of £5. This has the problems that the estimate is probably wrong and that cost and value are very different things, as most purchasers know.

Estimating percentage completion is also problematic. How complete is a house with walls but no roof? With the wall example, what time and cost were allowed for preparation and commissioning? Meredith and Mantel (2006) highlight four conventions:

- An estimate based on the time or cost spent against estimate. This is common but random and rather misses the point of measuring earned value.
- 50:50 estimate. It is assumed an activity is 50% complete as soon as it is started and 100% allocated only on completion. This is commonly used

as it is simple, but is a coarse measure and encourages starting activities to increase earned value. (As a note, this should not be confused with 50:50 estimates in Critical Chain, which have a completely different basis.)

- 0–100% rule: no earned value is allowed until the task is completed. This is pessimistic and coarse, but with the advantage that it encourages completion.
- Critical input use: where an expensive resource such as a machine or skilled labour is needed, value is credited according to how much of this is used. The only advantage of this is that it is a fine measure: not just 0–100 or 50–50. The logic behind using this applies only to very specific cases as it encourages spend, and early spend at that.

Earned value is a useful tool to look at a project as a whole and to compare several projects, where time and cost are key factors. It suffers from difficulty with base data, however, and no amount of complexity in calculation can correct that, so it should be used appropriately and with caution.

### Risk reporting

One of the most important elements of project management is risk management. Risk management and analysis using the risk and impact combination is valuable, but reporting risk is frequently done badly. A simple 'traffic light' system is usually sufficient. A typical division between risks would be:

- Green: highlighted as a potential risk but no action needed just now
- Amber: currently a problem or likely to become one unless action is taken
- Red: a problem with no remedy at the moment. Action is needed to change this or reduce the impact.



### Change and performance reporting

Changes in scope, quality, predicted cost and time should be reported and highlighted separately from the normal schedule and cost reports. The specification, timing, cost and resource of the project are likely to change and those agreed changes can be lost or ignored if left out of the reporting structure.

Project performance – predicted savings, predicted revenue or value improvements, output measures – should be an integral part of the reporting structure. Experience suggests that there are few things more boring than a complex project plan, few things more interesting than a substantial saving achieved.

### Soft factors

From study session 1 the importance of soft factors has been emphasised, yet this section has ignored them so far. The main reasons are that they are difficult to measure and rarely reported formally. How can morale or teamwork be measured? How can the momentum of the project be measured? There are ways of measuring these things, but accuracy is time consuming and hard to achieve. Even the idea of measuring these things might bring a traditional project manager to anger or despair: aren't there enough problems reporting on the hard factors? Most project management texts make no mention of measuring these factors and it is left as part of the 'black art' or the experience-based elements of project management.

The problem remains: project success relies heavily on soft factors, so if you are the project manager, how do you know morale and commitment are strong and that you have momentum? If you are the client or sponsor, how do you gauge whether those factors are in place? This is where the saying 'you can't manage what you can't measure' falls apart: you have to manage a range of factors you cannot measure, those soft factors are prime amongst them.

There are, then, no established, formal ways of reporting on soft factors beyond things like the stakeholder map, so as a suggestion for assessing these, a checklist for the end of each team meeting may help. After the team meeting, replay the discussions in your mind.

- For each team member, were they contributing, engaged, positive?
- What was the balance of enthusiasm for new work and excuses made for previous work late or neglected?
- What tells you there is momentum: what has been done since the last meeting? What has been completed and what has progressed?
- If you could change any members of the team, how many (and who) would it be?

The results are unlikely to be scientific or especially accurate, but they may be measures with impact.



### Self-assessment question 12.3

Write a training note for project managers on earned value. Explain where it is useful and potential problems.

*Feedback on page 198*

## 12.4 Different control processes, different days

Controls take many forms in projects: reports, meetings, presentations, discussions, arbitrary decisions, announcements or sudden actions. This section will look at a few of the control processes used and how they can apply, along with some ideas for successful control and how this might change through the project.

### Control processes

Meredith and Mantel (2006) identify three control processes: cybernetic or feedback, go/no go and post-control, or review.

## Feedback

The most familiar idea of the control process is the feedback loop (see figure 12.3). In this, a measure of the output is taken, then fed back so the process can be controlled.

**Figure 12.3:** A simple feedback loop

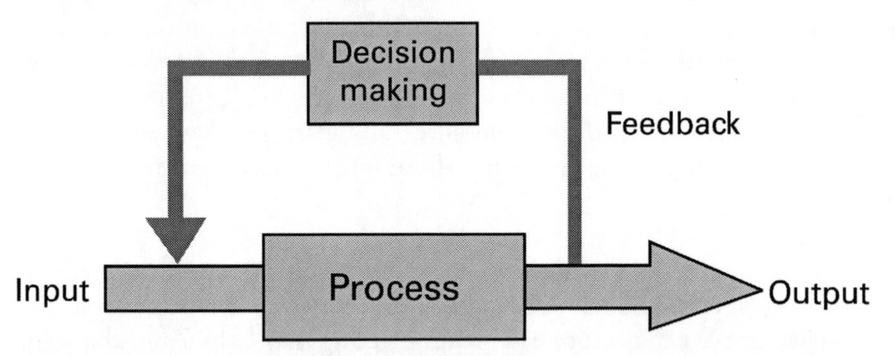


If we apply this simple schematic to a project, we might get figure 12.4.

**Figure 12.4:** A feedback loop applied to project management

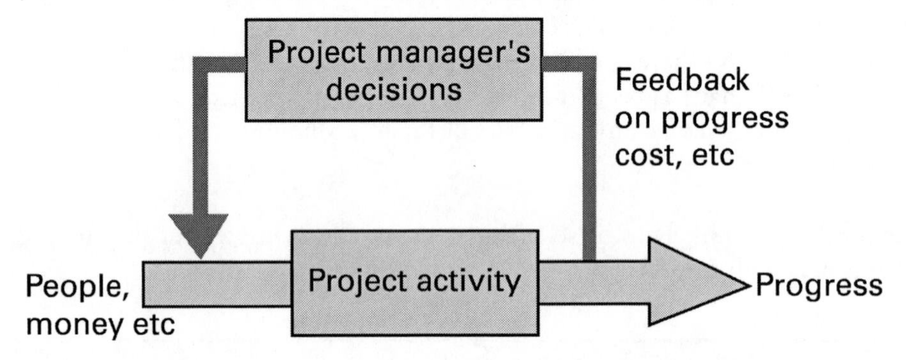


The idea is a simple and attractive one. Meredith and Mantel (2006) even bring in details of control theory to identify first, second and third order control systems. Much of the day-to day-management of the project and regular reviews follow this basic structure of feedback. The project is late, what do we do? Change schedules. The work is excellent, what do we do? Reward and congratulate. Feedback control is an excellent method of applying conscious decisions to the management of the project, within limits.

The main limit of this control is with decision making. Decision making is rarely based on entirely accurate feedback and entirely rational. People often make poor decisions and repeat them. The following is an example of a project where quality is absolute and cannot be reduced:

1. The project is running late. More staff are allocated. A fairly rational decision based on the cost-quality-time balance.
2. At the next review, the project is still late, the same feedback decision demands more resource, more staff. This still seems rational.
3. At the third review, the overrun has stabilised, so more staff are allocated temporarily to reduce it.

4 At the next review, the project is still late. Now something radical must be done so a team is sent in to find out what has gone wrong. More time and money are spent.
5 The team discovers that the original problem was that people were unclear on what to do so work was slow and poorly directed. Adding more staff actually made the problem slightly worse until a way of working emerged by trial and error.

The idea of feedback: looking at some output measures and changing the input works well for the field coils of a car alternator but ignores the complexity of a project which is a human system. The outputs can be measures of time or cost, but there is a need to understand a wealth of other elements, as described in section 12.3. The inputs can be more resource or time, but could be more human: a senior member of staff threatening dire consequences for failure, the results of which are unpredictable. Finally and most importantly, this model views the project management activity in the same way as a fixed system, like a car alternator. This simplistic view ignores the natural changes and developments and the ability of the project manager to change the system, the way the team work for example. This is frequently the most effective and valuable method of control. The final drawback of the model is that it seems to be description without implication. Once you understand the concept of feedback, it seems to offer little insight into managing projects, beyond the idea that measuring outputs and taking corrective action are of value.

### Go/no go controls

A go/no go control is a check whether a fixed set of criteria have been met. A common use of this is a project 'gateway' system. At set points in the project, the project is reviewed to see whether certain tasks have been completed. If not, the project cannot (in principle) progress to the next stage.

These checks or gateways are very useful for oversight and governance by sponsors or controlling stakeholders such as a project board: fixed points for review to check the correct process is in place or that the project still has a strong commercial justification.

Go/no go controls are also valuable for the project manager: by identifying some key milestones just before commitments are made, it allows a checklist of what needs to be in place: before launching the project we must have a skeleton team, a clear time plan, a strong business case and agreement from three key stakeholders.

### Post-control

Post-control refers to review processes where the result is not fed back to the activity of project management. The review stage at the end of a project or part is a very valuable element of the project, but does not help the control of that project. The value in learning is for other projects or to assess and manage the output: the product of the project. This area is dealt with in detail in study session 13.

### Learning activity 12.4

Produce a simple flow chart showing the steps in the process of introducing change in a project with which you are familiar or from a case.

If there is no clear process, identify some changes to the project, then map out the steps taken before the change was adopted.

*Feedback on page 198*

## Controlling change

Projects need to be flexible. Projects need to embrace change. The challenge is in controlling change so the project does not mutate wildly, while allowing for necessary or desirable developments.

Maylor (1996) suggests a multi-person process flow involving a change originator, a change coordinator, investigators and the project owner, carrying out nine activities. This is similar to prescribed civil engineering practice for large changes, but ignores two important exceptions. Small change decisions can and have to be made on site at the decision of an empowered engineer, and many changes avoid the process and are imposed, with mixed results.



It is unlikely that a single, fixed change control process will be successful. For small changes, empowering individuals to make decisions within limits is often appropriate, with the constraint that those changes are logged and reported. For larger changes, a simple control process will be useful, defining the basis of decisions, ownership and how those changes are logged. Stakeholders may still demand changes and controlling those is not a rigid process but a negotiation. As in the stakeholder example in section 2.4, if the sponsor unilaterally decides an e-auction will be held, it is possible to negotiate by explaining the impact, but an e-auction is likely to be held.

The most important element of change control is not the decision process, but logging what has been decided. Keeping track of the changes is vital for progress and future maintenance. Meredith and Mantel (2006) suggest control of change is one of the primary concerns of risk management.

## Simple reporting methods

Control and decision making rely on an understanding of the situation. Looking at the feedback model, control relies on measuring the outputs. A clear picture of the outputs and the situation relies on setting up some simple measures and a few ideas can help this:

- *Simple measures*: Focusing on a few simple measures or ratios reduces confusion and noise. How many buffer days are there? What is the ratio of earned value to cost? From the origins of project management simple measures have been used to drive performance: tons of earth dug for a railway, rivets driven for shipbuilding. Pick a few simple measures to give a basic view of what is happening.

- *Measuring what is important*: From the early identification of what will make the project successful comes a series of elements worth measuring. If time is critical, measures of cost overruns are common but of limited use. If the quality of output is key, then measures of adherence to schedule are secondary. The importance of different factors will change, so should the measures.
- *Control limits*: Setting limits or thresholds for action is an established way of simplifying decisions. For example: as long as we have 20 buffer days, no action needed, 15 days, investigate, eight days, panic. As long as earned value is above, for example 90% of cost, no action is needed.
- *Exception reporting*: If everything is going to plan, theoretically no action is needed, so the process of identifying exceptions helps reporting from team to manager and from manager to stakeholders.

### Self-assessment question 12.4

Return to your answer to self-assessment question 12.1 above. Given the information from this section and the rest of the session, how would you change your checklist for a project management information system to support the management of a complex project (see Meredith and Mantel, 2006: 552–8 and 540–41)?

*Feedback on page 199*



### Revision question

Now try the revision question for this session on page 321.

### Summary

Project success relies on control and monitoring, which relies on measurement. The barriers to effective performance measurement and control are many, from poor data, through the impact of measuring to the time it takes. Measurement is more challenging in a project than in other management activities, because there is no established system and the requirements are difficult to identify and changing.

The need for measurement remains and this complex situation can be tackled with some simple approaches:

- Measure what is important. This seems obvious but is often ignored, with easier measures taking focus. The importance of different measures will change through the project, for example cost takes second place to time as the deadline gets nearer. If soft factors are important, you should have some measure of how they are working.

- Different reports fit different audiences. As a rule of thumb, the absolute minimum information should be presented as a starting place, with supporting data as necessary.
- Use simple measures and ratios, together with control limits and exception reporting. Clear away the noise of too much data.

There may not be a perfect process for estimating progress, reporting, change control or measuring some factors, but an imperfect process is better than flying blind.

## Suggested further reading

- Clarke (1999).
- Eccles (1991).
- Fitzgerald et al (1991).
- Gregory M (1993).
- Kaplan and Norton (1992).
- Lock (2003); Chapter 20.
- Maylor (1996); Chapters 10 and 11.
- Meredith and Mantel (2006); Chapter 4.
- Palmer and Parker (2001).

## Feedback on learning activities and self-assessment questions

### Feedback on learning activity 12.1



Some of the negative aspects are outlined in this section: it can suggest a lack of trust, challenging what that person is doing and undermining confidence and loyalty. The feeling of 'big brother' or micro management is demotivating. Other aspects you may have touched on include:

- Spending time on creating reports which divert from the main task can kill enthusiasm.
- Being measured on 'the wrong things' while contribution is ignored will not help motivation.

There are of course positive aspects:

- Seeing progress.
- Seeing that work is recognised.
- Seeing that work is in the right direction.
- People working in 'cells' on their own particular tasks with no knowledge of the progress of the project are unlikely to be interested in how the project is progressing. Measuring and publicising the results can increase motivation.
- The process of collecting data means that the project manager will have to examine team members' activities and can encourage more effective management.

These will, of course rely on how the measurements are used.

## Feedback on self-assessment question 12.1

You may have identified a series of technical aspects: things the system must provide, such as:

- Gantt and PERT charts
- calendars for activities, departments or individuals
- budgeting information
- task lists and breakdowns in a structured way such as WBS.

There are probably some system aspects:

- ability to link with other systems: Sage accounting, Excel spreadsheets, Lotus Notes, MS Project, etc
- the flexibility to report in different, accessible ways
- back-up, support and training
- system compatibility with hardware.

And finally the 'soft' aspects:

- Will each group be able to access it as they need?
- Will they be able to use and adapt it?
- Will they want to: is it easy to use and effective?
- What is the balance between the cost of measurement and the benefit?

## Feedback on learning activity 12.2

The normal problems of evaluating suppliers still exist:

- Poor data availability: company systems have only partial records with limited reliability.
- The supplier will tend to give biased information.
- Attitudes of people who work with the supplier are frequently based on memory rather than fact: the one bad delivery or relationship overshadows years of success.
- The cost of evaluating: site visits, questionnaires or data analysis is high.
- Measures need to be very fresh to be useful: the older the date, generally the less valuable.

In addition there are project-specific problems:

- Your requirements of the supplier may not be clear and may change with the project.
- The project is new, the supplier may be untested with no history.
- The project is temporary, so there is little opportunity to build up information.

## Feedback on self-assessment question 12.2

1 You should have identified the need to monitor cost, quality and time of their output, but also some other factors, such as their attitude

or efficiency. Do not forget that this will need to be two way: the subcontractors need information on their performance, the rest of the project and so on.

2 There are several potential problems listed in this section and the learning activity, including cost, unavailability, inaccuracy, bias, the impact of measuring and the changing requirements.
3 The essential elements in working around these revolve around design. Accept that the reporting system will not be perfect. Balance the need to measure against the cost. Measure only the things which are very relevant: timing on the critical path may be vital, progress elsewhere needs less monitoring, for example. Finally, sharing responsibilities and motivation is important. People will resist reporting problems if they feel they will be blamed, but will measure, report and analyse if they have commitment, enthusiasm and understand the need and the reporting system.

## Feedback on learning activity 12.3

First there are all the issues mentioned in section 12.2, which make measurement difficult, but they have been discussed enough.

For earned value, there are the following problems: equating value to cost is a problem, a half-finished activity is not worth half a completed activity, estimating is difficult and a focus on cost ignores quality. All of these can be exacerbated by the relationship between a supplier and the project.

## Feedback on self-assessment question 12.3



This question does not call for an explanation of how earned value is calculated, it focuses on the applications and drawbacks.

Applications would include:

- projects where cost and time are key factors
- activities where cost can be measured fairly accurately
- organisations where accounts data is fairly up to date relative to the speed the project is progressing (three-monthly accounting periods are of limited value in managing a six-month project).

Potential problems:

- it relies on good accounts (see the points on applications)
- estimating completion is difficult
- it does not touch on future value, focusing on money spent
- an excessive focus on cost can lead to ignoring quality.

## Feedback on learning activity 12.4

This is frequently a difficult exercise as different changes can follow different paths. At the centre of this exercise is identifying who made the decision to change and how that decision was arrived at.

## Feedback on self-assessment question 12.4

There may be technical aspects which could be added to your original answer, for example:

- a log of changes
- an inbuilt process for change control
- the ability to set up gateways or review milestones
- risk reporting
- accessibility in different ways for different users
- whether it is easy to perform simulations or trial runs regarding scheduling, resources, etc
- whether it can offer some measures of soft factors.

System aspects might include more clarity on the way different reports need to be presented to different audiences, how measures and reports will need to be changed through the life of the project.

Once again, the system is useless unless it is adopted across the project, so the factors which encourage take-up will be central. Try to avoid having such a complex PMIS that more time is spent managing the PMIS than the project itself.

Study session 13

# Closure and evaluation: lessons for the future

To win a race you have first to finish it. In the same way, it is often the end of the project that delivers the benefits.

## Introduction

The end of a project is often the most useful part: most of the benefit is delivered, the product is handed over and the lessons are learnt for the future.

At the same time, the team is breaking up, new work will be found for the team and the project manager, many see the project as 'over' and have no interest in it, and there will be few of the breakthroughs that made the project so exciting. Much of the project work will involve tying up loose ends or completing activities people thought were finished.

With these tensions, closure and evaluation has exacting challenges: very important activities, many of them uninteresting, with low profile and limited resource.

This session looks at different ways to manage the end of the project for maximum success.

## Session learning objectives

After completing this session you should be able to:

13.1 Explain the purposes of project evaluation.
13.2 Appraise the uses of the project audit.
13.3 Explain the different methods of project termination.
13.4 Develop your own template for a final project report.

## Unit content coverage

This study session covers the following topic from the official CIPS unit content document.

### Learning objective

3.0 Develop and apply project management concepts, models, tools and techniques to create solutions to a range of practical project management problems.

3.1.5 Closure
- Obtain client acceptance
- Install deliverables

- Document the project
- Issue final report

3.1.6 Review, Evaluation and Learning
- Conduct project audit
- Lessons Learnt
- Communicate the review, evaluation and learning

3.2 Appraise the range of tools and techniques available to the project team in terms of appropriateness, selection and implementation.
- Appropriateness. Pick the right tools for the task
- Selection. Be aware of the limitations of tools and techniques
- Implementation. Be able to use the tools correctly

3.3 Utilise a range of tools and techniques to assist in robust and systematic data collection, analysis of options and decision-making.
- SIPOC
- 7 tools of quality control
- Financial appraisal
- Voice of the customer
- Quality function deployment
- Project initiation document (PID)
- Moments of truth
- Work breakdown structure
- Critical path analysis. Network diagrams
- Risk analysis and assessment. Mitigating risks
- Risk/Impact matrix
- Suitability/feasibility/vulnerability

## Prior knowledge



Study sessions 1 – 12.

## Timing

You should set aside about 6 hours to read and complete this session, including learning activities, self-assessment questions, the suggested reading (if any) from the essential textbook for this unit and the revision question.

## 13.1 'Those who do not remember the past are condemned to repeat it' (George Santayana)

### Learning activity 13.1

Select a recently completed project from within your organisation or from a detailed case and conduct your own evaluation.

Identify:

- what went right
- what went wrong

*(continued on next page)*

### Learning activity 13.1 *(continued)*

- lessons to be learned for future projects
- barriers to your evaluation.

*Feedback on page 213*

The core reason for evaluating a project is simple: to learn from it for the future. As the title suggests, if we do not learn from failures and successes, the failures are likely to happen again, while the successes are not certain to be repeated. Maylor (2003) uses the example of hedgehogs being run over by cars: they cannot learn and change their behaviour, so keep on curling into a ball for protection, a tactic ineffective against cars.

### Understanding outputs

The first and simplest reason for evaluating a project is to understand what it has done, what has been delivered, what are the outputs? The project may have been described at the outset, but the delivered product is likely to be different. What does that new database actually do? Is the new contract for energy likely to deliver consistently competitive pricing or will another project be needed in two years time? The review and evaluation process can bring out into the open aspects of the project that have not been clearly documented or handed over.

### Project management methods

Any comprehensive evaluation should look at the way the project was managed in order to understand what happened and why. The questions here need to look beyond the outcome towards causes and consequences. Was an activity late because of poor scheduling, estimating, communication or commitment? Did that complex Gantt chart put people off or give detailed insights? What were the key factors in making it go right, or wrong? The learning may be imperfect, as there are few absolutes in management, but a good evaluation will give insight into how, why and what to do next time.

### Governance

Effective governance needs evaluation for a range of things: understanding the output and the methods as above are important. Governance and the more general project environment are important factors in determining the management of projects in the future, so insights into the management and outputs are important. Understanding the project in context of others is easier from this vantage point: the output from this project will impact on others, now and in the future. Basic questions are important: Were the objectives set too high? What tools should we insist on and recommend? What are the 'turning points' or times of danger we should focus on especially? The evaluation for governance should reflect not just on the management and guiding this in the future, but on a critical appraisal of the governance. There is an almost overwhelming temptation to blame failure on individuals, predominantly managers and the team, and respond by making governance more rigid and prescriptive. Both these are barriers to better projects.

### Barriers to evaluation

It seems that evaluation is a vital part of project management, providing benefits well into the future, sometimes beyond the life of the direct project output. The benefits seem to be for everyone: the users, sponsors, governance and other stakeholders, and particularly the project team. And yet, evaluation is typically a brief afterthought or a little-read report at best, more often, just an informal reflection by the participants. There must be something in the way of effective evaluation.

1. The first barrier is the context. At the end of a project there is typically a rush to finish, people are leaving the team, previously ignored problems pop up. A calm, balanced reflection on the process and output is extra work at odds with the activities in hand.
2. The second barrier is failure. Failure is a great prompt for learning, but people tend to hide it. Shame, fear of blame and other discomforts stand in the way of understanding causes and remedies for failure.
3. The third barrier is uniqueness. Projects are unique, so management requirements are unique. Taking generally applicable lessons or rules from one case is difficult and sometimes dangerous.
4. The fourth barrier is the link between evaluation and resources. Most public sector funded projects demand evaluation but link future funding to successful outcomes. This promotes 'whitewashing', reports which accentuate the positive and ignore or diminish any negative aspects. If looking at failure is likely to reduce resources in the future, the evaluation is very likely to twist the truth to highlight success and lose much of its value.
5. The fifth barrier is the use of the evaluation. Once the team has gone and the project is wrapped up, who is there to read the project? Unless the need for and practical value of the evaluation are clear, there is little impetus to report effectively.



These barriers to effective evaluation are high, but not insurmountable. The most important factor in driving evaluation is governance. An environment where reports are filed unread and comprehensive evaluation is only used to apportion blame on minor players is unlikely to encourage learning. Learning is covered in more detail in study session 20, so a simple summary for now is that evaluation is about learning for the future and this is driven by the governance and environment.

### Self-assessment question 13.1

Write a one-page memo suggesting the value of a formal project evaluation process for your organisation or one you know well.

*Feedback on page 213*

## 13.2 Audits: beyond the grey

What does an audit conjure up in your mind? If you were managing a project and you were told a team was coming to audit the project, what would your response be?

If audit conjures up a vision of an interesting, valuable process, in place to ensure good work, you are probably quite unusual. Most people regard audits as something between necessary evil and an unnecessary bureaucracy carried out by grey-faced people who have no sense of balance or humour. Similarly, most people face audit with something between reluctance and dread.

Project audits are not the most exciting or attractive of topics, it seems. So if they are so unattractive, what do they bring to justify their existence?

### Audits? What are they?

Put simply, an audit is an assessment against set criteria of process or outcome. A financial audit, for example, may make sure money is spent according to set procedures, and might also measure whether the spend is effective and efficient by setting results against benchmarks.

Part of the reason for resistance to audit is that, being external, they have to rely on documentation and evidence. Financial management is very familiar with audits and accounting and financial systems are highly developed to provide evidence for them. Project management less so.

A project audit can answer two basic questions:

1. Has the correct project management process been followed?
2. Is the delivery of outputs as it should be?

As many projects devour a lot of resource and money, an independent review of the process and the outcome begins to seem more reasonable.

### Post control: using audits for closure and evaluation



The audit should be carried out by an external team or person, that is, they were not responsible for project management and delivery. The audit needs a clear brief: what it is examining, and against what criteria. It also needs the power to investigate access to records and commonly, individuals. It should happen soon after project completion for freshness of evidence and impact of findings.

The benefit of an audit as a review process is its rigour and independence. An independent assessment of the project against clear criteria ensures more objectivity than a narrative account provided by the team. The grey areas of assessment can be removed: either a project complies or it does not.

It also encourages good practice: the criteria need to be set, encouraging those involved in setting up and managing the project to define clearly the nature of the project and the project management process that will be used.

The difficulties of audit are threefold:

- Definition of the project and its objectives may be difficult and will change with time. An audit carried out against a set of objectives loosely written at the start reduces its value, while post-hoc comparison with benchmarks not available to the project at the time will lead to unfair comparison.

- To audit the project management process, it must be defined. In study session 7, different types of project and their different demands were identified. If one process cannot be applied across all projects, what will be audited. The tension between control and flexibility is apparent in many organisations.
- Audit itself is non-value adding to the project. That is, all the work auditing and documenting for audit has little direct impact on the outcome of the project, except to consume resource. Project management systems are less developed for accountability and audit, partly because projects vary so widely, partly because compared with accounting, audit is not legally necessary and financial transactions are easier to monitor than project management.

### Learning activity 13.2

Draw up a list of benefits that an organisation with which you are familiar would gain from a project audit.

*Feedback on page 213*

### Using audits within the project

The post-control audit has value. It can act as a review and encourage compliance, but earlier audits can catch problems early, while the project is still going on, and help to correct them.



Meredith and Mantel (2006) contains an extensive discussion of audits, so this section is restricted to a few key points:

- In-process audits have similar requirements to post-control audits, but tend to be briefer and less comprehensive.
- The focus should shift to highlighting problems to drive change in this project.
- The need for clear criteria remains, but the criteria can develop from audit to audit, allowing a more appropriate framework.
- The cost of audit in time and resource remains a factor and must be balanced against the benefit.

Audits can be used as 'gateways' through the process (see study session 12) bringing the same clarity and rigour, as they assess the same elements: has the process been followed, is the project still likely to deliver results.

Finally, where projects are subject to external post control audits, some organisations initiate their own audits throughout the process. This helps to ensure there are no surprises at the end and brings value from the audit process.

### Self-assessment question 13.2

Where are project audits most valuable and where are they less so? Draw up a list of factors which could determine the value of audits and briefly explain the impact of each.

*Feedback on page 214*

## 13.3 All good things come to an end: project termination

Projects are temporary by their very nature. How they come to an end varies and has a strong impact on their success, but come to an end they must.

### Learning activity 13.3

Suggest different ways projects might come to an end. What are the different demands of each?

*Feedback on page 214*

### Natural life termination

Some projects reach the end as planned or a little late and broadly deliver the objective. Termination is relatively straightforward, but completion, handover and break-up of the team must be carefully managed.

### The need disappears

Sometimes technology changes or the business environment shifts. A project on supplier development for a manufacturing company can become redundant once the decision to outsource production is made, a civil service project may become unnecessary overnight as policy changes through election or exigency. The case for termination is obvious and action should be swift. In this case, there is little to take away from the project however successful as it is part finished and learning may be limited. It is sometimes possible to move the team on to another project, but in most cases, the challenge is to disperse the team quickly and avoiding the negative impact of perceived failure.

### The project fails

Some projects simply fail. They may be mismanaged, ill-conceived or cannot overcome some technical or human obstacle. Once the failure is clear, termination should be rapid and clean. The impact on the team is likely to be negative unless a conscious effort is made to capture the lessons from the failure and celebrate the successes within the project. In some cases, team members describe a failed project as 'the best thing I have ever worked on'. A project by Goss Challenge to build a radical boat to break the world record for circumnavigation captured massive public interest and support. The boat failed repeatedly and never reached the start line, yet many of the team cite the project as a success just for the challenge and the teamwork.

### Running out of steam

In some cases, the project carries on, often making progress without meeting its objective until a decision is made to stop. The Common Cold Unit was set up on 1946 as a project to cure the common cold. In 1990, after more than 12,000 volunteers had been subject to experiments and millions of pounds had been spent, the decision was made to close the centre as success was still far away. For most projects in this situation, termination is hardly traumatic and merely puts an end to work for which the purpose is becoming less clear. There is a balance to be struck with this type of termination between increasing costs and declining likelihood of success. The point at which the decision to close is taken can be decided by a number of models, for example those in Meredith and Mantel (2006). Just because one project fades away, it does not mean others will not follow: other common cold projects have followed and more millions spent. In 1996, a new common cold centre was started at Cardiff University. Whether this shows that different approaches yield different results or that the funders cannot learn from failure, only time will tell.

### The detail of completing a project

There is a tendency for projects to drift towards completion and the management of exit has slightly different requirements from the rest of the project. The following are general pointers:

- *Speed up control*: Reviews and project meetings should become more frequent to redirect activity and bring urgency to completion.
- *Triage*: This is the process used in medicine usefully adapted to projects. For most projects, not everything will be completed: for example the last functions of the software will not be achieved, the contract will not be rolled out to every site. All the activity should be reviewed and divided into three types:
    - Things which are 'good enough'. They could be improved but will have little impact on the overall success of the project.
    - Things which will never be complete: there is not time or resource to achieve these.
    - Things which, if worked on now, will have a strong impact on the project success. All energy and resources should be focused here.
- *Change the project manager*: Many recommend that a different project manager is brought in. There are several reasons: it brings a fresh view, the skills of completion are very different from the skills of launch or management, the existing project manager is probably looking for his or her next project anyway. Typically a new project manager will inject new energy and investigate the project status then highlight a series of concerns and potential problems. This sometimes casts the old project manager in a bad light, but is likely to revitalise and refocus efforts and support.

- *Measure the results*: Understanding the impact and having strong data to support any claims is important but often ignored. Memories can be short and even strong success can become accepted as though it was always in place.
- *Communicate success*: One definition of success is the perceptions of stakeholders. Poor communication will damage the perception of stakeholders, while managed, even biased communication can make the most unpromising projects successes for the stakeholders. Perhaps the most commonly used example is the project to create Concorde. While a supersonic aeroplane was created, the project was an Anglo-French collaboration which ran massively over budget and deadlines. Even in 2006, long after flights have ceased, the call to 'bring back this great British success' can be seen in national newspapers.
- *Embed the results*: The product may be good, but the benefits depend on embedding it. Are the users trained? Are they using it? Can they update it as their needs change? That international contract for packaging with massive savings is useless if local sites drift back to their preferred suppliers .
- *Dissolve the team quickly*: Managing the break-up of the team may not be as difficult as building it but it has an impact on the individuals. The more cohesive and committed the team, the more is lost when it is dispersed and a quick, managed dispersal is better than a drifting, lingering break-up.
- *Celebrate*: Success or failure, the end of the project should be celebrated by party, recognition and reward. It marks the end, helps learning, allows participants to move on and frees attention for the next project.

### Self-assessment question 13.3

You have been given the task of managing a project which is progressing well and has just two months to run. Create a checklist of activity for exiting the project.

*Feedback on page 214*

## 13.4 What should the review look like?

So far this session has looked at the need for review and some of the uses and forms the review might take. This section aims to focus on the practical aspects of the review: what it will look like and how to complete it.

### Learning activity 13.4

Produce a questionnaire designed to identify necessary facts for a final project report and examine the performance of projects.

*Feedback on page 215*

### Start at the end

The first step in designing the review is looking at what will be done with it. This will guide the amount of time which should be spent, the style and some of the key aspects. If it is a review for other project managers, then practice on tools, techniques and teamwork may be most important. If the review is aimed at sponsors and other staff at high level, then a review of the output, success against objectives and any improvements to the definition stage and governance will take more prominence. In terms of style, few people like lengthy reports, and a one-page summary may be more appropriate for the sponsor, while a more detailed narrative may give the necessary subtleties for project managers.

### Identify the important measures

As mentioned, this comes partly from the audience, but will also depend on the context and what you believe is important. Maylor (1996) identifies a series of criteria and some very useful measures that could be used to review them.

**Table 13.1** Maylor's criteria and review measures

| Criteria | Review |
|---|---|
| Financial | variance from budget, return on investment |
| Time | customer satisfaction |
| Quality | customer perception |
| Human Resources | team spirit, motivation |
| Environmental | environmental impact assessment |
| Planning | cost, techniques used |
| Control | basis for improvement |



Frigenti and Comninos (2002) use a more extensive and specific list, giving a less structured series of items:

- Review:
    - the initial objectives
    - their soundness
    - the evolution of objectives from there up to the final form, and how well the team performed against them
    - the reasons for changes to objectives and which were unavoidable
    - the activities and relationships of the team
    - the interfaces, performance and effectiveness of project management
    - the relationships outside the team: within the organisation and with the client
    - the cause and process of termination
    - customer reaction and satisfaction
    - expenditures, sources of cost and profitability.
- Identify:

  - areas where performance was good and note the reasons and organisational benefits
  - problems, mistakes, etc and their causes.
- Comment on:
  - recommendations for changes to existing policies and procedures
  - the need for new policies and procedures to incorporate the lessons learnt.

This is a reasonably comprehensive list and could form prompts for a report. There are two central drawbacks of Frigenti and Comninos' (2002) approach: the items overlap and are badly distinguished, and they focus on changes to policy as the only output of a report, limiting its value.

Meredith and Mantel (2006) put forward JS Busby's framework for considering topics, focused on the process rather than the subjects:

- How do people learn?
- What do people learn?
- How worthwhile is it?

This brings the subject back to an instrumental view: what is the review for? A long review is likely to be expensive, unfinished and unread. Selecting the key factors for review is vital.

### Where does the data come from?

There are many ways of collecting data, the learning activity involved a questionnaire, but interviews, records such as accounts or the ERP system, observing the team, measurement of the outputs can all have their uses. This is not the place for a detailed look at research design, but a few key points are useful.

- Start with the easiest sources: records, people nearby. Only go further where you need to.
- A 'wash up' meeting where participants get together to discuss the project at the end is probably the single best source of data and learning, wrapped into one.
- The more data and the more detailed, generally the more expensive. Questionnaires are good for large numbers of respondents, but they are difficult and time-consuming to construct successfully. Interviews are flexible and provide a lot of detail but time-consuming to carry out.
- Do not forget to look at the client, users and other stakeholders. Too many reviews rely on internal perspectives.
- Start early. Perhaps the best method of writing a final report is to start when the project starts. This also helps focus work. Once the team has broken up and dispersed, memories will have faded and distorted.

### Whose truth?

Different participants will have different views. As has been mentioned, a very successful project for one stakeholder can be disastrous for another, people forget the progress made, imagining it has always been there. Where possible, triangulate. Triangulation involves getting two or more sources for each part of the data to reduce the problem of bias. It costs more but more than doubles the value of the data.

### What will you do with it?

Once you have the data, analysis and presentation are important, but beyond that, what happens? An unused report on file is a cost; recommendations in place or learning bring value. What will be done with the review to gain that value? Policies are one route, but most of the learning will be subtler and carried by individuals. Ask how will that learning move on to prompt what to do next.

### Self-assessment question 13.4

Write a memo to the chief executive outlining how and why the project final report should be retained by the company.

*Feedback on page 215*

## Revision question

Now try the revision question for this session on page 321.

## Summary

The last part of a project is generally the most valuable, the outputs and learning tend to be clustered towards the finish. Managing the termination therefore is a very important part of managing the project, yet many factors conspire to make it difficult: running out of time, money, people and momentum, for example.

The first part of closure is identifying the need to terminate and how the termination will take place. Will it be sudden, or a planned closure over a longer period? What will the impact be on the team and others involved? How can the benefits be maximised?

The project management needs change for the last part of the project. Taking a fresh view, perhaps with a new project manager, planning the final activities carefully and making sure the final phase has maximum impacts are all part of closure.

Finally, review and learning are extremely valuable and badly done. The barriers to successful review often stop the search for valuable lessons and the learning dies with the project. To gain the most from review requires a structured, managed, cost-effective process, whether through audit or other methods. Repeating the past mistakes is the true failure of project management.

## Suggested further reading

- Frigenti and Comninos (2002); Chapter 11.
- Maylor (1996); Chapter 14.

- Meredith and Mantel (2006); Chapters 12 and 13.
- Taylor (1996); Chapter 15.
- Winch (1996).

## Feedback on learning activities and self-assessment questions

### Feedback on learning activity 13.1

Your answer should begin to open up some of the benefits from evaluating a project: understanding the success and failure of methods tools and individual projects in detail.

The lessons may be in detail: use of one tool; personal: the strengths and weaknesses of a stakeholder or sponsor; or general: insight into managing a range of projects.

The insight into barriers to evaluation should also come out of this exercise. If you found the documentation of the project complete and easy to access and the participants open and willing to discuss all aspects without bias, then your case is unusual.

### Feedback on self-assessment question 13.1

There are a series of benefits from evaluation suggested above, your answer may touch on some of them but should not, of course, just be a copy. Start from the point that the reason for evaluation is to learn for the future. This should lead to the things the organisation needs to learn. As examples, what are the most important factors? The funding or structure of projects? The handover or documentation? Although the general points are useful, the particular benefits will depend on the organisation, its needs, weaknesses and structure.

From there, the question is specifically about a *formal* evaluation process: what would a formal process add compared to informal review? You could use the discussion on barriers to highlight the difficulties in ensuring evaluation is done, and ensuring the breadth of subjects is covered.

### Feedback on learning activity 13.2

There is some relevant information in the text:

> 'The benefit of an audit as a review process is its rigour and independence. An independent assessment of the project against clear criteria ensures more objectivity than a narrative account provided by the team...It also encourages good practice: the criteria need to be set, encouraging those involved in setting up and managing the project to define clearly the nature of the project and the project management process that will be used.'

As with the self-assessment question 13.1, the more important part is applying it to the organisation. Is there already a structured process and audit would 'close the loop'? Would it bring a different assessment from that which you currently use? Would it drive people to manage their projects more effectively? Would it fit with the existing culture or challenge a lack of rigour?

Finally, the question focuses on benefits. There may be outweighing drawbacks for your organisation, which you may have touched on in your answer.

### Feedback on self-assessment question 13.2

This question is not a comparison of in-process and post-control audits, but a look at the value of both types.

The benefits will vary and there is a wide range of possible answers.

Factors for audits include:

- if projects are similar, a standard process can be used
- project objectives and outcomes are well defined
- processes are well documented: good records are kept
- regulation requires them (for example, record keeping in the new product development process is a necessary part of much EU product certification)
- where people are used to audit.

Factors against include the reverse of the factors above, with some others:

- no experience in audits
- no resource for audits
- in a fast-moving, fast-changing environment where the lessons will come too late
- where enterprise is more important than process, for example in leading-edge commercial innovation.

A good answer would incorporate perhaps half of these factors, with perhaps some not mentioned in these lists.

### Feedback on learning activity 13.3

There is a reflection on different types in the remainder of this section but your types are unlikely to match these exactly. Meredith and Mantel (2006) take a different view: extinction, addition, integration and starvation, with 'projecticide': political project killings.

The important part is identifying the different needs, challenges and risks. As examples, the risk of cost and indifference as a project just fades away, the need to manage the dispersal of the team if the project fails.

### Feedback on self-assessment question 13.3

The list above 'the detail of completing the project' can form a basis, but you will probably add a range of activities of your own. For example, what needs to be done to plan and manage activities in the time left? How will you identify and manage key risks? How can you gain a picture of what success will look like?

## Feedback on learning activity 13.4

There is a series of points within this section and some ideas for subjects. Comparing your questions with some of the subjects may identify gaps or areas of particular importance to you. While drawing up the questionnaire, did you consider how it would be used? The application, analysis and future use of the information are prime considerations when developing a questionnaire.

## Feedback on self-assessment question 13.4

The benefits from the final review have been discussed throughout this session and may be covered briefly in the memo. Space is tight, however, so some other things should be covered:

- specifically what is important to the organisation
- how will it be assisted by the review
- what is the cost benefit balance (why is it not 'too much trouble')
- how the results will be carried forward: how will the learning take place.

Study session 14

# Systems thinking and process focus

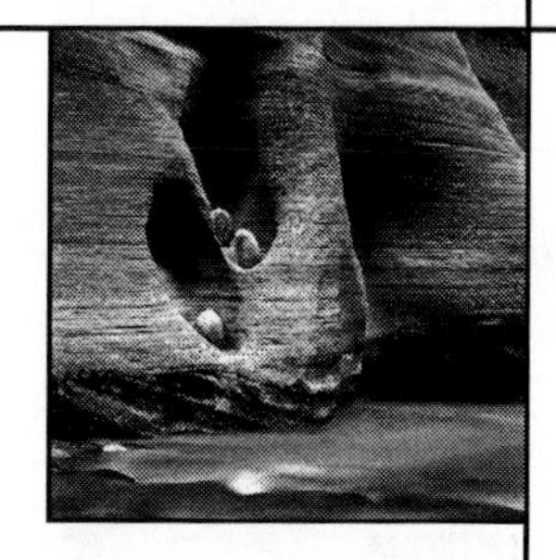

Greater than the sum of the parts: understanding the whole project.

## Introduction

There is an idea that to make a project work well, it takes a series of activities like time planning, risk management and stakeholder management. These are important but don't add up to managing a project. One part is missing if your project is built up from separate plans: the overview, the understanding of the whole. This session looks at the project as a whole and different ways of looking at dealing with the whole project.

## Session learning objectives

After completing this session you should be able to:

14.1 Explain the benefits of a systematic approach to the project planning process.
14.2 Identify the benefits and constraints of the work breakdown structure (WBS).
14.3 Apply basic methods of process mapping to project management (Maylor, 1996: 62–4).
14.4 Identify benefits and constraints of sequential and concurrent process models. (Maylor, 1996: chapter 3).

## Unit content coverage

This study session covers the following topic from the official CIPS unit content document.

### Learning objective

3.0 Develop and apply project management concepts, models, tools and techniques to create solutions to a range of practical project management problems.
3.2 Appraise the range of tools and techniques available to the project team in terms of appropriateness, selection and implementation.
- Appropriateness. Pick the right tools for the task
- Selection. Be aware of the limitations of tools and techniques
- Implementation. Be able to use the tools correctly

3.4 Demonstrate the approach of systems thinking and process focus, using process mapping techniques and procedures.
- Understand end-to-end processes
- Flow-chart the process
- Understand the interfaces. Swim lanes
- Critical Chain software

## Prior knowledge

Study sessions 1 – 13. Operations Management in the Supply Chain and Strategic Supply Chain Management modules would provide a clear link to this session.

## Timing

You should set aside about 6 hours to read and complete this session, including learning activities, self-assessment questions, the suggested reading (if any) from the essential textbook for this unit and the revision question.

## 14.1 Soup to nuts, holistic treatment, blinkers and systems thinking. What about your project?

A story about the building of the rail tunnel between France and the UK is used to explain some of the massive cost overruns and delays involved. When the group who were effectively the project team was formed, it was almost exclusively made up of civil engineers, with no railway-operating experts. As people naturally do, they focused on their understanding: the massive civil engineering challenge of tunnelling between the two nations. As a result, the rail commissioning part of the project was ignored and the civil engineering elements took all the available time, money and effort. They built a tunnel rather than a transport link. The work to commission the rail system had to be added on, increasing cost and delays.

This type of oversight is common and shows two examples of blinkered thinking. The project planning and management must go 'from soup to nuts'; from the very beginning until the last activity is complete. Secondly, if the team is dominated by a limited group of functions, it is likely the requirements of the other functions will suffer.

Systems thinking and holistic treatment are aimed at overcoming another type of blinkered thinking: optimising one part of the system but harming the rest. As an example, it might be possible to complete a project standardising all purchasing contracts and limiting suppliers to a very few. It is unlikely, but it might be possible. Purchasing would be optimised, with rapid, effective and efficient contracting. The impact on other functions might be disastrous: the new product team cannot engage new and innovative suppliers, the standard contract is a compromise and does not meet the business requirements of most departments, and so on. Optimising one part of the system should not be carried out to the detriment of the whole, as discussed by Meredith and Mantel (2006).

The final element of blinkered thinking is to focus on just one element of project success: hitting deadlines while the team suffers, making sure all stakeholders are engaged while making no progress, cutting costs until the quality of work and morale of the team drop away. The key is, as always, balance.

### Learning activity 14.1

The IT project 'Connecting for Health' is the world's largest computer procurements project, aimed at 'transforming the way the NHS works' in the UK. Over ten years, the aim was to connect 30,000 GPs to 300 hospitals and give patients access their personal health and care information.

Using press and official reports on the project, analyse the project for areas where 'blinkered thinking' could cause problems or has caused problems. Describe an example for each of the four general types of blinkered thinking:

- Not planning the process from start to finish: forgetting the railway commissioning for the channel tunnel.
- Focusing on one perspective: the example was civil engineer rather than transport experts.
- Ignoring the whole: failing to see the effect on linked systems.
- Focusing on one or two goals rather than balancing the different requirements.

*Feedback on page 226*

The problems with challenging all blinkered thinking are twofold:

- It is difficult to consider the wide spread of systems and functional concerns and bear them in mind with all decisions.
- Damaging the system is obviously wrong, but it is by no means proven that trying to optimise it as a whole is better than a step-by-step approach in practice, as demonstrated by Theory of Constraints and the TQM stepwise continuous improvement approaches.

The rest of this session looks at different aspects of attempting to overcome blinkered thinking: using a hierarchy of activities in the WBS, process mapping and concurrent engineering using cross-functional teams.



### Self-assessment question 14.1

List the key elements that should be contained in all successful project plans.

*Feedback on page 227*

## 14.2 All the project: the Work Breakdown Structure

In study session 8 the Work Breakdown Structure (WBS) was introduced as part of the definition of a project. The WBS is commonly described in project management texts (see further reading including Meredith and Mantel (2006), Lock (2003) and Taylor (1993)) and is seen as an essential step to form the basis of time, cost, resource and responsibility plans.

### Different attitudes to the WBS

Meredith and Mantel (2006) suggest 'its uses are limited only by the needs of the project and the imagination of the P[roject] M[anager]'.

Turner(1993) discusses the WBS 26 times on almost 10% of the pages of his book, without giving a completed example or clear direction on developing a WBS. Lock (2000) also gives it prominence as a hierarchy or family tree, with simple examples. Maylor (1996) recommends it for control. It is important it seems, because it breaks down in the project into all the activities involved in a structured way.

Working with people managing projects outside the 'hard' engineering environment, the creation of WBS has sometimes proved a barrier. The concept is understood, often by comparison with an organisation chart, a bill of materials or a mind map, depending on the individual's experience. The problems come in the construction. 'At the start of a project, how is it possible to define all the packages of work?' 'Is it necessary to define in detail all the work necessary towards the end of the project 2–3 years away? Things will have changed dramatically by then.' 'Do activities on each level need to be the same size?' 'If we define the areas of the project differently, the WBS comes out differently.' 'Most of the activities have sideways links: they could be in two or four areas and are closely linked to others.'

Identifying the breadth of activities involved and organising them somehow is valuable, perhaps driving towards a perfect hierarchy is less so.

### Learning activity 14.2

List the benefits of having a strong WBS and the barriers to achieving it.

*Feedback on page 228*

### Creating the WBS

Meredith and Mantel (2006) suggest 'list the task breakdown in successively finer levels of detail. Continue until all meaningful tasks or work packages have been identified and each task or package can be individually planned, budgeted, scheduled, monitored and controlled.' This seems reasonable until the scale of the task is seen: estimation was one of the real problems tackled by Critical Chain, uncertainty and novelty were part of the definition of a project.

Obeng (1996) has a structured and accessible method trademarked as 'Sticky Steps'. In this, by following a simple procedure repeatedly, it is possible to create a WBS with limited pain. It is an approach attractive to structured thinkers faced with a new project and allows gaps in understanding and unevenly sized tasks.

A common way to develop the WBS is to brainstorm all the known or predicted activities in a team using post-its, then group and re-group to build a structure. The brainstorming helps to draw out activities and gain a shared understanding of the project while freeing people's minds of the detail. Different people will have different ideas about what is involved. The structuring takes the list from a mass of activities to something that can be used to begin planning and separates big activities from detail. Estimating duration, cost, etc is probably best left for other stages of the planning process.

## Self-assessment question 14.2

Refer back to the definitions of project types in study session 7: radical, repeated change and traditional purchasing. Note briefly the suitability of WBS for each of these and what level of outcome might be expected.

*Feedback on page 228*

### 14.3 Understanding uncharted process territory: map it

One of the fundamental ways of understanding how businesses work is process mapping. Whether looking at the whole business and attempting to optimise whole processes, as in Business Process Re-engineering (BPR), or understanding individual flows and improving elements in turn, as with 'lean', or simulating processes to model and optimise, the act of mapping is a foundation and opens up understanding of what is happening.

Each project goes through a series of steps, which can be broken down into phases, as in the project life cycle, or further, into smaller steps. Many project managers recommend a 'macro plan' (see figure 14.1), which is a very simple form of process mapping. This can be carried out before any detailed level of planning to gain an overview of what will be needed.

**Figure 14.1:** A generic implementation macro plan

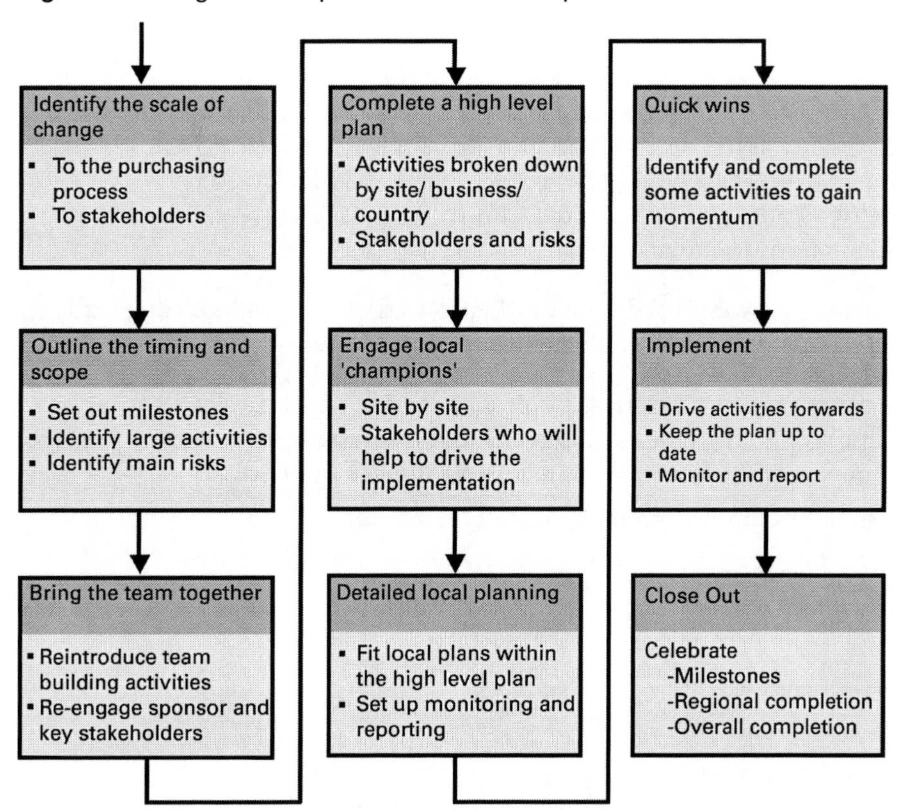


Research suggests that process mapping is an important part of project management. King and Wright (2002) concluded that 'there are many reasons why projects fail but that often failure to understand current processes is a major contributing factor. A relatively small investment in a mapping exercise can reduce risk in a project and help to engender the support from staff which is so essential.' Winch and Carr (2001) look at similar projects and conclude that a process map for each one to reflect how it is actually managed offers substantial benefits in risk and information management.

The balance between effort and benefit once again comes into the picture. Detailed process mapping is difficult and time consuming, for example incorporating it into the time plan as with GERT. Without process mapping, the process is vague and open to drift. For repeated processes, as in mass or flow production, the investment of detailed process mapping is repaid as the process is repeated many times. For repeated change or traditional purchasing projects, the repetition repays mapping. To a large extent, the more individual the process, the less detail is worthwhile. Maylor (1996) recommends Four Fields Mapping/Deployment Flow Charts, a complex method developed for repetitive processes.

## Learning activity 14.3

Write a memo to your boss detailing the benefits of mapping a process prior to detailed planning.

*Feedback on page 229*

## Adding complexity

Whatever process mapping tool is used, it is important that it is understood by the stakeholders who will need to use it. This may seem trivial, but even a 'one box four arrow' model such as IDEF0 (see IDEF: http://www.idef.com) or the common symbols used below can lead to substantial confusion and debate.

As a guide, start from the simplest (figure 14.2) and introduce complexity (figure 14.2) only when and where absolutely necessary.

The common flowcharting symbols described in figure 14.2 are part of a much larger family described in a US ANSI standard, covering a wide range of processes and commonly used for designing IT systems.

**Figure 14.2:** Common process mapping symbols

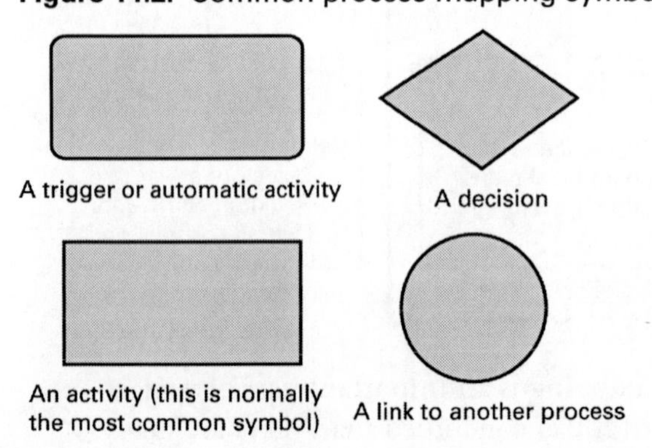

Using these symbols offers a structured, reasonably well-understood approach for charting a process. Figure 14.3 shows a version of probably the widest-circulated flowchart, designed for problem solving, particularly on machines.

**Figure 14.3:** Problem-solving flowchart

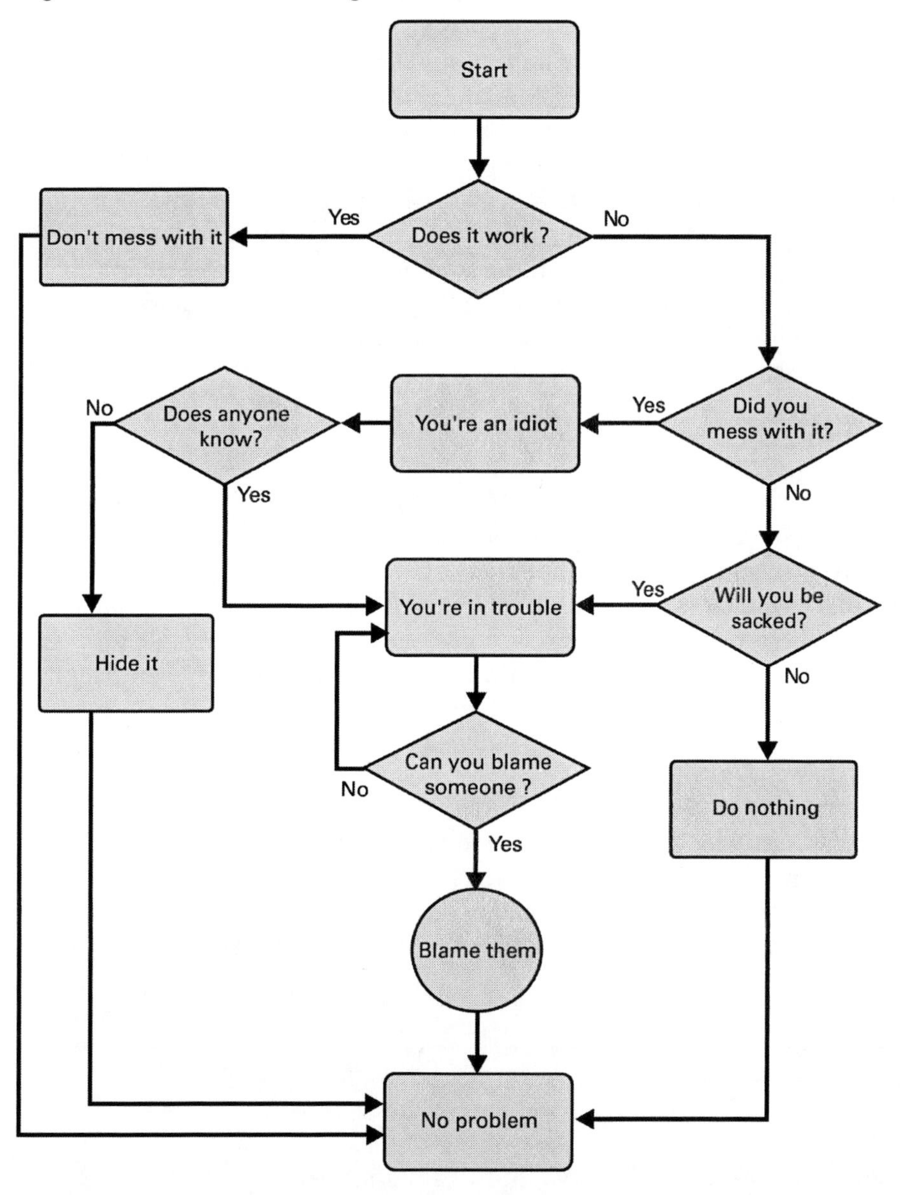


## Self-assessment question 14.3

Select a process with which you are familiar and identify the 8–20 high-level process steps involved from beginning to end. Apply the process mapping symbols to draw up a process map.

Compare this with the generic macro plan in figure 14.1 and suggest whether adding the complexity is worthwhile. If it is not, suggest under what circumstances would more complex mapping be of value.

*Feedback on page 229*

## 14.4 One at a time or all at once: sequential versus concurrent projects

### Scenario 1

Imagine you have an idea for a new way of purchasing maintenance which looks as though it could simplify the process, make costs more transparent and reduces downtime and the impact of maintenance. You discuss the idea, and your boss sends you away to get more information. You do this and your boss nods and suggests you work it into a full-scale business proposal. You do this and your boss takes the proposal to discuss with the decision makers involved. You get the go-ahead for a pilot and lead a small team to carry out a pilot and assess the results. The results are good and you hand over the project to someone from the facilities department to manage the project, which goes ahead successfully. The new transparency uncovers areas of potential saving and the need to invest in some cost-effective replacements.

### Scenario 2

Now consider a different scenario. Maintenance is a real problem and the downtime alone is costing millions, and direct costs are far above the industry average. A team from different departments gets together and identifies a whole range of causes, including old buildings and installations, poor suppliers, overcharging and lack of transparency in the whole process. Each cause is attacked at the same time by different people or teams from a range of departments who get together for coordination meetings every two weeks. The problems are radically reduced in six months and almost all the work is completed within a year.

These two scenarios are examples of sequential and concurrent project management. The first, rather like a gateway process (see section 12.4), has a series of stages. Once each is complete, the next can start. This is *sequential.* The second has a series of processes and projects happening together. This is *concurrent.*



### Learning activity 14.4

Refer to the two scenarios above (in this section). Identify why the different process types (sequential and concurrent) have been used and suggest why you might choose each of the two types in different situations.

*Feedback on page 229*

The concurrent or simultaneous process has been widely promoted as an important tool for new product development. Toyota and other automotive companies reportedly use it (Maylor (2001) and many others) and 3M, perhaps the most widely discussed case of new product development processes uses overlapping stages in a concurrent process to reduce time, using a strong cross-functional team to achieve results in reducing time to market (Handfield and Nichols (2002) and many others).

## Balancing risk

The advantages of sequential processes include control, for example through gateways, the ability to change or kill the project at each stage, and the focus on different aspects rather than fragmenting efforts in a range of areas. The drawbacks, in addition to the additional time, include the effect on morale and commitment: if the project can be killed at each stage, the attachment of the team to the project is reduced.

A slightly more complex drawback of the sequential process is that it relies on 'freezing' parts of the project before moving forwards. As a simple example, the concept of a car is frozen before it is passed to engineering for the design phase. The design is frozen before it can be passed to production and sourcing, the supply and production methods must be frozen before tooling up and running trials. This means that the concept was frozen well before the first car is sold, while technology, the competition and customer requirements are changing fast.

Concurrent processes, driven by a cross-functional team, can allow key design and sourcing decisions to be made far later, giving flexibility to adapt to external changes and problems with the design. The momentum of such a project is higher, with reported cuts in project times of 50% (Maylor, 1996). This process is more complex, with uncertainty carried through the project and decisions made later. However, in many cases, this may be a distinct advantage (Pender, 2001) with benefits in adopting technology, adapting to circumstance and avoiding rigid, incorrect choices. The core disadvantage is control: the sequential model is rational and fits established project management methods, with phases, milestones and gates. Maylor (1996) also highlights problems associated with a full-time cross-functional team: increased overheads if the project needs its own administration, cost of setting up a project office, cultural resistance and inappropriate application.

The two basic types have competing benefits and drawbacks, neither is 'better', as the benefits depend on the application. Many projects have a mix of both types, for example a building project which is planned sequentially but runs late, so for the end of the project, activities and phases are crushed together and happen concurrently.

As a general point, for the high-value-added activity of new product development, the concurrent process seems to have offered huge benefits in reducing time and increasing effectiveness. Purchasing and supply should be able to offer value to the organisation, yet most projects are sequential, with the corresponding delay in delivery. It may be time to adapt.

### Self-assessment question 14.4

Appraise a project with which you are familiar to determine whether a concurrent approach would have been beneficial.

*Feedback on page 230*

### Revision question

Now try the revision question for this session on page 321.

### Summary

This session started by looking at 'blinkered thinking': failing to see the whole project, focusing too much on a familiar part, or getting localised optimisation: efficiency in one part of the system while selling back the performance of the whole.

The subjects covered attack the problem from different directions. A system view can help to avoid localised optimisation, but will not help to identify activities. The WBS is a structure for identifying and organising activities, but does not explain how they will fit together. Mapping the process unlocks an understanding of a complex process, and can help improve it, while cross-functional teams working on a project scheduled to work concurrently can bring a balanced view, while reducing time taken, costs involved and allowing a previously unknown flexibility.

There is no one remedy or panacea for blinkered thinking, but a range of approaches can help you to build a transport link, rather than a hole in the ground.

### Suggested further reading

- Ayers (2004); Section III.
- Handfield and Nichols (2002).
- King and Wright (2002).
- Maylor (1996); Chapter 4.
- Maylor (2001).
- Meredith and Mantel (2006); Chapter 5.
- Pender (2001).



On BPR:

- Davenport (1993).

On Lean:

- Womack et al (1990).

On IDEF0:

- Idef0 page: http://www.idef.com/idef0.html.

### Feedback on learning activities and self-assessment questions

#### Feedback on learning activity 14.1

The range of options is large as this is a huge and complex project costing billions of pounds. You could have identified a wide range of potential or actual problems. The examples below are based on one report part way through the project: the review by the public accounts committee in June 2006.

- Not planning the process from start to finish: The original cost estimate was £6.2 billion (revised to £12.4 billion). The health minister Lord Warner suggested the total cost would be around £20 billion because the original estimates did not include training and ongoing local IT costs. By ignoring key parts of the project, between 40% and 60% of the cost was overlooked.
- Focus on one perspective: This project is extremely complex and has a huge range of powerful stakeholders. These include the public, a range of governmental agencies, doctors and other healthcare professionals, patients and health service managers and administrators. Though the overall aim is to benefit patients, it is not driven by patients and other benefits such as savings from centralised procurement are predicted. With this complexity it is extremely difficult to balance the different perspectives and the chance of bias is high. The committee heard that healthcare professionals expressing criticism or highlighting problems or risks had to meet in secret.
- Ignoring the whole: failing to see the effect on linked systems. This system needs to integrate with a huge range of other computer systems but also processes, such as scheduling appointments. Optimising patient choice can compromise efficiency or utilisation, for example. The focus on linking IT systems is certain to have a temporary negative impact on other activities, as all change does, and there is the potential for localised improvements which harm patient care as a whole.
- Focusing on one or two goals rather than balancing the different requirements. The project management was unable to provide any cost benefit analysis to the committee and cost estimates had at least doubled. The focus was on delivering to time, with other considerations taking second place. This may be a good tactic at this stage in the project, but with suppliers showing the strain and costs apparently increasing, there is the potential for problems over the project lifetime.



## Feedback on self-assessment question 14.1

This activity is not about describing a wide spread of elements covering every eventuality, but what is always essential given the points on blinkered thinking above.

Meredith and Mantel (2006: 241–2), for example, suggest that any project plan must contain:

- overview, including objectives and scope
- objectives (in more detail)
- general approach: managerial, such as deviation from standard procedures and technical, such as the relationship to available technologies.
- contractual aspects: subcontracting, intellectual property, etc
- schedules: including milestone events
- resources: mainly money, but can include machines, etc
- personnel: from recruiting to confidentiality

- risk management plans: to focus stakeholders on potential difficulties and 'lucky breaks'
- evaluation methods: how success will be measured.

This could be a useful starting place and is probably very appropriate for projects such as new product development. However, it is likely that projects will vary and deviate, of course. For example, an internal project to train people on a new purchasing system may be a low spend project so cost and resources are not a key factor. For a radical project, resources might be impossible to plan or readily available. A schedule and milestones may be unimportant to a project researching a new market. The technical and managerial approach could be unimportant for a category management project, because the technology is not yet known and the management processes are well established.

The 'universal' list for all projects might be limited to two or three items:

- a description of the project explaining what will be achieved, taken from different perspectives
- a breakdown of the activities involved
- some description of how those activities will be carried out: a time plan, responsibilities or a general approach.

And for different projects, there will be additions to this and detail appropriate to the needs.

## Feedback on learning activity 14.2

- The WBS is an identification of all activities needed: this helps ensure things are not forgotten or overlooked.
- A structured definition of the activities allows estimates of costs and time to be created by adding up the smaller activities into whatever level of detail is needed.
- By structuring activities into different areas, it is easy to allocate responsibilities.



On the description of barriers:

- It is difficult to identify all activities, at the start or indeed ever.
- It is time consuming.
- For a sizeable project in detail, it is complex and unlikely to fit on a manageable or accessible document unless that document is the size of a wall.
- It is difficult to set the hierarchy, groups of activities, etc.
- Whatever the grouping and hierarchy, positioning activities will always be imperfect and equivocal.

## Feedback on self-assessment question 14.2

### *Traditional purchasing*

This type of project has been done frequently before and involves many 'hard' activities. The definition of activities should be relatively straightforward. The challenges of allocating tasks and managing time and cost are also important and the WBS could be valuable for this. The outcome might be a well-structured WBS, in detail in most areas.

*Repeated change*

The experience exists, so by drawing on previous projects it should be possible to identify the majority of the activities. Soft activities and new areas, however, may prove a barrier to detail, so the detail of final implementation, for example, is unlikely to be possible. The outcome might be a fairly complete WBS for the early activities, high level only for those in the future. Detailed time and cost estimates are unlikely.

*Radical*

The identification of detail across the project is likely to be difficult except where a part has been done before. The 'radical' parts of the project will be difficult to pin down. The outcome is likely to be a high-level WBS, with gaps in knowledge identified, but the process is likely to help build agreement in defining the project and understanding of the task ahead.

## Feedback on learning activity 14.3

The benefits include:

- gaining an overview of the project
- highlighting important milestones, gateways or review points
- removing uncertainty as to the process
- the potential to streamline the process
- identifying information flows
- risk reduction.

## Feedback on self-assessment question 14.3

Your map will vary with your process, of course, but should give some insight into the practicalities of process mapping.

In general terms, if your process is fairly simple and linear, complexity adds little. Where branches and other information comes in, more complex mapping can be worthwhile.

## Feedback on learning activity 14.4

In the first case, a sequential process was used to test the value of the idea and reduce the risk of wasting resource on the project. In the second case, the problem was large and important and speed was more important than reducing the chance of wasted resource.

This gives the basic reason for choosing one or the other: risk.

Where resources are tight and the risk of wasting resources on a project which fails outweighs the risk of delay, a sequential process seems more valuable.

If the risk of being slow is more important than the cost of some false starts or resource wasted, then a concurrent process is better.

### Feedback on self-assessment question 14.4

The general points above (in this section) comparing the two types are a good starting point, but this assignment is about identifying how they balance in practice. Was your project high risk, with little cost to delay, or was delay expensive, while the project worked through the different stages and sign-offs?

Study session 15

# Tools and techniques for purchasing and logistics projects

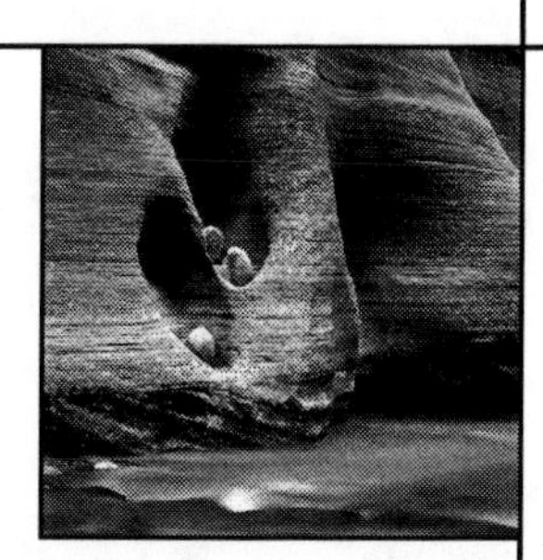

Getting past 'It won't work here': tools and techniques for our type of projects.

## Introduction

If you talk to a series of companies about their problems and challenges in purchasing and logistics, a pattern tends to emerge. Most companies highlight how unique their business is, with unique problems and challenges. Surprisingly, when those problems and challenges are discussed, many of them seem to be very similar. Every company is unique, but a core of the issues are the same or overlapping. In the public sector, every local council is unique, with unique challenges, yet the work of the 500 or so local government authorities is predominantly similar, directed by central government. The purchasing and logistics projects undertaken by organisations will each be unique, but an understanding of the characteristics can help to identify tools and techniques which can help and how they can be applied.

Study session 7 looked in general terms at the type of projects purchasing and logistics face. This session aims to take this further and explore the characteristics of purchasing and logistics projects and identify how tools, techniques and software can be used.

## Session learning objectives

After completing this session you should be able to:

15.1 Examine the key characteristics of a range of purchasing and logistics projects.
15.2 Identify characteristics that differentiate purchasing and logistics projects from projects in other functional areas.
15.3 Appraise the usefulness of some standard project management tools and techniques for purchasing and logistics projects.
15.4 Evaluate computerised project management systems for purchasing and logistics projects.

## Unit content coverage

This study session covers the following topic from the official CIPS unit content document.

### Learning objective

3.0 Develop and apply project management concepts, models, tools and techniques to create solutions to a range of practical project management problems.
3.5 Select and use a range of project management concepts, models, tools and techniques, which are relevant to purchasing and logistics projects.

- Assess the characteristics of purchasing and logistics projects
- Apply concepts to purchasing and logistics projects
- Apply models to purchasing and logistics projects
- Apply tools and techniques to purchasing and logistics projects.
- Apply project software to purchasing and logistics projects

## Prior knowledge

Study sessions 1 – 14. This section should relate to a number of modules at all levels that identify key issues and project-based solutions in supply management.

## Timing

You should set aside about 6 hours to read and complete this session, including learning activities, self-assessment questions, the suggested reading (if any) from the essential textbook for this unit and the revision question.

## 15.1 What characterises purchasing and logistics projects?

Study session 7 highlighted three general types of purchasing and logistics projects: traditional purchasing, repeated change and radical. Each had its own nature and requirements. Before taking that any further, it is useful to go back to what purchasing and logistics do, in order to identify the characteristics of the projects involved.

### Learning activity 15.1

Refer to the CIPS Purchasing and Supply Management model. Looking at the process from Strategic Sourcing Analysis onwards, describe what you believe will be the greatest and most important challenges in managing supply.

Pick no more than the ten greatest challenges and describe them with a sentence or two each.

*Feedback on page 240*

The feedback from the learning activity suggested that the key challenges lie in specialist purchasing analysis and the internal and external relationships.

This is based on the description of the task of purchasing in the CIPS model. Another aspect of the projects undertaken will be expectations of purchasing and logistics: what do the important stakeholders in the business expect of purchasing and what are the factors that will demonstrate that a purchasing or logistics project has succeeded?

### The expectations on purchasing

Many purchasing professionals complain about the lack of prominence of purchasing within their organisation. Frequently mentioned aspects include that CEOs are rarely from a supply background and that purchasing has traditionally been seen in an order fulfilment, operational role. Purchasing is not alone, operations professionals and engineers frequently make the same points. There are far more companies run by accountants than any of the other disciplines. Marketing typically attracts far more resources and training than purchasing in spite of the frequently cited comparison of impact on profit and value.

This historical position has been challenged by developments such as supply chain management over the past 20 years and category management over the past ten. The historical attitude is hard to shift however.

Fairly or not, purchasing has typically been confined to delivering value through cost reduction and availability or delivery conformance. If the specification and demand management are owned and controlled by other people, it is hard to offer other value. Engineering, operations, human resources, medical practitioners and regulators typically define specifications and purchasing delivers them. While the market knowledge of the sales and marketing function is used in defining products, the market knowledge of purchasing has less impact.

If the expectations of the organisation are focused on cost and delivery, then success will be defined in cost and delivery terms. If other forms of value are not expected, any value-purchasing projects add will exceed expectations, but will need to break down established attitudes and challenge the control of specifications.

### Summary: typical characteristics of purchasing and logistics projects

The two perspectives of this section lead to a series of characteristics which are likely to be present in purchasing and logistics projects:

- expectations on cost reduction and product delivery performance
- limited emphasis on other forms of value
- internal barriers to change, for example, specification challenge
- strong need for assent, compliance, support and commitment from internal stakeholders
- strong need for management of external stakeholders
- strong need for internal and external data from a range of sources.



### Self-assessment question 15.1

What makes relationships with suppliers important in projects to manage supply? Describe three or more ways supplier relationships can assist supply and logistics projects.

*Feedback on page 240*

### 15.2 Other people have all the fun: the difference between purchasing and other functions

If the expectations on purchasing are predominantly cost and delivery, how does this differ from other functions? How do the characteristics of marketing, operations, engineering or human resources projects differ?

#### Learning activity 15.2

#### Case study

You are not a purchasing professional: you work for the department for social services for a city council as 'special projects coordinator'. This means you look after the development projects for the department, but do not manage them. Project managers report to you. As always, the department has budget restrictions and increasing demands from clients (the public) and central government. You have three projects starting soon:

1. A project to contract overnight care for disabled children. You buy blocks of 'bed nights' from three providers, each providing different specialist care and the current cost is £2 million each year, all three contracts end in six months.
2. A project to build a hostel for homeless people in partnership with a charity. This will have 20 rooms and 60 beds, plus kitchen, common areas and offices.
3. A project to raise awareness of different services among the public. This is in response to an external audit identifying your department's weakness in this area.

What characteristics would you see as different between these projects? To prompt your thoughts, what are likely to be the challenges and the measures of success?

*Feedback on page 241*



#### The difference with purchasing

The learning activity looked at three different projects, one typically led by purchasing, one by facilities, one by marketing. These are just three fictional cases, but some points came out. Are the following points true?

- The output of purchasing projects is low visibility and commonly not well understood.
- The challenges of purchasing projects are not well understood.
- Purchasing projects serve other functions so rely on them for the specification.
- Other functions own the specification and can develop it within projects to gain better results.
- The potential for innovation is greater in other functions.
- The budget for purchasing projects is likely to be small, tight and inflexible.

Probably the best answer is 'sometimes'. Purchasing and logistics projects can be innovative and groundbreaking, but perhaps typically follow the list above.

## Self-assessment question 15.2

Consider the projects in purchasing and logistics that you are involved in or would like to be involved in. Draw up a checklist of their characteristics.

*Feedback on page 241*

### 15.3 Do the standard tools work?

Looking back over the different sessions, there are many tools and techniques discussed so far. This section takes a sample of them and looks at how they fit with the characteristics of projects put forwards in this section.

Looking back over the sections provides a series of different tools and techniques. A sample of ten is probably enough as a starting point.

1. Project definition: study session 8
2. Work Breakdown Structure: study session 8
3. Linear responsibility charts: study session 8
4. Stakeholder management: study session 2
5. Communications plan: study session 8
6. Risk management: study session 9
7. Gantt charts: study session 10
8. Network analysis: study session 10
9. Resource loading: study session 10
10. Gateways: study session 12.

## Learning activity 15.3

Examine the ten tools and techniques listed above alongside the characteristics of purchasing and logistics projects from self-assessment question 15.2 above.

Analyse each tool in turn: does it meet some need from the characteristics of projects? Make a note for each one on which characteristics it meets.

Are there any characteristics which are not covered well? If so, note what they are as they could indicate a requirement for using other tools or techniques.

**Table 15.1**

| The tools and techniques | The characteristics of purchasing and logistics projects |
|---|---|
| 1 Project definition: study session 8<br>2 Work Breakdown Structure: study session 8 | • Expectations on cost reduction and product delivery performance<br>• Limited emphasis on other forms of value |

*(continued on next page)*

15

Learning activity 15.3 *(continued)*

| The tools and techniques | The characteristics of purchasing and logistics projects |
|---|---|
| 3 Linear responsibility charts: study session 8<br>4 Stakeholder management: study session 2<br>5 Communications plan: study session 8<br>6 Risk management: study session 9<br>7 Gantt charts: study session 10<br>8 Network analysis: study session 10<br>9 Resource loading: study session 10<br>10 Gateways: study session 12 | • Internal barriers to change for example specification challenge<br>• Strong need for assent, compliance, support and commitment from internal stakeholders<br>• Strong need for management of external stakeholders<br>• Strong need for internal and external data from a range of sources<br>• The output of purchasing projects is low visibility and commonly not well understood<br>• The challenges of purchasing projects are not well understood<br>• Purchasing projects serve other functions so rely on them for the specification<br>• Other functions own the specification and can develop it within projects to gain better results<br>• The potential for innovation is greater in other functions<br>• The budget for purchasing projects is likely to be small, tight and inflexible |

*Feedback on page 242*

1. *Project definition*: Defining the project is generally useful or essential. It can be very valuable in agreeing the project with all those other stakeholders. The format may vary by project.
2. *Work Breakdown Structure*: A good understanding of the work involved in the project is useful and would be particularly valuable for construction or capital projects. Constructing a clear hierarchy of detailed activities may be difficult where the project is to negotiate a new contract, however, and where activities are blurred, the effort may be too big.
3. *Linear responsibility charts*: The characteristics include low visibility and understanding and a need to manage internal and external stakeholders carefully and well. A rigid responsibility chart is may be rejected or ignored by stakeholders until they are very committed to the project and their role is defined and accepted.
4. *Stakeholder management*: If internal and external stakeholders are characteristically key, then this is too.
5. *Communications plan*: As a central way of working with stakeholders, this is once again key.
6. *Risk Management*: High risk and innovation are not part of the characteristics, hence this may be unnecessary for some projects. Wherever the risk to the business is moderate or high, however, risk management becomes vital.
7. *Gantt charts*: These are a sound way of planning time and good for communicating the plan. Where people understand them, Gantt charts should be a valuable part of the project management.
8. *Network analysis*: This is suited to projects such as construction, where there are well-defined activities which have to be carried out in a certain sequence. This does not match the characteristics, although there will

be some purchasing and logistics projects which fit this description. More complex network analysis, such as PERT or GERT introduce probability and decisions. This complexity seems to add little but work, although the Critical Chain idea may be worth considering.

9 *Resource loading*: Resource loading is useful for managing those full time on the project. The resources needed in the characteristics are part-time assistance by a range of people from other functions. This will be by negotiation and depend on commitment and how important they believe the project is, rather than calculation.

10 *Gateways*: Using gateways can be valuable for governance where there is a well-defined project and oversight. It can show rigour in planning and management. There are few of the characteristics this approach meets directly, however, unless there is a strong budgetary element.

In summary the value will depend on the type of project but many do not fit the characteristics of 'typical' purchasing projects. Reflecting overall:

- Time planning is well developed but the tools are over complex for many projects.
- There seems to be little on the most important part: managing the stakeholders, getting commitment, providing an understanding about the nature of the purchasing challenge and potential benefits.
- Cost and finance are key factors, yet there is little on managing this except budgeting.
- Data is a key factor, yet this is not represented.

To manage projects successfully, some of the established tools can be adopted and adapted, but there are many areas under developed which will need to be managed, such as data, cost and commitment.

### Self-assessment question 15.3

Is the use of network analysis (PERT/CPM) appropriate in planning and managing a project to centralise purchasing for a major manufacturing company with several purchasing offices in different countries? Highlight the pros and cons and suggest where you believe the balance is.

*Feedback on page 242*



## 15.4 How can the computer help?

Project management has not been left behind in the shift towards IT that has swept the world of business since the 1980s. There are many different project management software products. For a review of a range of products, Meredith and Mantel (2006) reprint Fox and Spence's study from 1998. As they point out, software changes rapidly so a check through project management trade magazines or journals may lead to something more up to date.

### Microsoft Project

Similar to most project management software tools, MS Project uses a definition of activities as the basis and the core of the plan. Using this, several different tools are available:

- Work Breakdown structure
- Gantt chart with milestones indicated
- network analysis, including some advanced calculation
- calendar
- budgeting and cash flow based on activity costs
- earned value, based on the same costs
- resource loading based on defined resources and activity requirements
- a series of flexible reports based on the data used.

### Learning activity 15.4

Compare the characteristics of projects identified in section 15.2 above and the discussion of tools in section 15.3 above with the functions of Microsoft Project. What advantages and disadvantages of the software can you identify? If possible visit the Microsoft website or other sources to build up your understanding of the software.

*Feedback on page 243*

### Other software

There are other project management software providers and a range of products available, including direct competitors, simplified versions and far more complex systems which can embrace and manage many projects. Rather than a detailed report on those, it may be useful to consider other ways software can help purchasing and logistics projects.

### Software for coordination



Many projects involve people from different sites and different companies. Using a neutral but coordinated space for documents, plans and communications can help to foster involvement, information flows and coordination. Specialist providers such as [Projectplace: http://www.projectplace.com] offer low-cost websites which can be accessed by all and are owned by all. One useful feature is that it is possible to track different users to see whether each stakeholder is accessing material, what is valuable, etc.

### Software for communication

Intelligent use of email, Lotus Notes, Microsoft Outlook and other systems can help to make communication more effective. It is also very useful for record keeping. There are dangers; many project managers report that the distribution of emails has reached plague proportions with torrents of information – far too much to follow or digest – and key parts are lost. This is driven by a desire for safety: if problems occur subsequently, the excuse will be 'you had that information by email a month ago'.

### Software for information

Where a wide range of stakeholders could benefit from understanding the project, especially where change is involved, intranet or websites can have a high impact. Structured pages, the project plans, specifications and communications, weblogs, message boards and forums can offer people access to the project as and when they need it and demystify what is happening.

### Self-assessment question 15.4

Write a memo to your boss identifying what software (in general terms, not product specific) you would like to help manage a purchasing and logistics project of your choice.

*Feedback on page 243*

## Revision question

Now try the revision question for this session on page 321.

## Summary

One of the identifiable factors of projects is their uniqueness, so there cannot be one type of purchasing and logistics project. There are typical and common characteristics, however, which can be derived from experience or an analysis of the challenge of purchasing and logistics.

Typically, purchasing and logistics will be cost focused, rely enormously on internal and external stakeholders for data and support, and the understanding and priority within the organisation will be low.

The standard tools and techniques offer a starting point for project management but need careful adapting and application. They are biased towards time planning, to the detriment of stakeholder and data management.

When looking at how software can support purchasing and logistics projects, the standard software is only a limited starting place, far more is available.

## Suggested further reading

- Ayers (2004); Section III.
- Lock (2000); Chapters 12–14.

- Maylor (1996); Chapter 5.
- Meredith and Mantel (2006); Chapter 10.

## Feedback on learning activities and self-assessment questions

### Feedback on learning activity 15.1

The detail of the challenges will depend on your experience and current situation, but looking at the areas within the model:

- Process and competence analysis is important and while individual activities are difficult, the greatest challenges are frequently the search for information and working within the confines of the organisation.
- Spend analysis follows the same pattern. The analysis is frequently difficult, but getting the data is more of a barrier. In some organisations accurate spend data does not exist, in others it needs to be reconstructed from several sources. There are companies specialising in performing spend analysis as a service, but their projects face the same challenge: gaining access to data held by a variety of departments.
- 'Political' analysis, supply base analysis, supply/value stream mapping and 'generate options' rely once again on the data and information from outside. Given good information, the analysis itself becomes a matter of good practice. Generating options is a creative act, constrained more by the acceptance of the business and the freedom to implement than anything else.
- Manage Direct and Indirect Spend once again relies on cross-functional involvement, with training and support and some complex analysis also providing challenges.
- Acquisition pre- and post-contract again points towards cross-functional involvement and a strong relationship outside the business.

If this description is right, it seems that there is a strong requirement for the professional skills of analysis and mapping, but the biggest challenges lie mainly in managing internal and external stakeholders, gaining data, assent, support and commitment.

If your analysis highlighted other areas, it may be more accurate for your situation. As a check, reflect on the challenges you have identified and why you have selected them, in the light of the feedback.

### Feedback on self-assessment question 15.1

At a partnership level, the relationship is vital to delivering value to the organisation over the long term. This generally applies only to a few companies however, and your answer should not be confined to this area.

With suppliers in more generic markets, the relationship may be more distant and shorter, but the relationship is still important. Examples include:

- Suppliers can provide proposals for change to increase value.
- Suppliers can provide market information.

- Suppliers will often hold valuable information on your organisation: spend, market position, perceived attitude and maturity.
- Implementation and change will rely on a good working relationship, the supplier is important as an external stakeholder.

## Feedback on learning activity 15.2

Before discussing these projects, it is worth noting that purchasing could play a strong role in all three projects, although it is more likely to be leading the first, a typical purchasing project. The second is a facilities project, the third, marketing or promotion.

1. The project to contract is likely to be focused on fulfilling the specified need at best/reduced cost. Characteristics would include:
    - An expectation that less than £2 million will be spent next year.
    - Your understanding of the detail of the project is likely to be low. The output is a contract supply and difficult to assess, except by price.
    - Need to work internally to clarify specification.
    - Externally to negotiate contracts.
    - Gaining support from internal stakeholders is important, though their interest may be low.
    - The market is difficult: single suppliers in three niches, and as specified, the project gives little room for radical change.
2. This project is likely to have a substantial capital budget and be led by a specialist in facilities and construction. Characteristics include:
    - High visibility and understanding of the project: construction is an accessible project and the output is tangible.
    - Time is important, but not critical.
    - The budget could be flexible: if money runs out towards the end, more will be found, although this will be a form of failure.
    - A partnership, probably complex and a key part of the project.
    - The outline specification is set, but the detail is flexible and can be adapted to meet perceived needs.
    - A well-developed market: there are many construction companies.
3. This project is driven by a regulatory requirement:
    - Room for innovation.
    - High visibility, if not necessarily understanding of the detail of how promotion works.
    - The budget has yet to be set and while cost pressures exist, it needs to be done, so the project must adapt.
    - The specification is owned by the project team: how the promotion works is still flexible.

## Feedback on self-assessment question 15.2

The list at the end of section 15.1 offers a basis and there may be some points from this section to add to it. A simple combination of those would be:

- expectations on cost reduction and product delivery performance
- limited emphasis on other forms of value

- internal barriers to change, for example, specification challenge
- strong need for assent, compliance, support and commitment from internal stakeholders
- strong need for management of external stakeholders
- strong need for internal and external data from a range of sources
- the output of purchasing projects is low visibility and commonly not well understood
- the challenges of purchasing projects are not well understood
- purchasing projects serve other functions so rely on them for the specification
- other functions own the specification and can develop it within projects to gain better results
- the potential for innovation is greater in other functions
- the budget for purchasing projects is likely to be small, tight and inflexible.

The important part of this exercise is to challenge these, from both your own experience and intentions. Should the projects be badly understood and lacking in innovation, for example? Should the projects challenge the specification of the product and the project itself? A checklist of what purchasing and logistics projects *should* be like is as important as the status quo.

### Feedback on learning activity 15.3

There is a detailed discussion of each of the tools and techniques in turn below (in this section).

If you struggle to see the applicability, it suggests the tool may not be useful, but the key questions for each one are:

- 'If this had been used in the projects I have seen, would they have been better?'
- 'Would any improvement be worth the extra effort?'

If your answer does not match the discussion, check that you have understood the use of the tool, but it is quite likely your understanding of your projects is better than the general points made here.



### Feedback on self-assessment question 15.3

This question goes beyond the 'typical' characteristics outlined above. Network analysis cannot be dismissed completely for all purchasing projects because the variety is so wide.

Network analysis is valuable where activities are well defined and rely on one another in a complex sequence. It also demonstrates detailed planning and the complexity of the project to stakeholders.

On the other hand, network analysis is abstract and needs some training to understand. It does not give a clear visual understanding of when things will happen, unlike a Gantt chart or simple flow chart. It also takes time to construct and requires accurate estimates of tasks and dependencies.

The balance of value depends on the balance of these factors. Where activities are of fixed duration and depend on one another in a complex way, it is ideal. If the method is well known among stakeholders, it is ideal. If these are missing, value drops rapidly.

### Feedback on learning activity 15.4

There are fundamental advantages to using software:

- Calculations are automated: no need to analyse the network or complete the budget by hand.
- All reports and plans are in one place but can be copied and distributed easily to anyone with the software.
- Using standard software standardises plans, making each project plan easier to follow.

Looking at this software specifically:

- Time planning is there with as much complexity as most projects will need.
- Work Breakdown Structures are available.
- Budgeting (and earned value) can potentially be used to help control the money.
- Resources can be calculated.

The disadvantages are substantial, however. Fundamental to software is that:

- Full access to plans is available only to people with the software, a considerable investment.
- The plans are designed according to the software producer's view of what is needed: Microsoft Project is common in civil engineering and largely tailored to that sort of project.

Specific to Microsoft Project:

- Most importantly, it starts with fixed activities and a time plan. There is little on stakeholder management, communication, data and all of those things so central to purchasing and logistics projects.
- You may have discovered that many find the plans difficult to understand.

### Feedback on self-assessment question 15.4

The exact answer will depend on you and your choice of project.

Refer to the characteristics of your project and its requirements, then build up the need from there.

The common automatic response 'we need Microsoft Project for project management' may limit planning and effectiveness.

# Study session 16
# 'Hard' factors in avoiding project failure

## Introduction

If it's late, over budget and not what was wanted, it's not a success.

Projects vary and what makes a success varies with them. There are, however, some things that crop up again and again. The 'iron triangle' of cost, quality and time, management of risks and the factors that have made projects succeed in the past all offer different ways of seeing through the forest of project management problems to the clear ground of success.

In this session, four different sources are used to identify ways of managing towards that elusive success: the iron triangle, the contingency approach, understanding what makes projects fail and identifying success factors. None of these sources has the whole solution, but each gives different guidance and different perspective.

## Session learning objectives

After completing this session you should be able to:

16.1 Evaluate the elements and interdependency of the 'iron triangle' and the use of 'crashing' to ensure project success.
16.2 Contrast the 'iron triangle' approach with the contingency approach to project management.
16.3 Analyse and identify process-based factors in the most common causes of failure in purchasing and logistics projects.
16.4 Analyse and identify the most common process-based factors in successful purchasing and logistics projects.

## Unit content coverage

This study session covers the following topic from the official CIPS unit content document.

### Learning objective

4.0 Evaluate the key factors in successful project management in the context of today's business environment.
4.1 Evaluate the concept of the Iron Triangle (quality, cost, time)
- Quality, cost, time. Project objectives, Slack et al (2004)
- The balance between QCT. Contingent approaches

4.2 Contrast the Iron Triangle and other contemporary approaches
- Critical chains, Goldratt (1997) crashing project float

4.4 Apply the following concepts to purchasing and logistics projects:
- Greer (1999) Elements of project success
- Greer (2004) Ten ways that projects fail
- Other contemporary approaches to successful projects, Van Aken (1997), Grundy (2001), Gardiner (2005)

### Prior knowledge

Study sessions 1 – 15. The Strategic Supply Chain Management Strategy and Risk Management and Supply Chain Vulnerability modules should supply key linkages to this session.

### Timing

You should set aside about 6 hours to read and complete this session, including learning activities, self-assessment questions, the suggested reading (if any) from the essential textbook for this unit and the revision question.

## 16.1 Fighting with the iron triangle

### Learning activity 16.1

You are managing a project to introduce new software. The software is installed and available to almost all staff but there is a comprehensive plan involving training and roll-out. Time is getting short, the roll-out is behind schedule and you are under pressure to finish. The supplier who delivers the training says that they have difficulty delivering because the training specification is high and the skills of your users are low. This means the training is taking more time and can only be done by expert trainers. Most of their expert trainers are 'engaged on contracts with higher day rates'.

Make brief notes on two aspects of the project:

1. What is the supplier suggesting about the balance between cost, quality and time?
2. Do you believe their analysis of that balance?

*Feedback on page 257*

In section 2.2, the 'iron triangle' of cost, quality and time was introduced (see figure 16.1).

**Figure 16.1:** The 'iron triangle' of cost quality and delivery

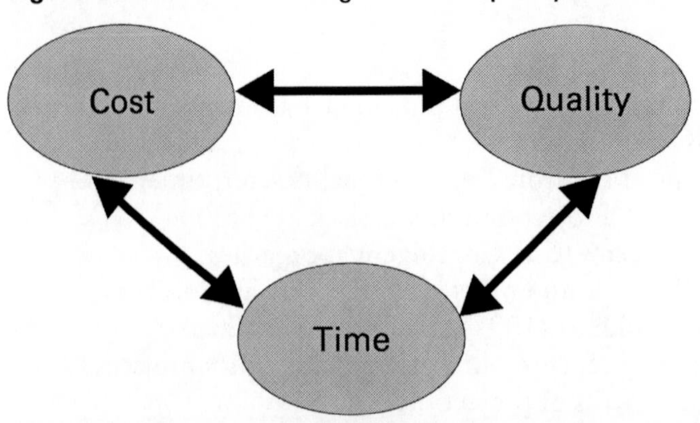


This is a standard idea used in many project management texts to define project objectives. The idea behind it is that there is a trade-off between the three factors and for each project the balance between the three is different.

There have been many challenges to these as a definition of project objectives and project success, many examples of projects which are seen as successful yet failed on one or more of these criteria, as has been discussed. Yet this triangle has lasted at least 50 years (see Oilsen, 1971) and crops up time and time again. There are probably several reasons why this imperfect triangle refuses to die:

- It looks at aspects which are relatively simple to measure. Time and cost can be measured with some degree of accuracy, and quality, if defined as meeting specifications, can be assessed.
- For projects such as small civil engineering, building or capital machinery projects, they are a reasonable starting place.
- For most projects they are a *part* of the story. Understanding the stakeholder requirements in terms of cost quality and time for your project and understanding how they develop is normally a useful part of project management.
- Pretending to stakeholders that there is an 'iron' relationship between the three is useful in negotiating for more time, money or changing specification or quality.

## Using the triangle

Exploring the importance of these measures with stakeholders and negotiating the level of input for the project can be very useful. Many stakeholders will have expectations for all three from the outset. Cost is frequently described in budget terms, but cost in terms of resources is frequently more important for purchasing and logistics projects. Deadlines are frequently set with comments about their importance but, from bitter experience, many people expect them to be overrun. Quality is more difficult to define, but some expression of specification and criteria is necessary to balance the other two.

At the outset, a clarification of all three and an understanding of the importance of each is useful. However, many stakeholders will have high expectations for all three and questions such as, 'If there was a choice between overspend and overrun, which would you prefer?' will merely trigger a fear of mismanagement and failure.

As the project develops, the importance of each develops too. A system implementation project in an organisation of 2,500 people was set up with a small team and limited budget, with a timescale of 18 months before the old software and hardware closed down and needed replacement. Costs were held down and quality requirements were maintained until three months before 'going live'. At this point, it was clear that the system must hit the deadline, yet progress was haphazard and well behind schedule. Quality requirements were radically reassessed and money and staff were reassigned to the project, multiplying the budget and increasing the staff by over 100%. Time became all important, the other criteria fell away.

Some change is almost inevitable, but the common pattern of keeping quality and cost fixed until the deadline looms, then casting controls aside can be a very inefficient way of running a project.

## Crashing a project

When time is pressing and the project is behind schedule, or the deadline is brought forward, 'crashing' the project is a way of adapting. Put simply, it involves paying more or adding resources to rush activities. For the example in the learning activity 16.1 above, paying more to bring in more trainers would be crashing the project.

Crashing is usually related to critical path and PERT methods, because in theory it is only worth crashing activities on the critical path. The process is a rational one:

- identify activities that can be done more quickly
- identify the cost per day (or unit) saved for each activity
- select the cheapest
- check all following activities can be brought forward
- check other paths have not become 'critical' and are now defining the project length.

As with all of PERT and CPM, crashing in this way relies on some fairly complex information, this time a calculation or, more likely, an estimate of how much it will cost to rush per day for each activity to allow a rational choice.

Some activities will have limits to how far hey can be rushed, of course. If an activity relies entirely on one person, it may be difficult to crash, or there may be physical constraints. Some activities may not have the potential for linear crashing: supplier A will deliver in six weeks, supplier B will deliver in three weeks, but it is a straight choice between the two.

## Summary

There is often a relationship between cost quality and time in projects. For building projects, that relationship may be a very useful expression of objectives. While the 'iron triangle' may be an imperfect expression of most projects and offers very limited criteria for success, there are strong reasons why it has survived and is in use in projects and project management training across the world.

As Atkinson (1999) suggested: cost, time and quality are 'two best guesses and a phenomenon'. It is important to manage all three, but the relationship between them is not rigid and their availability/demand can change through the life of the project.



## Self-assessment question 16.1

Refer back to the case described in learning activity 16.1 above. As project manager, outline a series of options for action on this project for your project board.

*Feedback on page 258*

## 16.2 It depends: the contingency approach

Section 16.1 above looked at the iron triangle and how the importance of the three factors might vary with project, stakeholder and time. If the three factors change in importance, then the importance of tools to manage these will change and different approaches will become more appropriate.

### Learning activity 16.2

Different project management approaches and tools can be more or less appropriate in different situations. List the factors you can identify which will determine how applicable the tools and approaches are.

*Feedback on page 258*

The learning activity looked at some of the factors which might effect the value of different ways of managing projects. If projects are so varied and the factors defining the best methods so mixed, it should not be a surprise that there is no one best way of managing projects. PRINCE2 might fit some projects and some environments, Critical Chain might fit others, PERT might really be useful in some situations. The discussions in study sessions 7 and 14 identified some general types of purchasing and logistics projects but there can be no 'purchasing and logistics project methodology'.

This is the basis of the contingency approach to project management. The approach is *contingent* on a range of factors which vary by project. The approach should vary by project.

### Contingency theory

The source for this idea is the use of contingency theory in leadership and organisational design. As an example Fiedler (1967) moved away from an idea of a 'best' way of leading to the suitability depending on two main factors: leadership style and situational control. Situational control was made up from three sub-factors: leader–member relations, task structure and leader position power.

Since 1980, this contingency approach has been adapted to project management, almost exclusively in the development of information systems and IT projects. Davis (1982) focused on the factor of uncertainty and proposed that different approaches could be selected on that basis. Gremillion and Pyburn (1983) use different factors: commonality, impact and structure in order to select the approach. Another way of tackling this problem is to have a 'contingency framework': essentially a loose framework of approaches rather than a methodology. The exact approach would be developed within this framework based on whatever factors are appropriate.

### Using a contingency approach

In very simple terms, a contingency approach involves examining the relevant factors and adopting a project management approach or methodology to match. Most project managers do this to some extent:

communicating with people in different ways, changing the approach from hard to soft activities. It is probably also true that most project managers are limited at adapting; their experience is based on a few projects and they do not have the ability to change radically according to the situation.

There have been many attempts to develop a generalised contingency approach, as mentioned above. The problems with this are fundamental and challenging. As in the learning activity, there are many factors and many states those could be in. Just as importantly, the understanding of links between situational factors and project management approaches are not fully understood. The final criticism of contingency approaches is that in order to make them work, the organisation and project manager must be able to apply a wide range of approaches. This is a tall order.

Although the contingency approach cannot determine exactly what to use or apply in any given situation, it does have some valuable insights. It challenges the idea of 'a project management methodology' and highlights the variety of approaches that are needed. It challenges the idea that managing cost quality and time are uppermost in project management. It explains why the results of different approaches are so varied and hard to understand: the situation determines what works and what does not. It links project management to the benefits of contingency theory on leadership, organisational design and motivation.

### Self-assessment question 16.2

Explain in no more than 100 words how the 'iron triangle' approach can work if the approach to project management is contingent on a range of factors.

*Feedback on page 258*

## 16.3 A process doomed to failure

### Learning activity 16.3

Identify two failed purchasing and logistics projects from reports in the media or trade press or your experience. Identify process-based factors which contributed to the failures, that is, mistakes in the project management process which contributed to failure.

*Feedback on page 259*

There are many studies looking at the ways projects fail and what helps them succeed. Different authors take different views.

Cooke-Davis (2002) identifies elements such as risk management and planning and keeping duration short, ideally below a year or dividing projects up as factors to avoid overruns. Cost is controlled by managing the way changes to scope are introduced and maintaining the performance baseline. Quality is not used as a criterion, but Cooke-Davis looks at success, which he defines as delivering benefits to stakeholders. This, he says, is dependent on the existence of a benefits delivery process linking the project to line management functions. Beyond this, consistent success relies on matching the 'suite' of projects to corporate goals, resourcing them well, measuring and controlling them in a balanced way and learning from each project experience.

Meredith and Mantel (2006) note the range of studies in the area and the differences between factors in different industries before citing four basic reasons:

1 A project organisation is not required. Setting up a project was wrong for the task or the environment.
2 Insufficient support from senior management.
3 Naming the wrong person as project manager.
4 Poor planning.

They state that: 'these, and a few others are the base cause of most project failures,' a statement raising more questions than it answers. They then identify a series of more specific causes of failures:

- failing to learn from previous projects
- estimates were not made by the people carrying out the work
- starting late, the project manager jumped into the tasks without adequate planning
- personnel moved or reassigned during slack periods then were unavailable
- project auditors were reluctant to carry out detailed meaningful evaluations
- the project was allowed to carry on long after it had ceased to make cost-effective progress
- evaluations failed to determine why problems were arising early in the project, due to inadequate risk management.

These are all sensible points, highlighting the need for monitoring and review, however they read more like the results of an enquiry into a single failure than points that can be used.

For a more direct approach, Greer (2004) offers ten ways to make your project fail:

1 Do not bother prioritising your organisation's overall project load.
2 Encourage sponsors and key stakeholders to take a passive role on the project team.
3 Set up ongoing committees focusing on management process.
4 Interrupt team members relentlessly.
5 Create a culture in which project managers are expected to 'roll over' and take it when substantive new deliverables are added halfway through the project.
6 Half way through the project, when most of the deliverables have begun to take shape, add a whole bunch of previously unnamed stakeholders and ask them for their opinions about the project and its deliverables.

7 Encourage the sponsor to approve deliverables informally. Never force sponsors to stand behind their approvals with a formal sign-off.
8 Make sure project managers have lots of responsibilities and deadlines, but no authority whatsoever.
9 Describe project deliverables in the vaguest possible terms so sponsors and reviewers have plenty of leeway to reinvent the project outputs repeatedly as the project unfolds.
10 Get projects up and running as quickly as possible.

## Failure factors in purchasing and logistics projects

Study session 15 explored the nature of purchasing and logistics projects, looking specifically at how different tools can be applied. Combining those same descriptions with the factors for project failure listed above, what are likely to be the most common causes of failure?

The 'typical' project characteristics fall into three general areas:

- Money-related: Expectations on cost reduction and product delivery performance but limited emphasis on other forms of value. Budgets likely to be small, tight and inflexible.
- Stakeholder-related: Strong needs for assent, compliance, support and commitment from internal stakeholders, for management of external stakeholders and for internal and external data from a range of sources.
- The position in the organisation: Purchasing projects serve other functions so rely on them for the specification and there are internal barriers to change, for example specification challenge. This can hamper innovation. The challenges and output of purchasing projects is low visibility and commonly not well understood. Logistics projects may be more visible.

The first area: money constraints can help with project success. If the budget is small and fixed, the activities can be more closely defined within those strict limits. If the expected outcomes are restricted to savings and product delivery, alignment to corporate goals and monitoring the project becomes easier. These characteristics will constrain the project's reach, scope and potential outcomes, which is a form of failure, but overall failure will be reduced.

The second and third areas are linked. If management of stakeholders is of very high importance, while purchasing and logistics are poorly understood, there is a double challenge. Looking back at Cooke Davis' points, unless the project includes a process for the management and delivery of benefits to the stakeholders, it is likely to head for failure. Both Greer and Meredith and Mantel highlight sponsor and senior management commitment as vital. If the project, its challenges and potential are poorly understood and regarded, commitment is likely to be tenuous.

Finally, the area of who manages the project and their ability and potential for successful planning and successful delivery. Meredith and Mantel mention picking the wrong project manager, Greer mentions the constant interruptions and expecting the project manager to 'roll over'. Typically, purchasing and logistics are not regarded as functions defining and leading major projects and change. Unless the project manager is well prepared to plan and manage effectively, the likelihood is that the 'day job', increased demands on the project and split resources will lead to failure.

As a final point, failure is to some extent unavoidable. If projects are to achieve novel, innovative outcomes, then they must risk failure and failure must be accepted. As mentioned in study session 13, the real failure of a project is to repeat mistakes, to fail to learn.

### Self-assessment question 16.3

What sort of process-based failures might you expect to encounter in the implementation of new distribution and automated sales replenishment systems?

*Feedback on page 259*

## 16.4 A process for success

As with factors for failure, there have been many studies and discussions about what makes projects succeed. Greer (1999) has 14 factors to balance out the ten ways to make projects fail:

1. Project managers must focus on three dimensions of project success: time, budget, and quality.
2. Planning is everything – and ongoing.
3. Project managers must feel, and transmit to their team members, a sense of urgency.
4. Successful projects use a time-tested, proven project life cycle.
5. All project deliverables and all project activities must be visualised and communicated in vivid detail.
6. Deliverables must evolve gradually, in successive approximations.
7. Projects require clear approvals and sign-off by sponsors.
8. Project success is correlated with thorough analyses of the need for project deliverables.
9. Project managers must fight for time to do things right.
10. Project manager responsibility must be matched by equivalent authority.
11. Project sponsors and stakeholders must be active participants, not passive customers.
12. Projects typically must be sold, and resold.
13. Project managers should acquire the best people they can and then do whatever it takes to keep the garbage out of their way.
14. Top management must actively set priorities.

Some of these link with the ten ways to fail and most have been mentioned before in this unit. Planning, identifying the need, setting deliverables are all well-established practice. Interestingly, Greer is very specific on the need for and nature of communication: 'urgency', 'deliverables and activities visualised and communicated in vivid detail'.

Pinto and Slevin (1987) created a series of Critical Success Factors, ranked in order of importance, from surveying experienced project managers:

1. Project mission: initial clearly defined goals and general directions.
2. Top-management support: willingness of top management to provide the necessary resources and power/authority for success.
3. Project schedule/plan: a detailed specification of the individual action steps for project implementation.
4. Client consultation: communication, consultation and active listening to all impacted parties.
5. Personnel: recruitment, selection and retention of the necessary personnel for the project team.
6. Technical tasks: availability of the required technology and expertise to accomplish the specific technical action steps.
7. Client acceptance: the act of 'selling' the final project to its ultimate end users.
8. Monitoring and feedback: timely provision of comprehensive control information at each stage in the implementation process.
9. Communication: the provision of an appropriate network and necessary data to all key actors in the project implementation.
10. Troubleshooting: ability to handle unexpected crises and deviations from plan.

Ignoring elements of bias in the ranking, for example project managers are likely to highlight support from those above them as a key factor, this provides an accessible checklist for developing success factors.

## Learning activity 16.4

Evaluate the extent to which the critical factors for project success above (Slevin and Pinto cited in Meredith and Mantel) might apply in particular to purchasing and logistics projects.

*Feedback on page 260*



In study session 7 three types of purchasing and logistics project were identified: radical, repeated change and traditional purchasing. Each type is likely to have a different balance of success factors, matching the different requirements touched on in study sessions 7 and 15. To look at purchasing and logistics projects in more depth, each type can be compared with the Pinto and Slevin list in turn.

### Traditional purchasing projects

These would typically be re-sourcing power supply for the company or procuring an office of fairly standard specification. The amount of money involved and potential impact of failure may be high, but the technology methods and stakeholders are identifiable and stable.

The following are from the Pinto and Slevin list.

*Still critical*

- The project schedule or plan is likely to be very important. Arranging for the office to be available or the power supply contract to be in place at the right time are measures of success.
- Communication will be important to ensure the people involved are aware of and involved in the progress.
- Monitoring and feedback will be needed to ensure the project runs smoothly.
- Client consultation will be essential to establish the business requirements, but given their stable nature, client acceptance should be more readily achieved.
- Troubleshooting is likely to be needed at some point.

*Less important*

- Technical tasks and availability of the required technology are still important, but given the nature of the project, are likely to be in place or easy to source.
- Project mission and top-management support are similarly important but are less likely to be in question in this type of project. The authority to negotiate a contract for energy, as an example, is likely to lie with purchasing.
- Assembling personnel for the project team will be more straightforward.

### Repeated change

These would typically be Six-Sigma or category management projects, individual projects in a programme of change. The general process can be well established, but the aims and objectives of each are individual.

*Still critical*

- As mentioned in study session 7, the project environment is critical and top-management support is important, but more than this, the ability and will to provide the right environment are central to programme success and within that, individual project success.
- Client consultation is important: there is little value in a category management project built on mistaken business requirements, for example while communication is necessary to gain and maintain commitment. If this is well done, client acceptance becomes more readily given, but it is still necessary to ensure the client recognises the success. Monitoring and feedback effectively becomes a part of this.
- Technical tasks are a core part of Six-Sigma and category management. The thriving specialist training in these areas demonstrate the value of specialist technical understanding.
- Troubleshooting and personnel: getting the right team is likely to be central to success.

*Less important*

- Project mission. The general aims of the projects will be identifiable and setting clear guidance and a brief at the outset, along with refining the objectives with stakeholders is less of a challenge for repeated change projects.

- A detailed project schedule/plan specifying each individual action step is useful but is frequently not done in detail without disastrous consequences. A plan for rolling out new sourcing procedures across different sites may need to be flexible, for example, with a good high-level plan and room to develop different schedules within that.

### Radical

The examples given were creating a new procurement department or developing a process for supplier collaboration where nothing exists and setting up a pipeline of new purchasing talent. The outline aim may be clear but what success will look like in detail is less easy to visualise.

#### *Still critical*

- Client acceptance: selling the end result to the people who will use it is critical. The results should be radical and the change may be hard for some to accept, yet acceptance is a defining factor of success.
- The project is likely to be difficult and have false starts or dead ends, so continued top-management support is essential.
- The right team: personnel will be necessary with a mix of vision, enthusiasm and capability to make things happen.
- Carefully managed communication will help make things happen. The changes involved may be threatening to some stakeholders, progress may be too slow for others. Managing those stakeholders will make the difference between success and failure.

#### *Less important*

- The more radical the project, the more client consultation changes. While delivering benefits is vital, the client's first requirements are likely to be moderated and adapted as the project progresses. This type of project is rarely about delivering exactly what the client specifies on day one.
- Project mission is similarly flexible. There can be no clear and comprehensive definition of deliverables where the project is radical.
- This flexibility in both objectives and process reduce the importance of detailed Schedule and specific technical ability. These will depend on the development of the project. Trouble-shooting becomes less important as deviation from plan is unremarkable.
- Monitoring and feedback is important but the idea of a strict audit against baseline measures loses its value. Monitoring must be flexible to accommodate innovation.



### Self-assessment question 16.4

Use the discussion in this section to develop a list of process factors which you believe are important to projects you could be involved in.

*Feedback on page 261*

## Revision question

Now try the revision question for this session on page 321.

## Summary

The lists of success factors tend to lean towards a prescription for success. They suggest that if you have top-management support, plenty of planning at the start and throughout, manage cost quality and time correctly and have a comprehensive communication plan, etc, your project will succeed. Each list varies a little with the experience used to compile it, the industries involved and the type of project. There is value in these lists and if the 'hard' factors are ignored, success becomes unlikely, especially in 'hard' projects like construction. The iron triangle provides insight, understanding risk is important and understanding success factors derived from previous projects is essential.

The hard factors are only part of the story, however, and success will be defined by perceptions of stakeholders rather than exact measures or ratios.

## Suggested further reading

- Atkinson (1999).
- Avison and Wood-Harper (1988).
- Butler Cox (1987).
- Cooke-Davis (2002).
- Davis (1982).
- Fiedler (1967).
- Gremillion and Pyburn (1983).
- Meredith and Mantel (2006); Chapter 13.
- Oilsen (1971).
- Saarinen (1990).

## Feedback on learning activities and self-assessment questions

### Feedback on learning activity 16.1

1

- They are suggesting that your high-quality specification is taking more time and using expensive trainers.
- You could reduce the quality, then the training would speed up anyway and they could use other (non-expert) trainers to speed things up further.
- You could allow more time, leaving the other two factors the same.
- You could possibly pay more to get those expert trainers off the other contracts.

2

- They may be right and there is a certain logic behind what they say. This position is fairly convenient for the supplier, however, and there are plenty of challenges available. As an example, if your users

16

are low skilled, why do they need the best trainers, especially for the first stages of training? There is no fixed reason why cost quality and time must always be traded against one another.

### Feedback on self-assessment question 16.1

Your options could refer to the balance between cost, quality and time provided by the supplier:

- Reduce the quality, then the training would speed up anyway and they could use other (non-expert) trainers to speed things up further.
- Allow more time, leaving the other two factors the same.
- Pay more to crash training.

It is worth remembering that there may be other options:

- Reduce quality by reducing the number of people trained.
- Reduce quality by delaying roll-out for non-critical staff.
- Challenge the supplier's analysis to drive the speed by changing the way training is done.
- Get someone else to train: users could train one another in a 'cascade'.
- You may be able to crash other activities: commissioning, documentation, etc.

### Feedback on learning activity 16.2

At the start of this section a few suggestions were given: the relative importance of the three factors, the requirements of the stakeholders, the type of project and the stage in the project.

Other factors that could have a bearing include:

- complexity of the project
- risk involved
- mostly hard or soft activities
- degree of change involved
- history of project management in the organisation
- novelty and uncertainty
- the preferences of individual stakeholders
- culture of the organisation
- national/regional cultural differences, and many more.

The overall conclusion is that the value of a style, approach, methodology or tool will vary according to a range of factors.

### Feedback on self-assessment question 16.2

The contingency approach suggests that different approaches work in different situations. There is no reason why the iron triangle approach should not work in some situations. Your answer should identify the overlap: that both can be correct, and the conflict, that according to the contingency approach, the iron triangle cannot be appropriate in all situations.

## Feedback on learning activity 16.3

There are many potential contributors to failure, compare your factors with the discussion below (in this section).

The difference between process factors and others are that they are likely to repeat: if one project fails because the process fails, others are likely to. A one-off mistake which is picked up quickly or a time overrun are not themselves process-based factors, but they may have been caused or exacerbated by them.

## Feedback on self-assessment question 16.3

This is a visible project with clear outcomes, so should not suffer from the lack of comprehension mentioned. However, success will rely on the integration of systems (always a difficult and complex operation) both within and external to the company. Some of the problems with this were discussed in section 14.1. This integration is likely to require huge amounts of coordination across internal functions from sales through to warehousing and distribution. Perhaps even more challenging is the integration with the systems of suppliers and other essential third-party providers. Automated replenishment is useless unless the suppliers can understand and respond to the requirements.

The impact of problems is potentially very high: failure could lead to stock-outs and lost sales, perhaps even lost customers. Risk and contingency planning is vital, for example back-up systems for maintaining service if the new system fails.

To put this in the context of the project management process, perhaps the best set of failure factors to use is Greer's:

1. *Do not bother prioritising your organisation's overall project load*: This project could drift down the organisation's priorities, leading to a lack of focus and resources in spite of the high cost of failure.
2. *Encourage sponsors and key stakeholders to take a passive role on the project team*: Unless the sponsors are engaged and committed, interest and support can wane, while the suppliers, for example, are key stakeholders here.
3. *Set up ongoing committees focusing on management process*: Possibly less likely in this case, but interruptions to look at how projects are carried out can be barriers to progress.
4. *Interrupt team members relentlessly*: The interruption of ongoing work, other projects and new activities would place a brake on progress.
5. *Create a culture in which project managers are expected to 'roll over' and take it when substantive new deliverables are added halfway through the project*: Any shift in deliverables is likely to cause a lot more work. Unless the system is clearly defined early on, the team will be chasing a moving goal and system development will stretch while delivery runs into the future.

6 *Halfway through the project, when most of the deliverables have begun to take shape, add a whole bunch of previously unnamed stakeholders and ask them for their opinions about the project and its deliverables*: This is linked to the points on stakeholder management. There is an internal and an external danger here. The first is that poor planning will exclude valid stakeholders, the second is that the brief changes part way through. For example, introducing the people responsible for the sales system and insisting that the system meets their needs as well, will cause severe disruption.
7 *Encourage the sponsor to approve deliverables informally*: Never force sponsors to stand behind their approvals with a formal sign-off. Again, changes to scope and measurements will move the goalposts.
8 *Make sure project managers have lots of responsibilities and deadlines, but no authority whatsoever*: Particularly in selecting and managing the team and managing powerful stakeholders such as local controllers of stock, warehousing and delivery and suppliers of software and hardware. Stakeholders soon recognise where a project manager has little power and are likely to ignore him or her, leading to severe problems managing the project.
9 *Describe project deliverables in the vaguest possible terms so sponsors and reviewers have plenty of leeway to reinvent the project outputs repeatedly as the project unfolds*: Failing to pin down what the system will and will not do early on will lead to rework and additional efforts. Does it integrate with all suppliers' IT systems/does it link with the sales system? Does it provide financial information such as stock values or cash flow?
10 *Get projects up and running as quickly as possible*: Time saved avoiding proper planning early on will have to be repaid many times over as the project hits problems and delays.

## Feedback on learning activity 16.4

- Project mission and top-management support are commonly discussed factors. The only drawback to focusing on these at the top of the list is that the mission may not be defined and top-management support may not be strong at the start of the project.
- Client consultation: Client acceptance and communication were discussed in section 16.3 and study session 13 amongst other places. Their importance is hard to ignore as purchasing serves operations, development and other functions.
- Personnel and technical tasks: As discussed, many projects will not have full-time team members so recruitment is not a contractual act but important nonetheless. The importance of purchasing and logistics specialist expertise is balanced by the need for help from different disciplines, for example in challenging specification.
- Project schedule/plan: Few would recommend running a complex project with no plan, although the time schedule may not be the most important element.
- Monitoring and feedback is part of the project management process. If sponsors are hard to engage in purchasing projects, this feedback is a central part of communication.
- Troubleshooting: ability to handle unexpected crises and deviations is likely to be useful.

Perhaps a summary would be that the factors are relevant. However, the importance will vary by industry and for purchasing and logistics projects, the ranking and detail may be difficult from Pinto and Slevin's findings.

### Feedback on self-assessment question 16.4

There are many factors discussed here (and previously). Start with the types of project you expect to be involved in then develop your own list.

Study session 17

# 'Soft' factors in achieving project success

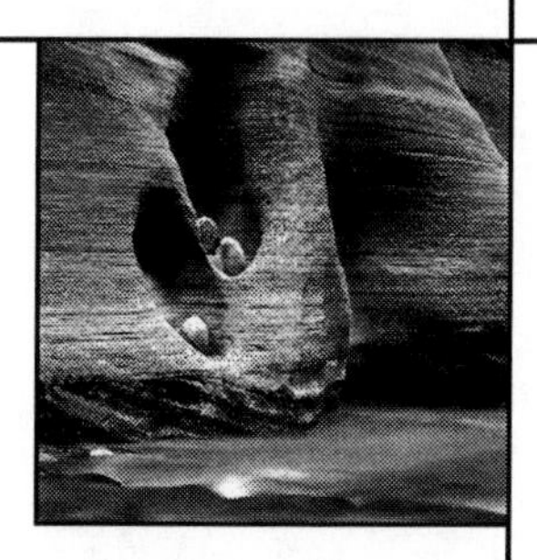

Collaborators, opposition, support and finally judges. People and their role in your success.

## Introduction

An understanding of the hard factors in avoiding failure is part of the story, but only part. Leading a project is not just about planning and management, good analysis and technical excellence. The teamwork, the direction, the attitudes and finally the judgement of the people involved will determine success.

## Session learning objectives

After completing this session you should be able to:

17.1 Explore the requirements of effective project leadership.
17.2 Identify the key stages in team development and key issues for management at each stage.
17.3 Analyse and explain the characteristics and importance of teamwork in a project.
17.4 Analyse the extent to which people management and leadership issues contribute to the most common factors of success or failure in projects.

## Unit content coverage

This study session covers the following topic from the official CIPS unit content document.

### Learning objective

4.0 Evaluate the key factors in successful project management in the context of today's business environment.
4.3 Recognise the importance of the human aspects of project management, including leadership, management, teamwork and communication.
- The role and skills of the project manager. Maylor, Meredith and Mantel, Lock
- Leading and managing projects. Managing in Four Directions, Buchanan and Boddy (1992)
- Teamwork, Belbin (1981), Body of Knowledge (2000)

4.4 Apply the following concepts to purchasing and logistics projects:
- Greer (1999) Elements of project success
- Greer (1999) Ten ways that projects fail
- Other contemporary approaches to successful projects, Van Aken (1997), Grundy (2001), Gardiner (2005)

## Prior knowledge

Study sessions 1 – 16. Leading and Influencing in Purchasing and Managing Purchasing and Supply Relationships together with Management in the Purchasing Function should all provide clear linkages to this section. In particular the latter should give a good foundation.

## Timing

You should set aside about 7 hours to read and complete this session, including learning activities, self-assessment questions, the suggested reading (if any) from the essential textbook for this unit and the revision question.

## 17.1 Leading the project

Leadership of the project is probably the best description of the role of project manager. Taking the lead in the direction of the project and providing leadership for the team involved are core activities in all but the simplest, most mechanical project. The leadership will be a key determinant of success and failure simply because it has an influence on so many of the factors for failure and success identified in study session 16. It is worth noting that project leadership is sometimes a development role: given as a test of potential and a training for functional leadership.

Back in study session 1 the difference between leadership and management was mentioned and the definition of projects as 'temporary organisations' (Cleland and Kerzner, 1985). These shift the role of project manager from someone who prepares and reports on detailed schedules to someone leading an enterprise. This also points to the two parts of project leadership: leading the team and providing direction for the project as a whole.

### Leading the team

Leadership is complex, challenging and extremely valuable for success. Good leadership is also hard to analyse effectively and very much depends on the context. If you feel your leadership is lacking and your vision of a good leader revolves around charismatic figures like Winston Churchill, Eva Peron or Margaret Thatcher, then it may be worth thinking again. Charismatic, dominant leaders work well in some circumstances but their value is limited in most projects.



### Followers make leaders

One of the easiest ways to look at leadership is not through a set of character traits or strengths but through the people who follow. As far back as 1938, the idea of authority was reversed from something given to a leader by position to something given by subordinates (Barnard, 1938). This introduced the idea that people choose to follow instructions if they understand them, it fits their personal interests, they believe it is good for the organisation and they are able (trained, have the time and freedom). For projects where the team is working only part time, this is a particularly useful view: the people involved can choose to do the work well, badly or even not at all.

## Learning activity 17.1

Identify two or more managers or leaders you believe are able 'to get things done', to get people to do what they want. What gives them the ability to get other people to work with them where others fail?

*Feedback on page 275*

The four conditions are not perfect: some people work far harder than they should for their health if other factors are strong, for example. The conditions are also not enough on their own: many people will still have a choice whether to spend more time on the project work or their normal role, so there must be other factors that make them decide.

These other factors will vary from situation to situation, from person to person and from culture to culture of course. The simplest way to approach this is to put yourself in the situation of someone being asked to work on the project then examine what factors would make you say yes and do the work well. There are many descriptions of the factors that make people follow, but the following is a simple list bringing together a few of them:

- Personal reaction: do you like or admire the person?
- Personal debt: do you owe this person something? Have they helped you in the past?
- Interest: does this person appear to have an interest in you and your participation?
- Reputation: does this person have a reputation as someone worth following?
- Role models: do other people you respect follow this person?
- Choice: do you feel they are offering you the choice to follow or do you need to assert that choice by resisting?

Too often leadership is seen as a commanding role and when project managers find people are not complying or helping the first reaction is to reach for power: getting senior management to apply pressure. Effective leadership is usually something far less formal and relies on a number of soft skills of persuasion, informal networking and even charm.

### Leading the project

Top of the list in Pinto and Slevin's 1987 description of project success factors is Project Mission: initial clearly defined goals and general directions. There is a tendency to translate this into specifying a very clear goal, scope and deliverables and expecting these to remain the same throughout the project. Even where scope changes are accepted as necessary, these are grudgingly admitted through a strict process to limit their impact.

This simple view of managing uncertainty by removing it can be useful for stable, well-defined projects such as the 'traditional purchasing' type. It begins to fall down once more projects are considered. Few organisations can predict what the demands on them will be in six months or a year, let alone exactly what they will deliver in terms of product type, specification and volume. Since the need for projects is often driven by a changing environment, it seems unreasonable to expect any project to be insulated from that environment and have far more certainty than the organisation that needs it. This is one reason why so many IT projects, for example, struggle with moving targets and deliver heavily compromised products: the need to adapt to change is resisted and fought.

The mission or goal of a project may be set, but detail on deliverables is dependent on negotiation with stakeholders such as the sponsor. Identifying requirements early on is an important part of the management process but that negotiation continues throughout the project.

Leading the project then becomes analogous to leading any organisation: matching the activities and performance of the organisation to the mission aims or goals, within the changing environment it finds itself in. This is not the place for a detailed examination of how strategy is developed and delivered, but two features of enterprise from Mintzberg (1998) are relevant: strong environmental knowledge on which to base decisions and the controlled boldness to take those decisions.

### Contingency in leadership

In study session 16, the contingency approach to project management was introduced with Fiedler (1967, 1971). He moved away from an idea of a 'best' way of leading and divided leadership style on two bases: task orientation: focusing on the work involved, and relationship orientation: focusing on relationships with team members, supporting, facilitating and encouraging.

This simple split hides a wealth of complexity but highlights a key point: different leadership styles suit different situations better. A task orientation is much more effective in an emergency or when things are going very badly, and also when things are going extremely well. Where people are conditioned to taking orders, task orientation is also valuable. For professionals and people used to autonomy, relationship orientation is frequently better. For example, academics are notoriously hard to order about. Taking over a project which is neither a disaster nor a huge success, relationship orientation might be better.

So what makes a good leader? Unfortunately the simplest answer is that it depends. Task orientation is better if things are going well or badly and for people who are used to it. Relationship orientation is better for other situations. Leadership must be matched to the situation.



### Self-assessment question 17.1

In one page, define what you believe would make a good project leader.

*Feedback on page 275*

## 17.2 Not just watching: managing the dynamics of your team

The Tuckman four-stage model for the stages of team development was discussed in section 11.2:

1. *Forming* describes when the group first comes together.
2. *Storming* follows.
3. When new roles and ways of working emerge the stage is called *Norming*.
4. If the team continues to develop, *Performing* is reached.

While the fourth stage, performing, is the most effective, with highest output, a team which reaches norming is more common and quite capable of achieving success in a project. If teams get stuck in the first two stages, progress is likely to be slow and painful and success will drift away.

The important aspects of this model become:

- How do we get the team to norming or performing as quickly as possible?
- What can I expect on the way?

### Learning activity 17.2

Work through the different stages of team development and identify what you believe a team leader should do at each stage to progress (or to maintain performance in the last two stages).

*Feedback on page 275*

### Moving between stages

The first thing to note is that moving forwards is not automatic and even when a team reaches a stage, it can still slip back.

### From forming to storming

If the team are uncertain about role, the project and the other team members, the key will be to challenge this and get beyond it. Expect a period of low output, but bring the team together frequently with tasks which involve collaboration and goals which can be achieved quickly. The team leader will frequently need to instruct the team: telling them what to do, but if the next stage is storming, the team will show when this instruction is no longer needed by resisting.

Things that will slow progress will include frequent changes in team membership, long gaps between working as a team and members unused to team work or embedded in other teams.

To move forward into storming will probably involve a period of disruption without increasing output.

### From storming to norming

This is the most dangerous stage: friction and slow output can prevent individuals working closely together. It does not need to last long, however. To move forward normally involves resolving conflict and achieving goals, even limited goals, while the team leader will frequently need to convince or inspire the team: reselling the project to them. Address conflict directly and effectively: aim for conflict resolution and planned team events. Ensure team members do not drift away by watching closely and re-engaging. Manage and celebrate achievements, however small. Focus on individual differences, strengths and needs. Some members may be stuck in a confrontational 'storming' mode and the team will have to develop around them.

Things that will slow progress include a natural reluctance to be involved in a 'storming' team, any failures or slow output and individual or group relationship problems.

### From norming to performing

This is an acceptable stage, though the team is not performing to its full potential, moving forward is often hard and will involve a balance between proactive management of tasks and group behaviour, and withdrawing instruction and direction to allow the team to develop. For most people, this withdrawal and 'letting go' is the hardest part as they lose control and direct influence. The leader's role will normally become less visible as the group moves towards participation: more collaborative work and decisions.

To move forwards: delegate, reduce direction, support and monitor progress and success, use individual and group strengths effectively. Maintain contact within the team, activity and achievement to prevent the team moving backwards to storming.

Factors slowing progress include no perceived need to progress, restrictive leadership and remaining lack of unity between individuals.

### Staying in performing

This is a difficult stage to achieve and without continued support, teams can move backwards to norming. Output is high and management input tends to be low. The team leader will need to delegate and allow the team members freedom to work together in the best way, maintaining a performing team involves balance between delegation and 'hands off' control, and support and guidance of achievement. The team will constantly need new tasks and challenges; ensure team members maintain collaboration. These challenges also help to prevent problems where cohesion is high but output is low: the team focuses on one another rather than the task in hand.

Factors pulling the team back to earlier stages include a lack of collaborative tasks, new disagreements between individuals, a natural drift and disruption to the team such as changes in membership.

### Self-assessment question 17.2

Review your own management strengths and identify:

- which stage of team formation best matches your strengths
- what you may need to consciously change in the other stages.

*Feedback on page 275*

## 17.3 It is the teams that make projects succeed, not the plans

It is a well established maxim that plans do not get the work done, people do. Yet most project management texts focus on time plans, risk management, project selection models, the organisation structure and financial aspects. Teamwork is dealt with by models such as Tuckman's. There are several factors behind this. It may be partly because most project management literature comes from engineering disciplines more at home with maths than motivation. It may be partly because teamwork is difficult enough to discuss without adding the complexity of a short-term and fluctuating team common to projects. The most important reason is that information on teamwork and management has been developed extensively elsewhere, from Henri Fayol (1919) through the breakthrough Hawthorne experiments of 1924–1933, the Human Relations school such as Maslow, Herzberg and MacGregor to the examination of TQM and lean practice in teamwork. There is enough information available, and this section will focus on what is particular or different about teamwork in projects.

### Learning activity 17.3

What are the features of teams in projects that make teamwork harder or easier? Outline two or three aspects of project teamwork which are different in projects compared with a team in a logistics department, for example.

*Feedback on page 276*

### The differences with projects

*Who is in the team?*

The first stage is to define what the team is. There is usually a core team of 2–20 people who meet regularly to manage the project, work more or less throughout the project and are formally recognised as 'the project team'. Within that, there may be a smaller group of people who make executive decisions to avoid the inertia involved in having to gather and consult the whole group. Beyond the formal or 'visible' team is a group of people who will work on the project, sometimes only for short periods. These people, anyone who works on the project, are part of the 'informal' or 'invisible' team. So in summary, there are two teams to manage, one within the other, and perhaps a small executive group. Already project teams begin to look complex.

#### *Temporary*

All teams are effectively temporary, but project teams have an end point fixed from the start. This can be double-edged: the temporary nature can reduce barriers or inhibitions, but as the team will not last, the incentive to commit can be reduced.

#### *Cross-functional*

If the team successfully involves people from different functions, it takes people away from their comfortable ways of working with established colleagues. Of course, purchasing and logistics professionals are expert at working with all functions within the business, but finance and marketing may have historic differences, development and production may have friction or rivalry built up from years of fighting over designs.

#### *Conditional*

While functions and departments are fairly resilient, the survival of a project relies on its success. If the team begins to fail, projects can be wound up quickly or ignored until they fade away. Put another way, for most projects the team is part time or seconded at most. Continued employment and promotion are likely to depend more on their commitment to their home function or 'day job'. The threat of the project disappearing has different motivational effects on different people ranging from rising to a challenge to refusing to commit as the team may disappear.

#### *Likely to face crisis*

Many projects, perhaps a majority, face crisis at some point. Some teams and managers push their projects into crisis. Crisis is more exciting and demanding to manage than a stable well-planned project. Crisis can raise the profile of the project itself. Crisis can release resources and finance previously denied to the project. Crisis can even bring a team closer together. Managing the team through the crisis or crises is an inherent part of project leadership. Understanding the nature and impact of the first failure or external changes is part of ensuring the team works well.



The typical impact of a crisis is to bind together the committed: the formal team or small functional groups, while the informal team fall back on contract, hide information and lose teamwork (Loosemore, 1998).

#### *Working remotely and 'virtual teams'*

Teams dispersed across sites, countries or continent are becoming more common as purchasing and logistics projects become more international in scope. This is partly because of the expansion of sourcing, for example to China and India, partly because more and more companies are trying to leverage their global purchasing through category management or integrated logistics. 'Virtual teams' is a description of teams which are geographically dispersed who rarely meet and typically do much of their communicating through the internet.

The impact on team development of rarely or never meeting is usually to slow that development. If the team never meet, getting an understanding of each other's needs and differences is difficult. If communication is mainly by email, it is difficult to resolve the friction of storming, instead, team members simply cut off communication. The problem of not meeting, losing the non-verbal communications and distance are exacerbated by the likelihood that the team has many different cultures.

There is no easy resolution to this problem. Some suggest 'there is no substitute for face to face', but the cost and time involved in flying team members around the world regularly is prohibitive. A limited number of meetings with maximum impact can be a good compromise, but a lot of conscious effort on team development and maximum use of the available communication technology and channels is the only widespread solution.

### Self-assessment question 17.3

You are discussing teamwork with a colleague who is just about to start a project involving a team whose individual members are located in different countries around the world, to coordinate the delivery of information to clients. She has a lot of experience in line management and feels that forming the team in this project will be the same.

Make a series of notes to discuss with her on the similarities and the differences between managing a co-located functional team and a dispersed project team.

*Feedback on page 276*

## 17.4 People and success

### Linking soft aspects and success factors

If it is the team that makes projects succeed, not the plans, as suggested, and the soft factors are important, then there should be a very close link between the soft factors, including teamwork and success factors.



### Learning activity 17.4

Examine Pinto and Slevin's list of project success factors from project managers and identify:

(a) Which relate closely to the team and teamwork
(b) Which are 'soft' factors.

*(continued on next page)*

### Learning activity 17.4 *(continued)*

Pinto and Slevin's list:

1. Project mission: initial clearly defined goals and general directions.
2. Top-management support: willingness of top management to provide the necessary resources and power/authority for success.
3. Project schedule/plan: a detailed specification of the individual action steps for project implementation.
4. Client consultation: communication, consultation and active listening to all impacted parties.
5. Personnel: recruitment, selection and retention of the necessary personnel for the project team.
6. Technical tasks: availability of the required technology and expertise to accomplish the specific technical action steps.
7. Client acceptance: the act of 'selling' the final project to its ultimate end users.
8. Monitoring and feedback: timely provision of comprehensive control information at each stage in the implementation process.
9. Communication: the provision of an appropriate network and necessary data to all key actors in the project implementation.
10. Troubleshooting: ability to handle unexpected crises and deviations from plan.

*Feedback on page 276*

The learning activity attempted to separate soft and hard factors for success, with the result that six out of ten appear to be soft. This separation is an interesting idea but may not tell the whole story. Looking at the remaining factors shows that hard and soft factors are inextricably linked.

1. Project mission: This is an expression of expectations from an important group of stakeholders. It is not always a rigid description handed down but defined and redefined in negotiation with the sponsor, client and other stakeholders. As an example, the initial goal for a project may be to save 12% of the purchase cost on a category, but investigation opens up better potential through increasing value.
3. Project schedule/plan. The ability to plan is important, but the plan relies on estimates, generally from the people doing the work, and Goldratt's Critical Chain (see study session 6) explores the difficulty of coping with the human aspects of this. A legal team may be scheduled to review and revise a contract in five days, but whether they do relies on a number of factors beyond the schedule.
6. Technical tasks. The availability of technical assistance and contribution relies heavily on the invisible team. Important data or specification flexibility can rely heavily on other functions and their help is contingent on their attitude to the project.
8. Monitoring and feedback: Measurement and feedback have an impact on what happens through people's reaction to it (see study session 12).

In summary, the soft and hard factors for project success are heavily intertwined. It is possible to identify elements which are purely one or the other, but a combination of both is important for success.

## What is success?

This session and the previous session are all about success factors in projects. To complete this look at success, it is useful to review what project success means.

Throughout this unit, different measures of success have been discussed. The 'hard' measures of time, cost and quality are attractive but projects can achieve on all three but be considered a failure, while apparently 'hard' failures (like Concorde) can be considered great successes. Baker (1983) suggests perceived success or failure is not a function of time or cost. The second problem with these 'hard' measures is that quality is difficult to define for a project. Conformance to specification relies on a clear fixed specification which matches what is wanted. Meeting client needs is difficult where the client is hard to define and they cannot define their needs. For example, is the client for an IT project the sponsor, the budget holder or the user? Each one will have different requirements and will find it difficult if not impossible to specify how the system should work. Meeting client expectations is a moving target: expectations change over time and can be as difficult to uncover as needs. Relying on hard factors for all project success is at best partially successful. An analogy would be recommending that all food sellers focus on weight, delivery time and specification. For a bulk grain trader that might work, for a Michelin-starred restaurant it would be less successful.

These problems have been highlighted and proposals put forwards (for example Lim and Mohamed, 1999; Atkinson, 1999). Most analysis accepts that hard factors play a part but attempts to expand with other aspects. Atkinson (1999) adds three factors: benefits to the organisation and other stakeholders combined with the information system. Lim and Mohamed separate the macro from the micro view and highlight that different stakeholders have different criteria and satisfaction is vital, therefore satisfaction criteria should be set at the start. Both of these have problems: Atkinson relies on an agreed, objective or rational assessment of benefits, Lim and Mohamed have the same problem with defining satisfaction criteria.

There seems to be no getting away from the problem that success is defined by the perceptions of the stakeholders, as noted by Maylor (1996). Hard factors play a part, the stakeholders' understanding of the project plays a part, benefits play a part, but the judgement on the project is made by the stakeholders based on their perceptions. Those perceptions may be based on twisted or wrong information, on an unrealistic dream of what the project could achieve or a strict adherence to the project specification. It makes no difference, success is based on perceptions of the stakeholders.



## Managing perceptions

The link between perception and success can explain why Pinto and Slevin found that client consultation, a clear mission and reselling the results were important to project managers: it is vital throughout the project to manage stakeholders' expectations and their perceptions. Communication and reporting, project and scope definition, change control, benefits delivery and handover are all part of managing stakeholders' perceptions.

### Self-assessment question 17.4

Identify three ways in which stakeholders judge success.

*Feedback on page 277*

### Revision question

Now try the revision question for this session on page 321.

### Summary

Project leadership is a complex task.

First it involves leading the team involved. Team development and dynamics tend to follow the 'orming' pattern common to teams in other situations, but there are several ways project teams tend to differ, including the likelihood that they will be spread around the country or the globe. The broader 'invisible' team is central to success and the success factors for projects are an inseparable mix of soft factors closely linked with hard factors: a time plan is only useful if it is accepted, good teamwork is only as effective as the definition of tasks needed.

Second, leadership involves directing the project in concert with the stakeholders and the environment. To expect these to stay constant is frequently unreasonable, project leadership has become more like leading a small temporary organisation. Finally, and frustratingly, it is the people involved, the stakeholders who decide whether your project succeeds or not. Project management is not just about delivering a specification or even benefits, but managing how people understand those benefits, outputs and the process itself.

### Suggested further reading

- Ayers (2004); Chapters 4, 12, 13.
- Lock (2003); Chapter 2.
- Maylor (1996); Chapter 9.
- Meredith and Mantel (2006); Chapter 3.
- Mintzberg et al (1998).

Selections from the *International Journal of Project Management* including:

- Atkinson (1999).
- Fiedler (1967).
- Fiedler (1971).
- Lim and Mohamed (1999).

## Feedback on learning activities and self-assessment questions

### Feedback on learning activity 17.1

There are many ways people gain 'compliance', or persuade people to do what they want.

Did your two cases follow the four conditions identified by Barnard of successful instructions? Those were: the person understood, it met their personal interests, they believed it to be in the organisation's interests, and they were able to do it.

Were there aspects beyond the four from Barnard? Are there personal attributes that you feel help, such as a commanding persona, charm or persuasiveness?

### Feedback on self-assessment question 17.1

This question asks for your opinion, so it is likely to vary from the description in this section, however several things should be present:

- What is meant by leading a project: is it just a team leader or does the project itself need leading?
- Some reflection on what a good leader of the team means in this context: what do you believe is needed in order to be a good leader?
- Some discussion on the impact of context: that different project types and situations have an impact on what will be successful leadership.

### Feedback on learning activity 17.2

There is some detail in this section which may help you to evaluate your answer. You may have identified other ways of promoting development, such as team days, social events or an external threat fostering group adhesion. These may well be useful and taking an overview there are really only a few key elements:

- The transition from a more directive style at the start towards invisibility in 'performing'.
- The focus on small achievements in the first two stages to gain momentum and as a platform for resolving differences.
- Expecting and managing the friction during 'storming'.
- Constant awareness and potential for intervention to manage how the team works.

### Feedback on self-assessment question 17.2

Your answer relies on your strengths but here are some suggested points.

*Forming*

If you are naturally good at drawing people together, managing the detail of tasks and directing people, this may be your best stage. You will need to focus on withdrawing and letting go as the team develops.

*Storming*

If you enjoy a daily challenge and firefighting and are good at conflict resolution, you may be good at working through storming. One challenge may be that managing a performing team seems boring by comparison and you may tend to create friction, unintentionally, to match your style.

*Norming*

If you like working with a well-organised team that understands its members and makes allowances, norming may be a good environment. As an example, you may get frustrated with the team in the first two stages with constant needs and low output.

*Performing*

This stage will appeal if you are comfortable standing back and letting people develop by making mistakes, carefully monitoring your input to keep dynamics on track. Many project managers are far more comfortable managing tasks rather than team dynamics, which is one of the difficulties of reaching this stage. If you are comfortable with this stage, the detail work earlier in team development may be less comfortable.

## Feedback on learning activity 17.3

There is a list in this section, compare how your examples fit with those provided.

## Feedback on self-assessment question 17.3

The first point is that her experience of teamwork and team development will almost certainly be very valuable. Team development has similar patterns in all sorts of areas and projects are not unique. A series of points could be made about the existing experience she could use, including the stages of development.

This question is also about the differences between her experience and what you expect to be the challenges of a dispersed project team or 'virtual team'.

- Possibly the most important feature is that the team is dispersed and working remotely, probably involving different cultures. The impact of this is likely to be great.
- This team may not be very cross-functional, but the temporary and conditional nature is likely to have an impact. This could be used to advantage, reducing inhibitions, providing a challenge and a sense of urgency.
- Finally, managing crisis may be something your colleague has met, but the combination of crisis with a dispersed team is likely to pose a complex challenge.

## Feedback on learning activity 17.4

(a) Apart from no 5: Personnel and perhaps 9: Communication, few relate directly to teamwork.

(b) Far more are closely related to soft factors, but not directly to teamwork. Including the two teamwork factors, the list becomes 2: Top-management support, 4: Client consultation, 5: Personnel, 7: Client acceptance, 9: Communication, and 10: Troubleshooting.

Six out of ten of the factors for success are 'soft' factors. This suggests that the project managers surveyed believed that soft factors were an essential part of success. There is, however, little consideration of teamwork. This could be because the people surveyed believed it was unimportant or believed it was always done well in projects. They were reflecting on their experience and it is of course possible they were wrong on either count.

### Feedback on self-assessment question 17.4

Although the judgement of success may be based on perceptions, those perceptions can come from a wide range of factors:

- by an objective measurement of cost, time or conformance to specification can be used
- compared against the original definition, or a carefully updated and generally agreed definition
- on a judgement of the benefits to them, such as prestige or an easier system
- on a judgement of the benefits to the organisation, such as savings
- by the satisfaction of their needs, whether they expressed them or not
- by reports from other people
- by the difficulty and disruption caused
- by whether they believe it was well managed.

This is by no means comprehensive, you could have identified three from this list or the wide range of others that people use.

Study session 18

# Organising to succeed

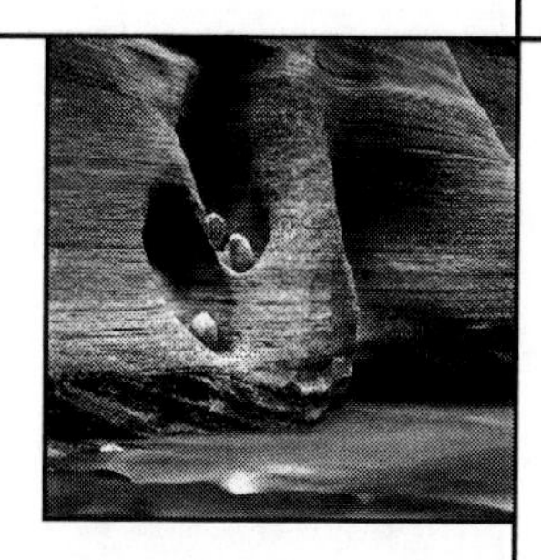

Boxing people in: organisational structure.

## Introduction

Once an organisation expands beyond 20–30 people it begins to need some management structure. Different structures have different impacts on the way people work, from the dominating hierarchy created by Henry Ford, to the decentralised units suggested by Fritz Schumacher (Schumacher, 1973).

As mentioned in study session 11, the structure of the organisation itself has an impact on loyalty, flexibility and readiness to adapt. The subject of organisational structure is quite a large one, but an understanding of the basic types can give some insight into what to expect.

If a project team grows to this size (beyond 20–30 people), it too will develop or need a structure and the design of that structure will have a strong impact on how people behave.

In essence, if you are managing a small project within an organisation with a fixed structure, then understanding the characteristics of different structures is of little benefit. If you are organising a large project with 20 or more staff, or looking at the project environment in your organisation, then understanding structure will give an understanding of the impact on behaviour.

## Session learning objectives

After completing this session you should be able to:

18.1 Evaluate the key characteristics of the functional organisation and the challenges facing project management.
18.2 Evaluate the key characteristics of the matrix organisation and the challenges facing project management.
18.3 Evaluate the key characteristics of the pure project organisation and the challenges facing project management.
18.4 Explain the key factors for consideration in choosing the best organisational structure for a project.

## Unit content coverage

This study session covers the following topic from the official CIPS unit content document.

### Learning objective

5.0 Evaluate project management processes and their relationship to current strategic practice.

5.1 Critically assess the architecture of project-orientated organisations: structures, cultures and project organisation and management.
- Function structures
- Matrix structures
- Process structures
- Culture and project approaches, organisational readiness, Hammer and Stanton (1995)

### Prior knowledge

Study sessions 1 – 17. The module on Strategic Supply Chain Management will provide some linkage and support to this session.

### Timing

You should set aside about 4 hours to read and complete this session, including learning activities, self-assessment questions, the suggested reading (if any) from the essential textbook for this unit and the revision question.

## 18.1 The commonest form? Functional structures

The functional organisation was introduced in study session 11. The identifying feature is that each member of staff is in a functional group.

**Figure 18.1:** A stylised diagram of a functional organisation

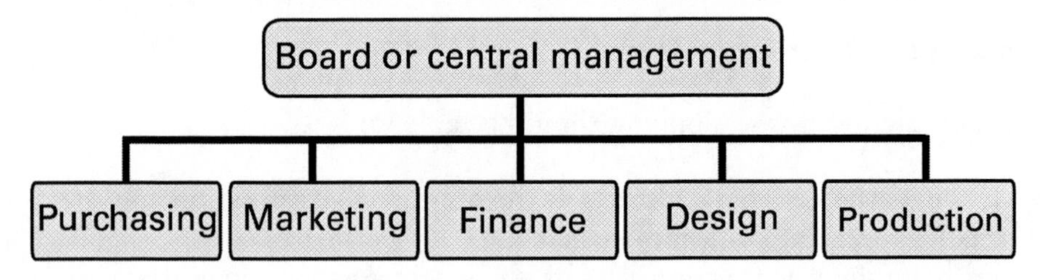


This combination of hierarchy and functional specialism was first identified as an ideal almost 100 years ago (Weber translated, 1947). There was a wealth of reasoning behind this ideal but from the point of view of function, there were a few essential aspects.

- It gives a clear structure for authority: it is clear who is in charge of which department and where different staff should report. Each person has only one manager.
- The specialism of departments helps to clarify each department's role: a 'closely defined sphere of competence'.
- There is a clear structure for promotion and advancement. Employment and promotion should be based on objective selection based on qualifications and experience.
- The structure separates the post from the person, making the authority of the post more important than personality, inherited power, etc.

### Learning activity 18.1

Identify strengths and weaknesses of functional structure for a project.

*Feedback on page 287*

The functional structure has frequently been criticised for its overriding failure: it organises people around function rather than on the basis of outputs, products projects or processes. Business Process Re-engineering and 'lean' have both challenged the functional organisation. In a functional organisation, there are always likely to be conflicts of loyalty and barriers to delivering projects effectively.

Most organisations are still in a roughly functional structure however, which suggests the benefits in managing people must be strong. To misquote: it is probably the worst type of structure there is, apart from all the others.

### Self-assessment question 18.1

Explain the circumstances where a functional structure would be the best organisation for a project team.

*Feedback on page 288*

## 18.2 Facing in two directions: the matrix structure

The problems of the true functional organisation become far worse where there is another strong division between different groups.

To take a clear example, consider the staffing of small health-care units dispersed around a city each providing care for 60–70 people. In each unit there will be a series of different professionals: nurses, psychologists, doctors, managers, occupational therapists and so on. These professionals must be coordinated and managed to some extent within the unit, so there must be some organisational structure in the unit. Professional conduct, development, promotion, etc cannot be organised within the unit and there is some resistance to mixed hierarchies: doctors prefer not to be managed by nurses and vice versa. This means there must be another organisational structure based on functional lines. This is a form of matrix organisation.

Transferring this to projects, an example would be where the cross-functional projects become so important and such a large proportion of the work that a functional structure could not cope. Where staff are working almost full time on one project, it makes sense for them to report at least in part to the project manager as in figure 18.2.

**Figure 18.2:** The matrix organisation

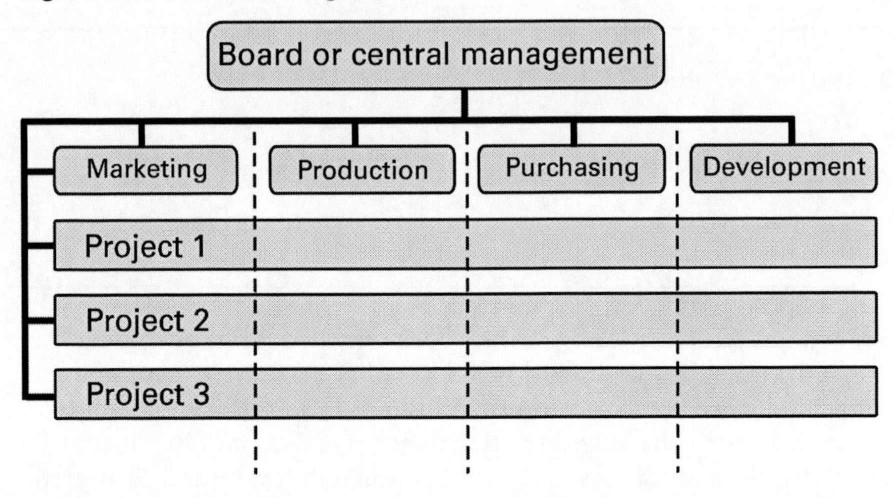


## Learning activity 18.2

Use your understanding of the benefits and drawbacks of functional structures to predict the advantages and disadvantages of a matrix structure for a project.

*Feedback on page 288*

The matrix organisation can offer a mix of benefits and problems. It allows for some project direction with some functional direction. Managing this is very difficult, however, and having multiple loyalties and direction can lead to confusion in decision making for individuals or groups and an increase in conflict.

There is a division sometimes made (Meredith and Mantel, 2006; Maylor, 2003) between lightweight, balanced and heavyweight matrix organisation.

In a lightweight matrix, the functional manager retains most of the control, in a heavyweight matrix, the project manager has more control. The balanced matrix is somewhere between the two. In practice, the balance of the matrix may be set overall as light or heavy, but the reality will vary from project to project and from person to person depending on personality, timing and need.

The matrix structure is in many ways a compromise between two idealised structures: the functional and the project (see section 18.3 below). As such it has the problems of a compromise with split reporting and the potential for achieving the benefits of both ideals or the disadvantages of both ideals. Few organisations fit an idealised structure, of course, and a compromise often fits a mixed situation.

## Self-assessment question 18.2

Write a memo to your boss explaining why a matrix structure would be optimal for a programme of projects to implement a new supply-chain

*(continued on next page)*

### Self-assessment question 18.2 *(continued)*

management system. The programme will involve around 50 people from different backgrounds and functions from across the company working full time on a range of projects.

*Feedback on page 288*

## 18.3 Projects as the focus: the pure project – organisation

In section 11.1, the 'pure project' structure was introduced. Instead of organising people by their function, they are organised by the project they are working for (see figure 18.3).

**Figure 18.3:** The pure project organisation

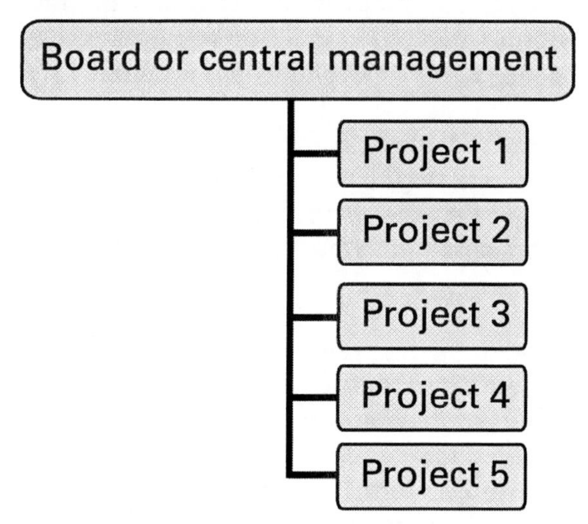


This is an idealised form, just as the functional organisation is, but with the opposite arrangement: instead of working in a logistics department with other logistics experts and professionals, reporting to a logistics manager or director, staff would be reporting solely to the project manager and working side by side with other functions.

### Learning activity 18.3

Using prior knowledge and the discussions in sections 18.1 and 18.2 above, identify strengths and weaknesses of a pure project structure compared to matrix and functional organisational structures from the project perspective.

*Feedback on page 289*



There are some other potential strengths and weaknesses.

- Comparing this structure with a matrix organisation, the problem of two managers and split reporting disappears and with it the difficulty of staff 'playing off' managers or being given conflicting orders.
- One of the great attractions is the transparency of projects. It is clear how much a project costs and how much work is involved

because that project is separate from the other projects and the rest of the organisation. This is very valuable both in identifying cost and controlling it: project managers tend to avoid employing staff unless they are essential, whereas in a functional organisation, the costs are blurred so there may be no penalty for adding work.

- For the whole organisation the project structure reduces the chance of departments growing and outliving their value as any overhead or non-project staff are highly visible. In the functional organisation, periodic restructuring is sometimes needed to reduce redundancy in the organisation.
- The constant restructuring involved in reorganising people around projects has its drawbacks. There is a cost to changing any organisation and the accounting, management and human resources systems must be flexible, efficient and effective to minimise this. Each time staff move to another project, the disruption involved in building a new team and adopting to new staff and management styles will reduce output for a time.
- There is the potential that as staff adapt to the frequent changes involved in moving from one project to the next they become more mobile and adaptable. As a result they can move to other companies more easily, which helps the organisation in terms of flexibility but reduces staff retention.

The pure project form is very attractive where projects are the main product of the organisation and those projects are long, typically a year or more. For engineering and construction companies, organising around projects is widespread. It is an idealised form and few organisations are unlikely to stick exactly to the pure project form, but where the benefits of flexibility and cross-functional alignment with the project outweigh the problems of frequent change and functional cohesion, it is a useful basis for organisational design.

### Self-assessment question 18.3

You are taking part in a large programme of projects across the organisation to move towards a lean orientation. Fifty people from different functions are employed full time on the programme of projects, each typically involving ten people and lasting two years. Write a memo to your boss suggesting why a shift from your current functional to a pure project organisation would be appropriate for the project team.

*Feedback on page 289*



## 18.4 One structure, the other or a mix?

The basic structures of functional, matrix and pure project reflect basic forms, but as always, most situations are not clear cut. Few organisations use the idealised forms exactly and the difficulties of managing a matrix organisation mean that it is rarely the first choice of structure. Structures tend to evolve and develop in response to needs and problems and most larger organisations have a mix of forms, for example the mixed organisation in figure 18.4.

**Figure 18.4:** The mixed organisation

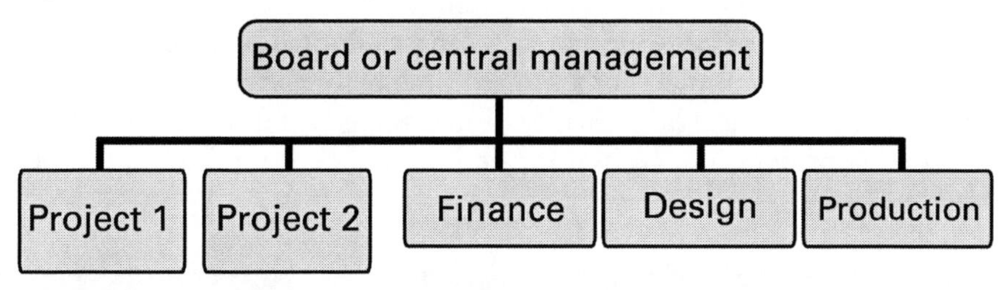


This structure may be used where large and important projects are set up alongside the 'normal' work of the business. The project might be to introduce a new ERP system, transform customer services or develop a radical new product, for example. Staff are seconded onto the project while it lasts and at the end of the project, may return to their old role, may move to a new vacancy or may be made redundant.

The mixed organisation separates some projects from the functional departments. As with a matrix organisation this mixes the benefits of functional and pure project organisations. It avoids the problem of two managers per employee, while offering project alignment for those in the projects and functional strength for those in the functions. The problems of reorganising staff after each project are reduced, as the functions can absorb or supply people to some extent.

There is one practical aspect not often discussed: being selected for the project can be seen as 'a place in the sun' or a punishment. Those selected to lead special projects can be a mix of the unmanageable, the rising stars and the incompetents who need to be sidelined.

## Learning activity 18.4

Use the benefits and drawbacks to identify a list of factors which influence the use of functional and pure project organisational forms.

*Feedback on page 290*

Learning activity 18.4 above gives a series of factors which decide whether the two idealised forms are appropriate, but that leaves the other two forms: mixed and matrix. Where are they appropriate? If it is true that most organisations use some form of mixed structure, why?

### Factors for a mixed or matrix structure

Where the different factors exist in one organisation, the ideals do not meet the needs well.

- Where the factors apply to most or all staff, as in the example of the health centre, a matrix structure can be appropriate. Its value does depend on the ability to cope with the ambiguity in management, however.

- Where some staff are fully engaged in projects over a long period and some staff are far more suited to a functional structure, the mixed structure can be the best option. This can be adopted temporarily, with staff seconded to a project for a limited time before a reversion to the functional structure. The difficulty of managing two different structures in terms of progression, accounting and lines of communication can be high, however.

### Self-assessment question 18.4

You work as logistics specialist for The Day After (TDA), a charity organisation which specialises in projects delivering international support after emergencies like floods and earthquakes.

Typically a team of people goes to the affected site 1–4 weeks after the disaster to provide medium-term help for 1–2 years. The help varies as you work closely with the local government and respond to their needs, but typically involves a lot of work sourcing and coordinating supplies then arranging transport, some rebuilding and some training and coordination activities. Most staff are cross-trained in a range of skills, but broadly there are project managers, sourcing and logistics specialists, civil engineering specialists, liaison and training specialists and some people who actually do the work.

TDA has grown from a few volunteers and now has 40 permanent staff and up to 60 on shorter contracts. At any one time there are around ten headquarters staff based in the Hague, the rest are in the field. The need for an organisational structure is becoming obvious.

Make a summary report of 1–2 pages suggesting what type of structure is appropriate and the possible drawbacks of your choice.

*Feedback on page 290*

### Revision question

Now try the revision question for this session on page 322.

### Summary

There are two basic idealised forms: organising around projects or functions. Whether either is appropriate relies on a range of factors including project type, the professions involved and history. The choice is generally not a straightforward one.

In general, projects are easier to manage in the project organisation and it is favoured by project-based organisations. This is not absolute and some projects are actually obstructed by the project organisation.

Many organisations do not fall neatly into one form. Where there are different needs in different parts of the organisation, a mixed structure can work well or be adopted for the duration of the projects; where all staff have functional and project responsibilities, a matrix structure can work well.

Understanding the organisation can be useful if developing a large project team or if you have the freedom to adapt the structure in response to project needs, however most projects will need to adapt to the organisation they find themselves in.

## Suggested further reading

- Lock (2003); Chapter 2.
- Maylor (1996); Chapter 9.
- Meredith and Mantel (2006); Chapter 4.

Organisational design texts such as:

- Zaidi (2006).

## Feedback on learning activities and self-assessment questions

### Feedback on learning activity 18.1

Because most organisations are structured at least partially in this functional way, it is a little difficult to identify its impact on work and projects. To try to identify strengths and weaknesses, it is useful to look from two perspectives: the management of people and the management of the project.

*Management of people in the functional organisation*

- Reporting and management lines are clear.
- Promotion routes are clear.
- Diffusion of technical good practice and professional management is easy because all the marketers are in one department, purchasing staff in another, etc.
- There is total flexibility for all staff to work on different projects: people in the different departments can spend any proportion of their efforts on any mix of projects without affecting the structure.
- There is no problem reallocating people to and from projects, because they never change department.
- There is continuity of control, employment and management.
- Attitudes and beliefs can become entrenched with the focus on department needs, seeing other departments as enemies.



From the perspective of managing the project, the fundamental problem is that a project must cut across these boundaries, drawing some resource from different areas:

- It is difficult to gain loyalty and commitment to the project as people remain in their departments.

- Different staff from the department may participate at different times, further damaging loyalty and reducing momentum.
- The amount of time spent on different projects is hard to assess and even harder to manage.
- Where parts of a project pass from department to department, the boundaries become particularly problematic. For example, a contract developed by central procurement and regionally signed by different sites, then passed to operations for implementation. At each department boundary the handover is likely to change the project slightly and there is likely to be friction and resistance.
- Encouraging staff who are fixed in functional departments to take a balanced view of other departments' needs is difficult.

## Feedback on self-assessment question 18.1

The main advantages lie in acquiring and returning staff. Since the staff never leave their department, disruption is minimised and theoretical flexibility is total. If the project is likely to involve change in the team, staff turnover or it requires the flexibility to move people from one piece of work to another, then a functional organisation is valuable.

The other advantages, such as professional and quality development of staff and clear lines of progression may have a limited impact on the project unless it runs for some time, more than a year, for example.

Given that most organisations follow some form of functional structure, it is familiar and acceptable to most people, so perhaps should be the 'default' structure. Unless there is an overriding factor pointing towards another structure, a functional structure is the natural choice for its flexibility.

## Feedback on learning activity 18.2

The main problem with functional structures is that they are not aligned with the project. Matrix structures add some alignment in that direction, while retaining the functional link. It could be predicted that many of the disadvantages of the functional structure are overcome: the barriers between departments are blurred, helping people to develop less factional views; the ability for project managers to exert some control is introduced. Meanwhile, many of the benefits of functional structures are introduced: people never leave their department so still have their colleagues for support and development and avoid the disruption of reassignment at the start and end of each project.

The overriding problem with matrix structures is ambiguity in management. Each person has at least two managers who can offer conflicting guidance or be 'played off' against one another. The influence of each manager can increase and decline over time. The 'dotted lines' of partial responsibility for staff are hard to manage effectively for both the manager and the managed.

## Feedback on self-assessment question 18.2

As there are many projects, all important to the programme success, shifting some control and management responsibility to the individual project managers would make the project management simpler and emphasise the importance of the projects.

The change in organisation would also begin to break down barriers between functions: logistics, warehousing, quality, etc. It will help to 'unfreeze' the structure and help change management. The resulting cross-functional relationships will be important given the requirements of supply chain management.

Because the projects vary and are not all clearly defined or long lasting, a shift to organising wholly around projects could lead to problems, so a matrix organisation is probably an effective mix.

There are drawbacks and dangers associated with the new structure detailed above in this section, for example the difficulty of managing with two managers per employee. These should be noted.

Finally, a shift to a matrix structure can be undone easily and simply, because the functional structure remains in place, so there is the potential to shift back with limited disruption once the projects are complete or if the structure fails.

## Feedback on learning activity 18.3

Some of the strengths and weaknesses were discussed in section 11.1.

The benefits noted there:

- far better alignment with the project
- the projects described do not have the problem of cutting across functional boundaries
- less theoretical flexibility than the functional structure: everyone is allocated to one project
- potential problems identified
- staff have to switch from project to project when each project finishes
- workload management is difficult as some staff will be needed by the new project before the old one finishes, while some will see a hiatus between projects
- projects which do not follow the standard type still have boundary problems: a project to improve procurement in a project engineering company has to work across many projects.

You may also have got beyond these and developed some of the points discussed below in this section.

## Feedback on self-assessment question 18.3

The factors towards the project organisation are that the projects are clearly defined and stable, requiring full-time involvement. Moving to a structure where each person has no ties apart from their project, sitting with the team, reporting only to the project leader will lead to far greater involvement and identity aligned with the team and help to break down any cross-functional friction.

In your memo you should probably deal with some of the problems outlined in this session:

- Staff have to switch from project to project when each project finishes.
- Workload management is difficult as some staff will be needed by the new project before the old one finishes. Some will see a hiatus between projects and need to be managed through that time.
- Any projects which do not follow the standard type such as quality improvement initiatives will struggle to work between the different projects.
- The constant restructuring involved in reorganising people around projects has a cost and the accounting, management and human resources systems must be flexible, efficient and effective.
- There is the potential for staff retention problems.

## Feedback on learning activity 18.4

Focusing on the positive: factors which make each structure more appropriate, rather than drawbacks, leads to a series of factors for each one.

*The pure project: structure*

- Projects are the main focus or product.
- The projects are one year or more long, otherwise change becomes too frequent.
- The organisation is large enough to align each person with a project; there is no need for the flexibility to split between projects as in the functional structure.
- The organisation has the capability to set up accounting, management, etc for each project, so the cost of change is not too high.
- Where a project structure is historically used and staff are used to it.

*The functional: structure*

- Where functions have a strong cohesion and a resistance to being managed by other professions, as with doctors, nurses and other health-care professions.
- Where the organisation is too small to devote each member of staff to one project.
- Projects are not the main focus of the business.
- The projects undertaken tend to be small, short or very varied in nature.
- Where a functional structure is historically used and staff are used to it.
- The cost of change is too high to reorganise staff for each project.
- Staff are uncomfortable with frequent change.



## Feedback on self-assessment question 18.4

The organisation has not had much structure so there is the flexibility to choose different types without too much upheaval:

- Most of the staff are engaged in similar projects of 1–2 years duration.
- The projects are dispersed around the world, so communication between professionals in different teams is necessarily limited.

- Staff are likely to be on just one project.
- Staff change where they are working at the end of each project, probably moving to another country.

This appears to be a clear case for a pure project organisation, with staff allocated to projects and line management carried out through those projects.

The exception could be the ten headquarters staff. If they need an organisation, a functional structure could be useful, as it could provide support across the projects, and also some leadership in the different specialisms.

The drawbacks would be as described in section 18.3:

- Staff have to switch from project to project when each project finishes.
- Workload management is difficult as some staff will be needed by the new project before the old one finishes, especially as the need for disaster relief is often pressing. Some will see a hiatus between projects and need to be managed through that time.
- Any projects which do not follow the standard type such as quality improvement initiatives will struggle to work between the different projects.
- The constant restructuring involved in reorganising people around projects has a cost and the accounting, management and human resources systems must be flexible, efficient and effective.
- There is the potential for staff retention problems.

Study session 19

# New paradigms in project organisation and management

Guaranteed competitive advantage or myths to make consultants rich? Maturity and Excellence in project management.

## Introduction

A good project manager can make one project succeed, but to achieve repeated success in projects depends on the organisation. In study sessions 6 and 7, senior management commitment and support were identified as important, in the discussions around success in study sessions 16 and 17, organisational factors appear again and again.

An understanding of how good your organisation is at achieving projects success is an attractive idea. Even more attractive is the concept of a prescription for success, a way of making projects succeed and deliver competitive advantage. There are many 'maturity' or 'excellence' models offering to help with both an understanding of what makes for competitive advantage and even more consultants, academics and 'gurus' offering to help implement them.

Are these new ideas of maturity and excellence in project management a route to success, good practice or myths developed to provide consulting work? All three of these views have been put forward. This session focuses on the models and their application to help assess their value.

## Session learning objectives

After completing this session you should be able to:

19.1 Analyse the extent to which project management maturity models help firms compare explicit competences at the programme and project level to a standard.
19.2 Critically evaluate the extent to which project management maturity models can actually provide a source of competitive advantage to firms.
19.3 Evaluate the relationship between the business excellence model (Kanji) and the project management excellence model (Westerveld).

## Unit content coverage

This study session covers the following topic from the official CIPS unit content document.

### Learning objective

5.0 Evaluate project management processes and their relationship to current strategic practice.
5.2 Utilise the Buttrick (2002), Project Management Maturity Matrix, and relate to contemporary project environments and issues.

- Maturity of organisations towards Project Management
- Unaware – sophisticated

5.3 Critically evaluate the use of the concept of project excellence (Westerveld 2002) and how it links to the principles of the business excellence model.
- The business excellence model
- The project excellence model, Westerveld (2002) and different approaches to project organisation and management

## Prior knowledge

Study sessions 1 – 18.

## Timing

You should set aside about 6 hours to read and complete this session, including learning activities, self-assessment questions, the suggested reading (if any) from the essential textbook for this unit and the revision question.

## 19.1 What is maturity?

There are many project maturity models, just as there are business process maturity models, marketing maturity models and software development capability maturity models. They all aim to do similar tasks: provide a framework for assessing how well an organisation has developed its ability in the field.

As mentioned in the introduction to this session, organisational factors are important in achieving project success, so a measure of the organisation's capability seems a useful tool in developing the environment for and ability in project management.

### Maylor's Maturity Matrix

Maylor (2003) describes an easily accessed description of maturity in terms of four groups of companies and suggests that their maturity can be described by their characteristics.

- *The Flatliners*: These treat each project as new, with little learning between projects or from outside. Project goals are poorly defined or not established.
- *The Improvers*: Some processes and systems in place resulting in some acceptable performance. Little learning from one project to the next, goals sometimes established and focused on conformance to objectives.
- *The Wannabes*: Systems imposed and processes well documented. Improvement based on copying the best but limited by the system. Goals routinely established but still focused on conformance to objectives.
- *The World Class Performers*: Processes mapped, and based around an ever-improving core. Learning evident and goals aimed at exceeding objectives and delivering the best project possible.

Ignoring the lack of substantiation or sources for this model of maturity, it provides some characteristics which could be measured and improved and follows this with some ideas on how to improve based on initiatives such as Lean, Business Process Re-engineering and benchmarking. Several questions could arise, for example where is the evidence that these four types exist and that the characteristics drive performance.

### Kerzner's five-level model

Kerzner (2001) provided a book with checklists to guide businesses in assessing and developing maturity. It cites five years of study in the development of the model.

#### *LEVEL 1: Common Language*

This is an 'awareness' stage based upon knowledge of the fundamental principles of project management and the associated terminology and is linked to understanding the project management body of knowledge by the Project Management Institute.

#### *LEVEL 2: Common Processes*

This involves a realisation that common methodologies and processes are needed and a concerted effort to develop processes and methodologies to support effective project management. It allows success on one project to be replicated to other projects and behavioural expectations to be set.

#### *LEVEL 3: Singular Methodology*

Level 3 involves total commitment to the concept of project management and adopting a singular project management methodology. The aims of this are synergism and process control.

#### *LEVEL 4: Benchmarking*

The organisation continuously uses a structured approach to benchmarking to compare their practices to recognised leaders. A key business process integrated into the organisation are critical factors.

#### *LEVEL 5: Continuous Improvement*

The top level involves the realisation that excellence in project management is a never-ending journey and using the information learned during the benchmarking information to drive the changes necessary for process improvement.

### Learning activity 19.1

Using the descriptions given in this section and any other sources, write a brief (less than 200 words) review of the Maylor and Kerzner maturity models highlighting similarities and differences between the models.

*Feedback on page 302*

### The Project Management Institute OPM3 Model

The Project Management Institute (PMI), based in the USA, put forward an Organization Project Management Maturity Model (OPM3) in 2003.

As with Kerzner's model, this was based on five years of development and is claimed to 'Translate Strategy into Success...Drive Business Improvement...Gain a Competitive Advantage', 'Just as individuals benefit from achieving personal maturity, organizations can now benefit from achieving organizational project management maturity. OPM3® is a standard unlike other contemporary maturity models.' (PMI website 2006: http://www.pmi.org).

This model is based on two aspects:

1 choosing the right projects to execute organisational strategies
2 implementing the processes, structures and behaviours necessary to deliver projects successfully, consistently and predictably.

The detail is complex and based on best practices, the capabilities that add up to the best practices, the outcomes of capabilities and the KPIs which measure the outcomes. In developing the model, 600 Best Practices, 3,000 capabilities and 4,000 relationships between capabilities were identified (Fahrenkrog et al, 2003). These have been to describe excellence in terms of a 'roadmap from lesser to more advanced capabilities'.

In order to help organisations increase in maturity, there is a cycle involving knowledge, assessment and improvement and all of this is supported by an extensive range of products including books and online tools which can be purchased by the organisation to assist it in understanding its maturity and how it can be developed.

### Overview of the maturity models

The idea of a maturity model is attractive and the wide range of work on them and tools, support and consultancy in applying them suggests that some organisations are open to adopting maturity models.

Most seem to rely on a similar basis, that adopting a standardised process and learning from project to project is beneficial. That learning offers benefits is rarely contested, standardisation appears at face value to conflict with the idea of adapting the project management approach to the project.

There is competition between the different models although there seems to be little variety, for example the PMI's claim that OPM3 'is a standard unlike other contemporary models' is hard to relate to the standard nature of the maturity models mentioned here.

The maturity models offer what is expected: clear descriptions of what maturity looks like which can be translated into assessment for the organisation, and often has. The outstanding question is: do they work? As yet there seems little empirical proof that described maturity independently leads to performance (Skulmoski, 2001), but this is hard to prove and may follow.

### Self-assessment question 19.1

Write a memo for an organisation of your choice suggesting whether it is appropriate to strive towards maturity as described by Maylor and Kerzner.

Use the similarities between models identified in learning activity 19.1 above to decide whether the maturity model would fit your organisation.

*Feedback on page 302*

## 19.2 Models look good, but do they work?

### Learning activity 19.2

From a reading of Jugdev and Tomas (2002), answer the following questions:

1. What do the authors suggest will be the impact of project management maturity on competitive advantage?
2. What basis or theories do they use to support their suggestion?
3. What challenges can you identify to their reasoning?

Critically appraise the usefulness of project management maturity modelling from reading set articles.

*Feedback on page 303*

### Learning activity 19.3

You may find it impossible to obtain the paper mentioned above in learning activity 19.2 above, in which case try this more limited activity:

1. Identify methods of gaining competitive advantage, preferably using established analysis of what gives a company that advantage.
2. Predict how project management maturity could provide competitive advantage in some form.
3. Suggest limitations to the ability of maturity to provide competitive advantage.

*Feedback on page 303*



The learning activity 19.2 above looks at one paper and its challenge to the competitive advantage provided by maturity models, but the value of the models in achieving that advantage is open to broader discussion. In this section there is only room to outline a few general points.

### What competitive advantage?

The maturity models suggest or claim increases in competitive advantage but rarely detail how that competitive advantage is gained. Reducing failures, aligning projects with strategy and streamlining the project process have been cited, but the larger impact of these on competitive advantage is less explored. The resource-based view used by Jugdev and Tomas is one example of describing competitive advantage, but there are challenging views.

### Contingencies and variety

The maturity models are based on some element of process standardisation. While standardising processes is essential in some industries, particularly high volume low variety, it can be disastrous where flexibility is key to competitive advantage. For some construction, the process used should essentially be similar each time, with variety only in design and the detail of implementation. This challenges the idea of projects as unique. The variety of projects has been discussed before and in section 16.2 the idea that management approach should vary – be contingent on the project – was put forward as a response to variety. The complexity involved in developing a standardised process with flexibility for contingencies increases very rapidly with variety. In summary, standardisation could be the lifeblood of some industries, death in others.

### Lack of proof

It is very difficult to make a causal link between maturity and success. There can be correlations and it seems logical that one should cause the other, but the variety of projects and industries makes the link between one definition of maturity and success very difficult. As an example, success might theoretically be a cause of maturity characteristics: if a company is successful, it might have the time and resources to standardise and codify processes and carry out benchmarking, while unsuccessful companies do not. There may be a third factor, for example industry type which drives both the maturity and success.

This lack of proof should not be seen as damning. As a comparison with other approaches, there are few empirical studies demonstrating the value of supply chain management (Mouritsen, 2002) or lean (Primost and Oliver, 2003).

### Temporary improvements

More challenging than the lack of proof is the possibility that any improved competitive advantage through developing maturity is attributable to a large scale 'Hawthorne effect'. This effect is that when interest is shown in groups of employees and something is done to change their situation, their performance increases independent of the value of the changes. The improvement is due to the attention, not the change, and dies away once the attention is removed. The attention paid to project management in developing maturity may be what gives the benefit. The often neglected implication of the Hawthorne effect is that continued attention leads to continued improvement. If continuous improvement involves continuous attention, the effect will be maintained.

### Self-assessment question 19.2

Summarise three criticisms of the suggestion that project management maturity leads to competitive advantage.

*Feedback on page 304*

## 19.3 Not mature but excellent

Maturity is one way of looking at an organisation's capability in project management. There are others and the idea of 'excellence' in project management or even in the business itself has been developed in a number of directions.

Excellence has been developed as an idea largely in the area of quality management. It is similar to maturity in that it looks at aspects of an organisation through measurable factors to assess it against criteria which are believed to reflect good management practice. The main difference is that while maturity models tend to be fairly prescriptive in how management is carried out, for example standardised written processes, excellence models cover general areas such as teamwork.

Two examples of excellence models are the Business Excellence model proposed by Kanji (1998) and the Project Excellence model proposed by Westerveld (2003). Kanji proposes a Total Quality Management based model for the whole organisation, while Westerveld proposes a model for application to individual (complex) projects, in effect treating the project as a temporary organisation.

### Learning activity 19.4

From a reading of Kanji (1998) and Westerveld (2003), answer the following questions:

1 How is excellence defined in each case?
2 What is the basis for the factors in each model: where did the authors get their factors?
3 How do the models relate to success or excellence in projects?

*Feedback on page 304*

### Learning activity 19.5

If you find it impossible to obtain the papers mentioned in learning activity 19.4 above, try the following activity.

1. Read learning activity 19.4 above and the feedback.
2. Use 300 words to compare the merits of the two models of excellence. Do not base this on application to one organisation but on their basis, how they might be applied generally and what they are expected to deliver.

Note: your understanding of the two models will be severely limited if you are unable to refer to the authors' descriptions given in the two papers.

*Feedback on page 305*

The two excellence models both aim to provide a framework for judging and improving management, Westerveld at a project level, Kanji at an organisational level. In certain areas they overlap: teams and management, customer/stakeholder satisfaction, for example. In other areas they diverge: Kanji's contention that all work is process is hard to relate to the project model, the 'narrow' factors in Westerveld are undeveloped by Kanji. To judge the two, some useful questions include: are they based on sound ideas? Are they straightforward to apply? Would you expect to gain from using these?

### The basis

As you may have noted in the learning activity, Westerveld bases his critical success factors and his factors for judging success on a wide spread of research, covering areas similar to study sessions 16 and 17. Although there is no explicit definition of what excellence is, it seems likely that understanding these factors will assist project success.

Kanji developed his own structure of factors, based on other work in TQM. He starts with the point that excellence involves achieving stakeholders' value, then notes in his conclusion that his model does not include stakeholders' value. He contends that the economic consequence of quality initiatives is straightforward to estimate and that business excellence exhibits a positive relation with customer satisfaction which increases the present value of the customer asset. These are arguable at best and seem poorly supported. Given this, the basis seems weak.

### The application

Applying Kanji's model to organisations, especially those involved in repetitive manufacturing work, would probably be straightforward. The measures and the areas fit with the type of organisation commonly implementing TQM, which makes a lot of sense. As covered in the learning activity, there are plenty of areas which would need development or to be adapted, such as continuous improvement and the concept of customers.

The model is specific in terms of the factors and measures, but those specifics may not be the best selection for projects or a project-based organisation.

Westerveld's model is derived from a TQM-based model of excellence, but only the framework is used, the contents are replaced by the factors derived from project management research. Unsurprisingly, this makes it more relevant and easy to apply to projects. It is also adaptable to a wide range of projects, offering some form of contingent flexibility. Moving up a level to applying this to an organisation running many projects goes beyond its intended purpose but is theoretically possible. It would then assess the overall capabilities in this area, but unlike maturity models, is not aimed at how the organisation manages the portfolio of projects.

### The pay-off

In essence, Kanji's model tests the organisation in some detail against TQM criteria and provides prompts for improvement. Unless TQM criteria are valuable for the project or the organisation, the pay-off may not justify the effort in implementation for a project or a project-based organisation.

Westerveld's model provides areas for examination for a project, supporting development of success criteria and the project organisation and management. There is limited detail in how to apply this, but the value is apparent.

### Summary of the two models

The two models are aimed at different things: one at the project level, one at the organisational level. It is conceivable that both could be used in the same organisation at the different levels, though in practice that may be difficult. One focuses on broad project-based factors, one on detailed TQM factors. The value of either depends on the factors which are important to the organisation.

## Self-assessment question 19.3

Which excellence model of the two used would be better suited to your organisation (or one of your choice)? Write a one-page memo recommending one or the other.

*Feedback on page 305*

## Revision question

Now try the revision question for this session on page 322.

## Summary

At the start of this session, the question posed was 'are these new ideas of maturity and excellence in project management a route to success, good practice or myths developed to provide consulting work?' Your answer will of course depend on your viewpoint but there are a few points derived from this session.

The maturity models are attractive and certainly there is a large business growing up around them, but there is also criticism. They may be very valuable in some situations, but are generally based on one idea of how projects should be coordinated and may conflict with the flexibility needed.

Excellence is an interesting idea, but again, the value of different models depends on the application. Each idea of 'excellence' is open to challenge.

It is probably very valuable to lift the focus above the best way of managing schedules, stakeholders, budgets and perceptions to evaluate how projects are managed at a higher level. Maturity and excellence are two vehicles for doing that. They may not be 'silver bullets' and cure everything, but they have insight to offer.

## Suggested further reading

- Fahrenkrog et al (2003).
- Kerzner (2001).
- Maylor 2003; chapter 15.
- Mouritsen et al (2002).
- PMI OPM3 page: http://www.pmi.org/info/PP_OPM3.asp.
- Primost and Oliver (2003).
- Skulmoski (2001).

## Feedback on learning activities and self-assessment questions

### Feedback on learning activity 19.1

The models have many differences: for example, the focus on characteristics in Maylor, attitudes ('realisation') in Kerzner, the number of stages, Maylor's identification of goals, Kerzner's reliance on benchmarking against Maylor's shift to 'world class'.

The basis for both is very similar:

- Both use clear stages in maturity against which an organisation could potentially be measured.
- Both rely on the idea that standardised processes lead to better projects,
- Both expect that an organisation that is self aware in the way it manages projects and improving using learning from project to project will get better at managing them.

### Feedback on self-assessment question 19.1

Application depends on the organisation, of course, but in basic terms, the applicability depends on:

- The importance of projects: why do it if projects are rare or unimportant?

- The standardisation of projects: if projects are widely varied, a standard process may not be appropriate, see study sessions 7, 14, 17 and 18.
- The likely response to the adoption of an externally created structured approach to learning and development: some organisations resist initiatives like this or are not ready for them and should focus efforts elsewhere.

Your answer probably didn't identify the three factors exactly as above, but should have touched on factors related to the basis of the models, such as standardising, learning and goal setting.

## Feedback on learning activity 19.2

1. This is stated in the abstract and the conclusions: that the models can lead to a temporary competitive advantage at best.
2. They use the resource-based view of competitive advantage: that competitive advantage is gained through resources that are not widespread among the competition and sustainability relies on the difficulty of the competition gaining similar resources.
   They do not attack the ability of maturity models to provide competitive advantage but define the maturity models as consisting of explicit, easily copied capabilities which are understood by many, therefore easily copied to erode competitive advantage.
3. This is probably the most complex part of the question, with many possibilities, but these are three general areas of argument:
   - The resource-based view may be wrong or inappropriate, for example competitive advantage may be based on other factors for some industries.
   - Their characterisation of maturity as explicit, easily copied capabilities may be wrong. The development of behaviour and ingrained processes is not the same as written descriptions of processes or expectations and it may be the hard-won applied processes and implicit knowledge embedded in that which gives competitive advantage. Just because you can describe and measure maturity in some ways does not make it easy to copy any more than describing or measuring human intelligence makes that easy to copy.
   - The widespread understanding of maturity may not lead to the ability to copy. As a comparison, the widespread understanding of Toyota's production system has not made it easy to copy or removed the competitive advantage Toyota has gained from it.

## Feedback on learning activity 19.3

1. There are many analyses of how competitive advantage is gained, through capabilities, etc. Central to most is the ability to provide for customers something competitors cannot, for example an innovation or market position, or to be better at providing the same thing, which delivers internal benefits, for example cost reduction. Key in most analyses is the sustainability of competitive advantage: how long it can be maintained.
2. Project management maturity can offer competitive advantage if it helps in one of the two ways suggested in (1). If it helps deliver projects which

meet customer needs, which are quicker, cheaper, meet more quality requirements than competitors, then there is competitive advantage.

3 The limits to this are many and you could have identified a wide range. Sustainability is questionable if maturity is well understood and easy to copy. More fundamentally, the benefit of standardising project management and expending effort on continuously improving is of value only where these deliver customer or internal benefits. As an illustration, maturity for projects in road building works well as they are similar and cost and time are factors of key importance to the client. For an organisation offering complex research and development, standardising projects and making them quicker and cheaper could damage the product by reducing flexibility and corroding the value in the customer's eyes.

### Feedback on self-assessment question 19.2

This question is not about a balanced review of whether maturity leads to competitive advantage, it asks only for the criticism.

There are four potential criticisms outlined above within this section that you could use:

- What competitive advantage?
- Contingencies and variety.
- Lack of proof.
- Temporary improvements.

But within the paper studied in learning activity 19.2 there are other criticisms. The central argument that competitive advantage will not be sustainable was discussed in the feedback, but there were other more general criticisms:

- Models are inflexible.
- Models are typically geared towards identifying problems without solving them.
- The models do not account for the rapid pace of change.
- The five (typical) levels do not allow enough detail to measure changes over time.
- They are overly disciplinary, impractical and overwhelming as methodologies.
- They focus on the process and ignore the human resources aspects.

If these criticisms are valid they would impact on the value and implementation of the models which directly affects the potential for competitive advantage through maturity.

### Feedback on learning activity 19.4

1 Early in the paper, Kanji defines achieving excellence as achieving stakeholder's values (p635) then later equates stakeholder's values to profitability (p642). This seems to equate excellence to profitability. Westerveld seems to equate excellence to managing a project successfully (p412) then later explicitly equates excellence as choosing the right project type.

2. Westerveld uses the framework of an existing model but all the factors are generated from a range of previous research in critical success factors in managing projects and factors which can be used in judging success. Kanji uses critical success factors 'based on well established theories and approaches' exclusively related to Total Quality Management (TQM), constructed into his own model supported by a survey he has carried out.
3. This is really the important part of the question.
   Westerveld provides a model linking the critical success factors for projects to the factors by which results can be judged. You probably found the general areas (stakeholders, resources, etc) familiar and directly applicable to projects. Westerveld suggests the model can be used to help define project success criteria and to evaluate the project organisation.
   Kanji's model is based on the ideas of TQM and looks at the whole organisation. You were probably able to relate some of the general areas to the project organisation, for example delighting the customer (if stakeholders are used as multiple customers), people-based management (it is hard to challenge the idea that management is based on people). You may have had more difficulty in relating a model developed for long-term organisations repeating the process of delivering products, to individual projects. For example, continuous improvement is a valid idea, but more valuable in terms of learning between projects than for the individual unique project. The drawbacks of Kanji's model rest in its value to projects. It needs to be developed or interpreted in order to apply it to individual projects, while for an organisation based on projects, there is little to suggest that it is applicable.

## Feedback on learning activity 19.5

You may have taken any of the elements of the feedback and developed them and there is some further discussion of the two in this section. Central to answering this is the comparison between the two. Check that you have answered questions such as:

- Do you accept either definition of excellence?
- What criticism can be levelled at the different bases?
- Does Kanji's model work for projects?
- Is Westerveld's model a synthesis of valuable factors or a jumble of previous work?
- Does the outcome of either model point towards competitive advantage?

## Feedback on self-assessment question 19.3

You could start from the summary to this section which suggests reasons for selecting one or another. It would be worthwhile considering the application and the pay-off as part of the justification. One key factor is what you want from 'excellence': one model effectively aims at project success across a broad set of factors, one aims at profitability through TQM.

## Study session 20

# The learning organisation and successful projects

'Funny how the new things are the old things.'
**Rudyard Kipling**

### Introduction

Projects do something novel and unique, there must be risks. If your project breaks new ground there is risk of failure, so some projects must fail. The important part of failure is looking back and taking the lessons.

Back in study session 4, reviewing and learning was introduced as part of the project life cycle, it is frequently highlighted as one of the most important parts because it can have a long-term impact on many projects.

In study session 13, review and learning came back and was emphasised as a vital part of project management. The review and audit were introduced as vehicles for learning.

Many millions of pounds have been spent on 'organisational learning' and the ability to learn is often used as a defining feature of being human.

Yet learning from projects is often haphazard, patchy and limited to the participants. The same mistakes happen again and again and people are limited to using the methods and ideas that worked once.

There has to be a better way.

### Session learning objectives

After completing this session you should be able to:

20.1 Explain what is meant by knowledge management and the requirements for a firm to become a 'learning organisation'.
20.2 Demonstrate the strategic benefits and advantages gained through knowledge management and becoming a learning organisation.
20.3 Appraise the impact of a learning organisation on the management of projects in purchasing and logistics.

### Unit content coverage

This study session covers the following topic from the official CIPS unit content document.

#### Learning objective

5.0 Evaluate project management processes and their relationship to current strategic practice.
5.4 Critically evaluate and apply the principles of knowledge management, knowledge communities, and organisational learning, and demonstrate

how this links to the successful implementation of strategy through projects, particularly in the purchasing and logistics areas.

- Knowledge management and links to project management – the role of ICT and special interest groups in capturing and disseminating good practice.
- Knowledge communities and knowledge creation, Nonanka and Tageuchi (1995)

## Prior knowledge

Study sessions 1 – 19.

## Timing

You should set aside about 8 hours to read and complete this session, including learning activities, self-assessment questions, the suggested reading (if any) from the essential textbook for this unit and the revision question.

## 20.1 What knowledge, what learning? The nature of the challenge

The idea that learning from projects is important seems uncontested. Many project management texts and project managers highlight the importance. How to learn is less clear. The suggestions are short and generally focus on end of project reviews or audits. Maylor (1996) goes a little further, describing knowledge management as:

- organisational learning
- explicit structure for sources of change ideas
- systematic evaluation of new ideas pre-implementation.

Obeng (2003) uses typically pragmatic descriptions of clarity in passing on information and focusing not on history and fairy tales, but on understanding and predicting the future.

What rarely appears in project management guidance is a more complex understanding of how to manage knowledge and how learning happens. There are two main reasons:

- The ideas behind the learning organisation and knowledge management are complex.
- As mentioned before, most of the potential learning in a project is left to the end, when everyone is most busy and leaving for other projects. It is also too late to help the project, so there is little immediate focus for learning.

There has to be a better way of learning from projects. However, it is likely to be fruitless to keep on stating how important learning is, recommending the same tools (review documents and audits) then hoping for better results.

Understanding a little more about knowledge management and learning may be necessary.

### Knowledge management

Knowledge management refers to the ways organisations gather, manage, and use the knowledge that they hold or acquire and is generally seen as active; to be successful requires active management of knowledge. CIPS (2003) uses a definition from PricewaterhouseCoopers:

> 'an integrated systematic approach to identifying, managing and sharing all of an enterprise's information assets including documents, policies and procedures as well as previously unarticulated expertise and experience held by individual workers.'

They noted that 83% of companies surveyed by PricewaterhouseCoopers claimed to be doing some sort of knowledge management, though relatively few had concrete objectives. While the active management of all knowledge in an organisation described in this definition might be ambitious, the value of knowledge management is widely reported and studies have found a link between knowledge management and company performance (Bontis et al, 2002). The CIPS paper divides knowledge management activities into three areas:

- implementing processes to carry out evaluations and capture outcomes, connect to people able to provide or generate new ideas and implement content management procedures for company information resources
- setting up structure and roles to leverage the abilities of individuals to work with knowledge management tools and facilitate learning processes
- tools to search for relevant resources (for example individuals and documents) and improve efficiency of analysis of data and other outcomes of work.

The more specific activities include:

- sharing across departments and geographical locations, where possible by moving people around
- providing accessibility across the organisation on procedures, policies activities and projects which cross boundaries.

### What knowledge?

There are two important types of existing knowledge, explicit, 'know what' such as documents and processes, and implicit 'know-how' held by individuals or groups but not in a form which can easily be communicated, such as how a process works. The first is relatively easy to share, the challenge is more in providing it in an accessible form. Tacit knowledge is more difficult to share or even identify. Nonaka and Takeuchi (1995) recommend changing implicit knowledge into explicit to manage it, but the exchange between the two is complex.

Beyond existing knowledge, for example knowledge contained by experienced project managers, is the knowledge that is created, for example from a crisis in the project or the project review.

### How to manage knowledge

IT can be valuable to knowledge management: databases, document management systems, online training, company 'yellow pages'; lists of who does what and knows about what. Beyond that, expert systems can be used to capture knowledge previously held by a few. There are less-formal methods of distributing learning: emailing, weblogs and 'wiki' sites (internet sites anyone can access to gain or update information). If the internet has helped spread knowledge around the world, then smaller, intranet-based methods can do the same within the organisation. One barrier is that the internet has succeeded in part through being organic and unregulated, organisations have a gnawing desire to control and impose regulation on their systems.

This is only part of the process and largely reflects explicit knowledge. More social methods such as working with colleagues, discussing problems, asking experts, the project review are all methods which can help to access other elements of knowledge, even tacit knowledge.

### Learning activity 20.1

Identify the knowledge which allows you to carry out your current role: know-how, professional knowledge, understanding the people around you.

Where possible analyse how you gained the knowledge: how did you get it? The end result should be a list of as many different ways you gained the knowledge as possible.

*Feedback on page 316*

### The learning organisation

Learning activity 20.1 above looked at learning for one role and how many different sources and methods of learning contributed. The learning in an organisation follows a similar pattern, with more complexity. Key to encouraging it is to accept and encourage learning in a very wide variety of forms. The learning organisation is a phase used to describe prescriptions of how organisations should adopt learning.

### One of the roots: Senge

While there is plenty of discussion about what a learning organisation is, much of the current understanding of the learning organisation can be traced back to Senge's 1990 book *The Fifth Discipline*. His description of the learning organisation is still probably the most widely quoted and involves:

1. *systems thinking*: understanding the interrelationships and impact of different actions and activities
2. *personal mastery*: the individual's proficiency and growth in their role, encouraged and supported by the organisation
3. *mental models*: understanding the deeply ingrained assumptions which direct our choices

4 *building shared vision*: a common understanding amongst employees of what the organisation is there to do
5 *team learning*: learning as a group and as part of different groups rather than solely relying on individual learning.

Senge states that unless all five are in place, the organisation cannot move forwards and learn, unless team learning is supported by individual learning and challenging the mental models already held, the organisation will be stuck with its existing knowledge, behaviour and a decreasing chance of success.

### Ideas that support the learning organisation

Different ways of learning are key. People have different preferences as to how they learn, but tend to use a mix. Structured courses and e-learning are useful for some subjects but learning through participation can offer a richer understanding and the chance to develop in different ways. One method is situated learning. This involves learning by being in the environment: a kitchen for a cook, in the field for a soldier, in the office with colleagues for the office worker. This allows change by habit and by relationship with others to happen and is a key part of training for cooks and soldiers, though often neglected in less manual roles. It is not the same as 'on the job' learning where learning comes through doing the job in reality. This is an important way of learning, but over-reliance can limit knowledge sharing and ingrain poor habits. The mix of methods is vital.

The understanding of tacit and explicit knowledge helps. There is a need to transfer tacit knowledge (know-how) from person to person. A common example of this might be driving a car. In order to drive safely and well you require a combination of explicit knowledge (the rules of the road and the controls of the car) and tacit knowledge, for example 'a feel' for how to use the controls in a particular car. An understanding of how to drive can be made explicit in books and the instructions of a driving instructor, but needs to be developed into tacit knowledge through practice and use. In the same way, know-how in the company needs to be transferred – know-how on process, on how to deal with customers and know-how on managing the business.

'Do you really have 20 years' experience or have you had the same year 20 times over?' is a question used to challenge rigid thinking. Senge emphasises the need for dialogue and 'thinking together' alongside the examination of mental models. More than an openness to change, the learning organisation requires an active attempt to understand assumptions, and understand the learning process as part of the drive for change.

### Self-assessment question 20.1

Identify and briefly describe the main barriers to knowledge management and becoming a learning organisation.

*Feedback on page 316*

## 20.2 What did learning ever do for us?

Becoming a learning organisation and managing knowledge is not straightforward. Self-assessment question 20.1 above reviewed some of the barriers. The question then is what does it offer? What lies behind those barriers?

### Learning activity 20.2

Suggest a series of ways in which external knowledge could help improve project management in an organisation of your choice.

*Feedback on page 317*

Learning activity 20.2 above touches on some of the benefits of learning from outside the organisation, but the potential is of course much larger.

### Competitive advantage

In section 19.2, the idea of maturity models was challenged as they could not provide long-term competitive advantage. The learning organisation offers something different: a capability which adapts to the environment and is difficult to copy.

Without delving into the extensive theories behind competitive advantage, the central need seems to be to offer consistently something different or differently. This is set against an environment which is changing. A new technology can offer advantage until someone copies or replaces it or consumers move on, a new market can offer advantage until competition joins in.

An organisation which excels at learning can gain an advantage which adapts to competition, which adapts to the environment and which continually brings innovation to provide that much sought after advantage.

A company which spreads learning about how to do projects across the organisation can lift all projects to the level of the best it has. It might reduce cost and increase speed, perhaps gain some of those other benefits which define success, maybe even becoming better than the competition. As soon as a project manager leaves to join the competition, much of that knowledge goes as well and soon the advantage is gone. An organisation which not only spreads best practice across the organisation but continuously experiments and adapts, using internal strengths and external influence, can maintain that advantage.

By its nature, learning offers something that adapts, hence the benefits can be long term. It is never the same for two organisations, so the capability is difficult to copy. Because achieving strength in learning and knowledge is difficult, it is a hard-won advantage which is hard for others to follow.

Becoming a learning organisation does not necessarily offer competitive advantage itself: the purchase decision for washing powder may not be influenced by the idea that the manufacturer is a learning organisation, for example. It is the ability to adapt and the innovations developed as a result of learning which offer advantage.

### The human impact

A focus on learning and development can offer benefits for employees which feeds back in a virtuous circle. Learning and self development is a motivator, at least for some people, and if a company is good at learning and encouraging Senge's 'personal mastery', motivation is increased, with increased chances of retaining the dynamic and innovative people who will be part of the constant need for learning.

### Learning as a definer of 'core business'

If there are areas in the business where learning cannot give competitive advantage, it may be a prompt that this is not core. As an example, learning and improving the activity of IT development and support, or managing a call centre may never offer competitive advantage over other organisations because there are many others who can do it as well or better. It may be better to outsource and focus efforts on learning about outsourcing as a strength.

### Self-assessment question 20.2

Suggest how consistent learning about project management can offer competitive advantage to an organisation.

*Feedback on page 317*

## 20.3 Making it work: learning from projects

This session started from the suggestion that learning was very valuable for projects but badly done. There are plenty of barriers to effective learning for projects (Williams, 2003), but the current methods do not seem to match up to the ideas of knowledge management and the learning organisation.

### Learning activity 20.3

List as many ways as possible that learning could be derived from projects: how could learning be spread and at what stages? Ignore the barriers and focus on the potential, and list rather than analyse. Aim for at least 20 different ways.

*Feedback on page 317*

Learning activity 20.3 above mentions some of the wide range of ways people can learn from projects, yet learning tends to be focused on just two things: the final report, mentioned so often in project management texts as a route for learning, and the experience the team, particularly the project manager, accrue over time (Smith, 2000).

This section aims to suggest ways of break out from the fixed and limited ways that project learning commonly happens, using the ideas of organisational learning and knowledge management.

There is an argument that in order to drive organisational learning from projects requires a learning organisation, and the learning from purchasing and logistics projects cannot happen in isolation. It may be the ideal solution to work within a learning organisation, but few situations are ideal, so the approaches to learning and knowledge management must work without that ideal.

### Tools

One of the simplest and most accessible elements of knowledge is 'who does what' and 'who to ask'. When many organisations lack an effective contract management system, maintaining a contact system for projects may seem excessive, but many project managers rely heavily on their 'black book'. Starting with the organisation and working outwards to other stakeholders, 'yellow pages' and contact logs can help to spread the explicit knowledge. Developing better use of electronic tools such as weblogs, emails and forums can offer user-driven learning.

### Processes

The final report is a common repository of the hopes for learning from projects, but learning is a process or a cycle. It is only by embedding the final report into a process that it becomes more than another ignored whitewash of what happened. If the report becomes part of a valued process, it is more likely to be a valued part of the project. Reports which are long, complex and hard to access are of no value. Publicly accessible digests of key learning points are more likely to be used. Some organisations run presentation sessions or series where project managers share experience from current or past events, with high pressure to attend and high pressure to present.

### Roles

Who is responsible for the knowledge transfer? Adding the job of capturing learning to the project manager's burden is fruitless and liable to bias. If no one is responsible for managing the processes and systems, they are unlikely to work.

A second aspect of roles is adding an applied knowledge of project management to your role. As purchasing and logistics professionals, 'personal mastery' of purchasing and logistics knowledge is part of the job. It is expected and supported. If leading or driving change is to be part of the role, then mastery of project management becomes an important part of the role.

### Multiple ways of learning

Training, situated learning, online access are all useful in different ways. As project teams are brought together then dispersed, there is the opportunity to draw on learning and to disseminate it with the team. As part of the 'forming' process, an active identification of knowledge and experience and building that into the project management can improve the process. Learning as a team, not just individuals can speed team development as well as output. As people leave, ensuring they are part of the review and carry learning onwards has more impact than many reports.

Experience is continuously cited as central to a project manager's development (Meredith, 2006; Weiss, 1992). This suggests that learning in the field and through experience is a central part of developing project management, so part of the learning organisation could be about moving that learning on from learning solely by being a project manager. This method condemns new project managers to learn through the same cycle of failures as all those in the past. Pairing old with new or the project manager of a new project with one nearing completion could offer more effective and ultimately cheaper routes to learning.

### Welcoming change

There are few managers who do not see the value of change and development, but effective learning demands something beyond that, according to Senge. Challenging mental models, ingrained assumptions and the results that come from them are necessary. Suggestion or 'Opportunity For Improvement' schemes can be a part of this, but are limited and unlikely to offer benefit alone. There is a suggestion that all innovation is destruction, and this is partly true, but it does not involve obliterating the learning from the past. Innovation and learning will involve false starts, painful truths, destruction of cherished beliefs and painful redevelopment. Until failure is a part of learning, rather than learning being the punishment for failure, mistakes will be hidden and continue to be repeated.

### Self-assessment question 20.3

Describe three things you would do as part of your next project to increase the learning for the organisation.

*Feedback on page 318*

## Revision question

Now try the revision question for this session on page 322.

## Summary

If learning from projects were easy it would already be done well. It is not. Organisational learning is complex and difficult. Even identifying the right knowledge to manage is a barrier. The reason for looking at learning is that it can offer truly sustainable benefits and perhaps even competitive advantage. Learning is what makes good organisations better and keeps organisations alive.

## Suggested further reading

- Bontis et al (2002).
- Nonaka and Takeuchi (1995).
- Obeng (2003).
- Senge (1990).
- Smith (2000).
- Williams (2003).

## Feedback on learning activities and self-assessment questions

### Feedback on learning activity 20.1

There are likely to be many different sources of the knowledge, with learning coming from different sources and through different routes. Here are a few examples:

- learned at school
- learned through CIPS
- saw someone else doing it
- a colleague helped
- on induction day
- from working with my colleagues over a long period
- from practice in my old job
- from reading the manual
- from that disaster: never do that again.

The learning for just one person's role is likely to involve a whole series of elements gained through many different routes.

### Feedback on self-assessment question 20.1

- The first barriers might be around what knowledge management and the learning organisation are. These are recently developed ideas covering intangible subjects and are hard to define exactly.
- There are likely to be some barriers around the volume of knowledge and potential volume of learning. There could be a comparison with the internet and how to structure a volume of knowledge so it can be accessible.
- The nature of the knowledge: trying to manage tacit knowledge, for example, offers barriers.
- There are personal barriers: people may resist giving up their knowledge or mental models.
- There are practical barriers: all of this knowledge management and learning takes time and money, effectively it is an investment.

## Feedback on learning activity 20.2

This question can be tackled in many different ways, but these are some suggestions for general points:

- Knowledge from outside can offer help in two areas: *how* things could be done and *what* can be a achieved and is being achieved. These are the fundamentals of benchmarking and market research.
- The knowledge can come from books or courses, from observation or from new recruits, for example.
- The new ideas can challenge existing norms, processes and targets and provide insight into how to meet those challenges.
- The knowledge can be adopted or adapted to the new organisation. The combination of external and internal knowledge may create something new and better.
- Even if the external learning is the unlikely outcome that your project management is the best in the world or even the industry, that knowledge is valuable and there are likely to be aspects of those inferior project management processes that can be adapted to keep you in the lead.

## Feedback on self-assessment question 20.2

The first way learning can offer competitive advantage is about *how* projects are managed. Continuously improving projects can increase the success factors discussed in study sessions 16 and 17: more satisfaction of the different stakeholders with less time, cost resources and disruption for example.

The second part of this question could look at *what* projects provide and deliver to the organisation. Constant development of project management can allow it to broaden the change in products, markets and the organisation in response to the environment.

## Feedback on learning activity 20.3

This question focuses on the learning from projects rather than external learning: from benchmarking, etc. As far as when learning can occur, as soon as the project starts there is the potential for valuable learning and this continues beyond the end. Even after the final report, reflecting on the project may bring out more lessons. You could suggest any point from the start onwards.

The ways of passing on learning should include the formal parts: the final reports, audits, interim reports, any lessons circulated, cases used in training. It should also include less-structured approaches such as the learning carried by all the people involved, working alongside colleagues, work shadowing, and discussions between project managers.

Combining the potential for learning in different ways and the potential for when this can happen opens up a wide range of potential routes for learning.

### Feedback on self-assessment question 20.3

The choice is wide. You could focus on the final review and improving the learning from that, or increase the learning at other stages, as discussed in this section. At the outset, learning from the set-up could seem presumptuous but is likely to be fresh information at the best time. Through the project, improving the learning of the team can be difficult, but lifts performance radically and ensures some of the learning is disseminated. Finally, giving the final review or report some impact by finding a process to make sure the lessons are learnt, transforms a document into innovation.

# Revision questions

### Revision question for study session 1

'What is a project anyway?' Use different definitions of projects to explore the concept of projects.

*Feedback on page 323*

### Revision question for study session 2

You are leading a one-year project to streamline logistics for a manufacturing company with 2,000 employees operating across three sites. This project will involve data collection, planning and implementation phases.

Identify three possible stakeholders in this project and suggest how their importance and attitude might change over the course of the project. The stakeholders can be groups or individuals.

*Feedback on page 323*

### Revision question for study session 3

Critically appraise the role of project managers and explain how it is different from that of functional managers.

*Feedback on page 324*

### Revision question for study session 4

Using the first and last stages of a project life cycle of your choice, analyse and discuss the most important issues for either end of the project.

*Feedback on page 325*

### Revision question for study session 5

The six problem-solving tools below each offer different outputs and fit different situations. For each one, answer two fundamental questions: where is this tool useful? What is the output?

- Pareto analysis
- 5 Whys
- brainstorming
- Lewin's force field

- Ishikawa or fishbone diagrams
- cause-effect-cause diagrams.

*Feedback on page 326*

### Revision question for study session 6

Critical Chain project management seeks to overcome established problems with time management.

1. What methods does it use? (20% of the question)
2. Critically appraise the potential success of Critical Chain in overcoming those problems. (80% of the question)

*Feedback on page 326*

### Revision question for study session 7

Standardised methodologies can simplify and assist project management. Discuss whether it is possible to develop a standard methodology or process for purchasing projects.

*Feedback on page 326*

### Revision question for study session 8

Critically evaluate the value of a clear and specific project specification agreed at the outset of a project.

*Feedback on page 327*

### Revision question for study session 9

Discuss some of the barriers to financial project selection, budgeting and financial risk management in projects.

*Feedback on page 327*

### Revision question for study session 10

Gantt, CPA, PERT and GERT all seem to be time planning tools. Discuss the different situations in which each might be applicable, examining the nature, requirements, strengths and drawbacks of each.

*Feedback on page 327*

### Revision question for study session 11

You are starting a project and the team selected for you to work with seems imperfect. In terms of Belbin team roles the team seems unbalanced and there is certainly no coherence or comradeship between the members who have been selected from a range of departments for the project.

Should you try to change the team make-up and balance the team or work with it? Explain the basis for your answer from the information you have.

*Feedback on page 328*

### Revision question for study session 12

Earned value can be a useful way of measuring project progress:

1 Explain how earned value measurement works. (30% of the question)
2 Evaluate the strengths and weaknesses of earned value. (70% of the question)

*Feedback on page 328*

### Revision question for study session 13

Auditing a project on completion appears a very valuable method of gaining understanding and learning.

Criticise the idea of using project audits in this way for every project.

*Feedback on page 329*

### Revision question for study session 14

'If you create a work breakdown structure with all the activities in the project, you have got the basis of really good project planning.' Suggest to what extent this statement can be supported or disproved.

*Feedback on page 329*

### Revision question for study session 15

Evaluate the usefulness of established project management tools and techniques for purchasing and logistics projects using examples of at least three of those tools and techniques.

*Feedback on page 330*

### Revision question for study session 16

The 'Iron Triangle' of cost, time and quality is cited by some as the central part of project management and criticised by others as a blinkered view of limited value. Justify the use of the iron triangle of factors in managing projects.

*Feedback on page 330*

### Revision question for study session 17

A manager has been successful managing a series of 'traditional purchasing' projects such as the development of a facilities management contract and re-sourcing energy supplies for the organisation. She has been selected to lead a 'radical' project to enhance the capabilities of purchasing teams across six sites for the organisation.

Predict the differences in role between managing the traditional projects and leading the new radical project in the future. Ensure your predictions are fully supported by analysis and examples.

*Feedback on page 331*

### Revision question for study session 18

You are leading a large project within your company to develop sourcing strategies for a range of purchasing categories. The company is functionally organised.

You believe that the project team should be moved to work full time on the project, effectively forming a new department. The company directors have suggested a matrix approach, in which the team will retain their functional management but work full time for you.

Develop an argument in support of your proposed pure project structure compared to the matrix structure suggested by the company directors.

*Feedback on page 331*

### Revision question for study session 19

Project management maturity has been proposed by many (including Kerzner and Maylor) as a route to competitive advantage through better project management.

Critically assess the ability of project management maturity to provide competitive advantage.

*Feedback on page 331*

### Revision question for study session 20

From the large number of repeated failures in project management, it seems that learning from project to project is poor. Diagnose the likely causes of this lack of learning in project management.

*Feedback on page 332*

# Feedback on revision questions

## Feedback on revision question for study session 1

As you will have picked up from the session, there is no one universal definition of projects, partly because of opinions, but partly because the understanding of projects is developing from its roots in engineering.

For a basic answer you should be able to use two or preferably more definitions of what a project is to show different views. For example, three definitions based on the simple 'achieving objectives on time and to budget' and discussing their differences effectively would be the absolute minimum. To demonstrate a fuller understanding, challenging the notion of fixed objectives, bringing in stakeholders and using more varied definitions would lift your answer from marginal to something better.

Beyond simply accepting the definitions, a more considered critical view would involve things like: drawing out hard and soft factors, demonstrating how projects have developed in response to the environment, for example increased change and global reach, or to apply those definitions to the purchasing and logistics environment.

## Feedback on revision question for study session 2

This is an open question and the important parts are as follows.

*Show you understand what stakeholders are*

You could use a definition to be absolutely clear, but selecting three different stakeholders should be sufficient.

There is a huge range of possible stakeholders from inside and outside the company.

Stakeholders inside the company could include suppliers, the sponsor, you, the project team, the company management team, the departments responsible for logistics, quality, production, despatch, and storage, as well as important individuals on three sites.

Stakeholders outside the company could include suppliers, regulators, transport pressure groups and even local government and residents around the sites.

*Show that they have differing importance and attitude*

You could use the Mendelow grid but it is not essential. The key is to demonstrate understanding of different stakeholders. As examples:

- The sponsor is likely to have high power and high positive interest at the start, for a range of reasons.
- Site logistics managers or similar may have high power to affect the project by helping or hindering, and could start out strongly resisting.
- Local residents may be irrelevant at the start of the project.

*Show how importance and attitude can change*

- The sponsor may have high power and high positive interest at the start, but interest may wane if there are problems, and once a plan is agreed their power to influence the outcome may be reduced.
- Site logistics power to affect the project by helping or hindering will be stronger in the data collection and implementation phases. They could start out strongly resisting, but be won over, or vice versa. A few suggestions on how they may be influenced by power, peers or persuasion would add to your answer.
- Local residents may be irrelevant at the start of the project with little interest or influence, but once the plan to consolidate loads from 7.5 to 44 tonnes is set, interest could rise and their power with it.

## Feedback on revision question for study session 3

It is worth explaining from the outset that many of the features and techniques of the two are the same, and that the two overlap: functional managers may be managing projects within or alongside their role.

There are many different ways of tackling this question successfully.

You could identify the project management tool and techniques such as time planning and stakeholder management, for a partial answer.

You could use definitions from sources such as Meredith and Mantel, the PMI or APM, etc as the basis, but these must lead into comparative discussions analysing the differences from functional management.

You could start with a definition of project management and work from there. The transformation model is hard to use here but the idea of projects being very high variety low volume could be useful: contrasting this with more repetitive functional work. The focus on uniqueness, time constraints and objectives from section 1.1 could form the basis of a comparison.

You could use the various elements described in section 3.3: 'achieving objectives which will change and develop while:

- managing changing resources such as people and money
- coping with time constraints

- managing complex situations and activities, frequently with interdependence on people, departments and stakeholders spread across and beyond the organisation
- planning and managing activities which are new, hence experience is limited
- managing human reactions to change.'

You could draw in authority and position in the organisation: a project manager is likely to have a temporary and changing position in the hierarchy and lines of reporting above and below can be confused and blurred. This can be useful or difficult for project managers. Line managers, by contrast, are likely to have a more clearly defined position and reporting links.

But of course this is only a basis for comparison, not the whole answer. Discussing and analysing it or comparing it critically with other definitions of project management would bring this towards what is needed for a really good answer.

## Feedback on revision question for study session 4

First, define what the stages are: your first could be inception, planning or development, starting from the first time the project idea is hatched until the start of serious work on the project activity or anywhere in between. The last stage could stop when completion is signed off, as in Meredith and Mantel, or be centred on development and improvement as in Maylor. You do not need to define which or whose life cycle you are using and definitely do not spend much time describing the other stages, but using an established life cycle like Maylor's, etc could save time and add clarity.

The central part of this question is demonstrating that you recognise the differences between the two different stages and can use that to build a picture of the different issues.

Some key issues may be the same: working to budget, time and with the possible resources is always an issue. The detail will change, however, for example:

- *Stakeholders*: At the start, many different stakeholders may have many different ideas of what the project will be and there may be indifference through lack of awareness. At the end the indifference may be because stakeholders are over familiar with it and want it to be finished, while the nature of the project is clear, so retaining help and support may be different.
- *Learning*: At the start, the focus is on gaining learning from other projects while there is no time to do it; at the end, the focus is on passing learning on to other projects while the team disperses and interest wanes.
- *Success*: At the outset, trying to find out what the objectives are and what success would look like is important; at the end, ensuring stakeholders and users accept the output, adopt it and recognise it as success are key.

## Feedback on revision question for study session 5

Your answers to the first four could be based on the ideas from self-assessment question 5.1. Ensure you differentiate between them clearly and identify what the output is, perhaps explaining what the output is applied to for clarity.

The last two are perhaps more difficult to differentiate. Both have an output, a network of linked causes. The key is in the name: cause-effect-cause links effects in a chain, where visible effects follow and lead to causes. You need to differentiate between the one-dimensional, though complex, problems of an Ishikawa diagram and the complex links in cause-effect-cause, then relate that back to their application.

## Feedback on revision question for study session 6

Part (1) can be answered fairly simply from Goldratt's work or from section 6.3: complex moving bottlenecks, estimates incorporating safety time, a tendency to overrun estimates, etc.

Part (2) is evidently the more important and taxing part of the question. Of course, the instructions 'critically evaluate' are key. To do this you can look at the basis, construction and use of Critical Chain critically; highlight potential strengths and flaws from any perspective.

You could discuss answers to the following questions:

- *The basis*: Is Goldratt's analysis of the causes of late running sound: is this why projects run late? It is hard to argue that a lot of projects do overrun, but is it because of estimating problems, overshooting targets and constraints?
- *The construction*: Does moving the safety time to the end of a project make sense? Is this likely to lead to better schedules? Is the idea of locally improving constraints sound? It conflicts with the idea of optimising the whole system rather than piecemeal improvements.
- *Implementation*: What are the potential difficulties of getting people to give '50:50' estimates? Is it feasible to protect the buffer for the whole project against management interference? If each activity is expected to overrun, then activities towards the end of the project will always run late to an undefined degree, is this tenable?

You could also refer to any studies or examples you have seen which shed light on the implementation of Critical Chain.

## Feedback on revision question for study session 7

The simple answer revolves around the suitability of standardised methodologies for the variety of projects in purchasing. To gain a pass you need to explain some different types of projects, perhaps using examples or the types developed in section seven, and their different management requirements, then provide a well-supported conclusion. If you can demonstrate that all purchasing projects will fit one methodology, the answer would be yes, but it is easier to argue that there is a wide range of purchasing projects so standardising a methodology would be a problem.

To go beyond the basic, you could, for example, refer to Six-Sigma and category management projects, each with their own standardised methodologies, which still vary from company to company. Another challenging task would be to identify some standard elements and highlight what would need to change.

### Feedback on revision question for study session 8

There are two areas you should cover in detail:

- a clear definition has a wide range of benefits including gaining agreement, basis for planning, etc
- the project is likely to change and develop, especially if it is radical, so the definition must be open to change and development also, with the needs that that brings.

### Feedback on revision question for study session 9

This question is centred on finance and your answer should centre on difficulties in financial assessment.

There are some generally applicable barriers which affect all financial assessments for projects. Projects predict into the future and are one-offs so inherently difficult to measure financially. Estimates are always loaded with the bias of the estimator or the estimating system: few people will estimate the cost of their work without a safety margin, for example. Focusing on finance is problematic where costs or benefits are hard to identify in financial terms.

You should also offer some barriers for each one.

Projects are often selected on other bases, so financial selection is applicable only to a few. For example, a project to build another production line with clear payback fits the selection model; long-term brand-building projects do not.

The problems with budgeting discussed in section 9.4 are useful here.

Self-assessment question 9.3 gives a series of barriers to financial risk management through the example of decision trees and expected value.

### Feedback on revision question for study session 10

The discussion in the summary to study session 10 gives a brief answer to this which you could build on, even adding examples, and you may have opinions on the breadth of applicability of the different tools.

One thing to emphasise is that while CPA, PERT and GERT all overlap to such an extent that using more than one in any situation is unlikely, Gantt offers different things and could usefully be used with any of the others.

### Feedback on revision question for study session 11

There is no correct yes or no answer to this question; it is an opportunity to demonstrate your understanding of teams, theories and practice.

First note that this type of team make-up is not unusual for projects and may be difficult to change anyway. Members are selected on availability, specialist skills, etc and rarely offer a perfect balance.

The Belbin types are only preferred roles and few people have seriously suggested it will be possible to create well-balanced teams. The benefit of understanding preferred roles is that once you have identified the bias you can consciously and actively manage to cope with it and encourage team members to do the same.

You could use the Tuckman model of team development, derivatives of it or other models to explain that expecting comradeship and effectiveness at the start is over-optimistic and that the team will develop, given effective management.

It may be worthwhile exchanging some team members but from the evidence given, the team you have is a perfectly sound starting basis.

### Feedback on revision question for study session 12

The explanation should be fairly simple but must explain the relationship between project progress, time elapsed and money spent.

The strengths are outlined in section 12.3. The main benefit is the combination of time and cost into one progress measure enabling progress to be compared against plan quickly and effectively.

The weaknesses are easier to expand upon:

- You could discuss the practical problems of reporting: getting up-to-date accounts, bias in estimating progress, etc.
- There are problems specific to earned value: it assumes a simple or linear relationship between cost and progress which is unlikely to be accurate, difficulty in estimating the cost of each activity in advance, etc.
- There is a challenge to the basis: half a bridge is not worth half the value of a whole, usable bridge, for example. The value to a customer is not the same as the cost put in by any stretch of logic.

To go beyond a merit and gain higher marks it is necessary to use more complex criticism of measurement with respect to earned value. You could use the discussions from study session 12 on measurement generally. The inherent problems in assigning cost to each element then managing the cost can lead to bias, ignoring far more important factors such as morale or work carried out internally for which the cost is low or zero. You could go further and use the general point that measurement changes the system, so measuring in this way will encourage people to behave according to the measurements. As a basic example, measuring according to critical resource use will encourage early and potentially inefficient or delayed and damaging use of critical resources.

## Feedback on revision question for study session 13

First explain what an audit is: a structured review against preset criteria by a body external to the project. This can form the basis for your answer.

It is worthwhile noting the potential value and what that is: clarity of understanding including assessment of a project, development of lessons learnt, removal of bias compared to an internal review, etc. You should emphasise what the audit can be used for.

Review potential problems: potentially huge cost both in auditing and preparing for audit, difficulty in setting criteria with emerging objectives, etc, the difficulty in providing an output from an audit which is attractive and easy to access so people will learn from it. There is also the point that an audit at the end is too late to allow for corrections and improvement in that project, it can only offer lessons for the future, these are only of benefit if they are used.

Conclude with a clear summary of the factors that make it worthwhile: large investment, distance from the client (as with public sector funded projects), clear objectives, etc. You could explain that final audits can be used in combination with other tools: final reports, in-process audits, etc.

## Feedback on revision question for study session 14

This is a strengths and weaknesses, for and against question.

First, describing WBS, possibly with a diagram, will help but it is not enough to pass, so do not spend too much time on it.

In order to answer this question, a brief analysis of the value of WBS in project planning is important, as is noting some of the drawbacks. You should identify that a WBS is not very useful on its own and not really a plan, but can form the basis of time plans, risk plans, responsibilities, etc. If you do this well and provide a cohesive conclusion which demonstrates this is true but doing it is difficult, you would have provided at least a basic answer.

To do better, more detail on the planning that can result would help: how the structure of the WBS can link with time plans, for example. The key part, however, is the challenge to WBS. It is hard to argue with the idea that a structured list of everything needed for the project would be useful but, for example:

- It is very difficult to do and guidance on how is pretty minimal.

- The project is likely to change, so a complete and perfect WBS is an impossible ideal.
- The whole idea of a fixed list of activities is far removed from the need to respond to the changing environment.
- There are many things ignored: focusing on activities and ignoring stakeholders can be fatal, for example.

You could use the discussion from self-assessment question 14.2, which looks at using WBS for different types of project.

## Feedback on revision question for study session 15

There are no clear right or wrong answers to this question; the central point is to demonstrate two things:

- You have a rich understanding of the nature of purchasing and logistics projects. Study sessions 7 and 15 have long discussions about different purchasing and logistics projects and you could use those as a basis for discussing different projects, adding in your own perspective or experience. You could alternatively argue that there are no 'typical' purchasing and logistics projects and that there should be no differentiation between purchasing and logistics projects and any other functions projects. This would require careful argument but offers a lot of potential.
- You understand where different tools and techniques can be useful within purchasing and logistics projects. Use your description from the first part along with a critical appraisal of different tools and techniques. There is some discussion of this in section 15.3.

## Feedback on revision question for study session 16

The key to this question is in recognising the iron triangle of factors as important but only part of project management.

To pass, you must demonstrate an understanding of:

- how the iron triangle is relevant to different projects with the importance of the different factors varying by project and with time
- a more complex understanding of factors in the project and project success, including stakeholder requirements other than these three.

The discussion of the iron triangle in Meredith and Mantel or any other text along with section 16.1 can be used to highlight the value of these three factors, not least because two of them are easily measured.

You do not need to demonstrate that the iron triangle covers the only factors measured for success, but that they are important in many and may even be central for some projects. As an example argument, the discussion for self-assessment question 16.2 examines the possibility that the contingent approach is consistent with using the iron triangle in some circumstances.

A discussion of different articles and views on project success and failure is not essential but may well enhance your answer.

### Feedback on revision question for study session 17

You should use this to demonstrate several aspects of knowledge:

- The difference in success between different projects: perhaps cost, quality and time for traditional projects, more complex understanding for radical projects.
- The difference between leading and managing projects.
- The potential for leading projects with uncertain and developing objectives and multiple stakeholders.
- The value of project management tools and techniques but the extension of project management into project leadership.

### Feedback on revision question for study session 18

You are effectively proposing a mixed structure, with a project basis for your team, but leaving the rest of the organisation unchanged.

The merits and problems of matrix and project organisations are discussed in detail in section 18. To gain a pass you should explain several different aspects on each, for example the problems of reporting to two managers against the problems of reassigning staff at the end of your project. You could also look at the 'weight' of the matrix: how much responsibility lies with each of the two managers the team members will have.

### Feedback on revision question for study session 19

First you should describe in outline what maturity is. You can use one model or the key points from several. Example points would be a series of maturity levels based around standardising practice and continuous improvement. A shift from conformance to specified requirements to exceeding expectations.

Sections 19.1 and 19.2 centre on critical reviews of the maturity models, so there is plenty to use in basic critical analysis of the models. Section 19.2 focuses on competitive advantage, using one paper as the start of a discussion.

Possible elements to include:

- Criticism of the basis, for example that standardisation improves project management. This is at odds with a wide variety of projects but might fit a company carrying out routine projects.
- Criticism based on theories or definitions of competitive advantage: section 19.2 discusses this.
- Criticism based on empirical evidence: there are few studies linking maturity to performance, or case-based discussion: 'it would not work in this example because…'.

## Feedback on revision question for study session 20

This is not a question on whether learning from project to project is poor, so avoid discussing that. Assume that it is poor and suggest why this *might* be, with justification.

To answer this question you need to show you understand two basic areas:

1 about learning and the learning organisation in general
2 about the barriers to learning from projects.

You could use any structure, perhaps chronologically, starting from the beginning of a project to the end, or looking at types of learning or how learning is passed on. You could use a comparative approach, explaining how learning from projects compares to learning inn repeated processes.

You should ensure you show broad understanding about learning and get well beyond the 'final report recommends changes to policy' process to include situated and tacit knowledge. Emphasise that learning can come from or into the project at any time, and that reports are only one (very limited) way of passing learning on. You could discuss the learning organisation, but do not spend too much time developing that idea as it is only partly related to the question.

In terms of barriers, discussion in this session and study session 13 should help. The uniqueness and variety cause problems for example, while the nature of project management, a rush to get started and a rush to get finished with the team dispersing, are barriers. More developed ideas will gain extra marks, for example: if project learning has always been poor, then this established behaviour will tend to carry on unless some large prompt to change emerges.

# References and bibliography

This section contains a complete A–Z listing of all publications, materials or websites referred to in this course book. Books, articles and research are listed under the first author's (or in some cases the editor's) surname. Where no author name has been given, the publication is listed under the name of the organisation that published it. Websites are listed under the name of the organisation providing the website.

Archer, MS (1995) *Realist Social Theory, a Morphogenic Approach*, Cambridge University Press

Atkinson, R (1999) 'Project management: cost time and quality: two best guesses and a phenomenon, it's time to accept other success criteria' *The International Journal of Project Management*, vol 17, no 6 pp337–42

Avison, DE and AT Wood-Harper (1988) 'Information Systems Development: A tool kit is not enough' *The Computer Journal*, vol 31, no 4, August

Ayers, JB (2004) *Supply Chain Project Management*, Florida: CRC Press LLC

Bennis, W and B Nannus (1985) *Leaders: The Strategies for Taking Charge*, New York: Harper and Row

Bontis, N, M Crossan. and J Hulland (2002) 'Managing an Organizational Learning System by Aligning Stocks and Flows' *Journal of Management Studies*, vol 39, no 4, pp437–69.

Burgess, R and S Turner (2000) 'Seven Key Features for creating and sustaining commitment' *International Journal of Project Management*, vol 18, pp225–33

Butler Cox (1987) *Using System Development Methods: Research Report 57*, Butler Cox Foundation

Chartered Institute of Purchasing and Supply, CIPS
Pareto Analysis, CIPS reference file, July 2003:
http://www.cips.org/BigPage.asp?CatID=206&PageID=332

Clarke, A (1999) 'A Practical Use of Key Success Factors to Improve the Effectiveness of Project Management' *International Journal of Project Management*, vol 17, no 3, pp139–45

Cooke-Davis, T (2002) 'The "real" success factors on projects' *International Journal of Project Management*, vol 20, pp185–90

Crosby, PB (1979) *Quality is Free*, London: McGraw Hill

Davenport, TH (1993) *Process Innovation*, Harvard Business School Press

Davis, G (1982)'Strategies for Information Requirements Determination' *IBM Systems Journal*, vol 21, issue 1 pp4–30

Davis, S (1996) *Future Perfect, 10th anniversary edition*, Harlow: Addison-Wesley Publishing Co.

Eccles, R (1991) 'The Performance Management Manifesto' *Harvard Business Review*, Jan/Feb, pp131–7

Fahrenkrog, S et al (2003) *The Project Management Institute's OPM3*, Project Management Institute Global Congress Europe

Fiedler, FE (1967) *A Theory of Leadership Effectiveness*, New York: McGraw-Hill

Fiedler, FE (1971) *Leadership*, New York: General Learning Press

Fitzgerald, L, R Johnson et al (1991) *Performance Measurement in Service Businesses*, London: CIMA

Frigenti, E, D Comninos (2002) *The Practice of Project Management*, London: Kogan Page

Goldratt UK: http://www.goldratt.co.uk

Grant, KP et al (1997) 'The Perceived Importance of Technical Competence to Project Managers in the Defense Acquisition Community' *IEEE Transactions on Engineering Management*, February

Gray, RJ (2001) 'Organisational climate and project success' *International Journal of Project Management*, vol 19, pp103–9

Greer, M (1999) *Handbook of Human Performance Technology*, Jossey-Bass San Francisco

[http://www.michaelgreer.com, Greer, M (2004), *10 ways to fail*]

Gregory, M (1993) 'Integrated Performance Measurement: A Review of Current Practice and Emerging Trends' *International Journal of Production Economics*, 30/3, pp281–96

Gremillion, L and P Pyburn (1983) 'Breaking the Systems Development Bottleneck' *Harvard Business Review*, March/April , pp130–7

Handfield, RB and EL Nichols (2002) *Supply Chain Redesign: Transforming Supply Chains into Integrated Supply Systems*, London: Financial Times Prentice Hall

Handy C (1998) *Beyond Certainty: The Changing Worlds of Organizations*, Boston: Harvard Business School Press

Handy, C (1989) *The Age of Unreason*, London: Random House

Johns, TG (1995) 'Managing the behaviour of people working in teams' *International Journal of Project Management*, vol 13, no 1, pp33–8

Jugdev, K and J Thomas (2002) 'Project Management Maturity Models; the Silver Bullets of Competitive Advantage?', *Project Management Journal*, December, vol 33, issue 4 p 4

Kanji, GK (1998) 'Measurement of Business Excellence', *Total Quality Management*, vol 9, no 7, pp 633–43

Kanter, RM (1990) *When Giants Learn to Dance*, London: Free Press

Kaplan, R and D Norton (1992) 'The Balanced Scorecard: the Measures that Drive Performance' *Harvard Business Review*, Jan/ Feb, pp71–9

Kerzner, H (2001) *Strategic Planning for Project Management Using a Project Management Maturity Model*, NJ: John Wiley & Sons Inc

King, D and D Wright (2002) 'Use Process Mapping' *Logistics and Transport Focus*, April, vol 4, issue 3, pp42–5

Kotter, JP (1990) *A Force for Change: How Leadership Differs From Management*, New York: Free Press

Kotter, JP (1985) *Power and influence: Beyond formal authority*, New York, Free Press.

Lewin, K (1943) 'Defining the "Field at a Given Time"' *Psychological Review*, vol 50, pp292–310. Republished in *Resolving Social Conflicts & Field Theory in Social Science* (1997) Washington DC: American Psychological Association

Lim, CS and MZ Mohamed (1999) 'Criteria of Project Success: an exploratory examination' *International Journal of Project Management*, vol 17, no 4, pp243–8

Lock, D (2003) *Project Management*, Hants: Gower

Maylor, H (1996) *Project Management*, Essex: Pearson Education

Maylor, H (2000) *Another Silver Bullet, a Review of the TOC approach to Project Management.* Presented at the 7th international conference of EUROMA, Ghent 2000

Maylor, H (2001) 'Assessing the relationship between practice changes and process improvement in new product development' *Omega: the International Journal of Management Science*, vol 29, no 1, pp85–96

Mendelow, AL (1981) 'Environmental Scanning – The Impact of the Stakeholder Concept', *Proceedings of the 2nd International Conference on Information Systems*, pp 407–17, Cambridge MA

Meredith, JR and SJ Mantel (2006) *Project Management: A Managerial Approach*, 6th edition, NJ: John Wiley & Sons

Mintzberg, H (1973) *The Nature of Managerial Work*, New York: Harper

Motorola: http://www.motorola.com

Mintzberg H, JB Quinn, S Ghoshal (1998) *The Strategy Process*, Bath: Prentice Hall

Mouritsen, J, T Skjott-Larsen and H Kotzab (2002) *The Supply Chain Management Integration Assumption- its Dilemma, Meaning and Validity*, 9th International Conference, EUROMA

Newbold, RC (1998) *Project Management in the Fast Lane: Applying the Theory of Constraints*, St Lucie Press Series on Constraints Management

Nonaka, I and H Takeuchi (1995) *The Knowledge-Creating Company: How Japanese Companies Create the Dynamics of Innovation*, Oxford and New York: Oxford University Press

Obeng, E (1996) *All Change the Project Leader's Handbook*, Essex: Pearson Education

Obeng, E (2003) *Perfect Projects*, Bucks: The Virtual Media Company

Office of Government Commerce (2005) *Managing Successful Projects with* PRINCE2, London: The Stationery Office Books

Oilsen, RP (1971) 'Can Project Management be Defined?' *Project Management Quarterly*, vol 2, issue 1, pp12–14

Palmer, E, and D Parker (2001)'Understanding performance measurement systems using physical science uncertainty principles' *International Journal of Operations and Production Management*, July, vol 21, issue: 7, pp981–99

Pande, P and L Holpp(2001) *What Is Six Sigma?*, London: McGraw-Hill Education

Pender, S (2001) 'Managing Incomplete Knowledge, Why Risk Management is Not Sufficient' *International Journal of Project Management*, vol 19, pp79–87

Pinto, JK and DP Slevin (1987) 'Critical factors in successful project implementation' *IEEE Transactions on Engineering Management*, February

Porter, M (1985) *Competitive Advantage*, London: McGraw Hill

Primost, D and N Oliver (2003) *Does Lean Production Enhance Financial Performance? The Case of UK Automotive Components Plants*, 10th International Conference EUROMA

Prince2: http://www.prince2.com

Project Management Institute (2000) *A Guide to the Project Management Body of Knowledge (PMBOK Guide Third Edition)*, PA: Project Management Institute

Saarinen, T (1990) 'System Development Methodology and Project Success: An Assessment of Situational Approaches' *Information and Management*, vol 19, pp183–93

Semler, R (1994) 'Why My Former Employees Still Work for Me' *Harvard Business Review*, January

Senge, PM (1990) *The Fifth Discipline*, London: Random House

Skulmoski, G (2001) 'Project Maturity and Competence Interface' *Cost Engineering*, vol 43, issue 6, pp11–19

Smith, G (2000) 'The black art of project management' *IEE review*, September, pp39–43

Taylor, JR (1996) *Handbook of Project Based Management*, London: McGraw Hill

Thamhain, HJ and DL Wilemon (1975)'Conflict Management in Project Life Cycles' *Sloan Management Review*, Summer

The Association of Project Management (2006) *The APM Body of Knowledge* (5th edition)

The IT Service Management Forum (ItSMF) (2004) *Project Management Based on Prince2: An Introduction*, Netherlands: Van Haren Publishing

Thomas, K and R Kilmann (1974) *Thomas-Kilmann Conflict Mode Instrument*, Tuxedo, NY: XICOM

Turner, JR (1993) *The Handbook of Project Based Management*, London: McGraw Hill

Turner, JR and R Muller (2003) 'On the nature of the project as a temporary organisation' *International Journal of Project Management*, vol 21, pp1–8

Weber, M (1947) *Basic Concepts in Sociology*, Illinois: The Free Press

Weiss, JW and RK Wysocki (1992) *5 Phase Project management, a Practical Planning and Implementation Guide*, PA: Perseus

Westerveld, E (2003) 'The Project Excellence Model: linking success criteria and critical success factors', *International Journal of Project Management*, vol 21, pp 411-18

Wheelwright, SC and KB Clark (1995) *Leading Product Development,* Free Press

Williams, T (2003) 'Learning from projects' *Journal of the Operational Research Society*, May, vol 54, no 5, pp443–51

Williams, TM (1999) 'The Need for New Paradigms for Complex Projects' *International Journal of Project Management*, vol 15, no 5, pp269–73

Winch, G (1996) 'Thirty Years of Project Management, What Have We Learned?' *British Association of Management Conference Proceedings*, London: British Association of Management

Womack, J et al (1990) *The Machine that Changed the World*, New York: Maxwell Macmillan International

Zaidi, R (2006) *Business Organisation Structure, Hierarchy and Staff Planning: A Policy Design, Discussion and Training Notebook*, London: Applied Management Research Ltd

# Index